British Pubs & Inns 2006

Les Routiers is an association of mainly owner-managed establishements. However, membership is not automatic. Many applications are refused because every establishment displaying Les Routiers' symbol must satisfy our rigorous quality criteria. All opinions included in the Guide entries are based upon the findings of external assessors.

Published in 2005 by:
Routiers Limited
190 Earl's Court Road
London SW5 9QG
Tel: 020 7370 5113
Fax: 020 7370 4528
Email: info@routiers.co.uk

Book-trade distribution:
Portfolio Books Ltd
Unit 5, Perivale Industrial Park
Horsenden Lane South
Greenford, Middlesex
UB6 7RL

ISBN 0-900057-22-X
Copyright © 2005 Routiers Limited

Maps © Routiers Limited 2005
Great Britain Digital Database and
Greater London Digital Data
© Cosmographics Limited.
Maps designed and produced by Cosmographics.
Reproduced by kind permission of Ordnance
Survey. Crown Copyright NC/01/365".
Including mapping content © Automobile
Association Developments Limited 2001 and
© Bartholomew Digital Database.
Greater London Map based on information
derived from satellite imagery and an original
ground survey by Cosmographics. Satellite data
provided by USGS and Infoterra Ltd.

Editor:
David Hancock
Production and design editor:
Holly Hall
Design:
Oliver Carter

Sub-editor:
Gill Wing

Editorial contributors:
Nick Channer
Natasha Hughes
Nicholas Stanley
Mark Taylor

Location photographers:
www.britainonview.com
Annie Hanson
Nicholas Stanley

Cover photography:
Claudia Riccio
Tel: 07990 604806

Pub Walks
Chris Bagshaw
Nick Channer
Neil Coates
David Hancock
Sue Viccars

Maps:
Cosmographics Limited, Watford

Printed in Italy by:
London Print and Design plc,
Warwick

For Les Routiers:
Chairman:
David Curry
Operations Director:
Imogen Clist
Marketing Manager:
Victoria Borrows
Membership:
Suzy Small

www.routiers.co.uk

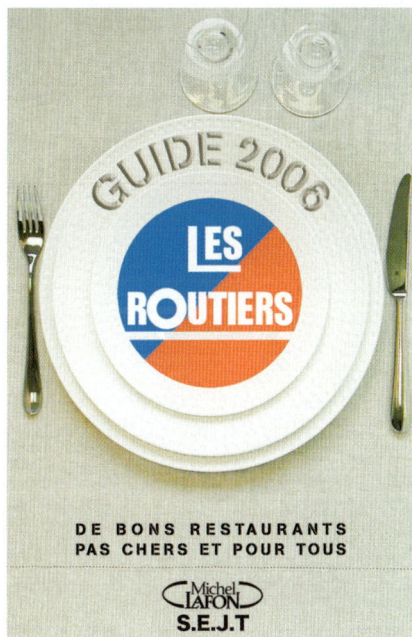

GUIDE 2006

LES
ROUTIERS

DE BONS RESTAURANTS
PAS CHERS ET POUR TOUS

Michel
LAFON

S.E.J.T

Les Routiers Guide – De bons restaurants pas chers et pour tous was originally written for truck drivers who were looking for fairly priced hotels and restaurants. It soon became popular with travelling salesmen, and French and foreign tourists.

Today, the red-and-blue Les Routiers sign has become a cult symbol, standing alongside the Gitanes pack and the Ricard logo as the essence of French style, and the Routiers' original concept of a warm homely welcome and affordable good value is as strong today as when it was first conceived.

Les Routiers Guide – De bons restaurants pas chers et pour tous is a boon for travellers in France, listing simple, inexpensive roadside restaurants and hotels for both truck drivers and motorists.

To obtain a copy visit:

www.routiers.com

Contents

About this guide   6
How to use this guide   10
Les Routiers Awards 2005   12

Features
Food, glorious local food   20
Raising the bar   30
Stanley's Highland fling   202

England   36
Scotland   168
Wales   186

Food Maps
Ivy House, Chalfont St Giles, Buckinghamshire   44
Brackenrigg Inn, Ullswater, Cumbria   62
Victoria Inn, Salcombe, Devon   66
The Wyndham Arms, Clearwell, Gloucestershire   76
The Cabinet, Reed, Hertfordshire   88
Red Lion Inn, Stathern, Leicestershire   98
Kings Head Inn, Bledington, Oxfordshire   118
The Crooked Billet, Stoke Row, Oxfordshire   122
The Camelot, South Cadbury, Somerset   130
The Holly Bush, Stafford, Staffordshire   134
The Fountain Inn, Tenbury Wells, Worcestershire   152
The Friar's Head at Akebar, Leyburn, North Yorkshire   158
Appletree Country Inn, Marton, North Yorkshire   162
Unicorn Inn, Kincardine, Fife   172
The Plockton Hotel, Plockton, Highland   178
Greyhound Inn, Usk, Powys   194
Felin Fach Griffin, Brecon, Powys   198

🛏 Accommodation   📕 Set menu

🍺 Range of real ale   ★ Award winner 2004

🫖 Teashop or café   ⭐ Award winner 2005

🌶 Food shop

Pub Walks

Hunters Rest, Bath, Bath & NE Somerset 210
St George & Dragon, Wargrave, Berkshire 212
Five Arrows Hotel, Waddesdon, Buckinghamshire 214
Rose and Crown, Romaldkirk, Co Durham 216
Old Inn, St Breward, Cornwall 218
Dukes Head, Armathwaite, Cumbria 220
Boot Inn, Eskdale, Cumbria 222
Fox Inn, Corscombe, Dorset 224
Plough & Sail, Paglesham East End, Essex 226
Plough at Kelmscott, Kelmscott, Gloucestershire 228
White Hart Inn, Winchcombe, Gloucestershire 230
Stagg Inn, Titley, Herefordshire 232
Alford Arms, Berkhamsted, Hertfordshire 234
Freemasons Arms, Clitheroe, Lancashire 236
Inn at Whitewell, Whitewell, Lancashire 238
Victoria at Holkham, Holkham, Norfolk 240
Pheasant Inn, Kielder Water, Northumberland 242
Bottle & Glass, Harby, Nottinghamshire 244
Cherry Tree Inn, Henley-on-Thames, Oxfordshire 246
Queen's Head, Brandeston, Suffolk 248
Ship Inn, Chichester, West Sussex 250
Sandpiper Inn, Leyburn, North Yorkshire 252
Clachaig Inn, Glencoe, Highland 254
Bell at Skenfrith, Skenfrith, Monmouthshire 256

Just off the motorway 259
Maps 269
A-Z index 281
Quick-reference guide 284
Reader report form 287

ABOUT THIS GUIDE

Individual, friendly, welcoming and value for money – you'll find all these attributes at Les Routiers' select collection of owner-managed pubs and inns around Britain. On their search of the regions, Les Routiers' inspectors look out for the most special places. Those that combine character, quality and have that special British quirkiness, be it a Russian tavern in the Scottish Isles, a country inn in the heart of the Dorset countryside or a city-centre gastropub, minutes away from Harrods.

Les Routiers' approach and philosophy is very much in tune with the discerning traveller, who wants style but informality, without the anonymous atmosphere and impersonal service of some of the larger pub chains. We are also committed to seeking out pubs that are passionate about the use of local and regional foods, whether it is a rustic country pub providing traditional home-cooked pub grub or a classic inn with comfortable rooms and modern takes on traditional British food. This means you get to enjoy foods in season when they're at their more flavoursome, as well as being assured of warm hospitality, comfortable, well-appointed bedrooms and excellent value for money.

How we go about it

Les Routiers has eight regional sales managers/inspectors. All have previously worked in the hospitality industry, either as publicans, food inspectors or hotel marketing managers. Pubs interested in applying for membership to Les Routiers are fully inspected and the benefits of becoming a member are discussed with the owner. Only those pubs passing our rigorous inspection process are accepted and invited to join. Pubs do pay to be included in the guide, and this annual membership fee assists in covering the inspection process and the high costs of producing the annual guidebooks.

LES ROUTIERS
Pubs & Inns 2006

Local foods

Over the last five years, the British public's interest in local, and often, organic food has developed as never before. In answer to this demand, pubs are serving more and more game, beef, fruit and vegetables from local estates, farmers, and fishermen.

In our headline feature Food, glorious local food, Mark Taylor looks at the gastropub revolution across Britain and investigates the growing trend for sourcing fresh ingredients from small local producers and suppliers. He goes behind the scenes at top Les Routiers pubs to find out the advantages and disadvantages in sourcing fresh, local produce.

Dotted throughout the guide are 15 food maps that identify our champions of local foods and highlight how 'local' their key suppliers are, be it a micro-brewery, a farm rearing rare-breed pigs, a smallholding that delivers organic fruits and vegetables to the pub door, or a fishing boat that lands fresh fish and crab on the quay.

Changing tastes – wine and beer

From the domination of Bass to a micro-brewery revolution and from the wine box on the bar to impressive, chalked-up lists of wines by the glass, Natasha Hughes, in the feature Raising the bar, explores the evolving pub scene. Notably, how the rise of the gastropub has triggered major changes in the quality and choice of wine and beer to be found in pubs and inns.

Classic inns – best for beds

An increasing number of pubs and inns now successfully combine a relaxed, informal atmosphere with good food and smart ensuite accommodation. They provide the discerning pub-goer with a quality alternative to a budget travel inn or a large, impersonal, expensive country hotel. Perfect for a long weekend, or a mid-week break, a number of our top inns feature on a full-page entry. To aid your rest and relaxation, we have included useful information on where to shop, local sporting activities and the top attractions to visit in the area.

Les Routiers' Nicholas Stanley hits the Highlands

Fuelled by thoughts of fine malt whisky and fond memories of his epic coast-to-coast walking adventure in 2004, Nicholas Stanley donned his boots once again (in the name of research) and headed north to tackle Scotland's famous West Highland Way. In Stanley's Highland fling he recounts his experiences during his 95-mile, week-long ramble from the Lowlands around Glasgow to the majestic mountains surrounding Fort William. Informative panels throughout the feature answer some of the most-asked questions about walking.

Perfect pub walks

To the walker, beer and beautiful countryside go hand-in-hand, providing the essential ingredients for a great day's ramble. Having stimulated a healthy appetite and a parched throat, the sight of a welcoming country pub will quicken the step of even the weariest of legs.

Our Pub Walks pages feature 25 beautiful walks (3-8 miles) across the country, including 10 new walks for 2006. All have been fully researched and provide detailed route directions, information on places of interest along the way, and essential notes on terrain and the Ordnance Survey map you should take with you. Many start from the front door of cosy inns with comfortable accommodation, so take your walking boots with you for the weekend and explore the surrounding countryside.

Just off the motorway

We've all been there: the motorway service station that shortchanges you on food, but charges the earth. Check out our nine motorway and A-road maps to find your detour to a Les Routiers member, who can offer you something more appetising. The members suggested are just a short drive from the main motorway junction, but miles ahead when it comes to food and accommodation.

Quick-reference guide

Here you will find pubs selected for the best gardens, stunning views and idyllic waterside locations, and pubs that offer wine or cookery courses. We also list the top pubs for seafood, game, cheese, wine, and those offering private dining facilities.

How to use this guide

Finding an establishment

Les Routiers Pubs and Inns 2006 is sectioned into England, Scotland and Wales. The countries are listed alphabetically by county, listing town and establishment name. There are four ways to track down an establishment.

1. If you are seeking a place in a particular area, first turn to the maps at the back of the book. County boundaries are marked in lilac and each establishment has a relevant marker alongside their listing town, shown in bold. Once you know the locality, go to the relevant section in the book to find the entry for the pub or inn.

2. Each page is colour-coded at the top so you can flick through the guide and find what you are looking for with ease. Turn to the contents pages for the colour key.

3. Turn to the index on page 281 where both establishment names and listing towns appear in alphabetical order.

4. Turn to the quick-reference guide on page 284 to help you find the places that will suit you, whether it be somewhere with riverside seating or beautiful views.

How to read a guide entry

A sample entry is set out on the facing page. At the top of the entry you will find the establishment's name, address, and telephone number and, if it has them, an e-mail and website address. Also, any symbols that may apply to the establishment; an explanation of what these symbols stand for appears beside the sample entry. The middle part of the entry describes accommodation, atmosphere, food, wines and so on, while the final section gives additional statistical information and a map reference.

Listing town and county: Many of our establishments are in the countryside, so their listing town may be a location several miles away. If you are unsure of the county, look up the town in the index and it will refer you to the correct page.

Telephone: Numbers include the international code for dialling the UK from abroad. To dial from within the UK, start the number with the 0 in brackets; from outside the UK, dial all numbers except the 0 in brackets.

Last orders: Times to order lunch and dinner by are given for the bar and restaurant where applicable. Where there is only an evening time given, the establishment serves food throughout the day.

Closed: Where 'Never' is stated, the establishment is open throughout the year. Where 'Rarely' is stated, the establishment is open throughout the year except on important holidays (Christmas, New Year). Otherwise, dates and days closed are stated.

Listing town

Name ♨🍺🍷

Address
Telephone: +44(0)111 000000
excellentpub@hotmail.com
www.excellentpub.com

This quintessentially English coaching inn dates back to the 18th-century and has been revamped by its new owners...

Rooms: 15. Double room from £72, single from £57. Honeymoon suite available.
Prices: Set menu £18. House wine from £9.95.
Last orders: Bar: 23.30. Food: 21.00.
Closed: 25th December to 2nd January.
Food: Modern British.
Real ale: Greene King IPA.
Other points: No-smoking area. Children welcome. Garden.
Car park. Licence for civil weddings.
Directions: Exit 22/M5. Turn right at the roundabout towards Weston-super-Mare. The hotel is one mile on the left. (Map 4, C6)

Symbols:
♨ Accommodation
🍺 Range of real ale
☕ Teashop or café
🍴 Food shop
🍷 Set menu
★ Award winner 2004
★ Award winner 2005

All symbols are in their country's colour, apart from the award-winner stars. We do not have a good-food or good-wine symbol, as it is part of our requirements for membership that all Les Routiers establishments serve good food and wine at reasonable prices.

Rooms: For establishments offering overnight accommodation, the number of rooms is given, along with the lowest price for a double/twin and single room. Where this price is per person it is indicated. Prices usually include breakfast. Where the price includes bed, breakfast and dinner, it is indicated.

Directions: These have been supplied by the proprietor of the establishment. The map reference at the end refers to the map section at the back of the guide.

Prices: Set meals usually consist of three courses but can include more. If a set meal has fewer or more than three courses, this is stated. Where no set lunch or dinner is offered, we give the price of the cheapest main course on the menu. House wine prices are by the bottle, unless otherwise stated.

Other Points:

Smoking The majority of establishments are either totally no-smoking or have a no-smoking area. However, we also indicate where smoking is allowed throughout.

Credit cards Very few places don't take credit cards; those that don't are stated here.

Children Although we indicate whether children are welcome in the establishment, we do not list facilities for guests with babies; we advise telephoning beforehand to sort out any particular requirements.

Dogs We indicate whether dogs are allowed in the public bar and/or overnight accommodation of the establishment. However, please mention this when booking.

Disabled: We indicate whether an establishment has wheelchair access. If this does not apply to the WC, this is also stated. However, we recommend telephoning the pub or inn of your choice to discuss your needs with the manager or proprietor directly.

Hospitality and Service Award

This year, we have introduced a new award for hospitality and service, sponsored by American Express. American Express consistently delivers new business and high-spending Cardmembers to its merchants, and works to support independent establishments across Britain. Good service deserves recognition. Offering customers a choice of payment methods contributes to good service, in both city centres and the countryside. Friendly, efficient staff and a slick front-of-house all make for a pleasant, stress-free stay or dining-out experience. We believe the winners of this award ensure customers feel at ease and are well looked after, from initial booking through to paying the bill.

Les Routiers Pubs and Inns Awards 2005

Our annual awards recognise members who excel at meeting the high standards required for Les Routiers' membership. There are five categories and, as always, it is a tough call to decide, as overall standards of accommodation, food and drink are excellent. Congratulations to our winners, who just had the edge, and will attend the Les Routiers' awards dinner.

Inn of the Year

Here we highlight some of Britain's great inns — the new breed of country hotels and restaurants. Our winners successfully combine a relaxed, informal atmosphere with superlative food, genuine warm hospitality, individuality and comfortable accommodation.

Dining Pub of the Year

Sponsored by Tabasco® Pepper Sauce
In recent years we have seen welcome improvements in the style and quality of pub food. Innovation, imagination and use of local, regional and fresh produce are the key ingredients in judging this award. All our winners offer first-class cooking.

Real Ale Pub of the Year

This award applauds those enthusiastic, even fanatical, landlords whose passion extends beyond their quest to offer a tip-top pint at every pull to only featuring local micro- and regional-brewery beers.

Wine Pub of the Year

For this award we look for passion and enthusiasm for wine, well-chosen wine lists, value for money and an exceptional range of quality wines by the glass. We have chosen pub members who put as much effort into their house selection as they do into choosing their fine-wine collection.

Local Food Supporters of the Year

Pubs winning this award are true champions of local produce, run by food-loving chefs or landlords who go out of their way to source, use and promote first-class food and drink from select suppliers in their immediate area.

INN OF THE YEAR

National Winner

London & The South-East – Swan Inn, Chiddingfold, Surrey

*'A hip hotel-meets-gastropub concept has breathed new life
into this expertly reincarnated 14th-century inn, providing chic,
Manhattan-style bedrooms, and impressive modern British menus.'*

Puesdown Inn

Regional Winners

Scotland – Plockton Hotel, Plockton, Highland
'Real food – local fish and seafood, Highland beef and cheese – and wine, real value
and, ultimately, real Highland hospitality make this a place that's hard to leave.'

The North – Pheasant Inn, Kielder Water, Northumberland
'Remote it may be, but the Kershaw family's appealing, all-round inn is spotlessly maintained,
the food honest and home cooked, and the hospitality genuinely welcoming.'

Wales & The Marches – Kinmel Arms, St George, Conwy
'Lynn Cunnah-Watson's rejuvenated pub in the beautiful Elwy Valley now has four stunning
suites, each with fantastic bathrooms, terraces and views – the best pub rooms for miles.'

Central & East Anglia – Cherry Tree Inn, Henley-on-Thames, Oxfordshire
'Impeccable, modern bedrooms in a converted outbuilding and great food draw the
discerning to this revitalised, 400-year-old brick-and-flint pub deep in the Chiltern Hills.'

The South-West – Puesdown Inn, Northleach, Gloucestershire
'John and Maggie Armstrong have renovated and refurbished this mellow stone inn with
style and panache, especially the three individually designed stable-block bedrooms.'

DINING PUB OF THE YEAR
Sponsored by Tabasco® Pepper Sauce

National Winner

South-West – Dartmoor Union Inn, Holbeton, Devon

'A revamped 16th-century building offering an incredible and untypical culinary experience in the heart of a typical Devon village, with innovative modern menus, and a real passion for local foods.'

Penhelig Arms

Regional Winners

Scotland – Unicorn Inn, Kincardine, Fife
'Tony and Liz Budde's lovely 17th-century inn draws discerning foodies for Tony's innovative menus that highlight the best-available local seafood, game and meat.'

The North – Golden Lion, Osmotherley, North Yorkshire
'Bustling dining pub in a picturesque village location on the edge of the North York Moors. Come for local Hambleton ales, roaring log fires and Peter McCoy's tremendous cooking.'

Wales & The Marches – Penhelig Arms, Aberdyfi, Gwynedd
'The Hughes' wonderful inn overlooking the Dyfi estuary just gets better and better. Stay the night and dine in style on delectable seafood, delivered to the door by local suppliers.'

Central & East Anglia – Three Horseshoes, Derby, Derbyshire
'Staff and loyal diners followed chef-landlord Ian Davison to this village local early in 2005. Why? Ian's food is imaginative, freshly prepared and draws on top-notch local produce.'

London & The South-East – The Countryman, Shipley, West Sussex
'Menus have moved with the times at this traditional, cosy inn tucked away down a country lane, with modern European dishes listed alongside excellent pub classics.'

REAL ALE PUB OF THE YEAR

National Winner

The North – Boot Inn, Eskdale, Cumbria

'Walkers head off the fells to refresh and refuel at this 16th-century farmhouse in the beautiful Eskdale Valley. Nine hand pumps dispense cracking pints of locally-brewed beers to accompany some hearty pub food.'

Tiger Inn

Regional Winners

Scotland – Grog & Gruel, Fort William, Highland
'With no fewer than 10 hand pumps lining the bar, active types can slake raging thirsts here by quaffing tip-top pints brewed in the Highlands and Islands.'

Wales & The Marches – Hunters Moon, Abergavenny, Monmouthshire
'Excellent Welsh beers from Cardiff brewer Brain's and local micro-breweries are tapped straight from the barrel at this historic pub tucked away in an isolated rural village.'

Central & East Anglia – Fisherman's Return, Winterton-on-Sea, Norfolk
'Top-notch Woodforde's and Adnams beers are beautifully kept and the ideal accompaniment to some hearty food at this consistently well-run and reliable coastal pub.'

The South-West – Cadgwith Cove Inn, The Lizard, Cornwall
'Smack on the coast path, the Cadgwith Cove Inn serves up some great seafood and five real ales. Relax on the terrace and savour the views with a cracking pint of Doom Bar.'

London & The South-East – Tiger Inn, Ashford, Kent
'Hidden down winding lanes beneath the North Downs, the rustic Tiger Inn draws the real ale aficionado for well-kept pints of Everards Tiger and micro-brewery guest beers.'

WINE PUB OF THE YEAR

National Winner

Central & East Anglia – Farmers Arms, Lincoln, Lincolnshire

'A quirky, 18th-century pub that's run by a couple with a passion for local food and wine. The wine list is well thought out, offers great value and choice (35 by the glass), and demonstrates real expertise in its selection.'

The Camelot

Regional Winners

The North – Freemasons Arms, Clitheroe, Lancashire
'Ian Martin has an intimate knowledge of wine and his global list of wines is just fantastic. The depth of quality and range of vintages is outstanding.'

Wales & The Marches – Felin Fach Griffin, Brecon, Powys
'Wines are carefully chosen and the list is packed with interest and character at the Griffin, which ranks among the new-breed of classy Welsh pubs.'

The South-West – The Camelot, South Cadbury, Somerset
'A fresh, new and innovative approach to dining in a country pub. A great wine list compliments everything from the traditional British to tapas Russian style.'

London & The South-East – The Dog Inn, Wingham, Kent
'Reasonable pricing, a global choice to suit all tastes, and nine wines by the glass highlight the extensive but not over-ambitious list at The Dog.'

LOCAL FOOD SUPPORTERS OF THE YEAR

The Swan at Felsted

Winners

Steam Packet Hotel, Isle of Whithorn, Dumfries & Galloway
'Fish, landed on the quay outside the pub, dictates the menu and chalkboards in the bar list the daily catch, be it langoustines or perfectly battered haddock.'

Sandpiper Inn, Leyburn, North Yorkshire
'Chef-landlord Jonathan Harrison has a genuine interest in sourcing local foods, with personal contact with the farmers and growers throughout Wensleydale.'

Black Bear Inn, Bettws Newydd, Monmouthshire
'Quirky, always inventive and often genuinely surprising, Stephen Molyneux's daily menus tap into the rich vein of local produce, be it pheasant, Usk salmon or locally reared lamb.'

The Swan at Felsted, Great Dunmow, Essex
'Imaginative food and a passion to source ingredients from local producers extends to listing individual suppliers on the menus at Jono and Jane Clarke's refurbished village pub.'

Victoria Inn, Salcombe, Devon
'Landlord Andrew Cannon works exceptionally hard to guarantee that, almost without exception, what is presented on the plate is as a consequence of careful local sourcing.'

Royal Oak, Poynings, West Sussex
'Paul Day's pub has everything, a glorious setting below the South Downs, a wonderful summer garden, and a menu that overflows with carefully sourced local ingredients.'

NO. **7** ON THE LIST OF
TABLES FOR TWO

Number 9 is in the dining carriage of the Orient Express.
Number 8 is in Monte Carlo in front of a croupier.
Number 7 however, you practically levitate above.
A white mud treatment washes away any traces of tension and with Membership Rewards®
picking up the bill, there's no stress on your wallet either. In fact the points Members earn on everyday
purchases can be redeemed for almost any indulgence – from mud packs to Margaux.

For more ideas visit americanexpress.co.uk/dreams

FOR WHATEVER DREAMS ARE ON YOUR LIST

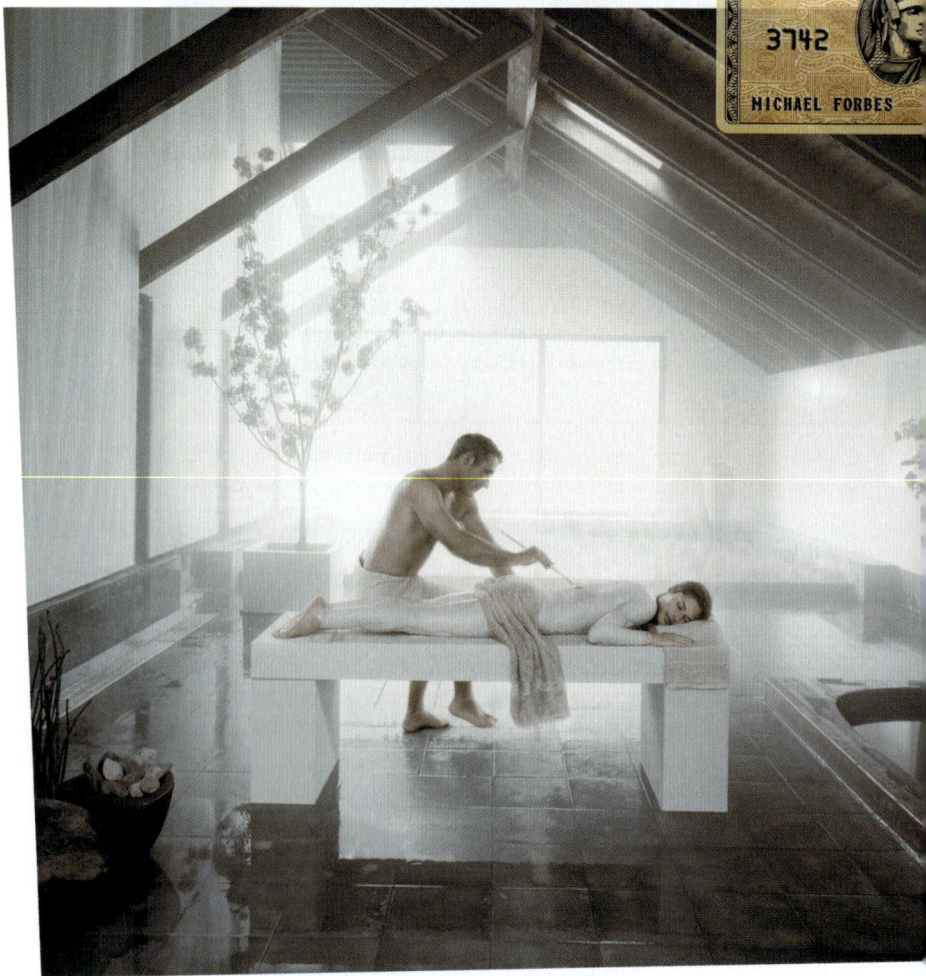

Hospitality and Service Award
Sponsored by American Express

National Winner

The Bell at Skenfrith, Monmouthshire

'This beautifully restored riverside pub-with-rooms oozes all the charming allure of an old Welsh inn and more, thanks to the dedication of hands-on owners William and Janet Hutchings. Rooms are luxurious, food and wine first-class, and guests are treated like friends.'

Food, glorious local food

by Mark Taylor
illustrations by Natalie Hall

As we tuck into our pan-fried, diver-caught scallops with cauliflower purée, washed down with a chilled glass of Sauvignon Blanc, it's easy to forget that, a few years ago, pub food used to be restricted to a pint of bitter and a pickled egg – if you were lucky.

Back in the 1960s, the pub-food canon consisted of a roll-call of cheap snacks – packets of pork scratchings, jars of cockles and whelks, pork pies, pickled onions – or stale cheese rolls sweating under plastic cloches perched on the bar. A decade later, with pubs aiming more at the family market, menus started to expand with pub-grub classics, such as chicken in the basket, and scampi and chips, followed by slabs of Black Forest gateau.

By the mid-80s, pub food was tapping into a more global cuisine, with Thai and South American dishes appealing to the broadening tastes of consumers. All the while, however, the majority of pubs were relying on bought-in 'freezer to fryer' foods that could be easily reheated in a microwave or a deep-fat fryer and served to customers as if it had been cooked to order by a team of busy chefs.

Although there had been a select few rural pubs cooking good food from fresh local ingredients, they were few and far between and it took the gastropub revolution of the early 90s to change the face of pub food forever. Suddenly, here were boozers with open kitchens and chefs cooking modern British and European dishes from fresh, locally sourced produce delivered on a daily basis.

The rise and rise of food-driven pubs has coincided with an increased consumer interest about where the food they are eating actually comes from. After health scares such as the BSE crisis, more and more people want to know exactly what they are putting into their mouths, as well as the mouths of their children. These days, more and more pubs are sourcing their produce from local farmers and suppliers, or even growing their own.

The Brackenrigg Inn at Lake Ullswater, Penrith, Cumbria, is well known for its increased use of local produce, which general manager Derek Mclean says is simply a question of responding to customer demand. 'I think people come to the area and want to eat the best that's available of the local cuisine,' he says. 'They want to escape the routine stuff they can get anywhere else in the country.'

> "They may not go as far as telling you the animal's name, but they provide a certificate with each carcass you buy, telling you the name of the breed, details of what its been fed on and where in the Lake District it spent its life."
> Derek Mclean, The Brackenrigg Inn

One of the most popular dishes at The Brackenrigg, not surprisingly, is Cumberland sausage, and the butcher who makes them, Adam Jackson, is in the same village as the pub. The pub also sources its meat from Milnthorpe-based Cumbrian Fellbred, a company that supplies the finest Cumbrian meat from the fells and dales of Cumbria and the Lake District. Derek Mclean says: 'They may not go as far as telling you the animal's name, but they actually provide a certificate with each carcass you buy, telling you the name of the breed, details of what it's been fed on and where in the Lake District it has spent its life.'

Ben Jones (with Sean Hope and Marcus Welford) runs two pubs – the Red Lion at Stathern, Leicestershire, and the Michelin-starred Olive Branch, Clipsham, Rutland. Both pubs source as much local produce as possible and, although using small producers can work out slightly more expensive than using larger suppliers, Ben is happy to pay extra for good quality 'because the produce is rarer, it's not mass-produced and small producers have to make a living.' He says: 'Regional and local is more important to us than organic. For us, the flavour is more important than the ethics, and often, free-range chickens can be better for flavour than the organic ones.'

Supply hasn't been a problem for Robert Whigham, who runs the Red Lion at Stodmarsh near Canterbury, Kent. Whigham has conquered the supply issue by sourcing vegetables from local allotment holders and meat from the closest farm. 'The allotment holders bring their produce in and it's the old bartering system – pints of bitter for a sack of potatoes,' he says.

"The allotment holders bring their produce in and it's the old bartering system – pints of bitter for a sack of potatoes."

Robert Whigham, The Red Lion

'I buy my baby vegetables and carrots from allotment holders 20 miles away and they bring them in as and when we need them. I've set them all up so they know what I want each week and we change the menu to what is available. One of our allotment holders grows seven types of organic lettuces for us. These people don't spray their allotments and they're very prudent about it. They pick this stuff at seven o'clock in the morning, it gets here by ten and the dew is still on the leaves. It couldn't be fresher than that, and it tastes wonderful, too.'

Since taking over the Appletree Country Inn at Marton, North Yorkshire, Melanie and Trajan Drew have found it increasingly easy to source local produce. 'Farmers will now approach us, rather than us looking for them,' says Melanie. 'It's not always cheaper, because there are a few unscrupulous people out there who think that, because everyone wants local produce, they can charge a bit more for it. But if the quality's there, we don't mind paying for it and quality is definitely on the increase.'

'We have two or three farmers who actually breed things for us and they're aware of what we want. We get our beef from a farmer called Anthony 'Tubby' Turnbull. He lives two farms away from us and he's a regular in the pub and plays in our domino team. We take one or two heifers from him each month, and a local abattoir hangs it for three to four weeks for us. We buy the whole animal and, because we do our own butchery, we get all the meat we need for pies, sausages, burgers and stocks.'

Builth Wells

THE FELIN FACH GRIFFIN

A470

A470

Black Mountains

A479

PF Sweeney family Butcher

Penpont

PenpontOrganic

Brecon

Bwlch

Welsh Venison centre

Crickhowell

A40

Black Mountain Smokery

A485

"We get our beef from a farmer called Anthony 'Tubby' Turnbull. He lives two farms from us and he's a regular in the pub and plays in our domino team."
Melanie Drew, The Appletree Country Inn

The Appletree also has a half-acre garden and an orchard with a plum tree, six apple trees, gooseberry bushes, cherry trees and crops of wild garlic. 'All the stuff we grow gets used in the pub,' says Melanie. 'We even make our own jams and chutneys, which we sell behind the bar.'

Another pub to go the self-sufficient route is the Felin Fach Griffin in Brecon. Owner Charles Inkin is a passionate advocate of using local Welsh produce and his award-winning restaurant menu features smoked salmon from the Black Mountains Smokery, local Welsh rib-eye steaks and an entirely Welsh cheeseboard.

A438

Hereford

A465

Bower farm Dairy

Grosmont

Abergavenny

A40

By using predominantly local producers, the kitchen still achieves a healthy gross profit, and Inkin's latest business idea has been to set up a kitchen garden at the rear of the pub.

'Last summer, we had a crop of beans, peas and salads, and we've just planted soft fruit trees. It's going to take a few years to make it profitable, but, aesthetically, it looks fantastic, with huge areas of colour.'

Situated in the National Trust village of Plockton, on the shores of Loch Carron in the Scottish Highlands, the Plockton Hotel exists almost entirely on local produce. Co-proprietor Dorothy Pearson says: 'We're using what's on our doorstep – I can see the langoustines and prawns being landed daily on the harbour, 100 yards away.'

'All our fish and shellfish comes from the local area or from nearby Kinlochbervie, our smoked fish comes from Andrew and Jenny Wiseman's Sleepy Hollow Smokehouse at Aultbea and the cheese comes from David Biss in the next village.'

The pub also uses the award-winning Skye Food Link Van. Launched in 2000, and subsidised by the Skye and Lochalsh Enterprise Company, the van collects produce from farms and small producers and delivers it to local households, pubs and restaurants twice a week.

'When tourists come here, they expect to see fish jumping out of the water and on to the plate and that's what we give them. We don't do anything fancy, we just give them well-presented fresh food, nothing complicated.'

"All our fish and shellfish comes from the local area or from nearby Kinlochbervie, our smoked fish comes from Andrew and Jenny Wiseman's Sleepy Hollow Smokehouse at Aultbea and the cheese comes from David Biss in the next village."
Dorothy Pearson, Plockton Hotel

The phenomenal rise in pubs sourcing fresh local produce is widespread across the country and on the increase. Several pubs have taken their commitment to local producers a step further by opening small produce shops in adjoining buildings, and there are also a number of pubs holding their own weekly farmers' markets. With more and more consumers demanding good-quality local ingredients, the gastropub revolution looks set to help cut food miles down to food inches.

What's the
catch?

A new wave of enthusiasm for different fish varieties means there is a wider choice of exciting dishes on restaurant menus. We net a rich source of species from our coastline, and our chefs have devised fabulous ways of serving them.

It is not only delicious and versatile, but seafood is low in calories, high in protein and rich in vitamins, minerals and natural oils – in fact it is one of the most nutritious foods we can eat.

Fish features in many different guises on menus around the world, and in the UK it has become the star feature on Les Routiers members' menus. More restaurants are creating superb fish dishes from fish caught off the British coast.

Apart from the national favourite – battered and fried fish served with chips – fish offers plenty of cooking possibilities. You can oven roast it whole, stuff it with aromatic herbs, a simple and fuss-free option, or lightly pan-fry fillets and serve with a butter or caper sauce. White fish is a brilliant canvas for absorbing a range of spicy and citrussy marinades, and once flavoured the fish takes no time to cook on the barbecue or under the grill.

The cooking possibilities are endless, especially as we are widening our fish choices and buying alternatives to the ever-popular cod and haddock. Sea bass, sea bream, halibut and monkfish are among the top choices. But that's not all. There are more than 21,000 species of fish in the world, and more than 100 varieties widely available in the UK.

Many of the fish varieties caught off our coastline are served at Les Routiers' establishments. In winter, try sea bass, coley, red gurnard and brill; in summer there are amazing fish such as flounder, hake, sardines, megrim, lemon or Dover sole. All year-round, we can tuck into marvellous monkfish, John Dory and mackerel. Just a few to look out for on menus or at fishmongers around the country.

Seafish was set up in 1981 and works to help consumers find out about the wide variety of seafood available and the many benefits that it offers, as well as to help all sectors of the seafood industry raise standards, improve efficiency and develop environmentally responsible practices.

A key date in the Seafish calendar is the annual Seafood Week, which is held every October. And the date is no coincidence, for it is this time of year when we have the best stocks of many different types of seafood available.

During the week, Seafish will be advising on buying and cooking fish and shellfish. It will be running special promotions with many restaurants and retailers. For information about events for this, and at other times of the year, check out its website at www.seafish.org.uk. It is a wealth of information, and a wonderful database of restaurants, pubs and fish and chip shops and even recipes to try for yourself.

'The rise (and rise and rise) of the gastropub has changed British drinking – and eating – habits forever.'

Raising the Bar

by Natasha Hughes

Those of us who were old enough to drink in pubs over a decade ago will have no difficulty in remembering the bad old days. By the bad old days, I'm harking back to an era when the only beers available were fizzy, tasteless lagers and ales brewed by numbers in vast factories owned by faceless corporations. And if, God forbid, you wanted a glass of wine, it was a dead cert that you'd be offered a Paris goblet of some thin, tasteless concoction that had been squeezed out of a bag in a box.

And, wherever you went, from the Outer Hebrides to the Isle of Wight, the same brand names would crop up again and again. Your wine would come from Stowell's of Chelsea and your beer from Bass. There was next to no chance at all that you could sample the ales, stouts, lagers or bitters made on the burgeoning local brewing scene. And as for the wheat beers, blondes and brunes of the Continent – you might as well expect to fly to the moon as expect the landlord of your local to offer you a trans-Channel brew.

In addition to the bland, generic nature of both beers and wines, there were other problems. Both drinks were often badly stored in unsuitable conditions and served either too warm or too cold, diminishing what little enjoyment there was to be had from them in the first place. And should you want to take your life in your own hands by ordering from a limited menu that probably included a ploughman's lunch, complete with a lump of sweaty Cheddar that had come straight out of a plastic packet, or a tasteless steak-and-kidney pie whose pastry had been microwaved into limpness, the idea of finding a drink to complement the food was laughable. Quite frankly, you were probably better off with a packet of pork scratchings washed down with a pint.

When it came to wine, the situation was much the same. A few big names dominated and there was little reflection of the fact that wine is made by thousands of producers working in hundreds of regions around the world. Nor was there much recognition that Britain has one of the most diverse wine markets in the world. These two facts alone should have allowed us the option to sample a South Australian Riesling or a Viognier from southern France, followed by an Argentinian Malbec or a Piedmontese Barbera, at the very least. Instead, we settled for Chardonnay or Merlot of unspecified origin. To make matters worse, even if your wine came out of a bottle rather than a bag, the chances were it had been open for days and that the liquid inside was now well on its way to becoming vinegar.

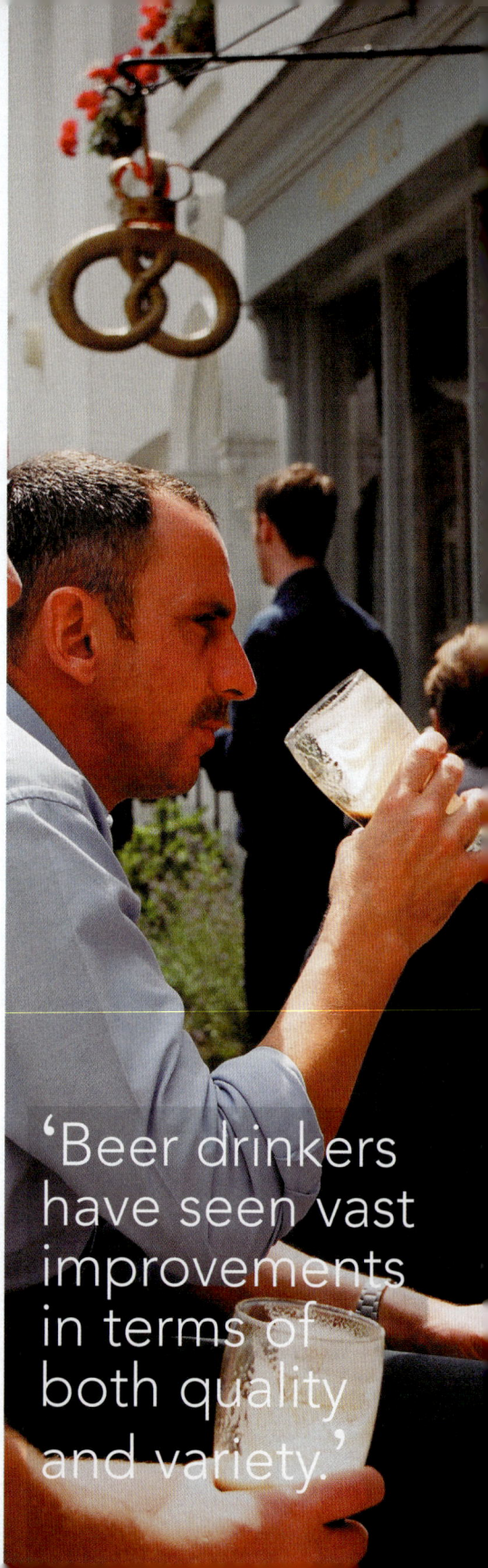

'Beer drinkers have seen vast improvements in terms of both quality and variety.'

Nowadays, as long as you pick your pub carefully – or let Les Routiers do the picking for you – you'll find that the situation has changed, quite dramatically, for the better. And these improvements are largely down to the coming-of-age of two key factors.

The Campaign for Real Ale (CAMRA) has been waging its war on mass-produced beers for 35 years now. And, while its organisers are the first to admit that there are battles still to be won (over a third of Britain's pubs are still owned by one of two huge companies), beer drinkers have seen vast improvements in terms of both quality and variety, thanks to the campaigns led by the organisation.

The growing interest in quality brewing has led to a flowering of independent micro-breweries, of which there are more than 400 scattered across the UK today. Not only does this mean that drinkers benefit from being able to order 'live' beers brewed locally, it also means that there is now an entire galaxy of different styles to choose from. International beers have also taken off – and I'm not talking about bland lagers from Holland or Denmark here. I mean Trappist beers, fruit beers, lambic beers and a whole host of other styles, many of which come from Belgium, a country with a brewing tradition as rich as that of the UK.

To add interest to the situation, the last bastion of beer-drinking is falling, as breweries start to invest in a range of glassware that will see we Brits supping from glasses with stems, glasses that hold a third of a pint and glasses with goblet- or tulip-shaped bowls. In short, everything but your traditional pint mug. There are a number of reasons behind this metamorphosis – not least of which is the fact that, having gone through all these efforts to create a range of tastes, the brewers want us to use glasses that will allow us to enjoy them.

The other important factor in the transformation of our drinking habits has come into play far more recently, although, arguably, its influence is even more pervasive. The rise (and rise and rise) of the gastropub has changed British drinking – and eating – habits forever. The trend kicked off in London, when David Eyre and Mike Belben opened The Eagle in 1991. So popular was the combination of simple, good-quality ingredients, low prices and relaxed atmosphere that, within a very short space of time, almost every town and village in Britain had at least one gastropub of its very own.

'Gone are the days when it was acceptable to have a sweet white, a dry white and a couple of reds on your list.'

The shift in emphasis has encouraged landlords to take a long, hard look at the drinks they serve alongside their new menus. Chalked-up wine lists now often reflect the personal tastes – and the travel experiences – of the landlord. Gone are the days when it was acceptable to have a sweet white, a dry white and a couple of reds on your list. You're far more likely to find a selection of wines from around the Med or a carefully picked selection that blends the New World with the Old. And all of these wines will have been chosen to match the style of food served up in the kitchen.

Although most pubs still have only a dozen or so wines on their lists, they're likely to have been chosen with care. And there are pubs that take their wine so seriously they have lists that can easily match those of nearby restaurants. Some will even haul out the good glassware for customers – are the days of the Paris goblet numbered?

The breweries are even getting in on the act – players both large and small, such as Greene King, Shepherd Neame, Coors and Hook Norton – are creating beers designed to be matched to food. What's more, they're training pub staff in the art of matching, so that they can pass on their new-found knowledge to customers.

There's still a long way to go before the pub trade can celebrate for encouraging British consumers to make adventurous drinking choices, but the first steps down a long road have been taken. Now its up to us, the drinking customers, to join them on the journey.

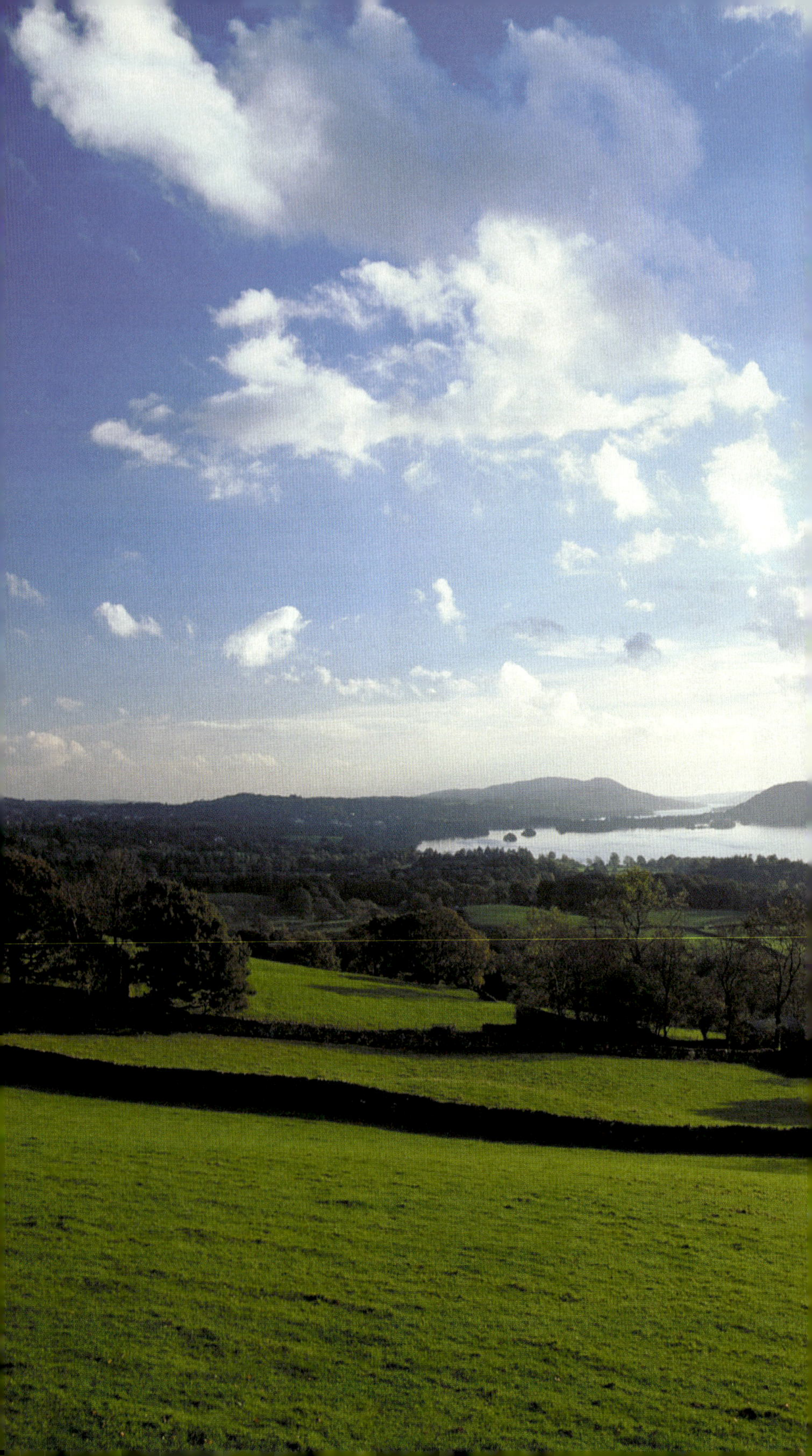

ENGLAND

Bath

The Hunters Rest Inn

King Lane, Clutton Hill, Bath BS39 5QL
Telephone: +44(0)1761 452303
paul@huntersrest.co.uk
www.huntersrest.co.uk

Persevere down winding country lanes to locate this isolated rural inn, built as a hunting lodge for the Earl of Warwick in 1755. Inside, a stone bar is surrounded by a number of interconnecting rooms; one leads into the bright conservatory. Old farm paraphernalia hangs from walls, and dried hops adorn the beamed ceilings' along with brass plates and hunting pictures. Food is traditional, and the specials locally sourced, and runs from hearty ploughman's lunches with locally produced cheddar to lamb with red wine, garlic and herbs. Tuna steak with lime, chilli and coriander butter may appear on the specials menu. Wednesday night is family night, and kids can make use of the miniature railway in the garden. All four bedrooms are individually decorated; each comes with bags of character and a teddy bear. See pub walk on page 210.

Rooms: 5. Double from £85, single from £60, family room from £125.
Prices: Set lunch £12.50 and dinner £18.50. Restaurant main course from £10. Bar main course from £7. House wine £9.25.
Last orders: Bar: lunch 15.00; dinner 23.00. Food: lunch 14.00; dinner 21.30 (Friday and Saturday 22.15).
Closed: Never.
Food: Traditional English.
Real ale: Bass, Butcombe, Otter Bitter, Bath Gem.
Other points: No-smoking area. Children welcome. Dogs welcome in the bar. Garden. Car park. Wheelchair access to the restaurant/pub.
Directions: Clutton Hill lies between the A39 and A37 south of Bristol. Call for directions. (Map 3, F2)

Ivinghoe

The Kings Head

Station Road, Ivinghoe, Leighton Buzzard, Bedfordshire LU7 9EB
Telephone: +44(0)1296 668388/668264
info@kingsheadivinghoe.co.uk
www.kingsheadivinghoe.co.uk

This 17th-century coaching inn more than holds its own in the charm and character stakes in the pretty village of Ivinghoe. It fills a prime site, impressively alongside one side of the village green. Low beams, oak panelling, antique furniture and period portraits create even more ambience. Enjoy a drink in the bars or head to the restaurant or up to the banqueting suite. Chef Jonathan O'Keefe cooks to suit all diners, from his Bon Appetit lunch menu to the carte. Three-course set-lunch menus feature starters of warm goat's cheese salad, followed by pan-fried fillet of sea bass and a selection of homemade puds. Vegetarians have a separate menu and the carte is another veritable feast of well-sourced dishes, from starters of fillet of red mullet to fillet of beef from Buccleuch and Aylesbury duckling. The banqueting suite, featuring paintings from Woburn Fine Arts, is available for business or pleasure and is an excellent setting for private functions.

Prices: Set lunch £16.95 and dinner from £33, including coffee. House wine £19.50.
Last orders: Food: lunch 14.15; dinner 21.30.
Closed: Sunday evening, 27-29 December.
Food: Modern British.
Other points: No smoking in the restaurant. Children welcome. Car park. Private banqueting. Wheelchair access to the restaurant/pub.
Directions: Exit M25. Take the A41 to Tring, turn right onto the B488 to Ivinghoe. The restaurant is on the right at the junction with the B489. (Map 3, D4)

Milton Keynes

The Swan

2 Wavendon Road, Salford, Cranfield,
Bedfordshire MK17 8BD
Telephone: +44(0)1908 281008
e.swan@peachpubs.com
www.swansalford.co.uk

Peach Pubs have done it again, carefully
identifying a corner of countryside crying
out for a decent dining pub, this time the
gastronomic desert around Milton Keynes,
and then finding just the right property. Just
10 minutes from the town centre, the Swan in
sleepy Salford has been given a new lease of
life. The attractive tile-hung Edwardian pub
was gutted and extended, and now sports a
comfortable bar, a new light and airy dining room leading out onto a smart terrace,
and a private dining-cum-meeting room in
a converted barn. Food combines classic
pub dishes with modern brasserie meals and
Peach Pubs trademark 'deli-board' offering nibbles of cheese, charcuterie, antipasti
and rustic breads. Expect starters of chilli
salt squid or crab-and-lime soufflé, then a
choice of chargrilled meats or calf's liver
with mustard mash and jus, or chorizo and
butter bean cassoulet. Good side orders and
delicious puddings - try the hazelnut parfait
with raspberry sauce.

Prices: Restaurant main course from £8.75. Bar snack
from £1.50. House wine from £10.50.
Last orders: Food: 22.00.
Closed: 25 December.
Food: Modern European.
Real ale: Fuller's London Pride, Greene King IPA.
Other points: No-smoking area.
Directions: Exit 13/M1. Take Bedford Road and almost
immediately left to Cranfield & Salford. The Swan is in
the middle of the village. (Map 3, D4)

Woburn

The Black Horse

1 Bedford Street, Woburn,
Bedfordshire MK17 9QB
Telephone: +44(0)1525 290210
blackhorse@peachpubs.com
www.blackhorsewoburn.co.uk

Peach Pubs are breaking into new territory
around Milton Keynes and the 16th-century
Black Horse in this upmarket village is their
latest acquisition. Located in the village centre, yet handy for the famous Safari Park,
it looks every inch a marketplace pub, the
traditional brick exterior giving way to a
rambling carpeted interior with a big wooden
bar, and neat rear garden. No doubt the décor
will change, but Peach's trademark 'deli-
board' menu is up and running, offering cold
cuts, cheeses, potted shrimps and pickles and
dips for nibbles, starters or as a main course
platter. For something more substantial, kick
off with crab, chilli and garlic linguine with
red-pepper oil, then move on to chargrilled
tuna with summer salad and herb dressing, or
roast pork loin with confit onion, apples and
black pudding. Finish with lemon tart and
a fine espresso coffee. To drink, you'll find
Greene King ales and 10 wines by the glass.

Prices: Restaurant main course from £8.75. Bar snack
from £1.50. House wine from £10.50.
Last orders: Food: 22.00.
Closed: Rarely.
Food: Modern British.
Real ale: Timothy Taylor Landlord, Greene King IPA,
Fuller's London Pride.
Other points: No-smoking area. Children welcome.
Dogs welcome in the bar. Garden. Car park.
Wheelchair access.
Directions: Exit 13/M1. Follow signs to Woburn. The
Black Horse is in the town centre by the pedestrian
crossing. (Map 3, D4)

Barkham

The Bull Inn

Barkham Road, Barkham, Wokingham,
Berkshire RG41 4TL
Telephone: +44(0)1189 760324
barkhambull@barbox.net
www.thebullatbarkham.com

At one time, this pub also doubled as the village blacksmith. The original forge still stands in the centre of The Bull's restaurant and scorch marks are visible on the adjacent beams. The main building was originally a brewhouse and the restaurant extension was the working blacksmith's forge from 1728 until it closed in 1982. You can eat informally in the bar or in the large attractive garden. In the restaurant, linen-clothed tables set beneath huge beams create a more formal setting for chef-proprietor Adrian Brunswick's traditional country cooking. Expect a modern twist to familiar dishes, perhaps calves' liver on a rocket-potato cake, and smoked haddock in a leek-and-prawn sauce. Chocoholics will appreciate the moist chocolate fudge cake with cream. As well as the hearty pies, chillies and battered fish, lighter dishes are available at lunchtime. Wife Susie oversees the attractively refurbished bar, dispensing Adnams ales and well chosen wines to locals and intending diners.

Prices: Main course from £7. House wine £11.95.
Last orders: Bar: lunch 14.50; dinner 22.50 (Sunday 22.20). Food: lunch 14.15; dinner 21.15.
Closed: Rarely.
Food: Traditional and Modern British and Continental.
Real ale: Adnams Broadside, Courage Best Bitter, Adnams Best, Old Speckled Hen. 1 guest beer.
Other points: No smoking in the restaurant. Garden. Car park. Dogs welcome in the bar.
Directions: Exit 10/M4. Head towards Wokingham and follow signposts to Barkham. The Bull Inn is in the centre of Barkham. (Map 3, F4)

Cookham

The Ferry

Sutton Road, Cookham, Maidenhead,
Berkshire SL6 9SN
Telephone: +44(0)1628 525123
www.theferry.co.uk

Another great location, another great refurbishment and, undoubtedly, another great success for Orange Pubs. Transformed from a Harvester pub to a swish gastro-pub in early 2005, the revitalised Ferry stands beside Cookham Bridge and a scenic stretch of the River Thames. The stylish 'Orange' formula has been replicated inside, so expect a contemporary feel to the decor and very comfortable furnishings. Beams have been exposed, walls painted with chic, earthy colours, fat leather sofas front huge open fireplaces, and chunky wooden tables fill the large dining area. Food is a mix of modern British and Italian, the latter evident in wood-fired pizzas, risotto and pasta meals such as crab, chilli and parsley linguine. Dishes are simple, freshly prepared and full of flavour, with robust main dishes like spit chicken with aïoli and calves' liver with mash and onion jam. A smart terrace makes the most of the riverside location and is the perfect spot for summer drinking.

Prices: Restaurant main course from £7.95.
House wine £12.
Last orders: Bar: 23.00. Food: lunch 14.30; dinner 21.30 (Sunday all day to 20.30).
Closed: Never.
Food: Modern British with Italian influences.
Real ale: Timothy Taylor Bitter, Fuller's London Pride.
Other points: No-smoking area. Children over 12 welcome. Dogs welcome. Garden. Wheelchair access.
Directions: Exit 15/M40. Go through Bourne End and over the bridge at Cookham. The Ferry is on the left. (Map 3, E4)

Newbury

The Bunk Inn

Curridge, Newbury,
Berkshire RG18 9DS
Telephone: +44 (0)1635 200400
thebunkinn@btconnect.com
www.thebunkinn.co.uk

Travel-weary M4 drivers in need of a bed can now pass over the Chieveley Travel Inn for a comfortable room at Mickey Liquorish's ever-popular Bunk Inn. All are kitted out with quality fabrics and fittings and smart en suite facilities. The accommodation should also appeal to those looking for a bustling and informal pub, and the present food set up should not disappoint either, as sound traditional favourites rub shoulders with modern pub dishes on the chalkboard menu and weekly changing carte. Take comfort in bangers and mash or a 'Bunk' long loaf snack. Or head for the conservatory dining room for ham hock and caper terrine with apple chutney, followed by half-shoulder of lamb with port and redcurrant gravy, with stem ginger brûlée or a plate of cheese to finish. Altogether, the newly extended beamed bar and front terrace with upmarket tables and chairs create a civilised atmosphere.

Rooms: 8. Double room from £85, single from £70.
Prices: Restaurant main course from £9.95. Bar main course from £5.95. House wine £13.50.
Last orders: Bar: 24.00. Food: lunch 14.30 (weekend 15.00); dinner 22.00 (Sunday 21.30).
Closed: Rarely.
Food: Traditional and modern British.
Real ale: Fuller's London Pride, Wadworth 6X, Arkells 3B's. 1 guest beer.
Other points: No smoking in the restaurant. Children welcome. Dogs welcome in the bar. Garden. Car park. Wheelchair access.
Directions: Exit 13/M4 Curridge is off the B4009 (Goring road) 3 miles north of Newbury. (Map 3, F3)

Waltham St Lawrence

The Star Inn

Broadmoor Road, Waltham St Lawrence,
Reading, Berkshire RG10 0HY
Telephone: +44(0)1189 343486
james@thestar-inn.co.uk
www.thestar-inn.co.uk

Sound investment by both Wadworth Brewery and enthusiastic tenants James Barrons-Ruth and Jayne Barrington-Groves has seen the fortunes of this unassuming local in pretty Waltham St Lawrence improve in recent years. Spick-and-span throughout the traditional pub interior, The Star draws folk from miles around for interesting wines and home-cooked pub food. Although the lunchtime menu offers pub favourites for speed and convenience, James refuses to serve chips or any deep-fried foods and prefers to prepare everything on the premises. Typically, chicken Caesar salad, ham ploughman's and freshly made chilli will accompany the home-baked pizzas on the lunchtime board. Expect a touch more imagination in the evening, with baked salmon with basil butter and rib-eye steak with peppercorn, cream and brandy sauce making an appearance on the seasonally changing menu. Tip-top Wadworth ales and good bin-end and monthly wine specials.

Prices: Restaurant main course from £11.95.
Bar main course from £5.95. House wine £11.95.
Last orders: Food: lunch 14.00; dinner 21.30.
No food Sunday evening.
Closed: Rarely.
Food: Modern pub food.
Real ale: Wadworth 6X, Henry's IPA.
Other points: No-smoking area. Garden. Well-behaved children welcome. Car park. Wheelchair access (not WC).
Directions: Exit 8 or 9/M4, A404 to White Waltham, heading west through Cox Green for two miles to Waltham St Lawrence. (Map 3, E4)

Wargrave

St George & Dragon

High Street, Wargrave, Berkshire RG10 8HY
Telephone: +44(0)118 940 5021
www.stgeorgeanddragon.co.uk

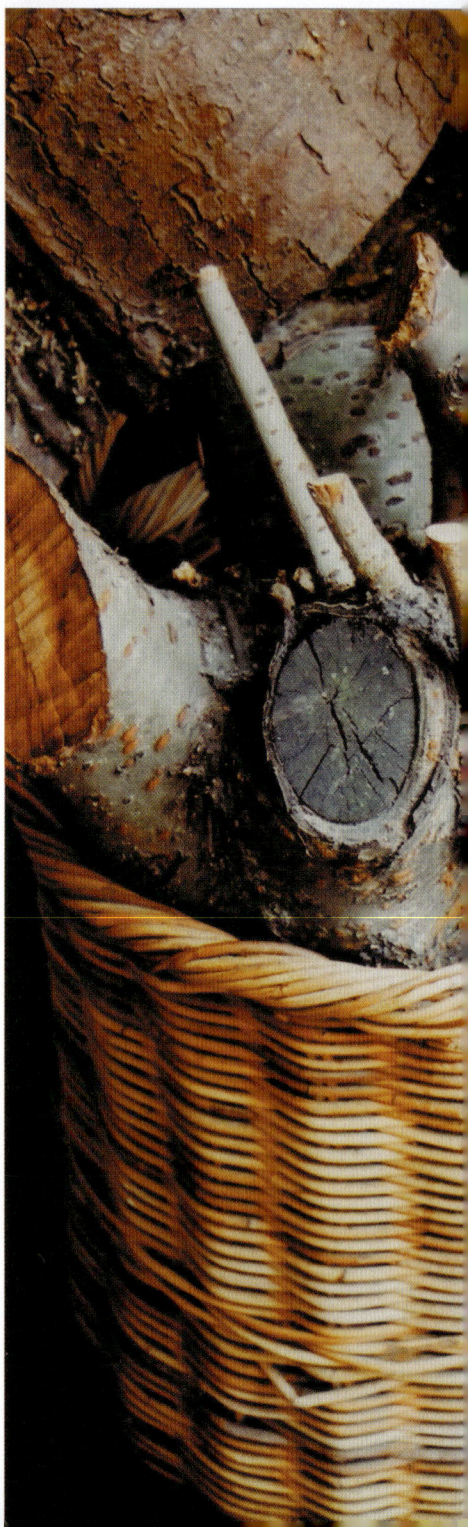

The quite brilliant 'Orange' pub concept, where run-down pubs are transformed into stylish gastro-pubs, now includes this impressive Thames-side pub. This winning formula - open kitchen and a contemporary, almost minimalist décor - has worked a treat here. The spacious, open-plan interior has been beautifully reworked, with simple muted colours, Asian art and wooden floors setting the style in the comfortable, yet very informal drinking and dining areas. Breads, cheeses and olive oils are on display and prepared at a deli-style counter, and all dishes are freshly prepared in the open-to-view kitchen. From an Italian-inspired menu, tuck into bowls of fresh pasta, pizzas from the oven (perhaps a traditional Margherita), Caesar salad, rack of lamb with peas, chorizo and new potatoes, or battered haddock with tartare sauce. On fine days, eat beside the Thames. See pub walk on page 212.

Prices: Restaurant main course from £8.95. Bar main course from £5.50. House wine £11.95.
Last orders: Bar: 23.00. Food: lunch 14.30; dinner 21.30 (Sunday 20.30).
Closed: Rarely.
Food: Modern British with Italian influences.
Real ale: Bass, Fuller's London Pride.
Other points: No smoking in the restaurant. Large terrace overlooking the river. Car park.
Directions: Exit8/9/M4 Take the M404 towards Maidenhead. At the roundabout take the A4 towards Reading. Wargrave is signposted on the right. Go through the village and turn right at the crossroads. (Map 3, E4)

Chalfont St Giles

The Ivy House

London Road, Chalfont St Giles,
Buckinghamshire HP8 4RS
Telephone: +44(0)1494 872184
www.theivyhouse-bucks.co.uk

This much-loved 17th-century brick-and-flint freehouse is set in the heart of the Chiltern Hills, with views across the Misbourne Valley. Spick and span, it sports an enlarged dining room, a smart patio for alfresco eating and five en suite rooms. The wood and slate-floored bar, with its old beams, cosy armchairs and wood-burning fires is full of traditional charm. A menu of modern British dishes reveals a happiness to experiment with ingredients to produce unusual dishes - look to the blackboard for the day's creations. Starter choices include homemade soups and giant prawns with basil oil and sweet chilli sauce. Main courses extend to ostrich with mango-and-orange sauce, and chargrilled steaks with a choice of sauces, plus winter casseroles, summer salads, pasta meals and homemade puddings, perhaps Baileys dark-chocolate truffle torte. Retire to one of the individually furnished bedrooms and wake up to a hearty breakfast.

Rooms: 5. Double room £95, single occupancy £75.
Prices: Main course from £7.75. House wine £11.50.
Last orders: Bar: lunch 15.00; dinner 23.00 (open all day at the weekend). Food: lunch 14.30; dinner 21.30 (all day at the weekend).
Closed: Never.
Food: Modern British and global.
Real ale: London Pride, Wadworth 6X. 3 guest beers.
Other points: No-smoking area. Children welcome. Dogs welcome in the bar. Garden and courtyard. Car park. Wheelchair access.
Directions: Exit2/M40. Situated directly between Amersham and Gerrards Cross on the A413. (Map 3, E4)

Denham

The Swan Inn

Village Road, Denham,
Buckinghamshire UB9 5BH
Telephone: +44(0)1895 832085
info@swaninndenham.co.uk
www.swaninndenham.co.uk

Weary M25 and M40 travellers should shun the faceless services for this creeper-clad pub in upmarket Denham, just a few minutes drive from exits 17 and 1 respectively. With fine houses and brick-and-timber cottages for neighbours, and a magnificent rear terrace and garden, the Swan must be the best motorway pitstop for miles. Like its stylish siblings (The Alford Arms, Frithsden; The Royal Oak, Marlow - see entries), the Swan's single bar and informal dining area has been refurbished with style, with a rug-strewn floor, sturdy tables, cushioned settles and a splendid log fire. A chalkboard menu and printed carte deliver modern pub food. 'Small plates' range from rustic breads with roast garlic, balsamic and olive oil for an appetiser, to starters/light meals such as beef carpaccio with onion jam. More substantial offerings include salmon fishcake with sorrel cream sauce and calves' liver with red wine and thyme gravy. Top-notch wines include 15 by the glass.

Prices: Restaurant main course from £9.75. House wine £11.25.
Last orders: Bar: 23.00. Food: lunch 14.30 (Sunday 15.00); dinner 22.00.
Closed: Rarely.
Food: Modern British.
Real ale: Courage Best Bitter, Wadworth 6X, Morrell's Oxford Blue.
Other points: No-smoking area. Children welcome. Dogs welcome in the bar. Garden. Car park.
Directions: Exit1/M40 and exit17/M25. From the M40 take the A412 Uxbridge to Rickmansworth Road and turn left in 200 yards for Denham. (Map 3, E4)

The Ivy House

Chef/proprietor Jane Mears and her team are always keen to try new recipes. They have sourced a wealth of local ingredients to achieve their exciting menus, which are modern British with a Mediterranean flavour. Here, Jane shares her top suppliers in the Chiltern Hills area.

Visit the local Farmers' Market

There is an excellent French farmers' market which comes periodically to both Amersham and Chesham, selling a great range of quality fresh produce, including olives, garlic and cheeses direct from France.

A413

A4128

Beechdean Ice Cream, North Dean

A404

High Wycombe

Beaconsfield

Beechdean Ice Cream
Old House Farm, North Dean, High Wycombe
Tel: 01494 562829
www.beechdean.co.uk

This rich, creamy ice cream is made on the family farm from fresh Jersey whole milk from the pedigree herd. Flavours run from the classic vanilla to sticky-toffee fudge, and you will find it served at everywhere from Buckingham Palace tea parties to the Royal Albert Hall, and sold in farm shops.

Godden Butchers
Tel: 01494 772997
Tel: www.goddens.co.uk

A local Chesham family butchers, which closed its high-street shop after the death of the founder Clive Godden. It continues to supply its favoured trade customers under the guidance of Clive's sons. Excellent steaks, ostrich, boar and award-winning sausages.

A416

Godden Butchers, Chesham

Tom Robertson Butchers
10 Chenies Parade, Station Road
Little Chalfont
Tel: 01494 763084

A long-established family butchers, with an outstanding reputation locally, from which The Ivy House buys top-quality game (including Balmoral wild venison), superb cooked meats and Gressingham duck.

A404

Amersham

Tom Robertson Butchers, Little Chalfont

G D Swerling & Sons Chalfont St Giles

The Ivy House, Chalfont St Giles

LES ROUTIERS

A413

G D Swerling & Sons
Upper Bottom House Farm,
Bottom House Farm Lane,
Chalfont St Giles
Tel: 01494 872492

These local farmers, owners of the fields opposite, have farmed the local area as long as anyone here can remember. Graham should have retired years ago, but won't give up his round, and supplies all of The Ivy House's milk and cream and many of its cheeses.

A40

D H Aldridge, Fruit and vegetables

Marlow

The Royal Oak

Frieth Road, Bovingdon Green, Marlow,
Buckinghamshire SL7 2JF
Telephone: +44(0)1628 488611
info@royaloakmarlow.co.uk
www.royaloakmarlow.co.uk

Fronted by a gravel terrace edged with rosemary, this lovely cream-painted cottage on the edge of Marlow Common has been refurbished with style. Beyond a cosy snug (open fire, rug-strewn boards, an array of scrubbed oak tables), piped jazz, and a buzzy atmosphere characterise the beamed bar and dining areas. Informality is the key here – eat anywhere with the choice extending to the landscaped garden in summer. Both chalkboards and printed menus promise food that reveals a lot of imagination at work in the kitchen. 'Small plates' take in twice-baked sorrel and Roquefort soufflé, while mains range from braised lamb shank with Italian bean stew to smoked haddock on champ with mustard sauce. Try the rustic breads with roast garlic and olive oil for dipping; there are freshly-cut lunchtime sandwiches and good puddings. Same ownership as The Alford Arms, Frithsden and The Swan at Denham.

Prices: Restaurant main course from £9.75.
House wine £11.25.
Last orders: Bar: 23.00. Food: lunch 14.30
(Sunday 15.00); dinner 22.00.
Closed: Rarely.
Food: Modern British.
Real ale: Fuller's London Pride, Brakspear Ales,
Marlow Rebellion.
Other points: No-smoking area. Children welcome.
Dogs welcome in the bar. Garden. Car park.
Wheelchair access.
Directions: Exit 9M4 and exit 4/M40. In Marlow, take the A4155 towards Henley and turn right in 300 yards to Bovingdon Green. (Map 3, E4)

Mentmore

The Stag

The Green, Mentmore,
Buckinghamshire LU7 0QF
Telephone: +44(0)1296 668423
reservations@thestagmentmore.com
www.thestagmentmore.com

The Stag stands in a picture-postcard village with a lovely garden, overlooking Mentmore House and is run by Mike and Jenny Tuckwood, whose fresh modern approach to running a traditional country pub has proved a great success. The classic bar is the place to sample Charles Wells ales and some good bar food: sandwiches (hot beef and onion), for example, and one-dish meals of local spicy sausages with onion gravy, or an evening dish such as Moroccan braised lamb. Imaginative, seasonally changing evening menus are served in the stylish two-tiered restaurant, which has direct access to the garden. A plate of buffalo mozzarella with balsamic and black-pepper strawberries makes an unusual starter. Thoughtful attention to inherent flavours produces main courses such as roast cod with coconut and lemon sauce. An alternative to dessert is a plate of British cheeses.

Prices: Restaurant set lunch £15 and dinner £28, main course from £16. Bar lunch £5.50 and dinner £8.50.
Last orders: Food: lunch 14.00; dinner 21.00;
Sunday 20.30.
Closed: Rarely.
Food: Modern British.
Real ale: Charles Wells Bombadier, Charles Wells Eagle.
Other points: No smoking in the restaurant. Children welcome at lunch and aged over 12 in the evening.
Dogs welcome in the bar. Sloping garden with seating.
Limited car park. Wheelchair access (no WC).
Directions: Five miles north east of Aylesbury off the A418 towards Leighton Buzzard. (Map 3, D4)

Stoke Mandeville

The Woolpack

Risborough Road, Stoke Mandeville, Aylesbury,
Buckinghamshire HP22 5UP
Telephone: +44(0)1296 615970
www.woolpackstokemandeville.co.uk

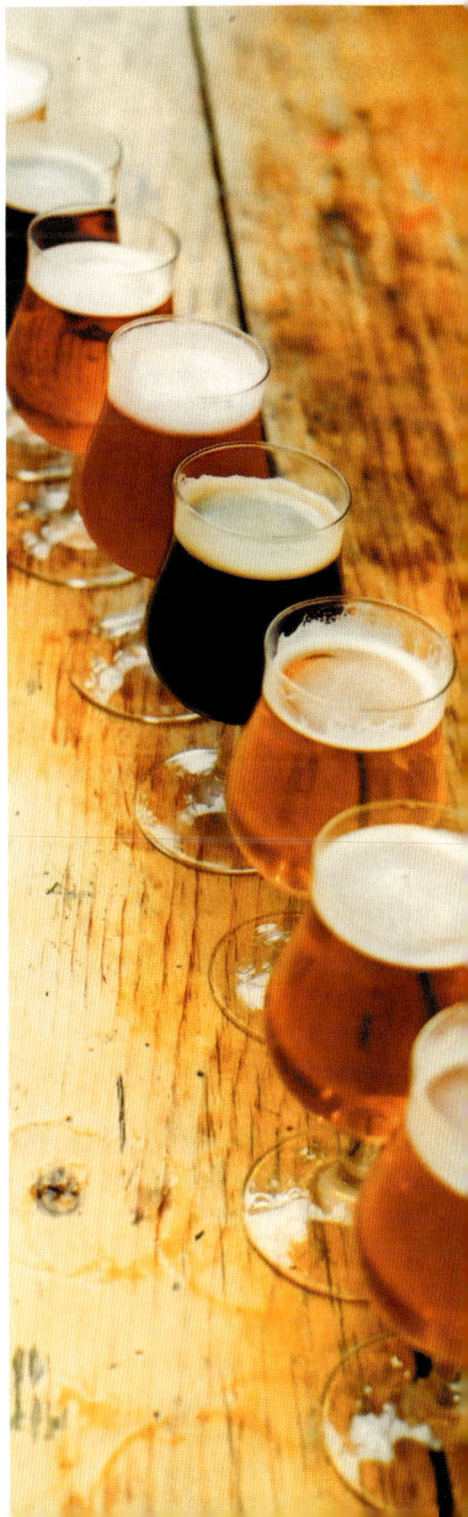

The dynamic Orange pub group headed south in 2004 and the Woolpack was the first of several faded country boozers to be stylishly revamped into upmarket dining venues. The concept is simple and impressive, with pubs stripped out and reworked with wood or rush-mat floors, squashy sofas and armchairs, chunky wooden furnishings, and a modern, minimalist look throughout. Trademark features include smart decked terracing, stone-fired ovens, and several dressers groaning with pasta jars, olive oils and baskets of bread. Italian-influenced menus are the same across the group, but everything is freshly prepared on the premises with chefs interpreting the dishes as they wish. 'Little dishes' include sardines with garlic and parsley, while 'leaves' feature Greek salad with feta, cucumber and thyme. There are also pizzas and pastas, more substantial dishes such as swordfish with Tuscan bean cassoulet and chorizo, and daily chalkboard specials. Good ales and first-class wines.

Prices: Restaurant main course from £8.95.
House wine £11.95.
Last orders: Bar: 23.00. Food: lunch 14.30; dinner: 21.30 (Sunday 20.30).
Closed: Never.
Food: Modern British with Italian influences.
Real ale: Bass, London Pride, Greene King IPA.
Other points: No smoking in the restaurant. Large garden and patio. Children welcome. Dogs welcome outside. Car park.
Directions: From Aylesbury, take the B4443 signposted to Stoke Mandeville. (Map 3, E4)

Waddesdon

Five Arrows Hotel

High Street, Waddesdon, Aylesbury, Buckinghamshire HP18 0JE
Telephone: +44(0)1296 651727
bookings@thefivearrowshotel.fsnet.co.uk
www.waddesdon.org.uk

Must-sees
Waddesdon Manor
Buckinghamshire Railway Centre, Quainton
Claydon House, Middle Claydon
Courthouse, Long Crendon
Ascott, Wing
Stowe House and Gardens
Pitstone Windmill

Pitstone Windmill

A delightful Victorian confection (think turrets, gables and balconies) built by the Rothschilds in 1887 to house the architects and craftsmen who were building Waddesdon Manor, set on a hill in the vast estate behind. Now a stylish small hotel-cum-inn, you enter straight into the bar, from which open several civilised dining rooms with rug-strewn floors, antique tables, and pictures from Lord Rothschild's collection. Locally sourced ingredients and home-grown herbs influence the menu, crayfish-tail salad with dill mayonnaise, for example. Thai marinated red mullet on soy noodles comes as a starter or main course, or there could be braised lamb shank with mint and sage gravy. To finish, choose between the cheese table or treacle tart. There are also blackboard specials and lighter lunchtime meals. The exceptional wine list majors on the various Rothschild wine interests, with eight by the glass. Eleven good-sized bedrooms, including two smart suites, boast all the modern comforts.

Rooms: 11. Double room from £85, single from £70.
Prices: Main course from £13.50. House wine £12.50.
Last orders: Bar: lunch 15.00; dinner 23.00. Food: lunch 14.30 (Sunday 14.00); dinner 21.00 (Sunday 20.30).
Closed: Rarely.
Food: Modern British and Continental.
Real ale: Fuller's London Pride.
Other points: No smoking in the restaurant. Children welcome. Garden. Car park. Wheelchair access.
Directions: Six miles north-west of Aylesbury beside the A41 in Waddesdon. (Map 3, D4)

Tourist information Aylesbury +44(0)1296 330559
Where to shop Aylesbury, Thame, Buckingham
Farmers' market Aylesbury (Tuesday)
Nearest golf course Aylesbury Park Golf Club

Cycling/walking
Quiet lanes criss-cross the gently undulating Vale of Aylesbury, linking attractive villages (Upper Winchendon, Brill, The Claydons) and places of interest (see above). See pub walk on page 214.

Best scenic drives
South-east into the Chiltern Hills via Great Missenden, Amersham, Beaconsfield, High Wycombe and Henley-on-Thames, returning via Stonor, Watlington and Thame. South-west to Oxford, Witney, Burford and the eastern Cotswolds.

Events and festivals
Workshops, wine tastings and events at Waddesdon Manor (all year)
Thame Festival (June/July)

Cambridge

The Green Man

Thriplow, Royston, Cambridgeshire SG8 7RJ
Telephone: +44(0)1763 208855
www.greenmanthriplow.co.uk

In the heart of a small Cambridgeshire village stands this traditional-looking village local, cream-painted with attractive window boxes. Decor within is traditional, with red-patterned carpet, deep red walls, stripped tables, a blazing open fire, and a comfortable dining area. Beers from micro-breweries change continually, so expect brews from Batemans, Milton and Wolf. The menus offer excellent value and evident passion in both compilation and cooking. Create your own dinner by selecting your main course, perhaps rib-eye steak or duck breast, your accompanying sauce, say, pepper or sweet-and-sour, then choose your desired side dishes. Precede with grilled goat's cheese with roasted pepper and tomato salad, and finish with a plate of European cheeses. In addition, chalkboards list a good choice of daily specials. At lunch, tackle the 'sandwich kit', or opt for the locally made sausages with red-wine gravy. Regular gourmet evenings with matching wines and Sunday lunches.

Prices: Set Sunday lunch £13.95. Restaurant main course from £7.50. Bar main course from £3.50. House wine £10.50.
Last orders: Bar: lunch 15.00; dinner 23.00. Food: lunch 14.00; dinner 21.00.
Closed: Sunday evening, all day Monday.
Food: Traditional and Modern British.
Real ale: Klas Act, Tolly Cobbold Original, Oakham, Slaters, Milton. 4 guest beers.
Other points: No smoking in the restaurant. Children welcome. Garden. Car park. Wheelchair access.
Directions: Exit 10/M11. Three miles south of the junction off B1368. (Map 4, D5)

Keyston

Pheasant Inn

Keyston, Huntingdon,
Cambridgeshire PE18 0RE
Telephone: +44(0)1832 710241
pheasant.keyston@btopenworld.com

The inn is housed in a row of classic 16th-century English cottages, with dark thatch, a mass of floral planters and alfresco tables and chairs out front making you a temporary part of a picture-postcard scene. Within, it is quintessentially 'olde England': leather upholstery, a mass of blackened beams, brick inglenooks, flagstone floor and stripped boards. The cooking, however, is bang up-to-date. Whether you eat in the informal lounge or in the more formal dining room, the menu's the same, with no restrictions as to how much or how little you eat. Jerusalem artichoke soup with truffle oil, pork cheeks with champ mash, baby capers and sage, Angus fillet steak with fat chips and béarnaise sauce, and warm lemon, almond and polenta cake for pudding is modern food cooked with skill and assurance, and based on prime raw materials. The delights of the wine list are a joy to behold, with 20 of the 100 well-chosen available by the glass.

Prices: Set lunch £14.95. House wine £12.50.
Last orders: Food: lunch 14.00; dinner 21.30 (Sunday 21.00).
Closed: Rarely.
Food: Modern British.
Real ale: Adnams. 3 guest beers.
Other points: No-smoking areas. Children welcome. Dogs welcome daytime only. Car park.
Directions: Village signed off the A14, 12 miles west of Huntingdon. (Map 3, C4)

Madingley

Three Horseshoes

High Street, Madingley, Cambridge,
Cambridgeshire CB3 8AB
Telephone: +44(0)1954 210221

The quintessential rural look of this very picturesque, thatched inn gives way to stylish country chic and a lively, cosmopolitan atmosphere as you step inside the early 1900s building. The Victorian orangery look does justice to the original architecture, mixing a light Mediterranean feel with period elegance through pastel-coloured, waxed wood and stripped boards. Moving through to the conservatory restaurant, though similar in design and with an identical menu to the bar area, white linen, wicker chairs and indoor plants create a relaxed mood. Richard Stokes's confident Italian-style cooking is a sound interpretation of the Huntsbridge Group's policy of seasonal food using prime raw materials. Thus, a typical meal could bring pea-and-mint soup with crème fraîche and pancetta, pan-fried salmon with chargrilled asparagus and salsa rossa, followed by chocolate-truffle cake with clotted cream. There's a superb choice of wines, offering the great and godly, as well as the unusual.

Prices: Bar main course from £9.50.
House wine £12.10.
Last orders: Bar: lunch 14.00; dinner 21.00. Food: lunch 14.00 (Sunday 14.30); dinner 21.00.
Closed: Rarely.
Food: Italian.
Real ale: Adnams Southwold. 1 guest beer.
Other points: No-smoking area. Restaurant no smoking. Children welcome. Garden. Car park.
Directions: Two miles west of Cambridge. From London leave the M11 at the A1303 exit. From the north take the A14, then the A1307. (Map 4, D5)

2

Tarporley

The Fox and Barrel

Forest Road, Cotebrook, Tarporley,
Cheshire CW6 9DZ
Telephone: +44(0)1829 760529
info@thefoxandbarrel.com
www.thefoxandbarrel.com

Named the Fox and Barrel after a former landlord let a pursued fox escape to the cellar, it is worth seeking out this thriving food pub for the genuine welcome, interesting seasonal menus and a tip-top pint of Bass. Beyond the snug bar, with its huge log fire, china ornaments and jugs and daily newspapers, the half-panelled dining area sports a rug-strewn wood floor and rustic farmhouse tables topped with church candles. Interesting menus list bar meals such as roast-ham platter, smoked-chicken Caesar salad, and chicken fajita. More inventive restaurant meals take in smoked haddock and chorizo risotto with pesto, Thai king prawn curry and lamb rump with champ and Mediterranean vegetables. Puddings include spiced raisin-and-ginger pudding with local Snugbury's ice cream. There's a good choice of wines, with 15 by the glass, malt whiskies, a secluded summer patio for alfresco eating, and live New Orleans jazz every Monday.

Prices: Set Sunday lunch £14.50. Main course from £8.25. Bar/snack from £4.25. House wine £9.95.
Last orders: Bar: lunch 15.00; dinner 23.00 (all day during the weekend). Food: lunch 14.30; dinner 21.30 (Sunday 21.00).
Closed: Rarely.
Food: Modern British with a Mediterranean influence.
Real Ale: Bass, Marston's Pedigree, John Smith's Cask. 1 guest beer changing every 2/3 weeks.
Other points: No smoking in the restaurant. Garden. Car park. Wheelchair access.
Directions: On the A49, close to Oulton Park race circuit, on the Warrington side of Tarporley. (Map 5, G4)

Romaldkirk

The Rose and Crown at Romaldkirk

Romaldkirk, Barnard Castle, Co Durham DL12 9EB
Telephone: +44(0)1833 650213
hotel@rose-and-crown.co.uk
www.rose-and-crown.co.uk

Must-sees
Barnard Castle
Raby Castle: a 14th-century castle built for the Nevill
   family and surrounded by 200-acre parkland.
Bowes Museum: a 19th-century French-style chateau
   with a fine collection of paintings and furniture
High Force: England's highest waterfall (70ft).
Killhope Lead-Mining Centre

High Force

Built in 1733 as a coaching inn, the imposing, stone-built Rose and Crown stands beside the Saxon church and one of the beautifully maintained greens in this most picturesque of Teesdale villages. High standards of hospitality, service and cooking have created one of the finest all-round inns in the country. Much of this success can be attributed to consistent cooking that is inspired by the seasons and backed by first-class local produce. Lunchtime filled baps are well presented and traditional favourites, such as salmon fishcakes with chive cream sauce, are always cooked with flair. Weekly changing menus may also list sea bass with red-wine jus, and belly pork with baked-bean cassoulet. Exemplary puddings are typified by sticky toffee pudding, but there are also perfectly selected local cheeses. Four-course dinners are served in the civilised, part-panelled restaurant. The spotlessly maintained en suite bedrooms have wooden floorboards, beams, well-chosen antique furniture, stylish contemporary fabrics, and a host of extras.   A class act!

Rooms: 12. Double/twin room from £120.
Prices: Set lunch £15.95 and dinner £26. Bar main course from £7.95. House wine £12.95.
Last orders: Bar: lunch 15.00; dinner 23.00. Food: lunch 13.30; dinner 21.30 (Sunday 21.00).
Closed: Rarely.
Food: Modern British.
Real ale: Black Sheep Best, Theakston Best.
Other points: No-smoking area. Children welcome. Car park.
Directions: Six miles north-west of Barnard Castle on the B6277 towards Middleton-in-Teesdale. (Map 6, C5)

Tourist information
Barnard Castle +44(0)1833 690909
Where to shop Barnard Castle, Durham
Farmers' market Barnard Castle (1st Saturday of month)

Best scenic drives
B6277 and unclassified road to St John's Chapel, A689, B6295 and B6305 to Hexham, return via B6306 and B6278. A66 and minor roads to Grinton and Reeth, B6270 to Keld, return to A66 via Tan Hill and Sleightholme.

Walking
See pub walk on page 216.

Events
Teeside Thrash - music and dance (May)
Barnard Castle Meet Annual Carnival (May)

The Lizard

Cadgwith Cove Inn

Cadgwith, Ruan Minor, Helston,
Cornwall TR12 7JX
Telephone: +44(0)1326 290513
enquiries@cadgwithcoveinn.com
www.cadgwithcoveinn.com

A fishing hamlet on the rugged Lizard coast-line is the appealing setting for this 300-year-old pub. In front of the whitewashed build-ing, a sunny patio affords drinkers views across the old pilchard cellar to the peaceful cove. Down the lane is the shingle beach and the colourful fishing vessels that provide the inn with freshly caught fish, and the best crab and lobster on the peninsula. Furnished sim-ply and decked with seafaring mementoes, the two bars, both with open fires, serve five real ales. Expect traditional homemade pub food, but note the delicious white crab-meat sandwiches or the crab soup served with crusty bread. Fish fanciers should look no further than the blackboard, which lists the daily catch, or plump for the beer-battered haddock. Alternatives include a real Cornish cheese lunch - perfect with a pint after a coastal walk. Simply equipped bedrooms.

Rooms: 7, 2 with private bathrooms.
From £25 per person.
Prices: Set lunch from £10 and dinner from £13.
Restaurant main course from £5.95. House wine £8.95.
Last orders: Bar: lunch 15.00 (Thursday 17.00); dinner 23.00 (all day during the weekend). Food: lunch 15.00; dinner 21.30.
Closed: Check for seasonal variations.
Food: Seafood and Traditional European.
Real ale: Wadworth 6X, Marston's Pedigree, Sharp's Doom Bar Bitter, Flower's IPA. Weekly guest beers.
Other points: Children welcome. Dogs welcome. Garden and patio. Wheelchair access (not WC).
Directions: Village signposted off the A3083, 9 miles south of Helston. (Map 1, G3)

Port Gaverne

Port Gaverne Hotel

Port Gaverne, Port Isaac, Cornwall PL29 3SQ
Telephone: +44(0)1208 880244.
Freephone 0500 657867
www.portgavernehotel.co.uk

Graham and Annabelle Sylvester's charming 17th-century inn is peacefully situated in a sheltered cove just 50 yards from the beach. The ship-shape, characterful, pubby bar has a polished slate floor, a big log fire, Sharp's ales on tap, and first-rate traditional bar food in the form of ploughman's lunches and seafood pie. A tiny snug bar with a genuine ship's table, and an equally beamed and pleasant restaurant lend a wonderful lack of formality. Noted for very fresh fish and a commitment to local produce, the Port Gaverne succeeds admirably in balancing good food and hospi-tality to all comers with a wholly acceptable degree of Cornish idiosyncracy. Dinner could produce homemade crab soup, grilled Dover sole with herb butter, and a selection of regional cheeses. Upgraded bedrooms have a fresh, comfortable look and gleaming modern bathrooms. There are wonderful coastal path walks and magical summer sunsets.

Rooms: 15. Double/twin from £79, single from £39.50, family from £79.
Prices: Set dinner £25. Sunday lunch £10.95. Bar main course from £4.95. House wine £10.95.
Last orders: Bar: 23.00. Food: lunch 14.30; dinner 21.30.
Closed: 1-14 February.
Food: Traditional and Modern British.
Real ale: Bass, Sharp's Doom Bar Bitter.
Other points: No smoking in the restaurant. Garden. Children welcome. Dogs welcome overnight. Car park.
Directions: Signposted from the A30 north of Camelford and the A389 from Wadebridge via the B3314. Follow the signs to Port Isaac. (Map 1, F3)

St Breward

The Old Inn

Churchtown, St Breward, Bodmin Moor,
Cornwall PL30 4PP
Telephone: +44(0)1208 850711
darren@theoldinn.fsnet.co.uk
www.theoldinnandrestaurant.co.uk

A low, white-painted stone cottage that claims to be the highest pub in Cornwall at 700 feet, set on the edge of Bodmin Moor in a true Cornish village. Parts of the bar date back over 1,000 years, when it was an ale-house for the builders constructing the parish church. The strongly traditional interior exudes charm and atmosphere, with slate floors, part-exposed walls, thick beams, oak settles, a roaring winter log fire, and a newly extended dining area. Food is wholesome, unpretentious and not for the faint-hearted - portions are very generous! Walkers, locals and moorland trippers tuck into hearty pub favourites such as ploughman's, homemade pies and Charlie Harris's garlic sausages and chips, all washed down with a tip-top pint of Sharp's local ale. Locally reared beef provides the excellent steaks, and fresh fish, notably the huge battered cod, is landed along the north Cornish coast. Note the Saxon cross set in the lawn. See pub walk on page 218.

Prices: Main course from £6.95. House wine £11.95.
Last orders: Bar: 23.00. Food: lunch 14..00.
dinner 21.00.
Closed: Rarely.
Food: Modern British.
Real ale: Sharp's Doom Bar Bitter, Sharp's Special, Bass.
Sharp's Eden Ale as guest beer.
Other points: No-smoking area. Garden. Children welcome. Car park. 120-seat restaurant available for functions. Wheelchair access.
Directions: Follow the signposts for St Breward from the A30. The Old Inn is adjacent to the village church. Also on the B3266 Bodmin to Camelford road.
(Map 1, F3)

Appleby-in-Westmorland

Tufton Arms Hotel

Market Square, Appleby-in-Westmorland,
Cumbria CA16 6XA
Telephone: +44(0)1768 351 593
info@tuftonarmshotel.co.uk
www.tuftonarmshotel.co.uk

The evocative conversion of this 16th-century building, which became a coaching inn in Victorian times, has been beautifully restored by the Milsom family. The ambience of the that period is reflected in the attractive wallpapers, lots of prints in heavy frames, drapes, old fireplaces and large porcelain table lamps. Light lunch and supper menus are served in the clubby bar, with a more formal choice available in the stylish restaurant with its conservatory extension. Cooking is of a high standard, be it rack of Cumbrian fell-bred lamb, or game from the local Dalemain Estate. Fish is delivered from Fleetwood, to create, perhaps, paupiette of lemon sole stuffed with smoked salmon with a dill white-wine sauce. There is a French accent to the carefully selected, well-annotated wine list of 160 bins. Bedrooms vary from suites with period fireplaces, antique furnishings and large old-style bathrooms to more conventional en suite rooms.

Rooms: 21. Double/twin from £95.
Prices: Set dinner £24.50. Restaurant main course from £9.75. Bar main course from £6.95. House wine £9.50.
Last orders: Bar: 23.00. Food: lunch 14.00; dinner 21.00.
Closed: Rarely.
Food: Traditional English and French.
Real ale: Boddington's, Worthington's Best.
Other points: Children welcome. Dogs welcome overnight. Car park. Licence for civil weddings. Wheelchair access (not WC).
Directions: Exit38/M6. Take the B6260 to Appleby via Orton. (Map 5, C4)

Armathwaite

The Dukes Head

Armathwaite, Carlisle, Cumbria CA4 9PB
Telephone: +44(0)1697 472226
hh@hlynch51.freeserve.com
www.dukeshead-hotel.co.uk

Henry Lynch's traditional whitewashed inn is a long-standing favourite in the beautiful Eden Valley among ramblers, bird-watchers and fishing folk. It retains an instant appeal for those with plenty of time to linger and reminisce, making it a peaceful base in this unspoilt area - cottagey bedrooms are simply and traditionally furnished. Downstairs, beyond the civilised lounge bar, with its stone walls, open fires and oak furnishings, you'll find a locals' bar, a neat dining room, and a glorious garden that borders the River Eden. One menu operates throughout, and offers a good range of dishes that make excellent use of local ingredients, including game in season. Begin with locally smoked salmon and prawns, followed by tuna loin with lime, coriander, chilli and garlic butter, or stuffed roast duck, and finish with bread-and-butter pudding. Sandwiches and salads are also available. See pub walk on page 220.

Rooms: 5, 2 not en suite. Double room from £52.50, single from £32.50.
Prices: Main course from £6.45. Sunday-lunch set menu £12.95. House wine £12.00.
Last orders: Bar: lunch 15.00; dinner 23.00.
Food: lunch 13.45; dinner 21.00.
Closed: Rarely.
Food: Traditional British.
Real ale: Jennings Cumberland Ale. 1 guest beer.
Other points: No smoking in the restaurant. Children welcome. Dogs welcome. Garden. Car park. Wheelchair access to the front.
Directions: Armathwaite is located off the A6 Penrith to Carlisle road, 7 miles south of Carlisle. (Map 5, C4)

Borrowdale

Scafell Hotel

Rosthwaite, Borrowdale, Cumbria CA12 5XB
Telephone: +44(0)17687 77208
info@scafell.co.uk
www.scafell.co.uk

Wordsworth and Coleridge stayed at this elegant, 19th-century hotel and walked the surrounding fells. It's easy to see the appealing mix of the hotel's attractions; the scenery is breathtaking and the food is along contemporary lines. Miles Jessop, who has been here for 40 years, is a welcoming host. Most of the bedrooms have good views, are comfortable and furnished in country style. A tempting table d'hôte is served in the dining room, and showcases local ingredients. Fresh farm chicken, Cumbrian pork and lamb are used in dishes such as cream of chicken and leek soup and pork with a mushroom and brandy-cream sauce. A simple 'cocktail' bar is set in one room around an open fire, while at the rear of the hotel is the public bar, which has slate floors and outdoor seating, serving good bar food and local cask ales.

Rooms: 24. Double from £145, single from £72.50. Rates are for dinner, bed and breakfast. Seasonal price variations apply.
Prices: Set lunch £11.95. Set dinner £20.50-£24.50 (five courses). Restaurant main course from £9.50. Bar/snack from £6.50. House wine £11.95.
Last orders: Bar: 23.00. Food: lunch 14.00; dinner 21.00.
Closed: Restricted bar hours January and early Feb.
Food: International.
Real ale: Coniston Bluebird, Jennings Cumberland Ale, Theakston Best.
Other points: No-smoking area. Children welcome. Dogs welcome. Garden. Car park. Licence for civil weddings.
Directions: Exit 40/M6. Take the A66 towards Keswick and then the B5289. (Map 5, D3)

Eskdale

The Boot Inn
(formerly the Burnmoor Inn)

Boot, Eskdale, Cumbria CA19 1TG
Telephone: +44(0)1946 723224
enquiries@bootinn.co.uk
www.bootinn.co.uk

An attractive, old, pebble-dash Lakeland inn, originally built as a farm in 1578, nestling in a tiny hamlet in the beautiful Eskdale Valley, a beautiful, lush and unspoilt part of western Cumbria. Converted to a pub in 1764, it has a homely bar with a crackling log fire and a row of handpumps dispensing tip-top local ales. Hearty food is served in both the bar and the cosy, cottagey restaurant, with dishes ranging from sandwiches to a Cumberland tatie pot of lamb, beef and black pudding. A specials board could list the likes of venison casserole and homemade puddings such as raspberry-and-apple pie, and own-grown herbs, summer vegetables and salads are a feature. Much of the menu is homemade, but if not, that fact is clearly stated. The nine bedrooms are simply furnished in a bright, rural style. Poor reception dictates the peace of a TV-free environment and all rooms have radios. Across the Esk are bridleways to Eel Tarn and Wasdale Head. See pub walk on page 222.

Rooms: 9. Room from £30 per person. Double room four nights for the price of three all year, and three nights for the price of two November-March.
Prices: Set lunch £12 and dinner £16. Main course from £7.50. Bar main course from £7. House wine £10.
Last orders: Bar: 23.00. Food: lunch 17.00; dinner 21.00.
Closed: Rarely.
Food: Traditional English.
Real ale: Jennings Bitter, Jennings Cumberland Ale, Black Sheep Best, Great Gable, Barngate's Ales, Tirril Ales.
Other points: No-smoking area. Garden. Children welcome. Car park. Bring your Les Routiers guide and receive a free drink. Wheelchair access to the restaurant and pub.
Directions: Exit 36/M6. Head to Broughton-in-Furness; then towards Ulpha, drop down into Eskdale and turn right into Boot. (Map 5, D3)

Hawkshead

Queen's Head Hotel

Main Street, Hawkshead, Ambleside,
Cumbria LA22 0NS
Telephone: +44(0)15394 36271
/+44(0)800 137263
enquiries@queensheadhotel.co.uk
www.queensheadhotel.co.uk

Set in the pedestrianised centre of a pretty, little Lakeland village, this 16th-century inn-cum-hotel appeals to visitors and locals alike. It has period character, from its black-and-white painted frontage to the traditional beamed bars with open fires. Ales are dispensed by bow-tied barmen, perhaps Robinsons Bitter or the aptly named Cumbria Way. The interesting menu travels far and wide, but they haven't forgotten how to do the basics well. A harvesters' platter of four generous wedges of organic cheese came with delicious walnut bread and salad. Other choices include the salad bar, which offers Cumbrian roast beef with watercress, chilli, radish and soy sauce, or the separate Herdwick lamb menu. Otherwise, a meal could include Westmorland pie, or Woodhall's cumberland sausage with ale and white-onion sauce. Prettily decorated bedrooms are charming, in a rural-chic style.

Rooms: 14, two not en suite, two with private bathroom. 1 four-poster beds and 2 family rooms. Double room from £34 per person, single from £47.50.
Prices: Main course lunch from £7.25.
House wine £10.95.
Last orders: Bar: 23.00. Food: lunch 14.30; dinner 21.30.
Closed: Rarely.
Food: Modern British.
Real ale: Robinsons Double Hop, Unicorn & Cumbria Way. 1 guest beer.
Other points: No-smoking area. Children welcome.
Directions: Exit 36/M6 Follow the A590 to Newby Bridge. Take the second right and follow the road for eight miles into Hawkshead. (Map 5, D3)

Penrith

The Highland Drove Inn

Great Salkeld, Penrith, Cumbria CA11 9NA
Telephone: +44(0)1768 898349
highlanddroveinnn@btinternet.com
www.highland-drove.co.uk

Set close to the church in a picturesque Eden Valley village, this archetypal inn resembles an old farmhouse, with its old wooden porch and abundance of flowers. Within, there are rustic tables and settles in the bar, a separate games room, and a lounge area with a log fire and tartan fabrics. The pub is renowned for its conviviality and popular food, the latter served in Kyloe's Restaurant upstairs. With its hunting lodge feel, it is the core of Donald Newton's business, but the bar is still very much a locals' bar. Utilising local produce, the kitchen produces satisfying country cooking that takes in mussels cooked in white wine and cream, then a main dish of duck with black pudding and cider sauce, with sticky toffee pudding to finish. Cracking beers, good wines, and nicely decorated bedrooms.

Rooms: 3. Soon to be 5. Double/twin from £50.
Prices: Set lunch £12.95 and dinner £18.50. Restaurant main course from £8.95. Bar snack from £4.95.
House wine £9.95.
Last orders: Bar: lunch 15.00; dinner 23.00 (open all day Saturday). Food: lunch 14.00; dinner 21.00 (Sunday 20.30).
Closed: Monday lunchtime.
Food: Eclectic bistro.
Real ale: John Smith's, Theakston Black Bull, guest beer.
Other points: No-smoking area. Children welcome. Dogs welcome. Garden. Car park. Wheelchair access to the restaurant and pub (no WC).
Directions: Exit40/M6. Take the A66 eastbound, then the A686 towards Alston. In four miles, turn left onto the B6412 for Great Salkeld. (Map 5, C4)

Sedbergh

The Dalesman Country Inn

Main Street, Sedbergh, Cumbria LA10 5BN
Telephone: +44(0)15396 21183
info@thedalesman.co.uk
www.thedalesman.co.uk

An unassuming, comfortably modernised 16th-century former coaching inn, festooned in summer with rampant floral displays. Stripped stone and beams, farmhouse chairs and log-effect gas fires set the scene in the rambling bar and dining room where you can enjoy good homemade food prepared from local produce. Arrive early for the excellent-value lunchtime menu that features beer battered fish and chips, a 'full Monty' breakfast, and hot bacon rolls. Evening bar food ranges from terrines and tiger-prawn starters to chargrills and lamb shank with red-wine gravy. Influenced by the seasons and changing fortnightly, the evening carte may extend the choice to chicken with bacon-and-mushroom risotto, and Aberdeen Angus steak with pepper sauce. For pudding, choose steamed ginger pudding, or Wensleydale cheese with cranberry sauce. Seven spacious and comfortably furnished bedrooms.

Rooms: 7. Rooms £30 per person.
Prices: Set lunch £10 and dinner £18. Main course from £8. House wine £8.
Last orders: Bar: 23.00. Food: lunch 14.00 (Friday, Saturday, Sunday 14.30); dinner 21.00 (Friday and Saturday 21.30).
Closed: Rarely.
Food: Modern British and traditional pub food.
Real ale: Black Sheep Best (on Bank Holidays), Tetley's Bitter, Dalesman. 1 guest beer.
Other points: No-smoking area. Children welcome. Car park. Wheelchair access (no WC).
Directions: On the A684 in village centre; 11 miles east of Kendal; 5 miles from exit 36/M6. (Map 5, D4)

Ullswater

Brackenrigg Inn

Watermillock, Lake Ullswater, Penrith,
Cumbria CA11 0LP
Telephone: +44(0)17684 86206
enquiries@brackenrigginn.co.uk
www.brackenrigginn.co.uk

The sweeping views across Lake Ullswater and the fells from the tranquil setting of the Brackenrigg are second to none. The vista is matched by an appealing homely feel throughout the unpretentious interior of this 18th-century inn. This is thanks in part to the attractive panelled bar with its polished floorboards, open log fire and cracking local ales. Both the dining rooms are traditionally appointed, and the latter also has splendid views. A sound local reputation for well-executed, contemporary food is certainly deserved. The bar menu is built around local produce and available in the bar, lounge and terrace. Choices include Cumberland sausage with apple mash, and steak, kidney and ale pie. The restaurant table d'hôte may list asparagus with feta and pine nuts, followed by calves' liver with Woodall's dry-cured bacon. En suite bedrooms are simply stylish.

Rooms: 17. Double from £28 per person. Single from £33. Superior rooms and suites also available.
Prices: Set Sunday lunch £9.95. Set dinner £24.95 Restaurant main course from £10.50. Bar main course from £8.25. House wine £10.95.
Last orders: Bar: 23.00. Food: lunch 14.30; dinner 21.00.
Closed: Never.
Food: Modern British.
Real ale: Black Sheep Ales, Jennings Cumberland Ale, Tirril Ales, Theakston Ales. 3 guest beers.
Other points: No smoking in the restaurant. Children welcome. Dogs welcome in the bar and overnight (in some rooms). Garden. Car park. Wheelchair access.
Directions: On A592 south-west of Penrith; 6 miles from Exit40/M6, overlooking Ullswater. (Map 5, C4)

Wasdale

Wasdale Head Inn 🍴 🛏 ☕ ★

Wasdale, Gosforth, Cumbria CA20 1EX
Telephone: +44(0)19467 26229
wasdaleheadinn@msn.com
www.wasdale.com

At the head of unspoilt Wasdale at the foot of Great Gable, in a setting of romantic grandeur with steep fells by way of backdrop, this is a famous, traditional mountain inn popular with serious walkers and climbers. Ritson's Bar, named after its first landlord (the world's biggest liar), has high ceilings, a polished slate floor, wood panelling, climbing memorabilia and stunning photographs of the surrounding fells. Here you can enjoy a pint of home-brewed Great Gable beer and hearty bar meals. Steak-and-ale pie, hotpots, thick soups and Cumbrian sausages from Woodalls of Waberthwaite served with onion gravy are perfect for tired walkers. Alternatively, spoil yourself in the restaurant, which puts together some of the best local produce in its excellent, four-course set-menu. Dinner may take in air-dried Cumbrian ham, local farm-reared Herdwick lamb or fillet steak, and classic puddings. The pick of the 14 bedrooms is the garden room, with its muslin-draped four-poster.

Rooms: 14. Room from £49 per person.
Prices: Bar meal from £7.50. Set dinner (four courses) £25. House wine £12.90.
Last orders: Bar: 23.00. Food: 21.00.
Closed: Rarely.
Food: Traditional British.
Real ale: A large range - Great Gable Brewing Company brews at the Wasdale Head Inn.
Other points: Totally no smoking. Children welcome. Dogs welcome overnight. Garden. Car park.
Directions: Wasdale Head is signed off the A595 between Egremont and Ravenglass. (Map 5, D3)

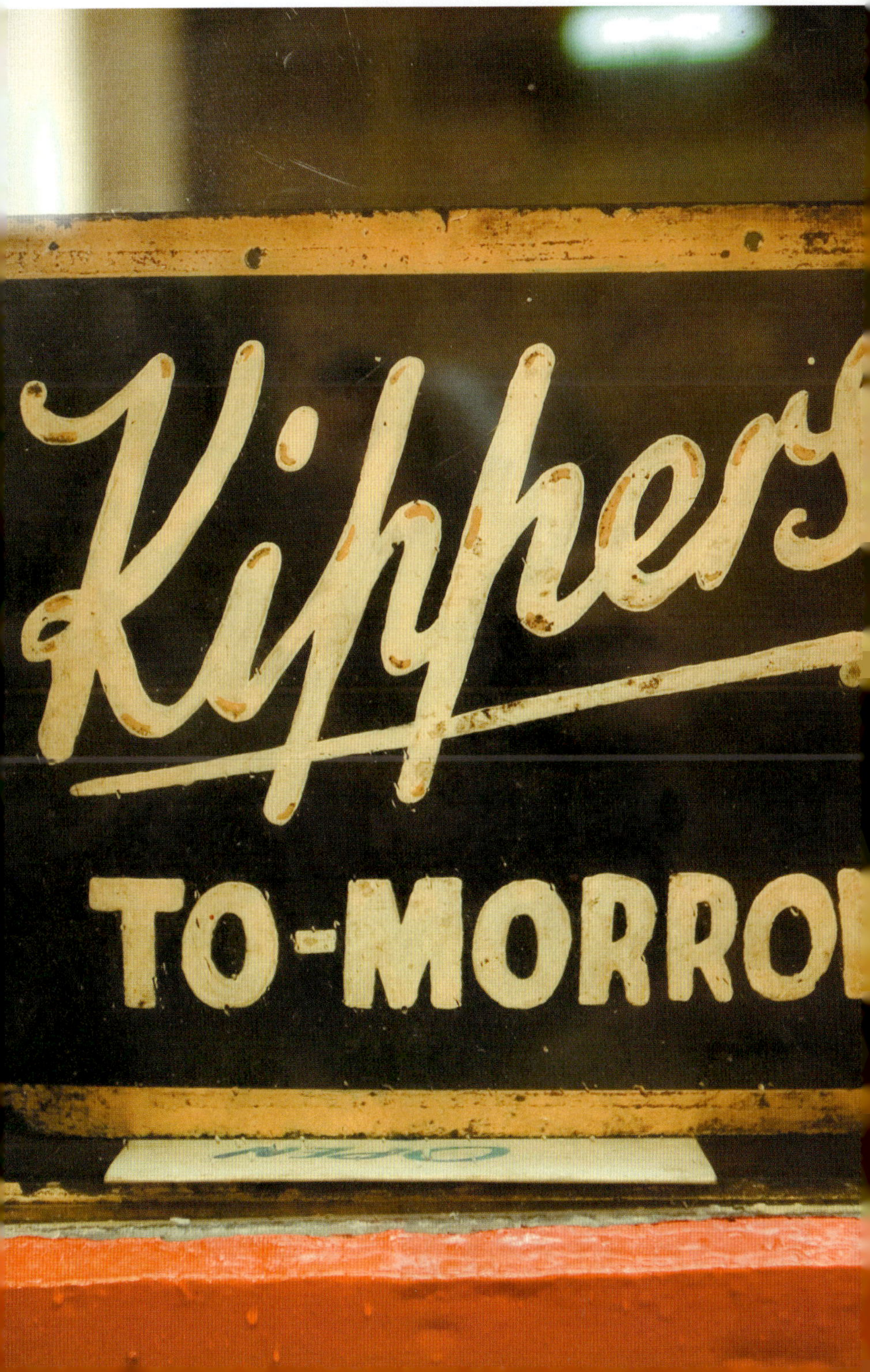
Kipper
TO-MORRO

The Brackenrigg Inn

A sound local reputation for well-executed, contemporary food has been built up over the years at this 18th-century inn. You can enjoy sweeping views across Lake Ullswater while supping a cracking pint of ale from Tirril or Jennings Brewery and tucking into some great pub food. Cumbrian produce is utilised to the fore on changing bar and restaurant menus, notably fantastic Cumberland sausages from Adam Jackson in the village and oak-smoked cheese from Carolyn and Leonie Fairburn at Thornby Moor Dairy.

Jennings Brewery
Castle Brewery, Cockermouth
Tel: 0845 1297190

John Jennings started brewing in the Lake District village of Lorton in 1828. The brewery moved in 1874 to its present site, an idyllic spot beside the River Derwent in the shadow of Cockermouth Castle, to tap into the abundant source of well water. It specialises in the production of cask ale, from the malty Jennings Bitter to the well-balanced dark brown Mild and the complex fruit, malt and roast flavours of the strong, dark brown Sneck Lifter. Jennings owns 130 pubs stretching across the Lake District to Cheshire and Yorkshire. Buy its bottled beers from the Brewery Shop after a guided tour.

Richard Woodall Ltd
Waberthwaite
Tel: 01229 717237

Famous for its traditionally cured hams, bacon and sausages, the seventh and eighth generation of family members use the same recipes and techniques as the Woodall's of over 170 years ago. The company farms its own herd of around 180 sows in large straw-filled barns with natural light and fresh air and in a completely chemical- and preservative-free environment. Woodall hams are the genuine article of real flavour and texture. Buy the air-cured meats, fresh meats and general groceries from the shop, which doubles as the village post office and still retains most of its original Victorian fittings.

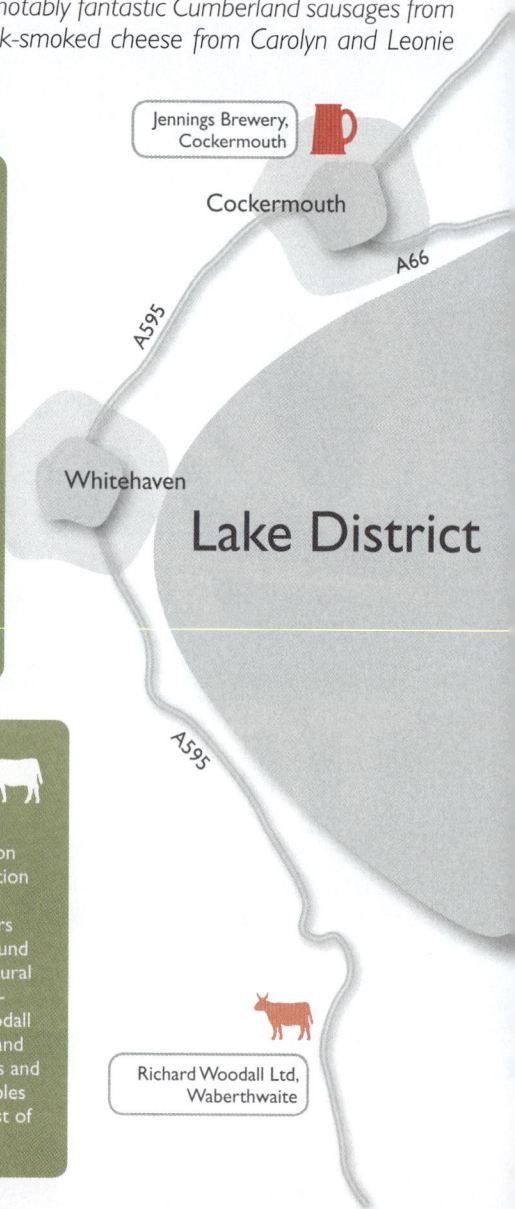

Jennings Brewery, Cockermouth

Cockermouth

A66

A595

Whitehaven

Lake District

A595

Richard Woodall Ltd, Waberthwaite

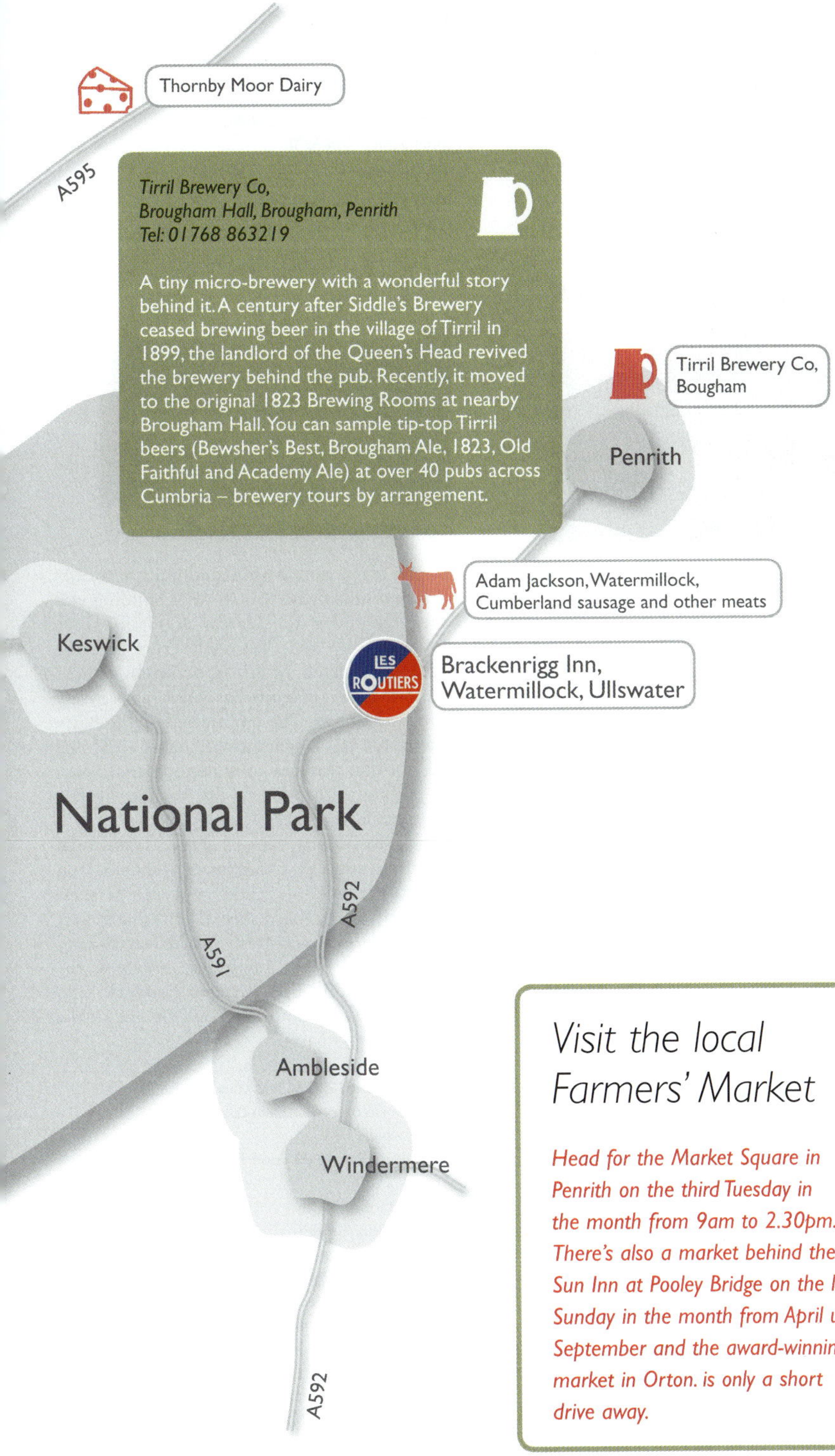

Thornby Moor Dairy

A595

Tirril Brewery Co,
Brougham Hall, Brougham, Penrith
Tel: 01768 863219

A tiny micro-brewery with a wonderful story
behind it. A century after Siddle's Brewery
ceased brewing beer in the village of Tirril in
1899, the landlord of the Queen's Head revived
the brewery behind the pub. Recently, it moved
to the original 1823 Brewing Rooms at nearby
Brougham Hall. You can sample tip-top Tirril
beers (Bewsher's Best, Brougham Ale, 1823, Old
Faithful and Academy Ale) at over 40 pubs across
Cumbria – brewery tours by arrangement.

Tirril Brewery Co,
Bougham

Penrith

Adam Jackson, Watermillock,
Cumberland sausage and other meats

Keswick

LES
ROUTIERS

Brackenrigg Inn,
Watermillock, Ullswater

National Park

A592

A591

Ambleside

Windermere

A592

Visit the local Farmers' Market

Head for the Market Square in
Penrith on the third Tuesday in
the month from 9am to 2.30pm.
There's also a market behind the
Sun Inn at Pooley Bridge on the last
Sunday in the month from April until
September and the award-winning
market in Orton. is only a short
drive away.

Derby

The Three Horseshoes Inn

Breedon-on-the-Hill, Derby,
Derbyshire DE73 8AN
Telephone: +44(0)1332 695129
ian@threehorseshoes.ndo.co.uk
www.thehorseshoes.com

The revitalised Three Horseshoes re-opened its doors in February 2005 with respected chef/landlord Ian Davison at the helm, who made a huge success of the Nag's Head at nearby Castle Donington. Staff and loyal diners have followed him to this village local, formerly a farrier's, which now blends the classic and the contemporary throughout its comfortably refurbished interior. Layers have been stripped back to reveal original features - imposing fireplaces, exposed brick, tiled floors - with a modern ambience reflected in seagrass matting, chunky tables and chairs and an eclectic mix of memorabilia. The real draw, however, is Ian's food, whether it be snacks of scallops with balsamic or pasta with salmon and dill cream, or inventive mains such as lamb shank with mustard mash or duck with stir-fried pak choi and curry oil. Food is freshly prepared from local produce, notably game from shoots and traditional Derbyshire cheeses. Bedrooms were due for completion in summer 2005.

Prices: Restaurant main course from £13.95. Bar/snack from £4.50. House wine £11.95.
Last orders: Bar: lunch 14.30; dinner: 23.00. Food: lunch 13.45; dinner 21.00 (no food Sunday).
Closed: 26 December to 2 January.
Food: Modern British.
Real ale: Courage Directors Bitter, Deuchars IPA, Theakston Ales, Marston's Pedigree.
Other points: No-smoking area. Dogs welcome in the bar. Garden. Car park. Wheelchair access.
Directions: Exit 23a/M1. Follow signs to Ashby and Breedon. (Map 3, B3)

Hardwick

Hardwick Inn

Hardwick Park, Chesterfield,
Derbyshire S44 5QJ
Telephone: +44(0)1246 850245
batty@hardwickinn.co.uk
www.hardwickinn.co.uk

Dating from around 1600 and built of locally quarried sandstone, this striking building was once the lodge for Hardwick Hall, which is owned by the National Trust, so the inn draws much of its trade from visitors exploring the magnificent park and lovely Elizabethan hall. The inn, owned by the Batty family for three generations, has a rambling interior that features good period details such as mullioned windows, oak ceiling beams, large stone fireplaces with open fires, and a fine, 18th-century, carved settle. Traditional bar food takes in ploughman's lunches, and a whole range of steaks and sandwiches, with daily blackboard specials offering hearty homemade pies, and fresh fish delivered daily from Scarborough. Look out for bass the orange and dill, beer-battered haddock, and game-and-ale casserole, or opt for one of the daily carvery roasts.

Prices: Set lunch £12.60 and dinner £13.60 in the carvery restaurant. Bar main course from £6.50. House wine £7.95.
Last orders: Bar: 23.00. Food: lunch 21.30 (Sunday 21.00).
Closed: Rarely.
Food: Traditional British.
Real ale: Theakston Old Peculiar & XB, Ruddles County Ale, Marston's Pedigree, Old Speckled Hen.
Other points: Totally no smoking. Children welcome. Garden. Car park. Wheelchair access to the restaurant/pub.
Directions: Two and a quarter miles from Exit29/M1. Take the A6175, then turn left and follow the tourist-board signs to the pub. (Map 6, G6)

Holbeton

The Dartmoor Union Inn

Fore Street, Holbeton, Plymouth,
Devon PL8 1NE
Telephone: +44(0)1752 830288

Negotiate the lanes through Holbeton and look for a polished brass plaque on the wall of a grey stone building to locate the Dartmoor Union - there is no swinging pub sign! Step through the solid wooden front door into a different world for this is no rustic Devon village local. Totally revamped, this 16th-century building is now a classy and very comfortable dining pub. Polished wooden floors and leather sofas fronting a blazing log fire in the bar set the scene for some first-class bar meals - crab and parmesan baguette, scrambled eggs with Dartmouth smoked salmon - accompanied by a pint of home-brewed ale. A meal in the inviting dining room, with its red walls and subtle lighting, may take in scallops with crispy pancetta, Ruby Red sirloin with red-wine sauce, and chocolate and orange-marmalade tart. A passion for local foods, excellent-value wines and courtyard seating complete the picture.

Prices: Set lunch £13.95. Restaurant main course from £9.95. Bar/snack from £6.95. House wine £9.95.
Last orders: Bar: lunch 15.00 (Saturday 17.30); dinner 23.00. Food: lunch 14.00 (Sunday 15.30); dinner 21.30 (Sunday 21.00).
Closed: Rarely.
Food: Modern British and French.
Real ale: Dartmoor Union Ales.
Other points: No-smoking area. Children welcome. Dogs welcome in the bar. Car park.
Directions: Exit A38 at Ivybridge. At the roundabout take the last exit. Turn left through Ermington onto A379, then take the left turn to Holbeton. (Map 1, F4)

Salcombe

Victoria Inn

Fore Street, Salcombe, Devon TQ8 8BU
Telephone: +44(0)1548 842604
info@victoriainnsalcombe.co.uk
www.victoriainnsalcombe.co.uk

From the outside, the Victoria has the look of a typical seaside-town pub but step inside and you'll find a swish, modern interior. Flagstones, heavy beams, chunky wooden furniture and crackling log fires feature in the cool bar area. Wind your way upstairs to a comfortable lounge bar and more formal dining area, both with stunning views across Salcombe Harbour. Menus state that everything is freshly prepared from Devon produce, so look out for local butcher meats, fresh fish landed along the coast and locally made cheeses. Lunch brings creamy shellfish chowder, crab open sandwiches, and plaice in crispy beer batter. In the evening, with that view to gaze at, tuck into braised pheasant with damson-and-port sauce or turbot with creamy white wine, shallot and chive sauce, leaving room for vanilla crème caramel. To drink, try a pint of Dartmoor Best or one of eight wines by the glass.

Prices: Set lunch £12.95, set dinner £19.95. Restaurant main course from £9.95. Bar main course from £4.95. House wine £10.75.
Last orders: Bar: 23.00 (Sunday 22.30). Food: lunch 14.30; dinner 21.00.
Closed: Rarely.
Food: Modern British.
Real ale: St Austell Tinners Ale, Tribute, Black Prince & Dartmoor Best.
Other points: No smoking in the restaurant. Children welcome. Dogs welcome in the bar. Garden. Wheelchair access.
Directions: Town centre. (Map 2, G5)

Aune Valley Meats
Loddiswell, Kingsbridge
Tel: 01548 550413

Third generation farmer Richard Windsor established his butchery business in Loddiswell over 25 years ago. Aune Valley Meats supply hotels, pubs and restaurants across the South Hams, and the public through their farm shop (Mon-Fri 8-5, Sat 8-1), with quality local meats. Angus beef is traditionally reared on Richard's family farm in nearby Ugborough and slaughtered in Ashburton (just 20 minutes' drive away), while lamb is sourced from farms within a 10-mile radius, and pork, chickens and duck are local and free range.

Langage Farm, Plympton
Tel: 01752 337723

Set amid the rich grasslands and rolling hills of South Devon, Langage Farm has remained a working farmstead for over 900 years. Today, with a herd of over 260 Jersey and Guernsey cows, the Harvey family produces an extensive range of high-quality dairy products. It is one of the few independent dairies left in Devon still producing 'real' Devon clotted cream. The high butterfat content of the milk produces a rich and thick clotted cream, and also helps make cottage cheese, live yogurts, soft cheeses, sorbets and quality ice creams at the dairy.

Langage Farm, Plympton

Plympton

A38

A379

The Victoria Inn

A typical seaside pub that has been stylishly updated by landlord Andrew Cannon. Step inside and you'll find modern decor, with chunky furnishings on flagstones and an open fire in the cool bar area; upstairs is a cosy lounge and the dining area, both with stunning views across Salcombe estuary. Menus state that everything is freshly prepared from Devon produce, so look out for local-butcher meats, fresh fish and seafood landed along the coast, and hand-cut chips from Devon potatoes.

Visit the local Farmers' Market

Kingsbridge farmers' market is held on the first Saturday of each month from 9am to 1pm.

Buckfastleigh

A38

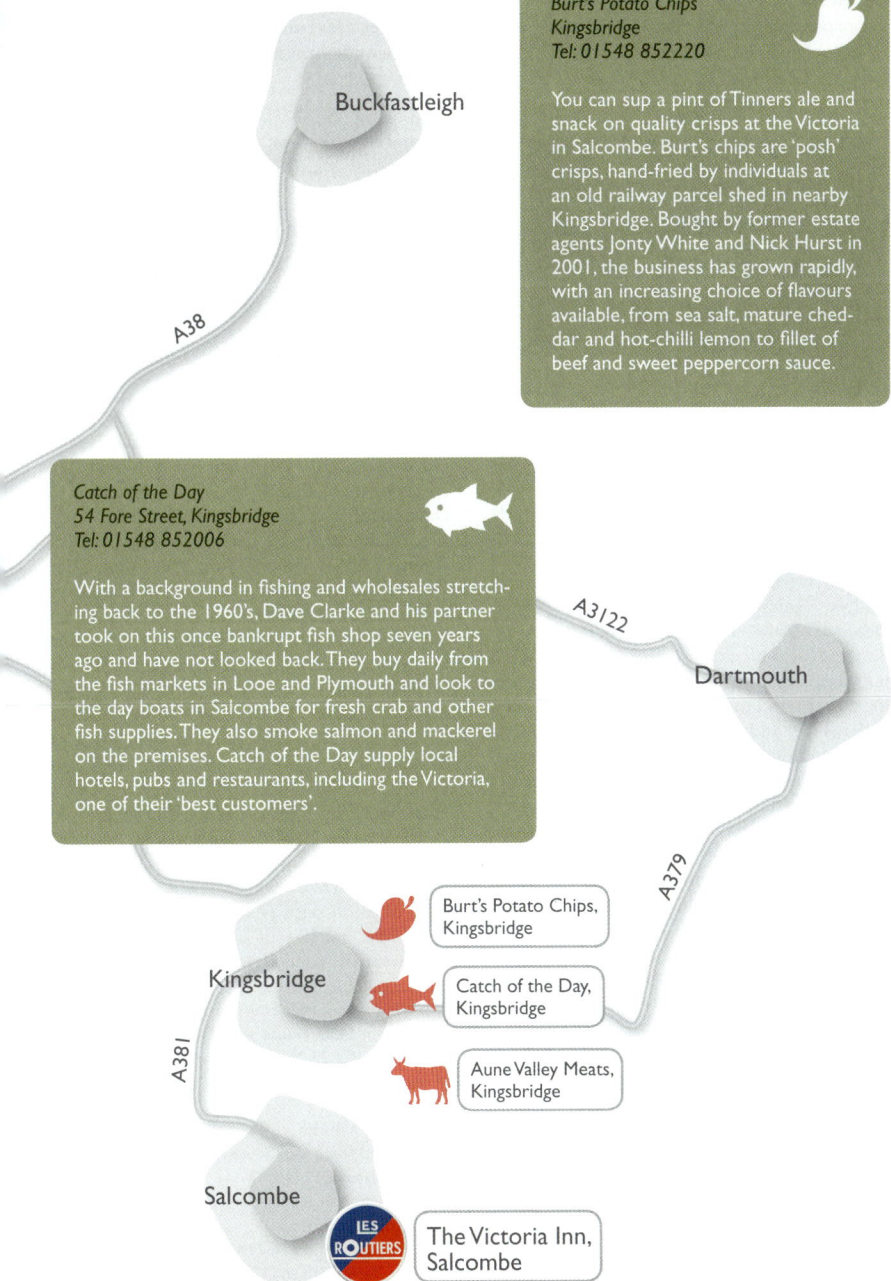

Burt's Potato Chips
Kingsbridge
Tel: 01548 852220

You can sup a pint of Tinners ale and snack on quality crisps at the Victoria in Salcombe. Burt's chips are 'posh' crisps, hand-fried by individuals at an old railway parcel shed in nearby Kingsbridge. Bought by former estate agents Jonty White and Nick Hurst in 2001, the business has grown rapidly, with an increasing choice of flavours available, from sea salt, mature cheddar and hot-chilli lemon to fillet of beef and sweet peppercorn sauce.

Catch of the Day
54 Fore Street, Kingsbridge
Tel: 01548 852006

With a background in fishing and wholesales stretching back to the 1960's, Dave Clarke and his partner took on this once bankrupt fish shop seven years ago and have not looked back. They buy daily from the fish markets in Looe and Plymouth and look to the day boats in Salcombe for fresh crab and other fish supplies. They also smoke salmon and mackerel on the premises. Catch of the Day supply local hotels, pubs and restaurants, including the Victoria, one of their 'best customers'.

A3122

Dartmouth

A379

Burt's Potato Chips, Kingsbridge

Catch of the Day, Kingsbridge

Kingsbridge

A381

Aune Valley Meats, Kingsbridge

Salcombe

LES ROUTIERS

The Victoria Inn, Salcombe

Slapton

The Tower Inn ★

Church Road, Slapton, Kingsbridge,
Devon TQ7 2PN
Telephone: +44(0)1548 580216
towerinn@slapton.org
www.thetowerinn.com

The 14th-century Tower Inn takes its name
from the ancient ruins of the tower it stands
beside, all that remains of a monastic college.
That has long gone, but the pub remains, as
charming as ever, tucked away in a sleepy village just inland from Slapton Sands. Visitors
will be warmly welcomed by Annette and
Andrew Hammett, who bought the pub in
December 2003. The welcome is followed by
pints of local ale and plates of good modern
pub food. Expect hearty sandwiches (try the
local crab) and more traditional dishes, such
as sausage and mash, at lunchtime. From
the evening menu, there are treats along the
lines of ham, leek and asparagus terrine,
followed by lamb shank, pheasant supreme,
salmon and sea bass. Stone walls, open fires,
scrubbed oak tables and flagstone floors
characterise the interior. There are three
cottage-style en suite bedrooms and a super
rear garden.

Rooms: 3. Single from £40, double from £60.
Prices: Restaurant main course from £9.
House wine from £10.
Last orders: Bar: lunch 14.30 (Sunday 15.00); dinner
23.00. Food: lunch 14.15 (Sunday 14.30); dinner 21.30.
Closed: Rarely.
Food: Modern British.
Real ale: Adnams Southwold, St Austell Tribute, Badger
Tanglefoot, Tower Ale. 1 guest beer.
Other points: No-smoking area. Garden and courtyard.
Children welcome. Dogs welcome overnight. Car park.
Directions: Off the A379 between Dartmouth
and Kingsbridge, or off the A381 between Totnes and
Kingsbridge. (Map 2, G5)

Stokenham

The Tradesman's Arms ★

Stokenham, Kingsbridge, Devon TQ7 2SZ
Telephone: +44(0)1548 580313
nick@thetradesmansarms.com
www.thetradesmansarms.com

Tucked away in the heart of the picturesque
old village, this 14th-century part-thatched
cottage is named after the men who traded in
Dartmouth and stopped at the pub for their
first night en route home to Kingsbridge.
Comprising a simply furnished main bar
with stone fireplace, wood-burning stove
and heavy beams, and an equally informal
dining room, it is now the domain of affable
landlord Nick Abbot. He's passionate about
offering good food and, in particular, locally
sourced produce. Meats and fish are smoked
on the premises, fish is from day boats at
Brixham and Plymouth, scallops are dived
for in Start Bay, vegetables are grown four
miles away, and Sutton Eddystone is brewed
along the road. This translates to scallops
with smoked bacon and red onions, smoked
haddock fishcakes, whole baked sea bass, and
rack of lamb with rosemary and redcurrant
jus. Light lunches of hot sandwiches, daily
curries and various omelettes.

Prices: Restaurant main course from £7.95. Bar main
course from £4.95. House wine £11.95.
Last orders: Bar: 23.00 (during summer months open
all day at the weekend). Food: lunch 14.30; dinner 21.30.
Closed: Rarely.
Food: Modern British.
Real ale: Brakspear Ales, South Hams Devon Pride,
Sutton Eddystone.
Other points: No-smoking area. Dogs welcome in the
bar. Garden. Car park.
Directions: Just off the A379, behind the village green
between Dartmouth and Kingsbridge, one mile inland
from Torcross. (Map 2, G5)

Cerne Abbas

The Royal Oak

23 Long Street, Cerne Abbas, Dorchester,
Dorset DT2 7JG
Telephone: +44(0)1300 341797

A thatched and creeper-clad pub nestling in a picture-book village below Cerne's chalk giant etched into the Dorset Downs. Built with stone from the nearby ruined Benedictine abbey, it dates from the 16th century and is now a thriving village local, with a traditional interior featuring flagstone floors, log fires, beams and bric-a-brac. It not only attracts hungry walkers and tourists on the Hardy Trail but local diners in search of hearty and genuinely home-cooked food that utilises first-class produce from local suppliers. The 'lighter bites' menu lists favourites such as ham, egg and chips and local venison sausages, while clam chowder, Dorset paté with gooseberry-and-coriander chutney, game pie, pot-roasted lamb shoulder, and fillet steak with Blue Vinney cheese appear on the main menu. Daily dishes extend the choice and may include pheasant in red wine. Secluded rear garden for summer sipping.

Prices: Starters from £3.95. Main course from £7.95. Snack from £4.25. House wine £10.65.
Last orders: Bar: lunch 15.00; dinner 23.00.
Food: lunch 14.00; dinner 21.30 (Sunday 21.00).
Closed: Rarely.
Food: Traditional and Modern British.
Real ale: Badger Tanglefoot, Badger Best, Fursty Ferret, Giant's Tipple. 2 guest beers.
Other points: No-smoking area. Courtyard garden and decking. Children welcome. Dogs welcome in the bar.
Directions: Village signed off A352 Dorchester to Sherborne road, six miles north of Dorchester. (Map 3 G1)

Corscombe

The Fox Inn

Corscombe, Dorchester, Dorset DT2 0NS
Telephone: +44(0)1935 891330
dine@fox-inn.co.uk
www.fox-inn.co.uk

Must-sees
Beaminster, Forde Abbey, Sherborne Castle, Mapperton Gardens, Abbotsbury, Maiden Castle

Best views
Pilsdon Pen, Golden Cap, Hardy's Monument, Eggardon Hill

Villages to visit Cerne Abbas, Abbotsbury, Evershot

Mapperton Gardens

A pretty little thatched pub of stone and cob, built in 1620 as a cider house, lost down a web of narrow lanes deep in unspoilt Dorset countryside. It's everybody's idea of the perfect country inn, with two charming beamed bars, one with a huge inglenook fireplace, stone-flagged floors and gingham-clothed tables, the other filled with old pine furniture and chatty locals quaffing pints of Exmoor Ale. No modern-day intrusions here or in the plant-festooned rear conservatory with its sturdy, long wooden table. The food is country-pub cooking at its best, with all dishes freshly prepared from quality produce, including local-estate venison with a rich game sauce, and rack of Dorset lamb with rosemary gravy, and the blackboard features fresh fish from West Bay, in such dishes as brill with sweet potato and coriander mash. Homemade puddings and lunchtime plough-man's are worthwhile. Tucked under the thatch are four cottagey en suite bedrooms. See pub walk on page 224.

Rooms: 4. Double room from £75, single occupancy from £55.
Prices: Main course from £8.50. House wine £10.50.
Last orders: Bar: lunch 15.00; dinner 23.00. Food: lunch 14.00; dinner 21.00 (Friday and Saturday 21.30).
Closed: Rarely.
Food: Modern British.
Real ale: Exmoor Ale, Fox Ale.
Other points: No-smoking area. Garden/conservatory. Well-behaved children welcome. Car park.
Directions: From Yeovil, take the A37 towards Dorchester. After one mile, turn right towards Corscombe and follow the lane for five and a half miles. Alternatively, take the A356 from Crewkerne to Maiden Newton for five miles. (Map 3, G1)

Tourist information Dorchester +44(0)1305 267992
Where to shop Sherborne, Beaminster, Dorchester
Farmers' market Bridport
Nearest racecourse Taunton
Nearest golf course Halstock

Local activities
Fossil hunting, horse riding, beaches, cycling, fishing

Best scenic drives
A35 between Axminster and Dorchester. B-roads between Beaminster and Lyme Regis.

Events and festivals
Yeovilton International Air Show (July)
Dorchester Music and Arts Festival (April)

Fontmell Magna

The Crown Inn

Fontmell Magna, Shaftesbury, Dorset SP7 0PA
Telephone: +44(0)1747 811441
crowninnfm@hotmail.com
www.crowninn.me.uk

The combined talents of Liz and Jon Neilson and chef Robin Davies have transformed this pub from a sleepy village local to a thriving food pub, where local produce, small suppliers and fresh food are taken seriously. Bread is baked on the premises, fish is delivered daily from Poole, meat is sourced from local traceable herds, farms in the Blackmore Vale supply dairy produce, and the cheeseboard features the local Ashmore cheddar. Robin's menus may list classic pub dishes - perhaps roast leg of Dorset lamb and rib-eye steak and chips - but the quality of the ingredients and presentation are first-class. Alternatives may include cod fillet with pesto crust and roast organic chicken with homemade bread sauce. Good puddings, Hall and Woodhouse beers, and excellent-value wines are all served in the comfortably refurbished bars and restaurant. Cosy bedrooms are light and airy with an old-fashioned and Victorian feel to them.

Rooms: 3 with private bathrooms. Double from £65.
Prices: Restaurant main course from £8.95. Bar main course from £6.95. House wine £8.50.
Last orders: Bar: open all day. Food: lunch 14.30 (Saturday and Sunday until 15.00); dinner 21.00 (Saturday 21.30).
Closed: Rarely.
Food: Classic British with traditional French influences.
Real ale: Badger Tanglefoot, Badger Best.
Other points: No smoking in the restaurant. Dogs welcome in the bar. Garden. Car park.
Directions: From Shaftesbury take the A350 to Blandford Forum, pass through Compton Abbas and the Crown is in the centre of Fontmell Magna. (Map 3, G2)

Braintree

Green Dragon

Upper London Road, Young's End, Braintree,
Essex CM77 8QN
Telephone: +44(0)1245 361030
info@greendragonbraintree.co.uk
www.greendragonbraintree.co.uk

You will find the Green Dragon hard beside the A131, close to the Essex County Showground. It's a classic 18th-century inn, formerly a private house and stables, the latter housing the Barn and Hayloft restaurants. Within the pub, the bars sport original beams, red carpets, banquettes and traditional pub furnishings, and provide a cosy atmosphere in which to relax with a pint of Abbot, or a decent glass of wine. Food from the blackboard and extensive printed menus are served throughout, but the range of light snacks to proper dishes offers great flexibility. Traditional pub staples are made from scratch with good ingredients, so tuck into cottage pie, filled baguettes, or home-cooked ham, egg and chips at lunch. Evening meals take in wild venison in red wine, slow-roasted rare-breed pork with cider sauce, and monthly specials such as supreme of pheasant with wild berry and port sauce and monkfish with mussels and chorizo.

Prices: Set lunch £12 and dinner £16.50. Main course from £7.50. House wine £9.
Last orders: Bar: lunch 14.30; dinner 21.00. Food: lunch 14.30; dinner 21.00 (Friday and Saturday 22.00, Sunday 20.00).
Closed: Rarely.
Food: Traditional British.
Real ale: Greene King IPA & Abbot Ale, 1 guest beer.
Other points: No smoking in the restaurant. Car park.
Directions: M11/Stansted exit. Take the A120 to Braintree then the A131 towards Chelmsford. At the fourth roundabout, take the exit to Young's End. (Map 4, D6)

Colchester

The Peldon Rose Inn

Mersea Road, Peldon, Colchester,
Essex CO5 7QJ
Telephone: +44(0)1206 735248
peldon@lwwinebars.com

Colchester-based wine merchant Lay & Wheeler have worked their magic in restoring this 600-year-old smugglers' inn. Conjure up images of discussions about contraband in the ancient bar, where old-world charm abounds in standing timbers, 'skull-shattering' beams, antique mahogany tables, huge log fires and, in the adjacent dining area, wonky timbered walls. The light and stylish rear conservatory is very contemporary by comparison. Bar food utilises locally sourced produce, notably Mersea Island fish and oysters. Follow pork-and-game terrine with, say, grilled Dover, whole local plaice, or braised venison with smoked bacon and field mushrooms. There's a good sandwich choice, pasta meals and ploughman's lunches, while puddings include chocolate pecan-nut tart. The short wine list is of superior quality, offering close to 20 by the glass. En suite bedrooms sport contemporary colours and furnishings.

Rooms: 3. Double/twin room from £70.
Prices: Restaurant main course from £7.75. House wine £10.95.
Last orders: Bar: 23.00. Food: lunch 14.15; dinner 21.00 (Friday and Saturday 21.30). During the summer, food is served until 21.30.
Closed: Sunday evenings 31st October-31st March.
Food: Modern and Traditional British.
Real ale: Adnams Bitter & Broadside, Greene King IPA.
Other points: No-smoking area. Garden. Children welcome. Car park. Wheelchair access.
Directions: On the B1025 south of Colchester, close to the causeway to Mersea Island. (Map 4, D6)

Great Dunmow

The Swan at Felsted ⭐

Station Road, Felsted, Great Dunmow,
Essex CM6 3DG
Telephone: +44(0)1371 820245
info@theswanatfelsted.co.uk
www.theswanatfelsted.co.uk

Looks can be deceiving and The Swan is no-exception. The imposing redbrick-and-timber pub dates from the 1900s, when the original Tudor building burnt down, and for years it was a rough boozer. Jono and Jane Clarke took on the Ridley's lease in 2002 and the transformation has been remarkable. Step inside to find a spacious, beautifully designed interior, featuring smart wooden floors, mustard-yellow walls hung with works of art, leather sofas in the bar, and a high-ceilinged dining area filled with chunky tables and high-backed dining chairs. Food is sourced locally and the imaginative menus offer a good choice of dishes, from lunchtime salads and sandwiches to main menu classics such as shepherds' pie, the Swan burger, and steak, ale and mussel suet pudding, both made with Barnston beef. Alternatively, go for one of the daily specials, perhaps duck breast with raspberry jus. Wines are well chosen.

Prices: Restaurant main course from £9.50. Main course bar/snack from £5.50. House wine £10.95.
Last orders: Bar: lunch 15.00 (Sunday 18.00); dinner 23.00 (Sunday dinner 22.30). Food: lunch 14.30 (Sunday 16.00); dinner 21.30 (no food Sunday evening).
Closed: Never.
Food: Modern British.
Real ale: Ridley's IPA.
Other points: No-smoking area in the restaurant. Children welcome. Dogs welcome in the bar. Garden. Car park. Wheelchair access.
Directions: Exit 8/M11. Take the A120 and then the B1256 towards Colchester, then turn right onto B1417 to Felsted. (Map 4, D6)

Paglesham East End

The Plough & Sail 🍺

Paglesham East End, Rochford, Essex SS4 2EG
Telephone: +44(0)1702 258242
mark.ollie1@btinternet.com

A peaceful location five minutes stroll from the bracing Essex marshes, a 400-year-old timbered and weather-boarded building full of character both inside and out, tip-top beer from the Mighty Oak Brewery, and hearty, traditional pub food, together make this coastal pub well worth a journey. Successive generations of the Oliver family have preserved the unique atmosphere of this local favourite, so expect low beams, nautical memorabilia and two blazing log fires. With views across remote fields, the garden is the place to while away a warm afternoon. Food takes in the tried and tested – ham and eggs, ploughman's lunches, steaks – but look to the board for Marianne's daily creations that utilise locally sourced meats and vegetables, and local seafood. Accompany a pint of Maldon Gold with a dozen local oysters, skate or Dover sole from local boats and lamb's liver with bacon. See pub walk on page 226.

Prices: Restaurant main course from £7. Bar snack from £3. House wine £8.95.
Last orders: Bar: lunch 15.00 (Saturday 15.30 and Sunday all day); dinner 23.00. Bar: lunch 15.00; dinner 22.30 (Sunday 20.30).
Closed: Rarely.
Food: Traditional and Modern British.
Real ale: Greene King IPA, Mighty Oak and, Maldon Brewery beers.
Other points: No-smoking area. Garden. Children over three welcome. Car park. Wheelchair access.
Directions: Exit 29/M5. Follow signs to Rochford from the A127 and then signs to Paglesham. (Map 4, 6E)

Cirencester

Wild Duck Inn

Ewen, Cirencester, Gloucestershire GL7 6BY
Telephone: +44(0)1285 770310
wduckinn@aol.com
www.thewildduckinn.co.uk

Creeper-clad with well-tended gardens, this fine Elizabethan inn creates a favourable first impression. The bar is brimming with character and atmosphere, with its backdrop of rich burgundy walls, covered with old portraits and hunting trophies, and large comfortable armchairs creating a warm atmosphere. The restaurant's labyrinth of rooms features dark beams, more burgundy walls and wooden tables and chairs; the same printed menu is available throughout, along with blackboard specials. The lively repertoire draws the crowds with its modern take and realistic pricing, perhaps a one-course lunch of fresh tuna burger, chicken Caesar salad or a classic fish pie. Dinner could run to roast duck with port-and-redcurrant sauce, slow-roast belly pork with cider gravy, and fresh Brixham fish. The globetrotting wine list offers some 30 by the glass, and the bar has five real ales. Twelve individually decorated en suite rooms await those not wanting to drive home.

Rooms: 12. Double room from £95, single from £70.
Prices: Main course from £6.95. House wine £11.
Last orders: Bar: 23.00. Food: lunch 14.00; dinner 22.00 (Saturday and Sunday all day until 21.30).
Closed: 25 December.
Food: Modern British.
Real ale: Bombardier Bitter, Smiles Original, Theakston Old Peculiar, Theakston XB, Old Speckled Hen.
Other points: Smoking by request, not in the restaurant. Children welcome. Dogs welcome overnight. Garden.
Directions: J15/17/M4. From Cirencester, take the A429 for Malmesbury. Left to Ewen at Kemble. (Map 3, E2)

Clearwell

The Wyndham Arms

Clearwell, The Royal Forest of Dean, Gloucestershire GL16 8JT
Telephone: +44(0)1594 833666
nigel@thewyndhamhotel.co.uk
www.thewyndhamhotel.co.uk

Set in several acres of glorious sloping gardens, woods and lawns, Nigel and Pauline Stanley's 600-year-old traditional inn stands at the heart of this medieval village. It is filled with oak beams, flagstones and exposed original red brick, the historic and very popular bar dispensing local Freeminer beers, decent wines and a fabulous range of malt whiskies. Local foodstuffs feature prominently on both the bar and fixed-price restaurant menus. These can include seasonal game from Lydney Park Estate, single-herd meats and Gloucester Old Spot pork products. They are also active in the community cooperative for supplies of vegetables, salads and herbs, and local farmhouse cheeses. Translated on the menu, this brings pot-roast Welsh lamb with rosemary jus, Gower sea bass with cockle prawn velouté, and Valhrona chocolate tart to finish. The spacious bedrooms are much more recent (1990s) and in an adjacent building.

Rooms: 18. Double room £65-£110, single £35-£65.
Prices: Restaurant main course from £12.50. Bar main course from £8.95. House wine £11.25.
Last orders: Bar: 23.00. Food: lunch 14.00 (Sunday 14.30); dinner: 21.30 (Sunday 21.00).
Closed: Rarely.
Food: Modern British.
Real ale: Freeminer Bitter. Monthly guest ale.
Other points: No smoking in the restaurant. Dogs welcome overnight. Garden. Car park. Licence for civil weddings. Wheelchair access.
Directions: Exit2/M48. Via A48 and B4228 signed Forest of Dean. From the A48 at Monmouth via A4176 and B4228, two miles from Coleford. (Map 3, E1)

Frampton Mansell

White Horse ⭐

Cirencester Road, Frampton Mansell,
Gloucestershire GL6 8HZ
Telephone: +44(0)1285 760960
www.cotswoldwhitehorse.com

Shaun and Emma Davies's White Horse is a
welcome beacon along the busy A419. The
pair have revived the pub's fortunes with
a smart makeover but, more importantly,
with their excellent food and drink. Brightly
painted walls, modern art and chunky tables
provide a fitting setting for the modern menu
built around fresh produce from quality
local suppliers. Meat comes from Butts Farm
butchers near Cirencester, game is from local
shoots, and fish is delivered twice-weekly
from Cornwall. Seafood has become quite
a focus, especially since a large lobster tank
was installed. As with other seafood, the lobster is simply served, as the quality speaks for
itself. Fine dining begins with pan-fried foie
gras, sweet-potato pancake, crisp pancetta
and a muscat butter, or rock oysters, then
moves on to mains of halibut with saffron
and a chive-cream sauce or venison with red
wine and ginger jus. Puddings are an equally
delectable bunch. Global wines focus on
smaller growers.

Prices: Restaurant main course from £8.95. Bar main
course from £4.95. House wine £11.75.
Last orders: Bar: lunch 15.00; dinner 23.00. Food: lunch
14.30; dinner 21.45 (Sunday 15.00).
Closed: Sunday evening.
Food: Modern British.
Real Ale: Hook Norton, Uley Bitter.
Other points: No smoking in the restaurant. Children
welcome. Dogs welcome in the bar. Garden. Car park.
Directions: Exit 15/M4 or exit 12/M5 Between
Cirencester and Stroud on the A419, not in the village
of Frampton Mansell itself. (Map 3, E2)

Kelmscott

The Plough at Kelmscott

Kelmscott, Lechlade, Gloucestershire GL7 3HG
Telephone: +44(0)1367 253543
plough@kelmscottgl7.fsnet.co.uk
www.theploughatkelmscott.co.uk

Tucked away down a dead-end lane in a
peaceful Thameside village and long a
favoured watering-hole among Thames path
walkers and the boating fraternity, the 17th-
century Plough operates as a gastropub with
rooms. Despite its isolation, the village and
the Plough bustle with visitors due to the
close proximity of Henry Morris's former
country home. The interior has a contemporary rustic look, mixing original flagstones,
log fires and exposed brick and timbers with
modern wooden chairs and tables. Matching
the surroundings is an imaginative modern
British menu. On the bar menu you may find
fresh cod in beer batter and local game casserole. Evening dishes produce game terrine,
herb-crusted cod with white wine and cream
sauce, and baked vanilla cheesecake. Eight en
suite bedrooms; one is decorated in William
Morris style. See pub walk on page 228.

Rooms: 8. Double from £75, single from £45, family
room from £85.
Prices: Restaurant main course from £9.50. Lunch and
bar snack from £4.95. Fish menu from £4.50.
House wine £10.50.
Last orders: Bar: lunch 15.00; dinner 23.00. Food: lunch
14.30; dinner 21.00 (Saturday and Sunday all day).
Closed: Rarely.
Food: Classic and Modern British and French.
Real ale: Hook Norton, Wychwood, Archers.
Other points: No smoking in the restaurant. Children
welcome. Dogs welcome overnight. Garden.
Wheelchair access (restaurant/pub).
Directions: Take the A416 Lechlade towards Faringdon,
then follow signs to Kelmscott. (Map 3, E3)

The Wyndham Arms

Next door to ancient Clearwell Castle and set in acres of glorious gardens, this 600-year-old traditional inn-cum-hotel draws a loyal clientele to its well-equipped modern bedrooms and freshly prepared food. Local foodstuffs feature on changing menus, notably farmhouse cheese, supplies of vegetables, salads and herbs from the community cooperative, and seasonal game from Lydney Park Estate. Here are some of their first-rate suppliers of food and drink.

Visit the local Farmers' Market

Friday is market day in the Forest of Dean. Cinderford is the venue on the first Friday of the month; Coleford on the second; Lydney on the third; and Newent on the last Friday of the month.

Charles Martell
Laurel Farm, Dymock

From an interest in reviving the Gloucester breed of cattle on moving to Laurel Farm in 1972, Charles Martell set about making cheese with their milk. Stinking Bishop is derived from a cheese once made by Cistercian monks in Dymock. They favoured the production of 'washed-rind' cheeses, cheeses that are washed in a variety of liquids. They are generally full-flavoured with lively aromas, and Stinking Bishop is no exception as it uses perry as its wash. It has a sticky yellow-orange rind, a soft and creamy texture and a delicious flavour, despite smelling of old socks!

Orchards Cider & Perry Company
Yewgreen Farm, Brockweir
Tel: 01291 689536

This formerly overgrown and disused farm in the picturesque Wye Valley is now producing top quality cider and perry. The 200-year-old property was bought by the fortuitously named Keith Orchard who discovered in the overgrown orchard a host of cider-apple and perry-pear trees. He now produces many varieties, winners of many awards, and sells them throughout the West Country to various shops, top pubs and restaurants.

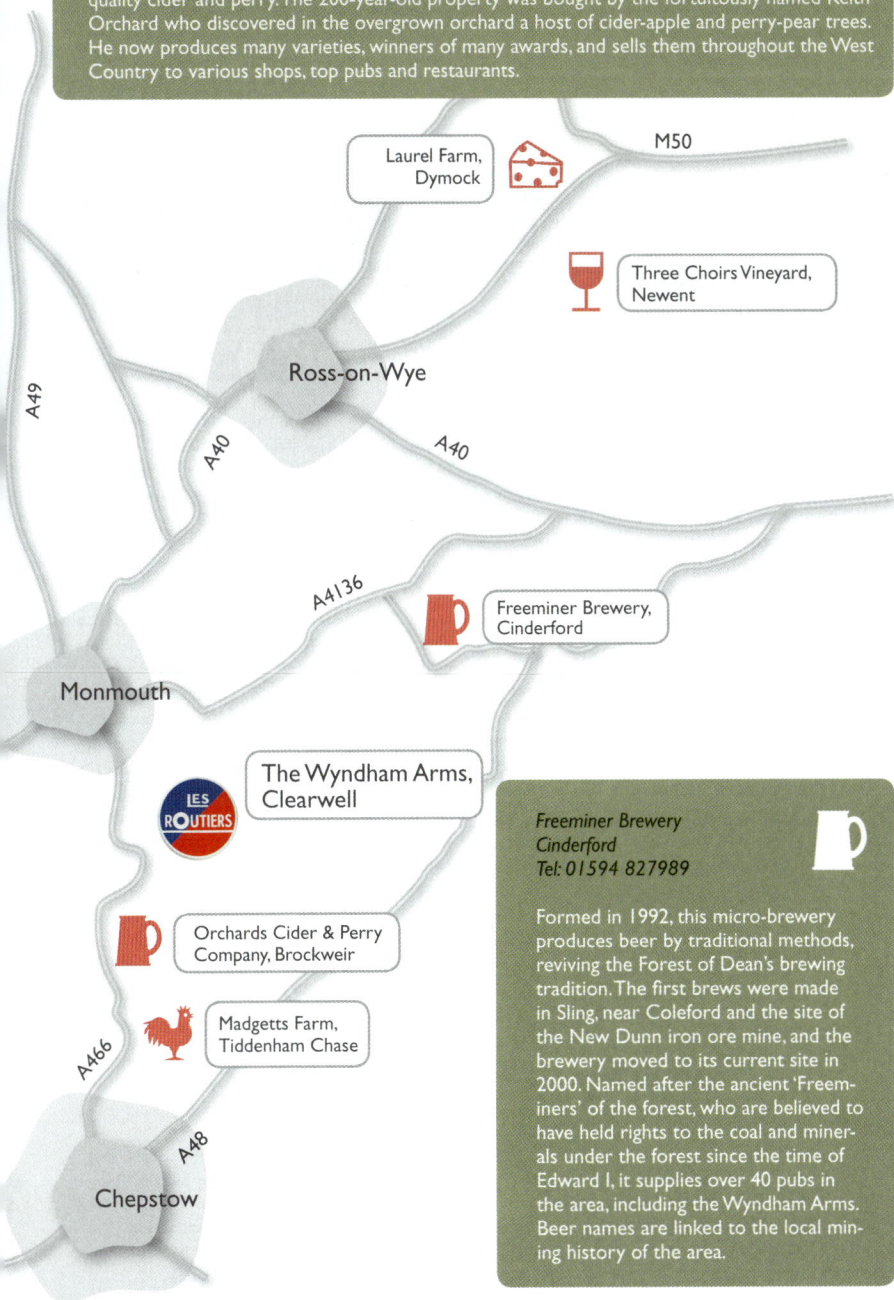

M50

Laurel Farm,
Dymock

Three Choirs Vineyard,
Newent

Ross-on-Wye

A49

A40

A40

A4136

Freeminer Brewery,
Cinderford

Monmouth

The Wyndham Arms,
Clearwell

LES ROUTIERS

Freeminer Brewery
Cinderford
Tel: 01594 827989

Formed in 1992, this micro-brewery produces beer by traditional methods, reviving the Forest of Dean's brewing tradition. The first brews were made in Sling, near Coleford and the site of the New Dunn iron ore mine, and the brewery moved to its current site in 2000. Named after the ancient 'Freem-iners' of the forest, who are believed to have held rights to the coal and miner-als under the forest since the time of Edward I, it supplies over 40 pubs in the area, including the Wyndham Arms. Beer names are linked to the local min-ing history of the area.

Orchards Cider & Perry
Company, Brockweir

Madgetts Farm,
Tiddenham Chase

A466

A48

Chepstow

Northleach

The Puesdown Inn

Compton Abdale, Northleach, Cheltenham,
Gloucestershire GL54 4DN
Telephone: +44(0)1451 860262
inn4food@btopenworld.com
www.puesdown.cotswoldinns.com

On a wild winter's night. this isolated former coaching inn, situated high in the Cotswolds beside the A40, is the perfect retreat. John and Maggie Armstrong bought the mellow stone pub in 2002 and have renovated and refurbished throughout with style, notably in the three individually designed stable-block bedrooms. The rambling bar and dining areas sport oak floors, warm, rich colours and deep sofas fronting log fires. Informality is the key and their hard work has paid off as the inn draws race-goers from Cheltenham, Cotswold walkers, and wine buffs and jazz fans for regular evening events. Food is freshly prepared by John, who sources quality ingredients, be it local game or fish from Brixham, for his daily menus. Expect the likes of sandwiches and lamb pie for lunch, while other options may take in mushroom and saffron risotto, baked bass with fennel and tapenade, and chocolate fudge terrine.

Rooms: 3. Double/twin from £80, single from £50. Family from £95.
Prices: Set Sunday lunch £16. Set weekday dinner £18.95 (Jazz evening). Restaurant main course from £13. Bar main course from £6.50. House wine £9.50.
Last orders: Bar: lunch 15.00; dinner 22.00. Food: lunch 15.00; dinner 22.00 (Sunday 21.30).
Closed: Rarely.
Food: Modern British.
Real ale: Hook Norton Best & 303. 1-2 guest beers.
Other points: No-smoking area. Dogs welcome. Garden. Car park. Wheelchair access.
Directions: Beside the A40 between Northleach and Cheltenham. (Map 2, C7)

Northleach

The Wheatsheaf Inn

West End, Northleach, Cheltenham,
Gloucestershire GL54 3EZ
Telephone: +44 (0)1451 860244
info@wsan.co.uk
www.wsan.co.uk

Quietly situated in this celebrated Cotswold 'wool town', the pretty stone-built 300 year-old coaching inn has been revamped by brothers Caspar and Gavin Harvard-Walls. Expect classic period features - worn flagstone floors, big oak beams, blazing log fires and chunky wooden furnishings - throughout the three, light and airy front rooms. The rustic bar deals in Hook Norton and guest ales, and has a blackboard menu. The classy, understated dining room is marginally more formal. Modern British favourites are inspired by what is available locally, Gloucester Old Spot pork tenderloin with parsnip mash, for example, or Bibury trout with watercress and bacon. Treacle tart, or apple crumble are classic desserts, with local cheeses making a savoury alternative. There are some impeccable choices on a globally inspired wine list. Eight en suite rooms have been refurbished along cool, white, Scandinavian lines.

Rooms: 8. Double/twin room from £60, single from £50, family room from £70.
Prices: Main course from £7. Bar/snack from £4. House wine £10.75.
Last orders: Bar 23.00. Food: lunch 15.00; dinner 22.00 (Sunday 21.00).
Closed: Never.
Food: Modern British.
Real ale: Hook Norton, Wadworth 6X. Guest beer.
Other points: No smoking in the restaurant. Children welcome. Dogs welcome in the bar. Garden. Car park. Licence for civil weddings. Wheelchair access.
Directions: Exit 15/M4. Just off A429 between Stow-on-the-Wold and Cirencester. (Map 3, E2)

Painswick

Butchers Arms

Sheepscombe, Painswick,
Gloucestershire GL6 7RH
Telephone: +44(0)1452 812113
bleninns@clara.net
www.cotswoldinns.co.uk

A mellow-stone pub dating from 1620 and originally a butchery for deer hunted in Henry VIII's deer park. Note the famous pub sign showing a butcher supping a pint of ale with a pig tied to his leg. It is worth negotiating the narrow lanes for the glorious views over the rolling Stroud Valley from the sunny front terrace. Added attractions include the good range of beers - try a pint of Wye Valley Ale - and an interesting choice of traditional and modern pub food. The homely, rustic bar and adjoining beamed dining room are the setting for cooking that relies on locally sourced raw materials, such as handmade sausages from Jessie Smith in Dursley and Texel lambs from Lypiatt Farm in nearby Miserden. For lunch, tuck into hearty homemade soups, decent ploughman's or spinach-and-ricotta cannelloni, while at dinner choose, perhaps, from prime steaks, beef Wellington, and salmon with sesame seeds and noodles.

Prices: Restaurant main course from £7.50. Bar snack from £4.95. House wine £9.95.
Last orders: Bar: lunch 14.30 (Saturday 15.00); dinner 23.00. Food: lunch 14.30 (Sunday 15.00); dinner 21.30.
Closed: Never.
Food: Modern and Traditional British and European.
Real ale: Hook Norton Best Bitter, Moles Best Bitter, Wye Valley Dorothy Goodbody's Golden Ale, Otter Ale. 3 guest beers.
Other points: No-smoking area. Children welcome. Garden. Car park. Dogs welcome in the bar. Wheelchair access, no WC.
Directions: Exit J11a/M5. Just off the A46 between Cheltenham and Stroud, near Painswick. (Map 3, E2)

Painswick

The Falcon Inn

New Street, Painswick,
Gloucestershire GL6 6UN
Telephone: +44(0)1452 814222
bleninns@clara.net
www.falconinn.com

Standing opposite the parish church, the Falcon is a handsome, stone-built, 16th-century coaching inn with a colourful history. It is also the unlikely setting in which to find the world's oldest bowling green. Interconnecting bar and dining areas are full of traditional character, the scene set by stone, tiled and carpeted floors, wood panelling, log fires, and an eclectic mix of furnishings. Jonny Johnston's careful sourcing of local produce, notably game from nearby shoots, locally grown vegetables, and butchers' meats, including belted Galloway beef, is evident in changing menus and daily chalkboard dishes. Expect the likes of organic pork loin with cider and honey, and braised venison with root vegetables, and fish dishes such as organic Cockleford trout with red pesto. Individually decorated bedrooms are split between the inn and the converted coach house.

Rooms: 12. Double room from £68, single from £45.
Prices: Set lunch £12 and dinner £16. Restaurant main course from £7.50. Bar snack from £4.95. House wine £9.95.
Last orders: Bar: 23.00. Food: lunch 14.30 (Sunday 15.00); dinner 21.30 (Saturday 22.00).
Closed: Never.
Food: Modern and Traditional British and European.
Real ale: Hook Norton Best Bitter, Greene King IPA, Wadworth 6X, Otter Ale. 1 guest beer.
Other points: No-smoking area. Children welcome. Dogs welcome overnight. Garden. Car park. Wheelchair access, no WC in the bar/restaurant.
Directions: Exit J11a/M5. On the A46 between Cheltenham and Stroud. (Map 3, E2)

Winchcombe

The White Hart Inn

High Street, Winchcombe, Cheltenham, Gloucestershire GL54 5LJ
Telephone: +44(0)1242 602359
enquiries@the-white-hart-inn.com
www.the-white-hart-inn.com

Must-sees
Sudeley Castle: An impressive old house blended into remains of a medieval castle. Rich furnishings, porcelain, fine tapestries and paintings, and a splendid garden.
Snowshill Manor: A typical Cotswold Manor filled with extraordinary collections, and a cottage garden.

Events & festivals
Winchcombe Horse Show (May)
National Hunt Festival, Cheltenham (March)
Prescott Speed Hillclimb Championship (May)

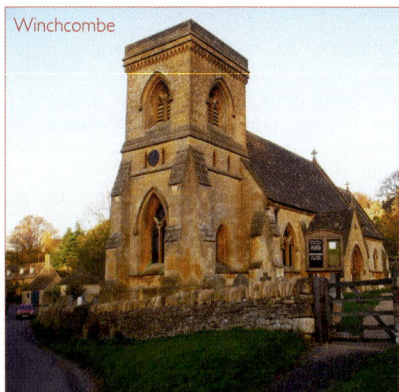

Winchcombe

Behind the 16th-century stone exterior of this Cotswolds town-centre inn, visitors will be treated to a taste of Swedish hospitality. Refurbished with impeccable taste by Nicole Burr, who hails from Stockholm, a cool Scandinavian influence runs through the minimalist dining room and upstairs to the eight beautifully decorated bedrooms. It also influences the contemporary menus. What is traditional, though, is the 'pubby' front bar where regulars quaff pints of local Stanney Bitter and tuck into ploughman's platters, big crusty baguettes, or the house speciality smörgasbord platter - Swedish cold meats, seafoods and salads. In the restaurant, order beef and pork meatballs with cream sauce, or something more traditional, perhaps monkfish with lobster and crab sauce. Beef and lamb come from the Sudeley Castle Estate. The Stable Bar offers Italian-style pizzas to eat in or take-away. Individually designed and decorated bedrooms offer a high level of comfort, with modern facilities and luxury en suite bathrooms.

Rooms: 8. Double from £70, single room from £55
Prices: Set lunch £12.95 and dinner £17.95. Restaurant main course from £11.95. Main course bar from £5.95. House wine £10.95.
Last orders: Food: 22.00.
Closed: Rarely.
Food: Modern British with Scandinavian specialities.
Real ale: Old Speckled Hen, Wadworth 6X, Greene King IPA, Stanway Stanney Bitter.
Other points: No-smoking area. Children welcome. Patio. Car park. Meeting facilities.
Directions: Exit 9/M5. In the centre of Winchcombe on the B4362 Cheltenham to Stratford road. (Map 3, D2)

Tourist information Winchcombe +44(0)1242 602925
Where to shop Cheltenham, Stow-on-the-Wold
Farmers' market Winchcombe (3rd Saturday of month)
Nearest racecourse Cheltenham
Nearest golf course Cleeve Hill

Where to walk
The Cotswold Way, a 100-mile path from Chipping Campden to Bath passes through Winchcombe, and some of the choicest scenery is to be found close to Winchcombe, notably between Broadway and Stanton and across Cleeve Common. From the town, you can follow the trail to Hailes Abbey and Belas Knap.
See pub walk on page 230.

Crondall

The Hampshire Arms

Pankridge Street, Crondall, Farnham,
Hampshire GU10 5QU
Telephone: +44(0)1252 850418
dining@thehampshirearms.co.uk
www.thehampshirearms.co.uk

Alan Piesse and Tim Dyer took over this 18th-century village pub in January 2005. In its time it had been a courthouse and then a bakery before becoming a pub to serve the community. Behind the unpretentious pub exterior, Alan and Tim have succeeded in sweeping away the pretentions that existed with regard to the atmosphere and style of food. Chef Colin McCavana produces fresh, well-presented food and now includes a lighter lunch menu in the bar featuring classic pub favourites, in addition to an imaginative carte. Typically, starters include mussels with white wine, shallots and herb butter or home-cured salmon with lime and honey dressing. Mains may offer whole bass with lemon balm, ginger and fennel, or lamb with coriander and apricot couscous. Leather sofas front the log fire in the informal bar area, which draws local drinkers in, while there's more formal dining in the newly refurbished restaurant. There's also a private dining room, and a terrace for summer alfresco eating.

Prices: Restaurant main course from £10.50. Bar main course from £7.50. House wine £12.50.
Last orders: Bar: lunch 14.30; dinner 23.00. Food: lunch 14.00; dinner 21.15. No carte Monday evening.
Closed: Sunday nights.
Food: Modern British.
Real ale: Greene King Abbot Ale, Ruddle's Best & IPA.
Other points: No smoking in the restaurant. Garden. Children welcome. Car park. Wheelchair access.
Directions: Exit 5/M3. Take the A287 for Farnham and turn off at Crondall. (Map 3, F4)

Fordingbridge

Rose and Thistle

Rockbourne, Fordingbridge, Hampshire SP6 3NL
Telephone: +44(0)1725 518236
enquiries@roseandthistle.co.uk
www.roseandthistle.co.uk

A delightful 17th-century thatched pub in a pretty downland village on the edge of the New Forest. It boasts two huge fireplaces with winter log fires and tasteful furnishings, with country-style fabrics, dried flowers, and magazines enhancing the civilised atmosphere. Quality pub food is up to date, and sensibly light and simple at lunchtimes. Note daily homemade soup, 'elegant' Welsh rarebit, local sausages and mustard mash, and ploughman's lunches. Evening dishes are more elaborate, featured on a monthly-changing menu and daily specials' board. Typically, tuck into pork with oyster mushroom and garlic sauce, local venison with chestnuts and spring onion, and fresh fish (also available lunchtimes), such as wild bass with prawns and capers. There is traditional bread-and-butter pudding and seasonal game from local shoots. Also, Sunday roasts, good ales and wines, plus a lovely rose-filled garden.

Prices: Restaurant main course from £11. Main course bar from £7.45. House wine £11.25.
Last orders: Bar: lunch 15.00; dinner 23.00 (Sunday 20.00 October - March). Food: lunch 14.30; dinner 21.30. No food Sunday evenings during the winter.
Closed: Rarely.
Food: Modern British.
Real ale: London Pride, Strong's Best. Guest beer.
Other points: No smoking in the restaurant. Children welcome. Dogs welcome in the bar. Garden. Car park. Wheelchair access to the restaurant/pub.
Directions: Follow signs off the A354 south of Salisbury, From Fordingbridge take the Sandleheath road and at the crossroads turn right to Rockbourne. (Map 3, G2)

Littleton

The Running Horse

88 Main Road, Littleton, Winchester,
Hampshire SO22 6QS
Telephone: +44(0)1962 880218
christineabrams@btconnect.com
www.therunninghorsepubrestaurant.co.uk

Considerable investment over the past two years has transformed this once run-down village pub into a stylish dining venue, but one that hasn't lost sight of its roots as a village local. Expect a smart interior featuring opulent Italian sofas, a marble-topped bar, plenty of stainless steel, slate floors and trendy wooden blinds, but the original fireplace and wooden floor remain. Light lunch in the bar may take in crab cakes with tartare sauce and seared scallops with caper dressing. In the evening, sit in the bar or restaurant to experience Joe Cathers' inventive cooking. 'Quality ingredients, well cooked - food the way it should be' is his philosophy and his freshly prepared dishes may include scallops, artichoke and grapefruit with truffle oil for starters, followed by roast Minstead duck with pak choi, broad beans and pink peppercorn sauce, and chilled vanilla rice pudding. There are also excellent wines, local Ringwood ale, and en suite rooms for 2006.

Rooms: 9. Double/twin from £85, family from £110.
Prices: Restaurant main course £15.50. Bar main course £9.95. House wine £12.95.
Last orders: Bar: lunch 14.00 (Saturday 16.00); dinner 21.30. Food: lunch 14.00 (Saturday 16.00); dinner 21.30.
Closed: Rarely.
Food: Modern British.
Real ale: Ringwood Best, Itchen Valley Fagin's Bitter.
Other points: No-smoking area. Dogs welcome. Garden. Car park. Wheelchair access.
Directions: Village signposted off the A272 Stockbridge road, just west of Winchester. (Map 3, F3)

Southampton

The White Star Tavern & Dining Rooms

28 Oxford Street, Southampton,
Hampshire SO14 3DJ
Telephone: +44(0)2380 821990
manager@whitestartavern.co.uk
www.whitestartavern.co.uk

Southampton's first gastropub, in a former seafarers' hotel close to Ocean Village and West Quay, has proved a great success, drawing both a lively drinking crowd and discerning diners. Smart front-bar lounge areas sport modern brown leather banquettes and cream walls adorned with shipping photographs and retro mirrors, yet retain the original flagstone floors and the period open fireplaces. Beyond lies the spacious, wood-floored and panelled dining rooms. Good use of fresh produce from Hampshire suppliers can be seen in 'light bites' such as chicken rillette and homemade piccalilli, or a classic Caesar salad, and, in the lunchtime carte, with smoked haddock and grain-mustard cream. In the evening, steamed mussels in black-bean sauce, and pork loin with confit root vegetables and mustard jus, show style, as do the homemade breads and puddings. Impressive list of cocktails, champagnes, and wines by the glass.

Prices: Restaurant Main course evening meal from £11.50, lunch from £4. House wine £11.50.
Last orders: Bar: lunch 15.00; dinner 23.00 (Friday to Sunday open all day, April to October open all day). Food: lunch 15.00; dinner 21.30 (Friday and Saturday 22.00, Sunday 21.00).
Closed: Rarely.
Food: Modern British.
Real ale: Fuller's London Pride, Bass, Courage Best.
Other points: No-smoking area. Children welcome during the day at weekends. Outside seating. Wheelchair access.
Directions: Exit J14/M3. Take the A33 to Southampton and head towards Ocean Village and the Marina. (Map 3, G3)

Wherwell

White Lion

Fullerton Road, Wherwell, Hampshire SP11 7JF
Telephone: +44(0)1264 860317

At the heart of a picture-postcard thatched village, just a short stroll from Hampshire's finest chalk stream, the River Test, this 17th-century coaching inn is a thriving community local with a loyal trade. It is also a popular lunchtime destination among Test Way walkers and cyclists exploring this beautiful valley. Traditional English pub food cooked on the premises from carefully sourced fresh ingredients is the key to the popularity of the food here. Eat in the beamed bar where a warming log fire burns in winter, or in one of the two homely dining rooms. Sample smoked trout from the Chilbolton Estate, handmade sausages from the renowned John Robinson butchers in Stockbridge, or home-cooked specials like steak-and-mushroom pie and pork steak with honey-and-mustard sauce. There are salad platters, ploughman's lunches, home-baked ham, egg and thick-cut chips, and popular Sunday roast lunches.

Rooms: 3. Double room from £49.50, single from £37.50.
Prices: Restaurant main course from £7.50. Bar main course from £5.50. House wine £9.95.
Last orders: Bar: lunch 14.30 (Saturday and Sunday 15.00); dinner 23.00. Food: lunch 14.00; dinner 21.00 (Sunday 20.30).
Closed: Rarely.
Food: Traditional English.
Real ale: Ringwood Best, Courage Best & Directors.
Other points: No-smoking area. Dogs welcome overnight. Garden. Car park. Folk club.
Directions: A303/M3. Wherwell is signed off the A3057 between Andover and Stockbridge. (Map 3, F3)

Kington

The Stagg Inn & Restaurant

Titley, Kington, Herefordshire HR5 3RL
Telephone: +44(0)1544 230221
reservations@thestagg.co.uk
www.thestagg.co.uk

Steve and Nicola Reynolds's rural local in tiny Titley plays host to farmers and avid foodies, the latter here for some of the best pub food in the land. Local boy and Roux-trained chef Steve has a real passion for food, delving deep into the fine raw materials that the Welsh Borders has to offer, notably rare breed meats and game from local organic farms, producing seasonally influenced menus. He makes just about everything on the premises. With his assured, yet restrained touch, dishes could include seared scallops with celeriac purée, followed by a hearty Herefordshire rump steak with béarnaise sauce. Puddings bring a lemon tart and a selection of 18 local, mostly unpasteurised, cheeses. Alternatively in the pine-furnished bar, tuck into organic pork sausages with a pint of Ralph's Radnor cider. Retire to one of the two en suite bedrooms, or stay at the Old Vicarage, where Steve's mum has two en suite rooms. See pub walk on page 232.

Rooms: 5. Double room from £70, single from £50.
Prices: Restaurant main course from £12.50. Bar main course from £7.90. House wine £12.50.
Last orders: Food: lunch 14.00; dinner 22.00 (Sunday 21.00).
Closed: Monday, the first two weeks of November, the Tuesday after a Bank Holiday and May Day.
Food: Modern British.
Real ale: Hobson's Best. 1-2 guest beers.
Other points: No-smoking in the dining rooms. Children welcome. Dogs welcome. Garden. Car park.
Directions: On the B4322 between Kington and Presteigne. (Map 2, B6)

Berkhamsted

Alford Arms

Frithsden, Berkhamsted,
Hertfordshire HP1 3DD
Telephone: +44(0)1442 864480
info@alfordarmsfrithsden.co.uk
www.alfordarmsfrithsden.co.uk

David and Becky Salisbury's pretty pub lies
secreted away on the edge of the Ashridge
Estate and is well worth finding for first-
class food served in an informal atmosphere.
Styled 'country pub and eating' on the menu,
it successfully blends a stylishly modernised
interior, with its tiled-and-wooden floors
and old scrubbed pine tables, with some
imaginative modern British cooking. Listed
on the carte or daily-changing chalkboard
are 'small plates' of, say, pancetta, leek and
parmesan risotto or warm squid, bacon and
rocket salad - ideal as a snack or starter.
Eclectic main courses range from sea bass
with roast aubergine and braised fennel to
beer braised beef stew with herb dumplings.
Chilled lemon tart is a typical dessert. Great
care is taken in presentation of dishes and
flavours shine through. Good ales and a raft
of wines offered by the glass. On warm days,
tables spill out onto the front terrace. See pub
walk on page 234.

Prices: Restaurant main course from £9.75.
House wine £11.25.
Last orders: Bar: 23.00. Food: lunch 14.30 (Sunday
15.00); dinner 22.00.
Closed: Rarely.
Food: Modern British.
Real ale: Brakspear, Marston's Pedigree, Morrell's
Oxford Blue, Flower's Original.
Other points: No-smoking area. Children welcome.
Dogs welcome in the bar. Garden/terrace. Car park.
Directions: From Berkhamsted High Street, follow
signs for Potten End and then Frithsden (Vineyard
signs). (Map 3, E4)

Flaunden

The Bricklayers Arms

Hog Pits Bottom, Flaunden,
Hertfordshire HP3 0PH
Telephone: +44 (0)1442 833322
goodfood@bricklayersarms.com
www.bricklayersarms.com

Coated in Virginia creeper, Flaunden's low,
cottagey-tiled pub is a peaceful, inviting spot,
especially in summer when its country-style
garden becomes the perfect place to enjoy
an alfresco pint of ale. On cooler days, the
refurbished, timbered and low-ceilinged bar,
replete with blazing log fires, old prints and
comfortable traditional furnishings, are popular with both local diners and walkers for
modern pub food. Alvin and Sally Michaels
have smartened up the place and offer a good
range of menus to suit all who visit. In the
bar, follow a country stroll with thick-cut
sandwiches or tuck into steak-and-kidney
pie or lamb shank with red wine-and-shallot
sauce. In the evening, come for home-smoked
fish with lemon-coriander butter and tomato
chutney, then follow with roast sea bass with
sweet-pepper cream sauce, and finish with
hot chocolate pudding. Don't miss the summer Sunday barbeques and live jazz in the
garden.

Prices: Restaurant and bar main course from £9.95.
House wine £10.95.
Last orders: Bar: 23.00. Food: lunch 15.00 (Sunday
16.00); dinner 21.30 (Sunday 21.00)
Closed: Rarely.
Food: Modern British and French.
Real ale: Fuller's London Pride, Greene King Old
Speckled Hen, Greene King IPA, Archers Best.
Other points: No smoking in the restaurant. Children
welcome. Dogs welcome in the bar. Garden. Car park.
Directions: 10 minutes from Exit18/M25. Three miles
south west of Hemel Hempstead. (Map 3, E4)

Reed

The Cabinet

High Street, Reed, Royston,
Hertfordshire SG8 8AH
Telephone: +44(0)1763 848366
thecabinet@btopenworld.com
www.thecabinetinn.co.uk

Transformed by TV chef Paul Bloxham from a tired boozer to stylish gastropub, this pretty, white clapboard, 16th-century pub retains its original low beams, cottagey windows and locals at the bar drinking pints of Adnams. For diners, there's a 'snug' smoking room with high-backed leather dining chairs, and a smart dining room with soft colours, crisp table linen and fresh flowers. An enthusiastic modern menu is built around local ingredients with 70 per cent purchased from local farmers, including 28-day aged Galloway beef and rare breeds such as Tamworth pigs. The bar lunch menu is a simplified version of what's available in the restaurant - perhaps a classic Caesar salad or ham hock and foie gras terrine. Dinner in the dining room brings chicken-liver parfait with red-onion jam, Welsh lamb shank with garlic and rosemary sauce, local Aylesbury duck with Roman sauce, and pan-roasted brill with crab and saffron risotto. *New owners as we went to press.*

Prices: Set lunch £15.95-£19.95. Restaurant main course from £13. Bar main course from £5. House wine £12.50.
Last orders: Bar: lunch 15.00; dinner 23.00. Food: lunch 14.30 (Sunday 16.00); dinner 22.30
Closed: Monday and Sunday night.
Food: Modern French/British with American influence.
Real ale: Nethergate, Adnams, Greene King, Guest beer.
Other points: No-smoking area. Children welcome. Dogs welcome in the bar. Garden. Car park.
Directions: The village is off the A10 betwen Buntingford and Royston. (Map 4, D5)

Watton-at-Stone

George and Dragon

High Street, Watton-at-Stone,
Hertfordshire SG14 3TA
Telephone: +44(0)1920 830285
pub@georgeanddragon-watton.co.uk
www.georgeanddragon-watton.co.uk

The 400-year-old George and Dragon dominates the centre of the village and you can't miss the pink-painted pebbledash exterior. There's character in spades within the homely bars, as exposed beams, log fires, yellow stained walls and old scrubbed tables create a quaint, rustic look. Welcome touches from caring landlords Peter and Jessica Tatlow include fresh flowers and the day's newspapers. Despite the rather gentrified trappings, this is still a real pub, offering local gossip and tip-top Greene King ales. On a changing menu and daily blackboards, starters include homemade soups and patés and, perhaps, a warm salad of asparagus, tallegio cheese and prosciutto. Braised ham hock with pea, cider and chive-cream sauce and seared red mullet on vegetable spaghetti with saffron and mussel sauce are typical main courses. Millionaire's bun, which is fillet steak in a toasted roll, is popular, as are lighter options, such as Greek salad and creamy tagliatelle with fresh parmesan.

Prices: Main course from £7.85. House wine £15 a litre.
Last orders: Bar: lunch 15.00; dinner 23.00. Food: lunch 14.00 (15.30 on Sunday); dinner 22.00. No food Sunday evening.
Closed: Rarely
Food: Modern pub food.
Real ale: Greene King IPA, Greene King Abbot Ale. 2 guest beers.
Other points: No-smoking in the dining area. Children welcome. Garden. Car park. Wheelchair access.
Directions: In the centre of the village, off the the A602 between Hertford and Stevenage. (Map 4, D5)

The Cabinet at Reed

You'll find low beams, cottagey windows and pints of Adnams Bitter at this pretty, 16th-century white-clapboard pub, but the real draw is TV chef Paul Bloxham's enthusiastic modern menus, which incorporate top-notch local produce. Around 70% of produce is sourced from local farmers, including 28-day-aged Galloway beef, rare-breed pork, and vegetables from an organic nursery. Paul is passionate about local, seasonal foods and is a regular visitor to Sandon Growers' Market, where many of his suppliers sell their produce direct to the public.

Visit the local Farmers' Market

In addition to the excellent, monthly Sandon Growers' Market (right), you'll find farmers' market stalls at Hitchin's general market every Tuesday.

Bury Lane Farm Shop
Melbourn, Royston
Tel: 01763 260418

Located on the Melbourn bypass (A10), Bury Lane is an extensive operation providing a unique range of fine foods, fruit and vegetables, cut flowers and plants. Fruit and vegetables are grown on the farm and sourced from local growers, with the more exotic varieties imported from around the world. Call in for asparagus during May and June, and pick your own strawberries from May to August, and apples and plums in the autumn.

Sandon Growers' Market
Sandon Village Hall
Tel: 01763 287216

Every third Saturday of the month, a collection of
representatives from Hertfordshire's farms and
nurseries offering the best in beef, lamb, pork,
chicken, preserves, game, eggs, vegetables, fruit and
cakes gather at Sandon Village Hall for the Sandon
Growers' Market. Among the stalls are many of the
food producers that help supply Paul Bloxham at the
Cabinet. For example, Beverly Burrows at Farrowby
Farm in Hinxworth supplies Paul with free-range,
organic Berkshire pork, while Highbury Farm in
Woodend supplies his lamb. They have their own
cold-room cutting facility so they can offer lamb
joints and cuts to meet individual requirements.

Bury Lane Farm Shop, Melbourn

Royston

Beverly Burrows, Farrowby Farm

A505

Sandon Growers' Market

LES ROUTIERS

The Cabinet at Reed

Brenda and Chris Risley, Green End Farm

A507

A1

A10

David de Bonville, Walkern Hall Farm

Yvonne Gear, Highbury Farm

Stevenage

Bembridge

The Crab & Lobster Inn

32 Forelands Field Road, Bembridge,
Isle of Wight PO35 5TR
Telephone: +44(0)1983 872244
allancrab@aol.com
www.crabandlobsterinn.co.uk

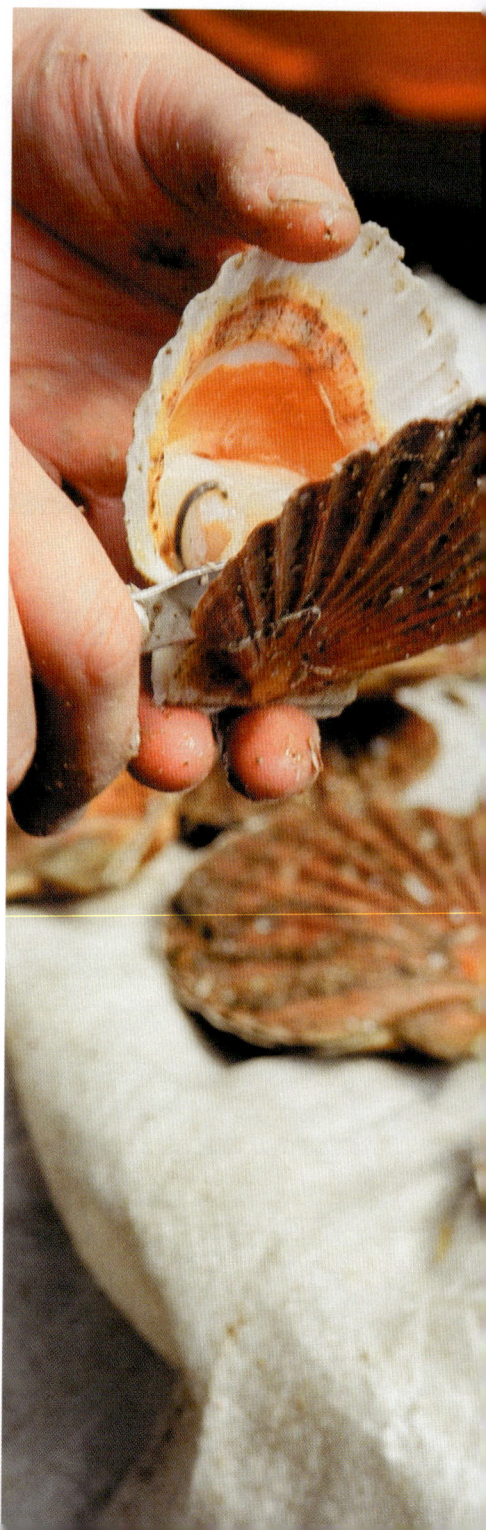

This popular cliff-top inn near the Lifeboat Station affords magnificent views across the Solent and English Channel. A popular watering hole for coastal-path walkers, it also attracts fish lovers for the fresh locally caught seafood listed on daily changing blackboards. Arrive early to bag a table, as the nautically themed and traditionally furnished bar and dining areas fill quickly. True to its name, house specialities are the crabs and lobsters that are caught on Bembridge Ledge and served every which way - crab cakes, sandwiches and salads, and enormous crab-and-lobster platters for two. Meaty alternatives on the straightforward bar menu include ham, egg, and chips, and chargrilled sirloin steak with mushrooms and fries. Wash them down with a pint of island-brewed Goddard's ale. From the restaurant carte, choose from a page of lobster specials or opt for whole Dover sole. Cosy en suite bedrooms enjoy stunning sea views, as does the summer terrace.

Rooms: 5. £35 per person per night including breakfast.
Prices: Restaurant main course from £8.25. Bar main course from £5.95. House wine £8.50.
Last orders: Bar: lunch 15.00; dinner 23.00 (open all day Saturday and Sunday). Food: lunch 14.30; dinner 21.30.
Closed: Never.
Food: Modern European.
Real ale: Flower's IPA, Greene King IPA, Goddard's.
Other points: No-smoking area. Children welcome. Dogs welcome in the bar. Garden. Car park.
Directions: The pub is in the centre of Bembridge. Follow signs to the Lifeboat Station. (Map 3, G4)

Ashford

The Tiger Inn

Stowting, Ashford, Kent T25 6BA
Telephone: +44(0)1303 862130
willettiger@aol.com
www.tigerinn.co.uk

The Tiger dates from 1676 and a bit of its history is preserved on the exterior - embossed into the rendering are the words Mackeson Hythe Ales. The single front bar is rustic, unpretentious and full of rural charm, with stripped-oak floors, wood-burning stoves, comfortable worn sofas, and sturdy scrubbed tables topped with candles, with a separate restaurant to the rear. Generally filled with locals, the atmosphere is relaxed and informal, and the home-cooked food hearty. Chalked up on the blackboard, dishes range from tiger prawns with red-curry sauce, and chargrilled chorizo salad with mint, coriander and sour cream salsa, to slow-roasted lamb shoulder with port and thyme sauce and Lincolnshire sausages with sage and apple sauce. Tip-top ales include Everards Tiger, naturally. Don't miss the summer barbecues, the annual beer festival, and the pub's famed live jazz every Monday evening. Super walks across the North Downs.

Prices: Main course from £10. House wine £10.30.
Last orders: Bar: lunch 15.00; dinner 23.00. Food: lunch 14.00; dinner 21.00.
Closed: Monday lunch.
Food: Global.
Real ale: Fuller's London Pride, Everards Tiger, Fuller's ESB, Shepherd Neame Master Brew Bitter, Shepherd Neame Spitfire. 1 guest beer.
Other points: No-smoking area. Children welcome. Dogs welcome. Garden. Car park. Wheelchair access.
Directions: Exit 11/M20. Go towards Canterbury on the B2068 for three miles, then turn left to Stowting. (Map 4, F7)

Bodsham

Froggie's at the Timber Batts

School Lane, Bodsham, Wye,
Kent TN25 5JQ
Telephone: +44(0)1233 750237

Chef Joel Gross built up a great reputation at Froggie's Restaurant in Wye, so when he headed deeper into the Kent countryside to the remote, 15th century Timber Batts, he knew they would follow. The place went from being just another rural pub to one with an authentic French restaurant attached. The beamed and timbered bars have blazing log fires, one in a huge inglenook, and comfortable seating. The restaurant has its own fireplace and old pine tables topped with candles. Local favourites - superb stuffed mussels, a classic duck confit salad, perfect rack of lamb with herbs - are staples of the printed menu. Profiteroles and tarte Tatin are classic puddings and there's a blackboard listing daily fish specials such as sea bass in white butter sauce, and bar snacks like sausage and mash. Sourcing is impeccable: game from local shoots, locally grown vegetables, but cheeses are as totally French, as is the wine list.

Prices: Set Sunday lunch £18. Set dinner £25.
Restaurant main course from £12. Bar main course from £6. House wine £12.
Last orders: Bar: lunch 14.30; dinner 23.00. Food: lunch 14.30; dinner 21.30. No food Sunday evening.
Closed: Monday, Tuesday after Bank Holiday Monday.
Food: Traditional French, Seafood and Game.
Real ale: Adnams, Fuller's, Harvey Sussex Best.
Other points: No-smoking area. Dogs welcome. Garden. Children welcome. Car park. Wheelchair access (no WC).
Directions: Exit 9 or 10/M20. Take A28 for Canterbury and follow signs to Wye. Continue on and through Hastingleigh, then turn left for the pub. (Map 4, F7)

Maidstone

Who'd A Thought It

Headcorn Road, Grafty Green, Maidstone,
Kent ME17 2AR
Telephone: +44(0)1622 858951
joe@whodathoughtit.com
www.whodathoughtit.com

You'll find plenty of glitz and glamour at this cosy country inn, built in the reign of Henry VIII. Whether you want a flute of Cristal or a pint of ale, you'll find your every whim catered for here. This inn is a fascinating mix of pub, champagne and oyster bar, tasteful restaurant and luxury accommodation. The rooms are finished to a very high standard; many have a four-poster, DVD and stereo. Downstairs, be it in the bar and brasserie, restaurant or attractive outside terrace, you will find food options to match your every mood. Colchester oysters and seafood are on offer in the brasserie. Start with king scallops with black pudding and Parma ham, then follow with wild sea bass with pak choi or garlic lobster, plus there are gourmet meat dishes such as chateaubriand. Balsamic strawberry mille feuille makes for an indulgent finish. The extensive wine list extends to a fine choice of cognacs and cigars.

Rooms: 9. Double/twin from £60, four-poster with double jacuzzi from £160.
Prices: Restaurant main course from £13. Bar/snack from £8. House wine £11.
Last orders: Bar: lunch 15.00 (open all day Sunday); dinner 23.00. Food: lunch 14.30 (Sunday 16.00); dinner 21.30 (no food Sunday evening).
Closed: Rarely.
Food: Modern British.
Real ale: Greene King IPA, Timothy Taylor Landlord, Fuller's London Pride.
Other points: No-smoking area. Garden. Children welcome. Car park.
Directions: Exit 8/M20. (Map 4, F6)

Stodmarsh

The Red Lion

The Street, Stodmarsh, Canterbury,
Kent CT3 4AZ
Telephone: +44(0)1227 721339
tiptop_redlion@hotmail.com
www.red-lion.net

Adjoining the famous Stodmarsh Nature Reserve, Robert Whigham's quirky 15th-century pub draws both twitchers and discerning foodies in search of fine ale and food. Within, low ceilings, stone-and-wood floors, hop garlands, fresh flowers, and an open fire, all add to the rustic charm of the tiny rooms. Beer is tapped direct from hop sack-covered barrels and the food is outstanding. A blackboard by the entrance displays a versatile, ingredient led menu, a mix of contemporary ideas and good country cooking. Local, free-range and organic ingredients make their way into the kitchen with game from local shoots and locally smoked ham all playing their part. Typically, tuck into pheasant and wild rabbit hotpot, lamb stuffed with rosemary and garlic, or tackle Robert's damned good breakfast - local butcher sausages, bacon, own eggs, mushrooms, grilled tomatoes, even kidneys and T-bone steaks (from a local beef farm). There are three simple double rooms (not en suite).

Rooms: 3, not en suite. Double room from £60.
Prices: Bar main course from £9.95.
House wine £10.95.
Last orders: Bar 23.00. Food: lunch 14.00; dinner 21.30.
Closed: Rarely.
Food: Traditional British using local produce.
Real ale: Greene King Old Speckled Hen & IPA.
Other points: No smoking in the restaurant. Dogs welcome in the bar. Car park. Wheelchair access to the restaurant/pub.
Directions: Take the A257 from Canterbury and follow signs to Stodmarsh. (Map 4, F7)

Wingham

The Dog Inn ⭐

Canterbury Road, Wingham, Canterbury,
Kent CT3 1BB
Telephone: +44(0)1227 720339
thedoginn@netbreeze.co.uk

Realising that there was plenty of life in the 'old Dog' yet, Richard and Sherry Martin took on this ancient hostelry and have begun scraping away years of grime to expose the impressive features of the original building, which dates back to the 13th century. Superb heavy beams and panelling blend well with the antique oak floors throughout the character bars, and there's a historic function room and renovated en suite bedrooms under the eaves. It's early days and there's still plenty to do, but it's a promising start and the building has huge potential. Upgraded menus feature game from Godmersham Estate, organic meats from Chandler and Dunn in Ash, and fish from Whitstable. This translates as Romney Marsh lamb with rosemary jus, rib-eye steak with pepper sauce, baked trout with parsley butter, and upmarket lunchtime bar snacks. One to watch!

Rooms: 9. Double/twin from £69, single from £40. Family from £89.
Prices: Set lunch £15. Set dinner £20. Restaurant main course from £8.95. Bar main course from £6.95. House wine £12.95.
Last orders: Bar: open all day until 23.00. Food: Lunch 15.00 (open all day Saturday and Sunday); Dinner 22.00.
Closed: Never.
Food: British Eclectic.
Real ale: Courage, Adnams, Greene King IPA, Marston's Bitter, Shepherd Neame.
Other points: Totally no-smoking. Dogs welcome. Garden and BBQ. Children welcome. Car park. Licence for civil weddings.
Directions: On A257 east of Canterbury. (Map 4, F7)

Clitheroe

The Freemasons Arms

8 Vicarage Fold, Wiswell, Clitheroe,
Lancashire BB7 9DF
Telephone: +44(0)1254 822218

Ian Martin sold the Red Cat in Crank in 2004 and, with his amazing cellar of wines, headed up the M6 to this tiny pub tucked down an unmade village lane at the foot of Pendle Hill. Originally three cottages, it became a pub in 1850 and remains a traditional village local with a cosy bar and upstairs dining area decorated in rich greens, soft reds, fresh flowers and contemporary prints. Local foodies are beating a path to the door for Ian's exemplary cooking and a raft of wines that includes 120 clarets and some great vintages. The draw is Ian's fresh, modern menu, which reflects his enthusiasm to source everything locally, including loin of Bowland pork with black pudding and a cider-and-mustard sauce. Come for the great value two-course lunch, or choose seared scallops with chilli jam, followed by beef fillet with foie gras, wild mushrooms and Madeira sauce. Don't miss the well-organised wine dinners. See pub walk on page 236.

Prices: Set lunch and dinner £9.95 (two courses).
Last orders: Bar: lunch 15.00; dinner 20.30. Food: lunch 14.00; dinner 21.30.
Closed: Monday and Tuesday.
Food: Modern British.
Real ale: Bowland Hen Harrier, Moorhouses Pride of Pendle, Black Sheep Best.
Other points: No-smoking area in restaurant. Children over three welcome. Wheelchair access.
Directions: A59, two miles south of Clitheroe. Take the A671 to Blackburn and first left to Wiswell. (Map 5, E4)

Whitewell

Inn at Whitewell

Whitewell, Forest of Bowland, Clitheroe, Lancashire BB7 3AT
Telephone: +44(0)1200 448222

Must-sees
Clitheroe Castle and Museum
Ribchester Roman Museum
Slaidburn Heritage Centre
Forest of Bowland

Fishing
Hotel residents have access to seven miles of the
River Hodder

Farmers' market
Clitheroe (fortnightly on Wednesday mornings)

Bowland

Standing next to the church, overlooking the River Hodder in the wild beauty of north Lancashire, this magnificent inn is far from the hustle and bustle of town life. The atmosphere is unique, thanks to Richard Bowman and his staff, who imbue this ancient hostelry with warmth and personality. Inside, it's relaxed with a haphazard arrangement of furnishings, bric-a-brac, open log fires, heavy ceiling beams and colourful rugs throughout the stone-floored taproom, rambling dining areas and library. The bar supper choice may include pork medallions with mustard sauce, with salads and substantial sandwiches featuring at lunchtime. The evening carte majors on quality local ingredients, perhaps breast of Goosnargh duck with tomato and bean cassoulet, fantastic puddings and British and Irish cheeses. Individual bedrooms are furnished with antique furniture, peat fires and Victorian baths. Eight miles of fishing, a superlative wine list (and wine merchant), an art gallery and a shop selling homemade foods complete the picture.

Rooms: 23. Double/twin room from £89.
Prices: Restaurant main course from £12. Bar main course from £7.50. House wine £9.50.
Last orders: Bar: lunch 15.00; dinner 23.00. Food: lunch 14.00; dinner 21.30.
Closed: Never.
Food: Modern British.
Real ale: Marston's Bitter, Taylor's Ales, Copper Dragon Ales.
Other points: No-smoking area. Children welcome. Dogs welcome overnight. Garden. Car park. Licence for civil weddings. Fishing. Wheelchair access throughout.
Directions: Exit 32/M6 to Longridge. Centre of Longridge follow signs to Whitewell. (Map 5, E4)

Tourist information Clitheroe +44(0)1200 442226

Where to walk
An insight into the wild beauty of the Forest of Bowland can be enjoyed with walks along the River Hodder, across Dunsop Fell, up Wolf and Fairsnape Fell from Chipping, and through Beacon Fell Country Park. Cross the Ribble Valley for an invigorating ramble up Pendle Hill. Follow the Ribble Way for gentler strolls through the Ribble Valley. See also pub walk on page 238.

Events & festivals
Royal Lancashire Show, Ribchester (July)
Hodder Valley Agricultural Show (September)

Nether Broughton

The Red House

23 Main Street, Nether Broughton, Melton Mowbray, Leicestershire LE14 3HB
Telephone: +44(0)1664 822429
bookings@the-redhouse.com
www.the-redhouse.com

Must-sees
Belvoir Castle, Burrough Hill Country Park
Great Central Railway, Leicester Museum & Art Gallery
DH Lawrence Birthplace Museum
Sherwood Forest Country Park & Visitor Centre

Events & festivals
Flower Festival, Belvoir Castle (May)
Robin Hood Festival, Edwinstowe (July/August)
Nottingham Carnival (August)

Belvoir Castle

An impressive, stylishly revamped early Victorian house that now functions as a modern and very individual pub-restaurant with rooms, and which successfully combines a relaxed atmosphere with contemporary luxury. The bar has a traditional feel, where blackboards offer the day's bar menu, which includes tuna and salmon fishcakes with creamed spinach, bangers and mash, and a steak and red onion sandwich. But modern styling distinguishes the restaurant with, for example, a bar that consists of a pine-wood frame filled with old books. Or, head for the adjoining dining room that's filled with light from patio doors that look on to the teak-decked courtyard. Here you can choose pan-roasted scallops with chorizo, roast suckling pig with Calvados jus, and iced white Malteaser parfait from a seasonally-inspired menu. The global wine list is expansive and keenly priced. Eight en suite bedrooms are imaginatively designed and feature DVDs and a host of goodies. Old Stables houses both the Garden Bar and Grill.

Rooms: 8. Twin/double room from £50 per person.
Prices: Restaurant main course from £9.95. Bar snacks from £5. House wine £12.
Last orders: Bar: 23.00 (Sunday 22.30). Food: lunch 15.00 (Sunday 17.00); dinner 22.00 (Sunday 18.00).
Closed: Rarely.
Food: Modern British.
Real ale: Marston's Pedigree, Beaver Bitter. Guest beers.
Other points: No smoking in the restaurant. Children welcome. Dogs welcome in the bar. Car park. Outside garden bar and open kitchen. Meeting room. Marquee facility. Wheelchair access to the restaurant/bar.
Directions: Exit 25/M1, the A52, then the A606 to Melton. Situated on the A606 between Nottingham and Melton Mowbray, five miles north of Melton. (Map 3, B4)

Tourist information Melton Mowbray
+44(0)1664 480992; Nottingham 0115 915 5330
Farmers' market
Melton Mowbray (every Tuesday and Friday)

Where to walk
Take a stroll along the Grantham Canal towpath around Hose, Plunger and Redmile in the heart of the Vale of Belvoir. Excellent forest trails and marked walks through Sherwood Forest.

Stathern

Red Lion Inn

Red Lion Street, Stathern,
Leicestershire LE14 4HS
Telephone: +44(0)1949 860868
info@theredlioninn.co.uk
www.theredlioninn.co.uk

Informality, real ales, fine wines and good-quality, innovative and traditional food using local produce sums up the philosophy of the hugely successful Rutland Inn Company, the mini-pub empire that includes the eponymous Olive Branch at Clipsham and this refurbished 16th-century village pub. The converted skittle-alley dining room comes with low beams, terracotta walls and wood-burning stove, and the informal bar also buzzes with diners and local drinkers. As the back of the menu indicates, there's a passion for quality suppliers: Brewster's Bitter is brewed in the village, game comes from the Belvoir estate, and cheese, sausages and fruits are sourced from local farms and dairies. There's something for everyone on the daily menu, including, perhaps, chicken-and-pheasant terrine with homemade chutney, scallops with chorizo, butter bean and sweet chilli fondue, calves' liver with celeriac mash and onion gravy, and rich chocolate tart.

Prices: Set lunch £15. Restaurant main course from £8.95. Bar main course from £5.25. House wine £10.50.
Last orders: Bar: lunch 15.00; dinner 23.00. Food: lunch 14.00 (Sunday 15.00); dinner 21.30.
Closed: Sunday evening.
Food: Modern pub food.
Real Ale: Brewster Vale Pale Ale, Grainstore Olive Oil. Guest beers.
Other points: No smoking in the restaurant. Garden. Children welcome. Dogs welcome in the bar. Car park.
Directions: A1. A52 towards Nottingham. Left towards Belvoir Castle; Stathern is signposted. (Map 3, B4)

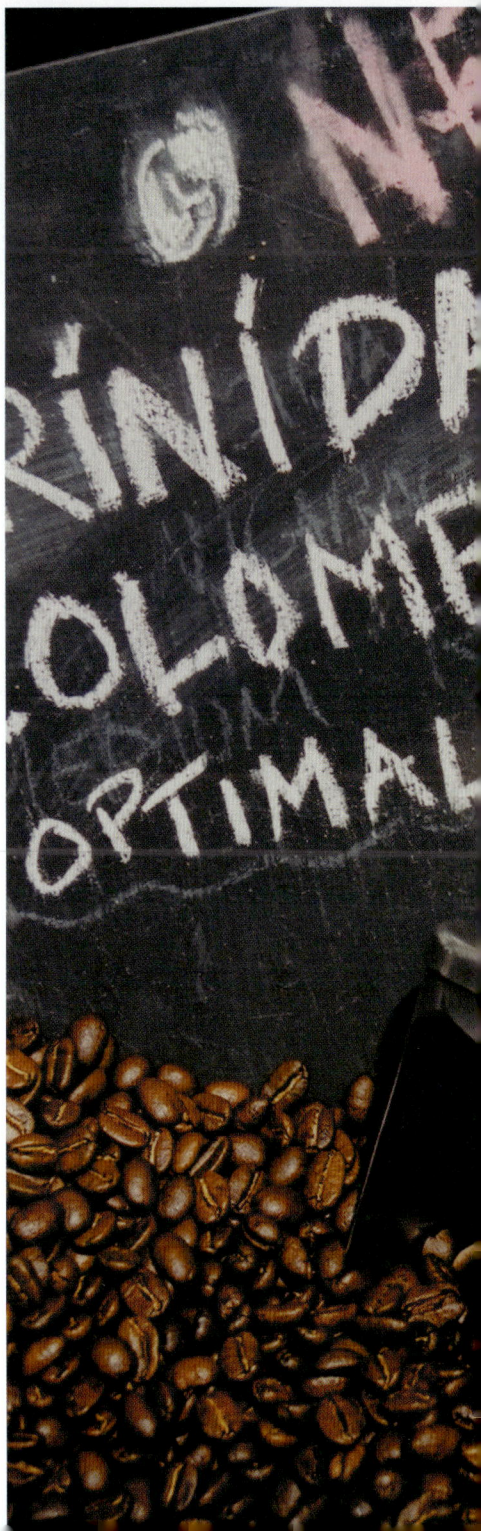

Cropwell Bishop Creamery
Tel: 0115 989 2350
Colston Bassett Dairy
Tel: 01949 81322

Cropwell Bishop and Colston Bassett are two of the seven dairies in the world licensed to make Stilton cheese. By law, Stilton can only be made in the three counties of Derbyshire, Leicestershire and Nottinghamshire. It is still made in much the same way as it was 250 years ago, with traditional methods being used as much as possible. The milk is taken every day from the same pastures and the same farms it has always been, despite production rates currently at over one million Stiltons per year. The Red Lion is a passionate supporter and, whether it be White Stilton, Shropshire Blue or the 'King of Cheese', the Blue Stilton, it always takes pride of place its cheese platter.

Brewsters Brewery
Stathern
Tel: 01949 861868

Just round the corner from the Red Lion, Brewsters Brewery was set up in 1998 by Sara Barton – Brewster is the old English word for a female brewer. With Sara brewing, selling and delivering the beer, the brewery developed from a five-barrel plant to a 10-barrel brewery in 2002 and now brews around eight beers that are supplied to over 250 pubs throughout central England. No wonder Sara won the Small Business category of Country Living magazine's Enterprising Rural Women awards in 2000.

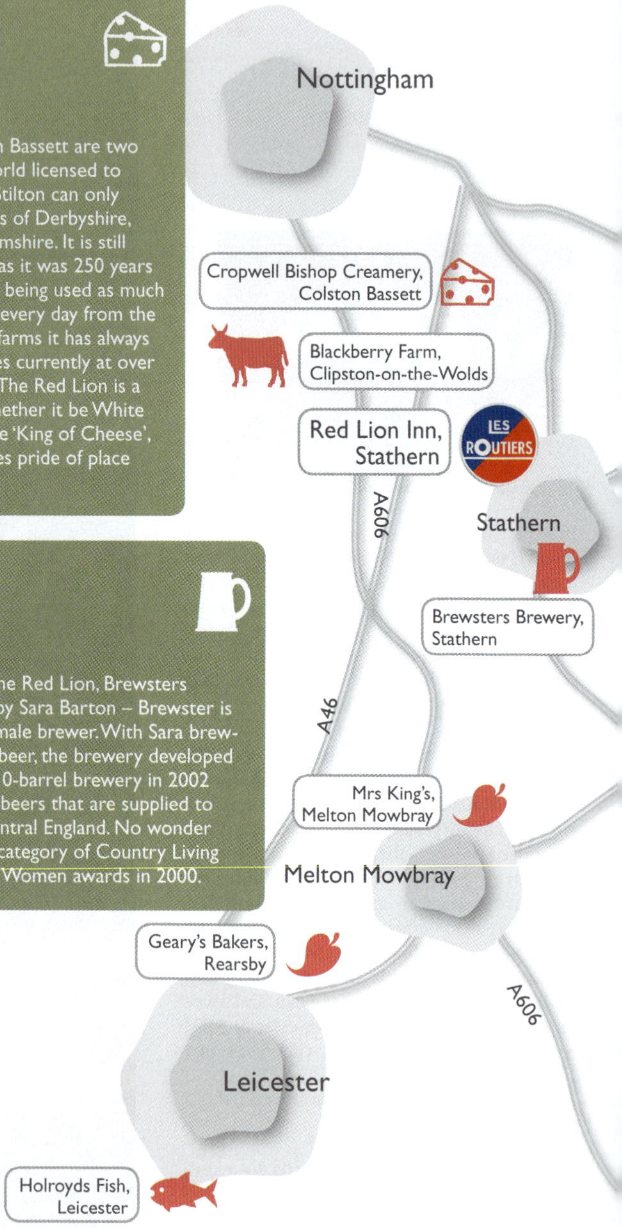

Nottingham

Cropwell Bishop Creamery, Colston Bassett

Blackberry Farm, Clipston-on-the-Wolds

Red Lion Inn, Stathern

Stathern

Brewsters Brewery, Stathern

A606

A46

Mrs King's, Melton Mowbray

Melton Mowbray

Geary's Bakers, Rearsby

A606

Leicester

Holroyds Fish, Leicester

The Red Lion Inn

Informality, real ales, fine wines and good-quality local produce sum up the philosophy of the Rutland Inn Company, which also owns the Michelin-starred Olive Branch at Clipsham. There's a real passion for using quality local suppliers, as one glance at the back of the daily-changing menus will reveal. Beer is brewed in the village, game comes from the Belvoir estate and all cheeses, vegetables and fruits are sourced from local farms and dairies. The Olive Branch and the Red Lion have set a trend for others to follow.

A52

Belvoir Fruit Farms,
Belvoir

Grantham

A607

Visit the local Farmers' Market

The former poultry shed at Melton Cattle Market is the location of Melton Mowbray's Farmers' Market every Tuesday and Friday.

Belvoir Fruit Farms
Belvoir
Tel: 01476 870286

Fresh fruits, flowers and spices grown on the farm are pressed, infused and cooked to create health-giving cordials, presses and crushes. Founded in 1984, this family business is thriving due to the demand for soft fruit drinks that have real, honest fruit flavours. Belvoir cordials are devoid of artificial colours, flavours and sweeteners.

Blackberry Farm
Clipston-on-the-Wolds
Tel: 0115 989 2260

The farm shop at Blackberry Farm (closed Sunday & Monday) sells quality produce that has been naturally reared, much of it sourced from the surrounding area, with lamb, turkey and beef being reared on the farm. The latter is derived from prime-quality livestock that is fed on natural foods, with no added hormones, additives or growth promoters. There's full traceability on individual animals and beef is hung on the bone for a minimum of seven days, with steak joints hung for a minimum of 21 days to ensure flavour and tenderness.

Grainstore Brewery,
Oakham

Oakham

Belvoir

The Chequers Inn

Main Street, Woolsthorpe-by-Belvoir, Grantham, Lincolnshire NG32 1LU
Telephone: +44(0)1476 870701
justinnabar@yahoo.co.uk
www.chequers-inn.net

Must-sees
Belvoir Castle
Belton House (NT)
Woolsthorpe Manor (NT)
Grantham Museum
Crossroads Farm Museum, Eastwell

Grantham

Just a stone's throw from Belvoir's magnificent castle, the Chequers is a 17th-century coaching inn that has been stylishly refurbished by Justin and Jo Chad. Decor blends the old and new, with bold colours on the walls, leather chairs, sturdy oak tables and a blazing log fire in the smart, beamed lounge, and a light and airy restaurant lined with modern artwork. Outside, you'll find teak furniture and lovely views of the castle. Food is taken very seriously, the philosophy being 'to use the freshest ingredients to create modern, simple dishes with exciting taste and texture'. Expect home-baked breads, herbs from the garden, lamb from neighbouring farms and game from the Belvoir Estate. Typically, tuck into a rib-eye steak sandwich or fish and chips at lunch, with evening additions taking in seared monkfish with herb risotto, and whole lemon sole with prawn ragout. First-class wines and local Brewster's beer. The contemporary feel extends to the four en suite bedrooms.

Rooms: 4. Double from £59, single from £49.
Family from £69.
Prices: Set lunch £12.50. Set dinner £13.95 (Monday evening only). Restaurant main course from £8.95. Bar snack from £7.95. House wine £11.
Last orders: Bar: lunch 15.00; dinner 23.00. Food: lunch 14.30 (Sunday 16.00); dinner: 21.30 (Sunday 20.30).
Closed: Rarely.
Food: Modern British.
Real ale: Brewster's Belvoir Bitter.
Other points: No-smoking area. Children welcome. Dogs welcome overnight. Garden. Car park. Wheelchair access.
Directions: A1. Take the A607 towards Melton Mowbray and follow the Heritage Trail signs towards Belvoir Castle. (Map 6, G7)

Tourist information Grantham +44(0)1476 406166
Where to shop Melton Mowbray, Grantham, Oakham
Farmers' market Melton Mowbray (every Tue & Fri)
Nearest racecourse Southwell, Nottingham
Nearest golf course Belton Park, Grantham

Where to walk
Picturesque small villages dotted around the Vale of

Belvoir are linked by a a good network of footpaths and bridleways. The towpath beside the Grantham Canal provides an easy and level route to explore the Vale, notably around Hose, Plungar and Redmile.

Events & festivals
Flower Festival, Belvoir Castle (May)

Lincoln

Farmers Arms

Market Rasen Road, Welton Hill, Lincoln,
Lincolnshire LN2 3RD
Telephone: +44(0)1673 885671
farmersarmsuk@yahoo.co.uk
www.farmers-arms.co.uk

For this imposing, 18th-century pub to have survived and thrived on the wind-blown and flat farmlands north of Lincoln is testament to the hard work and genuine hospitality of Andrew Bennett and Vicky Herring. Customers are drawn to this hamlet on the A46 for the pub's quirky interior, the impressive range of micro-brewery beers, freshly prepared food that favours produce from quality local suppliers, and the mind-boggling list of wines. The latter offers good tasting notes, 35 wines by the glass, and you can buy a case or two from Andrew's wine shop next door. Come for lunch and tuck into a baguette filled with Lincolnshire sausage and red-onion jam, or opt for the lamb casserole or bacon chops with mustard cream. Evening diners could start with scallops with lemon beurre blanc, then follow with Lincoln Red sirloin, and finish with the impressive cheeseboard - try the Lincolnshire Yellow Belly, made by a local farmer.

Prices: Set lunch £15. Set dinner £23. Restaurant main course from £10.95. Bar main course from £4.95. House wine £9.95.
Last orders: Bar: Lunch 15.00; dinner 21.00. Food: lunch 14.00; dinner 21.00
Closed: Mondays and Sunday evening.
Food: Modern British.
Real ale: Adnams, Fuller's, Theakston Ales, Tom Wood, Shepherd Neame.
Other points: Totally no-smoking. Garden. Children welcome. Car park. Wheelchair access. Wine shop.
Directions: A1. Take the A46 towards Lincoln, then head towards Market Rasen. (Map 3, A4)

Spalding

The Ship Inn

154 Reservoir Road, Surfleet Seas End, Spalding,
Lincolnshire PE11 4DH
Telephone: +44(0)1775 680547
Shipinnsurfleet@aol.com

On the banks of the tidal River Glen and with a history dating back some 400 years, the Ship has long been a favourite among fishermen and ramblers. Although rebuilt two years ago, every effort has been made to recreate the original ambience of the old pub, with original features retained and collections of nautical memorabilia adorning the beamed downstairs bar. Sink into one of the Chesterfield sofas with a pint of Adnams and a decent sandwich, or head upstairs to the bright, modern dining area and linger over cod in beer batter or fillet steak with pepper sauce, while enjoying the views over the surrounding wetlands. Menus take in good bar snacks such as steak-and-ale pie, and more imaginative dishes, perhaps rack of lamb with rosemary crust. Food is freshly prepared using locally sourced produce, notably fish caught by the local fleet and landed at the door. There's a super summer terrace and four comfortably appointed en suite bedrooms.

Rooms: 4 Double/twin from £65, single from £50.
Prices: Restaurant main course from £8.95. Bar main course from £5. House wine £9.75.
Last orders: Food: Lunch 14.00; dinner 21.00.
Closed: Never.
Food: Modern British
Real ale: Adnams, Eccleshall Slaters Supreme.
Other points: No-smoking area in restaurant. Dogs welcome in the bar. Car park. Wheelchair access.
Directions: On the A16 north from Spalding on the main Boston Road. (Map 6, G8)

London

The Bridge Pub
and Dining Rooms

204 Castelnau, Barnes, London SW13 9DW
Telephone: +44(0)20 8563 9811
thebridgeinbarnes@btinternet.com
www.thebridgeinbarnes.co.uk

A 10-minute walk across the Thames from Hammersmith Tube and you will be in leafy Barnes. The Bridge Pub used to be a dingy, down-at-heel locals' bar until it was beautifully refurbished in late 2002, creating an upmarket gastropub that appeals to modern foodies. Beyond the long, stylish bar is the cosy, red-walled lounge, and the 'Dining Room' bit, a tad more formal, with french windows overlooking decking. Modern, Italian-influenced food is freshly prepared on the premises using first-class ingredients. Monthly changing menus may include pork-and-leek sausages, imaginative salads, and Thai salmon fishcakes at lunch, with the likes of pork belly confit, white-bean stew and red wine jus in the evenings. Expect a raft of wines and cocktails to challenge any West End bar, and Wells Bombardier on handpump. Spend lazy summer weekends and long lunches out on the wonderful garden terrace - well worth the trip out of the city.

Prices: Restaurant main course from £10.
House wine £11.50.
Last orders: Bar: 23.00. Food: lunch 15.00; dinner 20.30.
Closed: Rarely.
Food: Modern British with Italian and Australian influences.
Real ale: Marston's Pedigree, Bombardier Premium Bitter, Ruddles Best.
Other points: No-smoking area. Garden and decked seating area. Children welcome.
Directions: Travelling from Hammersmith, the Bridge Pub is 200 yards over Hammersmith Bridge on the left. (Map 4, E5)

London

The Bull's Head
and Stables Bistro

373 Lonsdale Road, Barnes, London SW13 9PY
Telephone: +44(0)20 8876 5241
jazz@thebullshead.com
www.thebullshead.com

The Thames side setting of this imposing 17th-century pub would be a draw in itself, but what really pulls crowds from miles around is the top-class modern jazz and blues groups that have made The Bull's Head internationally famous for over 40 years. Nightly concerts are from 8.30-11pm (also 2-4.30pm on Sundays), held in a separate room with a genuine jazz-club atmosphere. Back in the bustling bar, alcoves radiate around the island servery, which dispenses Young's ales and some 240 bottles of wine, 30 offered by the glass. All the food is freshly cooked and served from noon until it's finished (and they will then make sandwiches). Typical choices include soup and ciabatta, roast of the day, steak-and-kidney pie, and treacle tart. The former Stables Bistro now houses Nuay's Thai Bistro, but you can also order at the bar in the pub and be served there, or order authentic Thai food to takeaway.

Prices: Main course from £4.50. Thai main course from £4.75. Wine from £10.50.
Last orders: Bar: 23.00. Food: 22.00.
Closed: Rarely.
Food: Traditional British served at lunchtime.
Thai food served in the evening.
Real ale: Youngs Bitter.
Other points: No-smoking area. Children welcome in daytime. Wheelchair access (no WC).
Directions: Five minutes' walk along the river from Barnes Bridge station. (Map 4, E5)

London

Freemasons Arms

32 Downshire Hill, Hampstead,
London NW3 1NT
Telephone: +44(0)20 7433 6811
www.freemasonsarms.co.uk

The Orange Pub Company's London out-post enjoys an unrivalled position beside Hampstead Heath and boasts the largest pub garden in London - a landscaped deck area and a beautifully secluded courtyard with alfresco bar. It's just the sort of place you could spend all day in. Follow a winter walk on the heath with a pint by a blazing log fire in the large and very stylish bar, replete with oak floor, deep leather sofas and a smart, contemporary decor. The atmosphere is friendly and relaxed and appeals to a young clientele. An open kitchen serves great Italian inspired food, including pasta, cassou-let, warm salads and wonderfully authentic wood-fired pizzas, say, Siciliana, with ham, artichoke, olives, mozzarella and tomato. If you're lingering over a long lunch, start with chilli-cured salmon with dill and tequila, then follow with spit chicken with garlic, lemon and aïoli or rib-eye steak with fries and Café de Paris butter. A triumph for 'Orange'!

Prices: Main course from £9.
Last orders: Bar: 23.00. Food: lunch 14.30; dinner 21.30 (Sunday 20.30).
Closed: 1st January.
Food: Modern British with an Italian influence.
Real ale: Greene King IPA, Timothy Taylor Ale.
Other points: No-smoking area. Garden. Courtyard. Alfresco bar.
Directions: West Hampstead underground station. (Map 4, E5)

London

Swag and Tails

10-11 Fairholt St, London SW7 1EG
Telephone: +44(0)20 7584 6926
theswag@swagandtails.com
www.swagandtails.com

Secreted away in a warren of pretty residential mews in Knightsbridge village, the Swag and Tails is well worth seeking out after a hard day's shopping. Beyond the magnificent, flower-adorned facade lies a civilised yet informal bar, with original panelling, stripped wooden floors and open fires and, to the rear, a cosy, quieter dining area. Business folk, shoppers and well-heeled locals quickly fill the bar at lunchtime, attracted by the welcoming atmosphere and the modern, Mediterranean-style dishes listed on the blackboard menu. Pop in to peruse the papers over a pint and a sirloin-steak sandwich with garlic mayonnise, or linger longer over something more substantial. Follow roasted red-pepper soup with Parma ham and pesto with roast duck leg with white-bean cassoulet, and finish with date sponge pudding, or a plate of Irish cheeses. A good list of wines. Note: the pub is closed at weekends!

Prices: Main course from £10.95. Bar/snack from £7.50. House wine £11.95.
Last orders: Bar: 23.00. Food: lunch 15.00; dinner 22.00.
Closed: Saturday, Sunday, all Bank Holidays and 10 days over the Christmas period.
Food: Modern British.
Real ale: Marston's Pedigree, Bombardier Premium Bitter, John Smith's.
Other points: Dogs welcome in the bar in the evening. Wheelchair access to the pub only.
Directions: Harrods is the nearest reference point. On the opposite side of the road, turn into Montpelier Street and take the first left into Cheval Place and then the second right and first left. (Map 4, E5)

Brancaster Staithe

The White Horse

Brancaster Staithe, King's Lynn,
Norfolk PE31 8BY
Telephone: +44(0)1485 210262
reception@whitehorsebrancaster.co.uk
www.whitehorsebrancaster.co.uk

The evocative call of the curlew and memorable views across breezy salt marsh are among the magical treats that await you at this stylishly refurbished inn on the North Norfolk coast. Drinkers will find a welcoming atmosphere within the light and airy bar, kitted out with scrubbed pine. The conservatory dining room, with its adjoining summer sun deck and one of the finest views in Norfolk, is the place to linger over dinner. Reflecting the view, colours throughout are muted and natural, and Nick Parker's modern menus focus on fresh local fish and seafood. Start, perhaps, with salad of confit duck with balsamic dressing, move on to black bream with tomato dressing, or lamb rump with sweet onion and creamed leek tartlet. Sandwiches, salads and chargrilled rib-eye steak are available for lunch. Original bedrooms are in the grass-roofed extension facing the marsh. Those upstairs feature handsome modern furniture, simple clean lines, and soft colours.

Rooms: 15. Double room from £90, single supplement £20 per night.
Prices: Main course from £9.50. House wine £10.80.
Last orders: Bar: 23.00. Food: lunch 14.00; dinner 21.15.
Closed: Rarely.
Food: Modern British.
Real ale: Adnams Southwold, Fuller's London Pride, Woodforde's Wherry. Guest beer.
Other points: No smoking in the restaurant. Children welcome. Dogs welcome overnight. Garden. Car park. Wheelchair access.
Directions: Midway between Hunstanton and Wells-next-the-Sea on the A149 coast road. (Map 4, B6)

Hevingham

Marsham Arms Inn

Holt Road, Hevingham, Norwich,
Norfolk NR10 5NP
Telephone: +44(0)1603 754268
nigelbradley@marshamarms.co.uk
www.marshamarms.co.uk

Set back from the B1149, with an attractive creeper-clad facade, this 18th-century country inn was built by local landowner Robert Marsham as a staging post for drovers travelling to Norwich market. In the comfortably modernised interior you'll find local Adnams and Woodforde's ales on tap and a varied menu listing traditional home-cooked bar food that relies on local lines of supply. Expect sound pub favourites such as grilled bacon baguette, garlic mushrooms, seafood mornay, and steak-and-kidney pie with shortcrust topping. Steaks come from the local butcher, who also provides the meat for an excellent mixed grill; there's a popular help-yourself salad bar, and daily fish dishes on the chalkboard. Those looking for comfortable accommodation will find 10 well-equipped en suite bedrooms housed in a purpose-built block. A good base from which to explore Norwich.

Rooms: 10. Double room from £70, single from £48.
Prices: Lunch main course from £7.50.
House wine £9.50.
Last orders: Bar: 23.00 (Closed Monday and Tuesday between 15.00-17.00). Food: lunch 15.00; dinner 21.30.
Closed: Rarely.
Food: Traditional and Modern British.
Real Ale: Adnams, Woodforde's, Bass, Greene King IPA. Guest beers.
Other points: No-smoking area. Children welcome. Garden. Car park. Wheelchair access to the restaurant/pub.
Directions: Four miles north of Norwich airport on the B1149 and two miles north of Horsford. (Map 4, B7)

Holkham

The Victoria at Holkham

Park Road, Holkham, Wells-next-the-Sea,
Norfolk NR23 1RG
Telephone: +44(0)1328 711008
victoria@holkham.co.uk
www.victoriaatholkham.co.uk

Viscount Coke's beautifully refurbished inn-cum-chic hotel stands at the entrance to Holkham Hall estate. An imposing brick building, built in the early 1800s to house the entourage of gentry visiting the hall, it now offers accommodation in ten individually decorated bedrooms. All are furnished with unique furnishings sourced from Rajasthan, alongside luxurious bathrooms. The colonial theme extends to the informal bar and brasserie: carved-wood furniture, huge sofas, and a wealth of Indian artefacts. Menus focus on fresh, local produce, notably beef and seasonal estate game, as well as seafood from the Norfolk coast, with lunch bringing risotto of Thornham mussels with saffron and chives or Holkham venison burger with cranberry chutney. Dinners might include sea bream with citrus-and-basil dressing, rib-eye steak with béarnaise, and caramelised lemon custard with gingerbread ice cream. See pub walk on page 240.

Rooms: 10. Low season £55 and high season £70 and mid-season £70 - prices are per person per night.
Prices: Restaurant main course from £7.
House wine £12.
Last orders: Bar: 23.00 Food: lunch 14.30; dinner 21.30 (Friday and Saturday 22.00).
Closed: Never.
Food: Modern British.
Real ale: Woodforde's. 2 guest beers.
Other points: No-smoking area. Children welcome. Dogs welcome in the bar. Car park. Licence for civil weddings.
Directions: On the A149, 3 miles west of Wells-next-the-Sea. (Map 4, B6)

Itteringham

Walpole Arms

The Common, Itteringham, Aylsham,
Norfolk NR11 7AR
Telephone: +44(0)1263 587258
goodfood@thewalpolearms.co.uk
www.thewalpolearms.co.uk

Discerning foodies travel to this unspoilt brick-and-timber cottage in sleepy Itteringham for first-class modern British and Mediterranean-inspired food. With talented chef Andy Parle at the stove, daily menus reflect his passion for fresh local produce, notably Morston mussels, Cromer crab, lamb from the Walpole estate, and venison from nearby Gunton Hall. Typically, starters may feature bouillabaisse, rouille and gruyère, or baked brioche, crab and basil 'pudding'. Mains include a sizeable serving of Morston mussels steamed with onions and thyme, sea bass with saffron mash and gazpacho salsa, and lamb shank with peas and mint. Round off with chocolate parfait with poached apricots. There's the choice of dining in the rustic opened-up bar, which retains plenty of original character, or booking a table in the more formal dining room. Excellent ales and top-notch wines.

Prices: Restaurant main course from £9. Bar main course from £5. House wine from £11.90.
Last orders: Bar: lunch 15.00; dinner 23.00. Food: lunch 14.00 (Sunday 14.30); dinner 21.30.
Closed: Rarely.
Food: Modern British.
Real ale: Adnams Broadside, Adnams Best, Wolf Walpole. Guest beer.
Other points: No smoking in the restaurant. Children welcome. Dogs welcome in the bar. Garden. Car park. Wheelchair access.
Directions: Off the A140 Norwich to Cromer road. Go through Aylsham, past Blickling Hall, then take the next right turn. (Map 4, B7)

Norwich

The Wig & Pen ⬤★

6 St. Martins Palace Plain, Norwich,
Norfolk NR3 1RN
Telephone: +44(0)1603 625891
info@thewigandpen.com
www.thewigandpen.com

Arrive early, bag a window seat, or a table on the sunny front terrace, and savour the fabulous cathedral views over lunch at this old beamed pub opposite the cathedral close. Log fires crackle in the original bar, where legal related prints adorn the walls, and the welcoming atmosphere extends through to the modern dining extension. Expect to find lawyers and locals supping pints of ale at the bar, shoppers and tourists popping in for lunch and, in the evenings, a young, lively crowd, here for the beer and live sport on the TV. Real-ale enthusiasts are spoilt rotten. Brewery badges on the six hand-pumps may feature Oulton Ales Wet and Windy and Adnams Old Ale. All are kept in tip-top condition, great beer to wash down some hearty, traditional pub food - sandwiches, ham, egg and chips, or a home-cooked special such as steak-and-kidney pie or fresh battered fish.

Prices: Restaurant main course from £7.50. Bar main course from £3.00. House wine from £8.95.
Last orders: Bar: 23.00. Food: lunch 14.30; dinner 21.00.
Closed: Sunday evening. Christmas Day, New Years Day.
Food: Traditional and Modern British.
Real ale: Adnams Best Bitter and 5 guest beers
Other points: No-smoking area. Children over 14 welcome. Garden. Wheelchair access (not WC).
Directions: Adjacent to Norwich Cathedral. 100 yards from Maids Head Hotel Tombland. Walking distance from the River Wensum. (Map 4, B7)

Old Buckenham

The Gamekeeper Freehouse 🛏

The Green, Old Buckenham, Attleborough,
Norfolk NR17 1RE
Telephone: +44(0)1953 860397
richardashwell@thegamekeeperfreehouse.com
www.thegamekeeperfreehouse.com

Set by the largest village green in East Anglia, this attractive 17th-century inn has a lovely rural feel and fits perfectly into the picturesque village of Old Buckenham. In the winter, there's a blazing log fire in the rambling bar, where chunky church candles and hop-strewn beams create a cosy atmosphere, and in summer, you can dine alfresco in the garden. The restaurant menu is comprehensive and includes many local ingredients in season. Appetisers take in crayfish, asparagus and shallot tart or smoked haddock chowder, while main dishes include fillet steak with all the trimmings and chicken with asparagus and parmesan risotto. In the bar, you can feast on fish and chips, chicken tandoori and steak burger. And if you want to extend your stay, there are three comfortable rooms, complete with DVD players, although the bathroom is shared.

Rooms: 3 with private bathrooms (not en suite). Double room from £45, single from £30.
Prices: Restaurant main course from £8.95. Bar snack from £7.50. House wine £10.95.
Last orders: Bar: 23.00. Food: lunch 14.30 (Sunday 17.00); dinner 21.00 (Friday and Saturday 21.30). No food Sunday evening.
Closed: Never.
Food: Traditional British.
Real ale: Adnams, Wolf Brewery Ales. Guest beer.
Other points: No smoking in the restaurant. Garden. Children welcome in snug and garden. Dogs welcome overnight. Car park. Wheelchair access to pub.
Directions: Exit the A11 at Attleborough, then follow the B1077 to Old Buckenham. (Map 4, C7)

Snettisham

The Rose and Crown

Old Church Road, Snettisham, King's Lynn,
Norfolk PE31 7LX
Telephone: +44(0)1485 541382
info@roseandcrownsnettisham.co.uk
www.roseandcrownsnettisham.co.uk

Built in the 14th century to house the crafts-men working on the parish church, the Goodrich's splendid, flower-decked inn hides a warren of bars with heavy oak beams, uneven red-tiled floors, huge inglenook fire-places and comfortable settles, and a small informal dining room. To the rear, there's a large garden room leading directly onto the walled garden. The kitchen makes good use of the best seasonal and local produce, notably Cromer crab, Brancaster lobsters, oysters and mussels, and Sandringham Estate beef. At lunchtime, expect decent sandwich-es, chargrilled burgers and classic dishes such as steak-and-kidney pudding. Evening addi-tions range from smoked haddock kedgeree cakes to roast duck breast with hazelnut jus. Puddings may include rice pudding with rhu-barb compote. Six real ales and 20 wines by the glass complement the food. Stylishly en suite bedrooms are individually decorated.

Rooms: 11. Double room from £45, single from £55.
Prices: Set lunch £10 (two courses Monday-Friday).
Restaurant main course from £8. House wine £11.
Last orders: Bar: 23.00. Food: lunch 14.00 (14.30 Saturday and Sunday); dinner 21.00 (21.30 Saturday and Sunday).
Closed: Rarely.
Food: Modern British.
Real ale: Adnams, Greene King IPA. 4 guest beers.
Other points: No-smoking area. Children welcome. Dogs welcome overnight. Garden. Car park. Wheelchair access to the restaurant/pub.
Directions: Off the A149 between King's Lynn and Hunstanton, 10 miles north of King's Lynn. (Map 4, B6)

Winterton-on-Sea

Fisherman's Return

The Lane, Winterton-on-Sea,
Norfolk NR29 4BN
Telephone: +44(0)1493 393305
fisherman_return@btopenworld.com
www.fishermans-return.com

After a long, bracing walk across the dunes, the friendly and unpretentious bars of this 17th-century brick-and-flint pub, replete with warming wood-burners, are a welcome retreat in which to find good East Anglian ales and some hearty home-cooked food. Formerly a row of fisherman's cottages, it is a tradi-tional village pub where locals, fishermen and tourists exploring the coast are made truly welcome by John and Kate Findlay. There's a good summer family room (Tinho) in a tim-bered rear extension, and a lovely enclosed garden with a pets' corner and an adven-ture playground. The printed menu sticks to the traditional, but look to the chalkboard for hearty homemade soups and casseroles, Caister crab, mussels and mackerel, winter game dishes, boozy beef pie, and fresh fish such as whole Dover sole, skate with capers and mushroom sauce, and hot Winterton smoked salmon. Upstairs are three clean and modestly comfortable en suite rooms.

Rooms: 3. Double from £70, single room from £45.
Prices: Main course from £8.25. House wine £10.75.
Last orders: Bar: lunch 14.30; dinner 23.00 (all day during the weekend). Food: lunch 14.00; dinner 21.00.
Closed: Rarely.
Food: Traditional English and Continental.
Real ale: Woodforde's Wherry & Norfolk Nog, Adnams Best & Broadside. Guest beers.
Other points: No-smoking area. Children welcome. Dogs welcome overnight. Garden. Car park. Wheelchair access to the restaurant/pub (not WC).
Directions: Eight miles north of Great Yarmouth off the B1149. (Map 4, B7)

Bulwick

Queen's Head

Main Street, Bulwick, Corby,
Northamptonshire NN17 3DY
Telephone: +44(0)1780 450272

Situated in the heart of a pretty village, opposite the church, this quaint 17th-century stone pub has bags of character, and it's a great pit-stop if you're travelling on the nearby A43. From the front door you enter a tiny bar warmed by an open fire and dominated by plenty of timber joints and beams, with those wonky, uneven walls indicating great age. You'll find a good range of ale, and quality pub food that utilises the best local produce. Menus are modern British with influences from the Mediterranean, with imaginative offerings such as pork tenderloin with roasted shallots and caramelised apple, and calf's liver with pancetta mash and red-onion marmalade. Lunchtime meals include ploughman's and filled ciabatta sandwiches. Food is served in three small adjoining rooms, each strewn with rugs and furnished with classic wood furniture and knick-knacks. Interesting bin-end wines and a delightful terrace for summer dining add to the appeal.

Prices: Restaurant main course from £10.95. Bar main course from £4.95. House wine from £10.25.
Last orders: Bar: lunch 14.30; dinner 23.00. Food: lunch 14.30; dinner 21.30. No food Sunday evening.
Closed: Monday.
Food: Modern British and Mediterranean.
Real ale: Shepherd Neame Spitfire, Church End, Slaters, Newby Wyke. Guest beers.
Other points: No smoking in the restaurant. Children welcome. Dogs welcome in the bar. Garden. Car park. Wheelchair access in the restaurant/bar.
Directions: Just off the A43 between Stamford and Corby. (Map 3, C4)

Oundle

Falcon Inn

Fotheringhay, Oundle,
Northamptonshire PE8 5HZ
Telephone: +44(0)1832 226254

Standing close to the grand parish church in this historic village, the Falcon is a great village pub. Candles, fresh flowers, Windsor chairs, high-backed tapestry-covered chairs, some exposed stone, and discreet, soft colours define the bar. The double conservatory dining room provides a slightly more formal setting, filled with a mix of director's chairs and Lloyd Loom chairs. There's a snack menu chalked up on a board, but the printed, monthly-changing menu is offered in the bar as well as the dining room. This fits the bill nicely, aware of the rural location and tastes, but managing to be thoroughly modern. Thus, a March meal could open with chicken-liver parfait with red-onion jam. Sea bass with roasted fennel and tomato stew could follow, with coconut pannacotta with chilli-roasted pineapple, making a great finish. Don't miss the bargain lunch menu. The first-class wine list offers an eclectic, esoteric and stimulating selection.

Prices: Set lunch £16.75. Restaurant main course from £9.95. Bar main course from £8.95. House wine £12.50.
Last orders: Bar: lunch 15.00; dinner 23.00. Food: lunch 14.15; dinner 21.30.
Closed: Rarely.
Food: International.
Real ale: Adnams Best, Greene King IPA. Guest beers.
Other points: No smoking in the restaurant. Children welcome. Dogs welcome in the bar. Garden. Car park.
Directions: Village signposted off the A605 between Oundle and Peterborough, one mile north of Oundle. (Map 3, C4)

Kielder Water

The Pheasant Inn

Stannersburn, Kielder Water, Hexham, Northumberland NE48 1DD
Telephone: +44(0)1434 240382
enquiries@thepheasantinn.com
www.thepheasantinn.com

Where to walk
The Hadrian's Wall Path National Trail runs for 84 miles from Wallsend to Bowness-on-Solway and is a great way of seeing one of the country's most famous monuments at close hand. The Cheviot Hills are perfect for exhilarating hikes, and the great tract of Kielder Forest is a super recreational area, with self-guided forest walks from numerous points along the road through it.

Events & festivals
County Show, Corbridge (May)
Rothbury Traditional Music Festival (July)

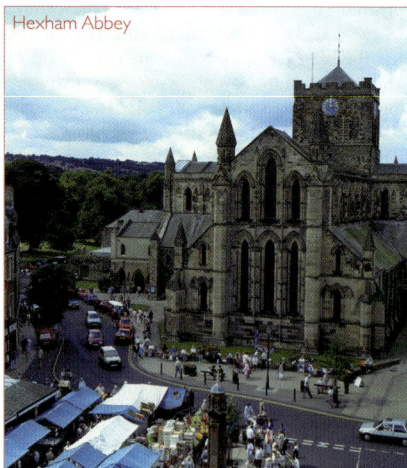

Hexham Abbey

A 400-year-old former farmhouse, the Pheasant Inn lies deep in unspoilt Northumberland countryside, just a mile from Kielder Water. All areas of this well-maintained building are meticulously clean, the decor cottagey and entirely appropriate to the style of the building and area; indeed, the Pheasant wears its comfortable look well. Polished wood tables and chairs add to the country look of the low-ceilinged dining room. The menu delivers sound, traditional country cooking, with the most popular dish being roasted Northumberland lamb with a rosemary and redcurrant jus. Lamb, beef and game come from a local butcher and fresh fish is from North Shields. Typically, start with grilled asparagus with a balsamic dressing, move on to game and mushroom pie, or sea bass with herb-butter sauce, and round off with lemon and lime chesecake or a plate of farmhouse cheeses. There are homemade bar meals and super Sunday roasts and excellent accommodation in eight, light and prettily decorated en suite rooms. See pub walk on page 242.

Rooms: 8. Double/twin from £65, single from £35 and family from £75.
Prices: Evening main course from £9.25, lunch main course from £6.75. House wine £9.95.
Last orders: Bar: lunch 15.00; dinner 23.00. Food: lunch 15.00; dinner 21.00
Closed: Monday and Tuesdays from November to March.
Food: Traditional pub food.
Real ale: Black Sheep Best, Timothy Taylor Landlord, Greene King Old Speckled Hen.
Other points: No-smoking area. Children welcome. Dogs welcome. Garden. Car park. Wheelchair access to the restaurant and pub (no WC).
Directions: Follow signs to Kielder Water from B6320 at Bellingham, 17 miles north of Hexham. (Map 5, B4)

Must-sees
Corbridge Roman Site & Museum
Hexham Abbey
Hadrian's Wall -- Housesteads Fort (NT) & Vindolanda
Kielder Water (Tower Knowe Visitor Centre)
Hareshaw Linn Waterfall, Bellingham

Tourist information Hexham +44(0)1434 652220
Where to shop Newcastle, Hexham
Farmers' market Hexham (2nd Saturday of month)
Nearest racecourse Hexham
Nearest golf course Bellingham

Longframlington

The Anglers Arms

Weldon Bridge, Longframlington, Morpeth,
Northumberland NE65 8AX
Telephone: +44(0)1665 570271
johnyoung@anglersarms.fsnet.co.uk
www.anglersarms.com

Set in an idyllic spot beside the old stone bridge over the River Coquet, this grand 18th-century coaching inn is perfectly located for fishing and walking in the Cheviot Hills. Bar and lounges are spacious and handsomely appointed, with wood panelling, log fires, antique ornaments and some fine old prints. Cosy up with a pint and a good old-fashioned bar meal, perhaps cod and chips or steak-and-ale pie, prepared from quality local ingredients. For quite a different dining experience, book into The Carriage restaurant, where fine foods are served in a refurbished Pullman carriage. Starters take in French onion soup and Thai-style fish cakes, while mains may include fillet of pork stuffed with apricots and prunes and wrapped in prosciutto. Puddings are the hard-to-resist variety such as hot chocolate fudge cake. En suite bedrooms have lovely rural views.

Rooms: 5. Double room from £60, single from £40, family from £90.
Prices: Restaurant main course from £14.95. Bar main course from £7.95. Set menu on request.
House wine £12.50.
Last orders: Bar: lunch 14.00 (Sunday 14.30); dinner 21.30 (Sunday 21.00). Food: lunch 14.30; dinner 21.30.
Closed: Rarely.
Food: Traditional British.
Real ale: Timothy Taylor Landlord.
Other points: No smoking in the restaurant. Children welcome. Dogs welcome overnight. Garden. Car park. Licence for civil weddings. Wheelchair access.
Directions: A1. A697 to Woller & Coldstream, carry on to Weldon Bridge and follow signposts. (Map 6, A5)

Seahouses

The Olde Ship Hotel

9 Main Street, Seahouses, Alnwick,
Northumberland NE68 7RD
Telephone: +44(0)1665 720200
theoldeship@seahouses.co.uk
www.seahouses.co.uk

Run by the Glen family for more than 100 years, the character inn is attractively decked out with nautical memorabilia. The bar offers superb views over the harbour and across to the Farne Islands and the famous Longstone Light. Food is local and hearty, from a well-honed menu of around six starters, six mains and a range of puds and cheese. Homemade soups, a salmon medley, followed by Bosuns' fish stew or roast leg of lamb, with saucy lemon pudding or clootie dumpling to finish make for a formidably satisfying meal. Well-priced wines, in the main European, add up to excellent value all round. The hotel's other trump card is its accommodation that comes in all shapes and sizes; from the single with a built-in bunk like a captain's cabin to the beautifully decorated four-poster room with original stone fireplace and period furnishings. There's also a self-contained bungalow and apartments. You'll find plenty to explore in this part of the Northumberland coast.

Rooms: 18. Double/twin from £90, single from £45.
Prices: Set lunch £11. Set dinner £19. Restaurant main course from £8.75. Bar main course from £6.75.
House wine £9.95.
Last orders: Bar: 23.00. Food: lunch 14.00; dinner 20.30.
Closed: Mid December to end of January.
Food: Traditional British.
Real ale: Bass, Ruddles County Ale, Hadrian and Border Farne Island Pale Ale, Black Sheep Ales.
Other points: No-smoking areas. Garden. Children over 10 welcome. Car park.
Directions: Take the B1340 off the A1 eight miles north of Alnwick. (Map 8. F8)

Harby

The Bottle & Glass

High Street, Harby, Newark,
Nottinghamshire NG23 7EB
Telephone: +44(0)1522 703438

Steve Horbury has brought this distinctive freehouse back to life. It's an impressive 16th-century building set in a pretty village near Lincoln and the atmosphere is sophisticated, but relaxed and unpretentious. Both bar areas are cosy with brick fireplaces, while the separate dining area is light and airy with a modern feel. Cooked with flair and beautifully presented, dishes are certainly a cut above your normal pub grub, with starters of grilled black pudding with haricot beans and red-wine sauce, or pigeon breast with pak choi, chilli, artichoke and a soy sauce. Mains are just as exquisite, with roast cod on stir-fried savoy cabbage or pan-roasted duck breast with apple mash. The selection of puddings covers indulgent whims, from cream to chocolate, or you could try the excellent local cheeses. Add in good coffee, great breads and friendly service, well-kept real ales and first-class wines and this pub is really going in the right direction. See pub walk on page 244.

Prices: Restaurant main course from £9.50. Bar/snack from £5.50. House wine £10.50.
Last orders: Bar: lunch 14.00; dinner 23.00. Food: lunch 14.00; dinner 21.30 (Friday and Saturday 22.00). No food Monday.
Closed: Monday lunchtime.
Food: Modern British.
Other points: No-smoking area. Children welcome. Dogs welcome in the bar. Patio. Car park.
Directions: A1 Lincoln exit. From Newark follow the signs for Collingham, and go through to Besthorpe. Turn right and follow the signs for Harby. (Map 3, A4)

Tuxford

Mussel and Crab

Sibthorpe Hill, Tuxford, Newark,
Nottinghamshire NG22 0PJ
Telephone: +44(0)1777 870491
musselandcrab1@hotmail.com
www.musselandcrab.com

Pubs and restaurants in land-locked Nottinghamshire are not renowned for offering great seafood, but this busy, energetic country pub is clearly bucking the trend. They aim to provide the freshest fish, whether native or exotic, with much of it delivered daily from Brixham. Choose from starters of crab bisque or oysters with chilli relish. Main courses might be grilled sea bass and salmon with avocado, pineapple and mango salsa, or baked swordfish with pesto sauce. Meat-eaters will not be disappointed with the huge mixed grill or game from local shoots. The stylishly refurbished interior offers various eating areas, a couple of bars with welcoming log fires, a mass of specials blackboards, and has all the wine list out on display. There are two distinct restaurant areas, one a sheer, vibrant Mediterranean, with terracotta and ochre hues. Gents, note the live goldfish in the plastic cistern above the urinals in the 'buoys' room.

Prices: Main course from £11. House wine £10.50.
Last orders: Bar: lunch 14.30 (Sunday 14.45); dinner 22.00 (Sunday 21.30). Food: lunch 14.30 (Sunday 14.45); dinner 22.00 (Sunday 21.00).
Closed: Rarely.
Food: Modern British.
Real ale: Tetley's Cask.
Other points: No smoking in the restaurant. Children welcome. Dogs welcome in the bar. Garden. Car park. Wheelchair access.
Directions: From junction A57/A1 (Markham Moor), take the B1164 to Ollerton/Tuxford. The pub is 800 yards on the right. (Map 6, G7)

Bledington

The Kings Head Inn

The Green, Bledington, Kingham, Oxfordshire OX7 6XQ
Telephone: +44(0)1608 658365
kingshead@orr-ewing.com
www.kingsheadinn.net

Must-sees
Stow-on-the-Wold: a handsome market town.
Chastleton House
Rollright Stones, Little Rollright: a dramatic Bronze Age
stone circle.
Batsford Arboretum, Moreton-in-Marsh: a private
collection of over 1000 rare species of trees spread
over 50 acres. Also home to the Cotswold Falconry
Centre: flying demonstations.
Bourton-on-the-Water: a touristy Cotswold village.

Bledington

Tourist information
Stow-on-the-Wold +44(0)1451 870083
Where to shop
Stow-on-the-Wold, Burford, Cheltenham, Oxford
Farmers' market
Stow-on-the-Wold (2nd Thursday of the month)

Classic cotswold villages
Take time to visit: Lower and Upper Slaughter; Adlestrop;

Facing the village green with its brook and border-patrolling ducks, this is surely the quintessential, 15th-century Cotswold pub. Inside, the original bar is charming, full of low beams, ancient settles and flagstone floors, and a huge log fire burns in the inglenook, while the separate dining area is an informal setting for some imaginative pub food. Archie and Nicola Orr-Ewing are passionate about local, free-range and organic ingredients, and, along with the fresh Cornish fish, all feature on the ever-changing menus. Start, perhaps, with scallop and Parma ham brochette with chilli-onion marmalade, then opt for rack of lamb with apricot and thyme jus, or whole lemon sole with minted pea puree. Finish with lemon mousse with raspberry coulis, or regional cheeses. Chalkboards list the lighter lunchtime choices. There is tip-top Hook Norton on hand pump and an interesting global wine list. Beautifully refurbished en suite bedrooms are split between the inn and the converted barn.

Rooms: 12. Double room from £70.
Prices: Set lunch from £15 and dinner from £20. Main course from £8.95. House wine £10.95.
Last orders: Bar: lunch 15.00; dinner 23.00. Food: lunch 14.00; dinner 21.30 (Sunday 21.00).
Closed: Rarely.
Food: Traditional and Modern British.
Real ale: Hook Norton Best Bitter, Bass. Guest beers.
Other points: No-smoking area. Children welcome. Dogs welcome in the bar. Garden. Car park. Wheelchair access to the restaurant/pub (no WC).
Directions: On the B4450 between Chipping Norton and Stow-on-the-Wold. (Map 3, D3)

The Wychwoods; The Rissingtons; Cornwell. Head further afield to explore the charming small towns of Burford, Chipping Campden and Charlbury.

Events & festivals
Gypsy Horse Fair, Stow-on-the-Wold (May)
Cornbury Music Festival, Charlbury (July)
Moreton Agricultural Show, Moreton-in-Marsh (September)

Chipping Norton

The Chequers

Goddards Lane, Chipping Norton,
Oxfordshire OX7 5NP
Telephone: +44(0)1608 644717
enquiries@chequers-pub.co.uk
www.chequers-pub.co.uk

The 16th-century Chequers has a strongly traditional look, with low ceilings, open fires and rugs on flagstone floors giving it a very cosy feel, and the location, in the middle of a bustling market town, certainly draws some appreciative customers. Fuller's ales' perfectly kept by landlord John Reid and food freshly prepared by wife and former home economics teacher Kay add to the appeal of this bustling pub-restaurant. In the conservatory-style restaurant, formerly an open courtyard, you'll find a popular menu that utilses fresh produce from select local suppliers. Start, perhaps, with Thai fishcakes with sweet-and-sour dipping sauce, then tuck into a roast half-shoulder of lamb with mint gravy or pork-and-leek sausages with mash and onion gravy. Blackboard specials and lunchtime sandwiches, ploughman's and salads extend the choice. Accompany a good meal with a pint of Pride or one of 16 wines available by the glass.

Prices: Restaurant main course from £8.95. Bar main course from £7.50. House wine £9.95.
Last orders: Bar: 23.00. Food: 14.30 (Sunday 17.00); dinner 21.30.
Closed: Rarely.
Food: Traditional/Modern British.
Real ale: Fuller's London Pride, Fuller's Chiswick, Fuller's ESB. Guest beer.
Other points: No smoking in the restaurant.
Directions: On the A44 between Oxford and Evesham, and Oxford and Stratford. (Map 3, D3)

Faringdon

The Snooty Fox Inn

Littleworth, Faringdon, Oxfordshire SN7 8PW
Telephone: +44(0)1367 240549

Initially, you walk into a large, mainly open-plan room with plenty of space, a few private dining areas with lots of oak beams, and wooden tiled flooring to the rear. Walking further into the pub, you come across the modern-looking bar, a huge wine rack beside it, and lots of comfy sofas opposite. The main part of the restaurant is more open, has real wood flooring, timbered ceilings and a big brick fireplace with an open fire (blazing in cooler months). Chalkboards offer a wide-ranging list of reasonably priced wines, and seasonal menus may deliver scallops and king prawns cooked in garlic butter with creamy cabbage and smoked bacon for a starter. For a main dish, try the half-shoulder of lamb with honey and rosemary gravy, pasta carbonara, or one of four Thai curries. Sandwiches, filled baguettes and a popular 'light eating' section of, say, home-cooked ham, egg and chips, are also available.

Prices: Restaurant main course from £9.95. Bar snack from £7.95. House wine £11.
Last orders: Bar: lunch 15.00; dinner 23.00 (open all day during the summer). Food: lunch 14.30; dinner 21.30 (Friday and Saturday 22.00).
Closed: Rarely.
Food: Modern brasserie food.
Real ale: Greene King IPA, Adnams. 2 guest beers.
Other points: No-smoking area. Children welcome. Dogs welcome. Garden. Car park. Wheelchair access, (no WC).
Directions: Exit16/M4. On the A420 Swindon to Oxford road, two miles east of Faringdon. (Map 3, E3)

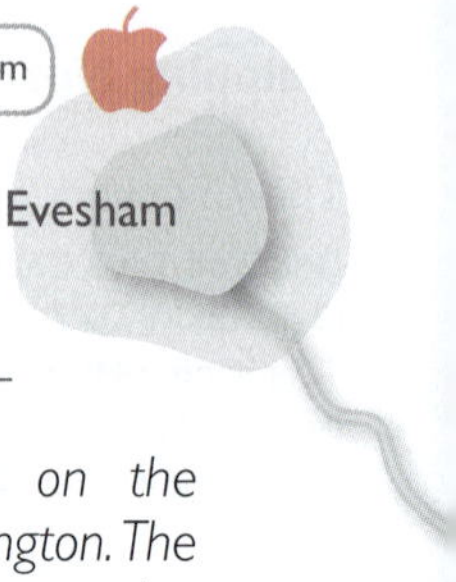

A M Bailey, Evesham

Evesham

The Kings Head Inn

The quintessential Cotswold country pub stands smack on the Gloucestershire border in the immaculate stone village of Bledington. The atmospheric bar is chock full of low beams, flagstones and worn settles, and a winter log fire burns in the big inglenook. Come for top-notch Hook Norton beer and some imaginative pub food. Ever-changing menus focus on local produce, notably free range and organic ingredients, with meats sourced from a respected local butcher and game from nearby estates.

Visit the local Farmers' Market

Nearby Stow-on-the-Wold operates a farmers' market in the main square on the second Thursday of the month from 9am to 2pm.

Haynes, Hanson & Clark Wine Merchants, Stow-on-the-Wold
Tel: 01451 870808

Founded in 1978, this thriving independent wine merchant sources wine direct from growers, which ensures excellent value and allocations of the finest-quality wines. It is best known for Burgundy Domaines, as well as extensive Bordeaux listings, great Loire Domaines, wines from the Clare Valley in Australia, and Spain's finest syrah – the Finca Sandoval. You can sample its wines at the Kings Head and order a case or two from either Stow or London shops.

A40

W J Castle & Jesse Smith Butchers, Burford
Tel: 01993 822113

Occupying one of Burford's historic timber-framed houses on the High Street, this traditional butchers has a good reputation for high-quality goods. Here you will find Hereford and Buccleuch beef alongside Gloucester Old Spot pork and locally farmed lamb. Cheese, olives, handmade sausages, and roast meats are also available from laden deli counters.

...for the latest news

Fifield House Farm
Fifield

The Orr-Ewings use as much local free-range and organic produce as possible and this includes their own Aberdeen Angus beef, which is reared on the family farm a few miles from the Kings Head. Although not organic, it is entirely grass fed – no additives – and is hung for 21 days to enhance its unique flavour.

Bensons Apple Juice
Sherborne
Tel: 01451 844134

Founded in March 1999, Bensons is based near Burford, in the heart of the Cotswolds. Rather like a single-grape variety wine it produces single-variety apple juice: the traditional Cox, with a sweet, full flavour; Bramley, one of its driest juices and an award winner ('Brammy Award' for the best Bramley Apple Juice in 2000); and supreme Jonagold, with a flavour that lies between the two. It also recently branched into some more adventurous concoctions - apple and raspberry or elderflower for the summer, or rhubarb and cinnamon warmed up - delicious in the winter. You will find Bensons juices at local farmers markets and you can drink this pure English nectar at the Kings Head.

A429

A44

Haynes, Hanson & Clark,
Stow-on-the-Wold

Stow-on-the-Wold

Chipping Norton

B4450

The Kings Head Inn,
Bledington

A429

A424

Fifield House Farm

Bensons Apple Juice,
Sherborne

W J Castle & Jesse Smith
Butchers, Burford

Burford

Henley-on-Thames

The Cherry Tree Inn

Stoke Row, Henley-on-Thames, Oxfordshire RG9 5QA
Telephone: +44(0)1491 680430
info@thecherrytreeinn.com
www.thecherrytreeinn.com

Pull off the M40 at junction 6 to locate this collection of 400-year-old brick-and-flint farm cottages deep in rolling Chilterns countryside - you won't be disappointed! With impressive CVs behind them, Paul Gilchrist and chef Richard Coates have worked wonders in bringing this old pub bang up-to-date. Bar and dining areas have been elegantly refurbished - think relaxing, earthy tones to the decor, subdued lighting and modern furnishings, yet original features such as worn flagstones, low beams and open fireplaces remain and blend in beautifully. Equally stylish and modern is the cooking. With an emphasis on simplicity and fresh, seasonal ingredients daily menus may take in starters of crab and brandy bisque or mussels in white wine and garlic cream sauce, and mains such as rack of lamb with grain-mustard sauce, or roast cod with parsley and oyster cream sauce. Good puddings or local cheese to finish. Brakspear ales, select wines and wonderful accommodation in four impeccable bedrooms complete the picture. See pub walk on page 246.

Must-sees
Basildon Park (NT)
Mapledurham House & Mill
Grey's Court, Rotherfield Greys (NT)
River & Rowing Museum, Henley-on-Thames
The Living Rain Forest, Hampstead Norreys
Stonor House & Park

Where to walk
Stroll beside the River Thames (Thames Path Trail) between Henley-on-Thames and Sonning and around South Stoke near Goring. The south Chilterns have a wealth of paths exploring beechwoods, rolling farmland and chalk hills, notably around Stonor and Turville. A glorious walk with far-reaching views across the Thames Valley is to follow a section of the Ridgeway Trail. See pub walk on page 248.

Rooms: 4. Double from £65.
Prices: Restaurant main course from £8.95. Bar/snack from £5.50. House wine £12.95.
Last orders: Bar: 23.00. Food: lunch 15.00 (Saturday and Sunday 16.00); dinner 22.00.
Closed: Rarely.
Food: Modern European.
Real ale: Brakspear Ales.
Other points: No-smoking area. Children welcome. Dogs welcome in the bar. Garden. Car park.
Directions: Exit 6/M40. Go towards Watlington. Take the B480 towards Nettlebed and then the B481 towards Reading. Turn right at Highmoor. Stoke Row is one mile away. (Map 3,4E)

Tourist information Henley-on-Thames
+44(0)1491 578034
Where to shop
Henley-on-Thames, Reading, Oxford, Marlow
Farmers' market Reading (3rd Saturday of month)
Nearest golf course
Huntercombe Golf Club, Nuffield

Events & festivals
Royal Windsor Horse Show (May)
Henley Royal Regatta (June/July)
Henley Festival (July)
Swan Upping, Abingdon (July)
WOMAD, World Music & Arts Festival, Reading (July)
Reading Festival (August)

Oxford

The Fishes

North Hinksey Village, Oxford,
Oxfordshire OX2 0NA
Telephone: +44(0)1865 249 796
www.peachpubs.com

New owners Peach Pubs are gradually upgrading this attractive village pub, built as a house in the 1800s and located just minutes from Oxford and the A34. Throughout the large, airy and traditionally furnished bar the atmosphere is friendly and down-to-earth, while the conservatory dining room has a relaxed rural meets Mediterranean feel. Menus follow suit, with robust British classics listed alongside hearty Italian-inspired dishes. Peach's novel deli-board menu offers nibbles or starters of cheese, fish, charcuterie and dipping oils with breads. Alternatively, start with duck spring rolls with plum sauce or Caesar salad. Portions are generous, so arrive hungry to tackle the 35-day dry-aged rump steak with pepper sauce or the sausages of the week served with mash and onion gravy. Lighter options include warm smoked haddock and chorizo salad, and roasted vegetable and feta cheese tart. The large garden is perfect for children.

Prices: Restaurant main course from £8.75. Bar snacks from £1.50. House wine from £10.50.
Last orders: Bar: 23.00. Food: lunch 22.00.
Closed: Rarely.
Food: Modern British.
Real ale: Fuller's London Pride, Greene King IPA, Timothy Taylor Landlord.
Other points: No-smoking area. Children welcome. Dogs welcome in bar. Car park. Wheelchair access.
Directions: North on the A34, take the left junction after Botley Interchange signed to the rugby club. From south, exit the A34 at Botley and return to the A34 south, then continue as above. (Map 3, E3)

Stoke Row

The Crooked Billet

Newlands Lane, Stoke Row, Henley-on-Thames,
Oxfordshire RG9 5PU
Telephone: +44(0)1491 681048
www.thecrookedbillet.co.uk

Tucked away down a leafy country lane, Paul Clerehugh's well-hidden little gem is a typically quaint village local that has upgraded itself to pub-restaurant status, and is well worth uncovering. It has the feel of a great winter pub, with small intimate rooms with low, heavy-beamed ceilings, rustic furnishings, and the roar of burning logs in the inglenook fireplace. The lengthy, cosmopolitan and adventurous menu has plenty of interest and the food is unpretentious with a rustic, homely quality that doesn't lose sight of its surroundings. From the carte or the set lunch menu choose, perhaps, baby squid marinated with chilli and garlic and served with chorizo and spinach, followed by sea bass and king prawns with Thai herbs and bok choy, or excellent game dishes in winter. For pudding, try the lemon tart with raspberry coulis, or a plate of local cheeses. Expect an enthusiast's wine list, and quality live jazz on Sundays. Booking essential.

Prices: Set lunch £14.95. House wine £12.
Last orders: Food: lunch 14.30; dinner 22.00.
Closed: Rarely.
Food: Modern British.
Other points: Garden. Car park.
Directions: Exit 8/9/M4 and follow signs for Henley, then A4130 to Nettlebed. Turn left and follow signs to Stoke Row. (Map 3, E4)

Brookleas Fish Farm, East Hendred, Wantage
Tel: 01235 820500

The Fish Farm was established in 1979 on the beautiful site of an old mill on the East Hendred Brook at Ludbridge. From the farm shop you can purchase fresh trout, locally caught crayfish, oak-smoked trout and smoked-trout paté. Brookleas also has a stall at Henley Farmers' Market, among others across south Oxfordshire and Berkshire.

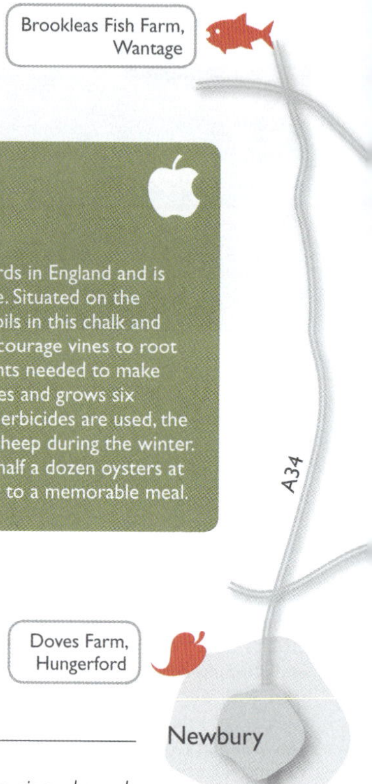

Brookleas Fish Farm, Wantage

Boze Down Vineyard, Whitchurch-on-Thames
Tel: 0118 984 4031

Boze Down is one of a few hundred vineyards in England and is one of even less producing world-class wine. Situated on the sheltered slopes of the Chiltern Hills, the soils in this chalk and flint area provide excellent drainage and encourage vines to root deep into the chalk and bring up the nutrients needed to make excellent wine. The vineyard covers five acres and grows six varieties of white grape and four reds. No herbicides are used, the vines being fertilised organically by grazing sheep during the winter. Sample a glass of English 'Champagne' with half a dozen oysters at the Crooked Billet – a wonderful precursor to a memorable meal.

A34

Doves Farm, Hungerford

The Crooked Billet

Newbury

Built in 1642, this smashing country pub remains largely unchanged, with masses of rustic appeal. Of the three rooms, two have darkwood beams, fireplaces, flag or wooden floors, and walls lined with bottles of wine. The cosmopolitan menu delivers unpretentious, rustic cooking that's based on careful sourcing of raw materials, much of it local, such as water-buffalo mozzarella from Camp Farm in the village.

Visit the local Farmers' Market

Henley has a market in the new Falaise Square every Thursday that combines with a popular Farmers' Market on the last Thursday of each month.

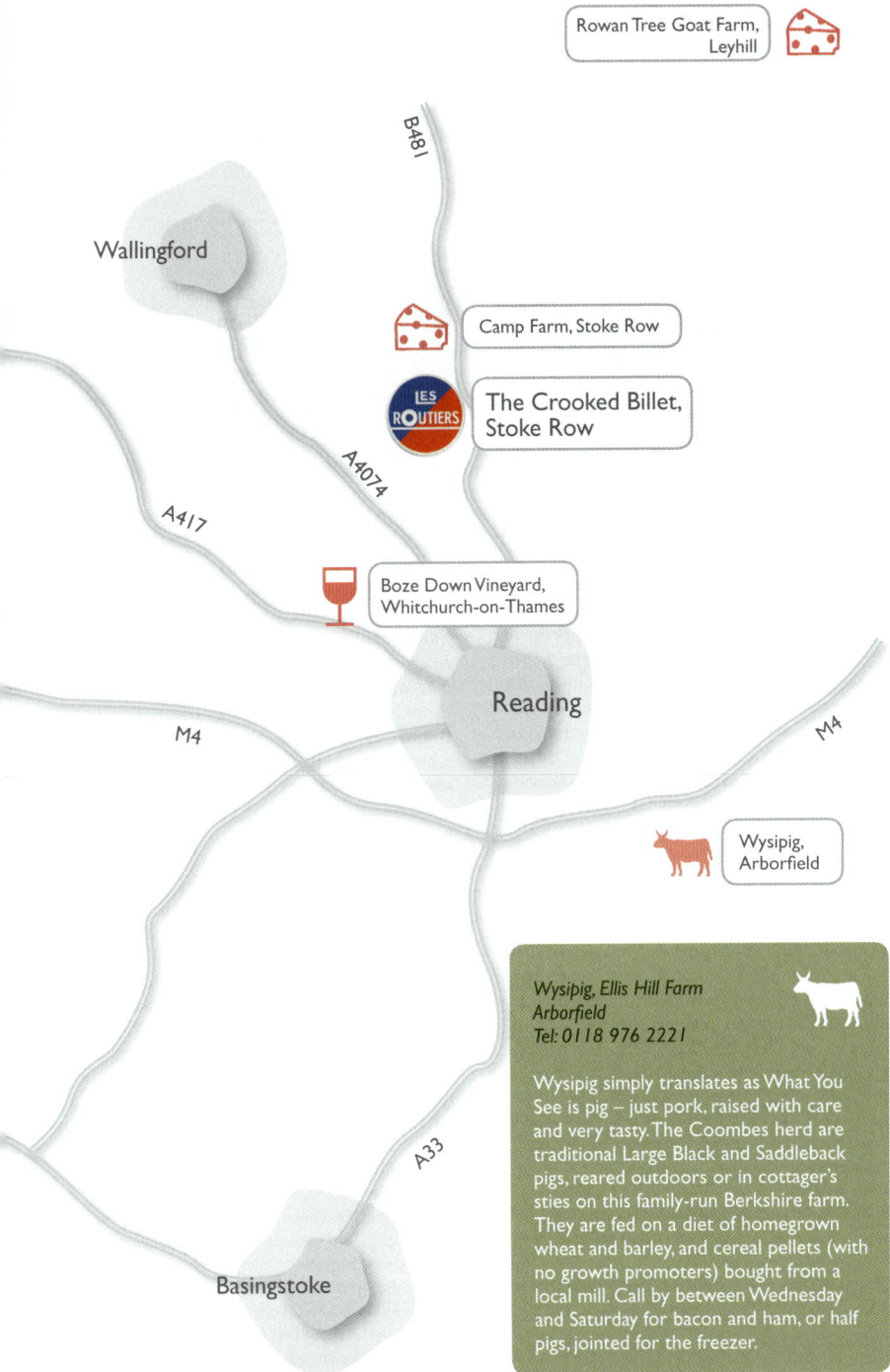

Rowan Tree Goat Farm,
Leyhill

B481

Wallingford

Camp Farm, Stoke Row

LES ROUTIERS

The Crooked Billet,
Stoke Row

A4074

A417

Boze Down Vineyard,
Whitchurch-on-Thames

Reading

M4

M4

Wysipig,
Arborfield

Wysipig, Ellis Hill Farm
Arborfield
Tel: 0118 976 2221

Wysipig simply translates as What You
See is pig – just pork, raised with care
and very tasty. The Coombes herd are
traditional Large Black and Saddleback
pigs, reared outdoors or in cottager's
sties on this family-run Berkshire farm.
They are fed on a diet of homegrown
wheat and barley, and cereal pellets (with
no growth promoters) bought from a
local mill. Call by between Wednesday
and Saturday for bacon and ham, or half
pigs, jointed for the freezer.

A33

Basingstoke

Thame

The Birdcage

4 Cornmarket, Thame, Oxfordshire OX9 3DX
Telephone: +44(0)1844 260381
birdcagepub@hotmail.com
www.twokiwisltd.co.uk

Thame's oldest pub dates from around 1300 and it's a quaint, black-and-white beamed-and-timbered place, listed by English Heritage and oozing history. In medieval times it was used to detain petty thieves and criminals, even lepers on the upper floors, and during the Napoleonic Wars it housed French prisoners. Sympathetic refurbishment in the rambling, wooden-floored bars has revealed thick oak beams from beneath modern plaster and the two oak-framed windows are of historic importance. The drinks menu is impressive. Quaff real ale or quality Belgian beers - Leffe, Hoegaarden, Blanc - or choose one of 50 wines available by the glass. There are few pretensions on the food front. Sausage lovers will struggle to choose a favourite from the 50-strong list that takes in the exotic (wild venison), house favourites (hot garlic) and the traditional (Cumberland) - all served with mash and gravy. Alternatives meals include a choice of pasta, steaks and seafood.

Prices: Restaurant main course from £9.50. Bar main course from £4.95. House wine £10.20.
Last orders: Bar: 23.00 (24.00 Wednesday and Thursday, 01.00 Friday and Saturday). Food: lunch 15.00 (16.00 Sunday); dinner: 22.30.
Closed: Rarely.
Food: Traditional British, specialising in sausages.
Other points: No-smoking area. Dogs welcome in the bar. Pavement dining area.
Directions: Exit 6 or 8/M40. Take the A418 to Thame. (Map 3, 4E)

Thame

The Old Fisherman

Mill Road, Shabbington, Thame,
Oxfordshire HP18 9HJ
Telephone: +44(0)1844 201247
dick@theoldfisherman.com
www.theoldfisherman.com

Built on the site of an old mill and much extended in 1996 and 2004, the Old Fisherman enjoys a tranquil waterside location in the picturesque Thame Valley. With the Oxfordshire Cycle Way and the Thame Valley Walk passing the door, the extensive riverside garden is popular on sunny summer days. Inside, new bar and dining areas sport big oak beams, quarry-tile and carpeted floors and an eclectic mix of furnishings, which blend well with the original two-roomed pub. Fresh food 'cooked as fast as we can' draws a loyal drinking and dining trade. There's something for everyone here, from pub favourites such as sandwiches and Bicester Royal sausages with mash and onion gravy to seared chicken salad, whole sea bass and a range of 'house specials', perhaps fresh crayfish from the river in summer.

Prices: Restaurant main course from £8. Main course bar/snack from £5. House wine £10.95.
Last orders: Bar: lunch 15.00; dinner 23.00. Open all day Saturday and Sunday and every day from 1st June to mid September. Food: lunch 14.15; dinner 21.00 (Saturday 21.30, Sunday 20.30).
Closed: 26 December.
Food: British and Mediterranean.
Real ale: Greene King Old Speckled Hen, Greene King IPA, Greene King Ruddles County Ale.
Other points: No-smoking dining room and some pub areas. Riverside garden. Children welcome. Car park. Private dining room. Wheelchair access.
Directions: Exit 7/M40. Follow signs to Thame. Turn left onto the A418 at the first roundabout. After one mile, turn right to Shabbington. (Map 3, E4)

Witney

The Fleece

11 Church Green, Witney,
Oxfordshire OX28 4AZ
Telephone: +44(0)1993 892270
fleece@peachpubs.com
www.peachpubs.com

The Witney outpost of the hugely successful Peach Pub Company is a 10-bedroomed inn overlooking the church green. Refurbishment is ongoing but the company's unique and stylish formula has been replicated here. The trademark leather sofas around low tables, and mirrors and modern artwork on warm, earthy coloured walls, a laid-back atmosphere, and a Continental-style opening time of 8am for coffee and breakfast sandwiches have certainly proved a hit among Witney residents. Equally popular is the all-day sandwich, salad and deli-board menu, the latter offering starters or nibbles of charcuterie, cheese, fish and unusual antipasti. Modern main-menu dishes range from smoked salmon fishcake with caper sauce and sea bream with lemon peas and fennel chips to lamb noisette with roasted vegetables and pesto. En suite bedrooms have warm, vibrant colours and chic fabrics and furnishings.

Rooms: 10 Double/twin from £75, single from £65 and family from £85.
Prices: Restaurant main course from £7.50. Bar main course from £1.35. House wine £10.50.
Last orders: Bar: 23.00.
Closed: Rarely
Food: Modern European.
Real ale: Greene King IPA, Old Speckled Hen, Morland Original Ale.
Other points: Children welcome. Dogs welcome. Garden. Car park. Wheelchair access to the restaurant/pub and one bedroom.
Directions: In the town centre. Witney is just off the A40 Oxford to Cheltenham road. (Map 3, E3)

Clipsham

The Olive Branch

Main Street, Clipsham, Oakham,
Rutland LE15 7SH
Telephone: +44(0)1780 410355
info@theolivebranchpub.com
www.theolivebranchpub.com

While retaining all of its pub qualities - space for just having a drink and a casual relaxed style - Sean Hope, Ben Jones and Marcus Welford are to be congratulated for putting flesh on a brilliant gastropub vision. Success is down to a philosophy of offering good-quality innovative and traditional food using first-class local produce. Chalkboards list lunchtime sandwiches and the very good value set lunch. Otherwise, grab a menu and a table anywhere in rambling bar and dining areas. Kick off a memorable meal with smoked chicken and confit shallot terrine with lemon pickle, move on to tandoori-baked halibut with Bombay potatoes, and finish with mango tarte Tatin with coconut ice cream. Wine is obviously a passion, with blackboards detailing house specials, classics and up-and-coming producers. This unpretentious old stone pub is a boon for travellers on the A1. Don't miss the pub shop.

Prices: Set lunch £15. Restaurant main course from £8.95. Bar main course from £6.75. House wine £11.50.
Last orders: Bar: lunch 15.00 (Saturday and Sunday open all day); dinner 24.00. Food: lunch 14.00 (Sunday 15.00); dinner 21.30 (Sunday 21.00).
Closed: Rarely.
Food: Modern pub food.
Real ale: Grainstore Olive Oil. 2 guest beers.
Other points: No smoking in the restaurant. Children welcome. Dogs welcome in the bar. Garden. Car park. Wheelchair access to the restaurant/pub.
Directions: Two miles off the A1 at the B668 junction north of Stamford. (Map 3, B4)

Oakham

The Old Plough

2 Church Street, Braunston, Oakham,
Rutland LE5 7DH
Telephone: +44(0)1572 722714
info@theoldplough.co.uk
www.theoldplough.co.uk

You're guaranteed a warm welcome from proprietors Claire and David Cox at their charming character inn, a converted stone house, rebuilt in 1838, which dates back to Tudor times, when the site was used to produce malt barley for brewing. It majors in superb ales and good home cooking. Depending on your mood and the weather, you can dine in the bar beside an open fire, in the light and airy conservatory, or on the garden patio. At lunch and on certain evenings, there's a good-value plat du jour set menu. Start with soup or pâté and move on to lamb's liver and mash or steak-and-ale pie. Daily specials such as Barnsley lamb chop or salmon fillet also hit the spot, as do the selection of steaks and other meats from the grill. If you like real ale, you've come to the right place, as they offer excellent ales from The Grainstore Brewery.

Rooms: 5. Double room from £65, single from 55.
Family room from £75.
Prices: Set lunch £13.95 and dinner £14.95.
Restaurant main course £7.95-£16.
Bar main course £4.95-£6.50.
Last orders: Bar: 23.00. Food: 21.30.
Closed: Never.
Food: Traditional English.
Other points: No-smoking area. Children welcome.
Dogs welcome. Garden. Car park.
Directions: From Oakham High Street, go over the level crossing and bear left. Take the second left towards Braunston, driving for 2 miles. (Map 6, H7)

Telford

The Hundred House Hotel

Bridgnorth Road, Norton, Shifnal, Telford, Shropshire TF11 9EE
Telephone: +44(0)1952 730353/0845 644 6100
hundredhouse@lineone.net
www.hundredhouse.co.uk

Must-sees
Wightwick Manor: reflects the style and influence of
  William Morris and the Arts and Crafts Movement.
Boscobel House: where Charles II hid from
  Parliamentary troops in 1651.
Ironbridge: offers an insight into the origins of the
Industrial Revolution.
Aerospace Museum, Cosford.
Dudmaston: 17th-century house containing fine
  furniture and Dutch flower paintings.
Severn Valley Railway: take a classic ride on a restored
  railway.

Bridgnorth

From the outside, the Hundred House is an unassuming, red-brick Georgian inn. It is a very different story once you step inside: quarry-tiled floors, exposed brickwork, huge fireplaces, and some fine oak panelling show signs of sympathetic restoration. Herbs and dried flowers from the inn's wonderfully luxuriant gardens adorn beams and tables. The personality of the inn gains from the inimitable input from the Phillips family since 1986. This enthusiasm extends to the excellent food prepared by Stuart Phillips, who sources local produce and cooks both a brasserie-style and full restaurant menu. Expect such dishes as beef fillet with blue cheese risotto and beef jus, sea bass with basil cream sauce, and lighter dishes such as venison casserole and lasagne. Delicious home-made puddings include apple, walnut and sultana crumble. You'll also find five real ales and a well-chosen list of wines. Both names and colour schemes in the 10 enchanting en suite bedrooms reflect the garden.

Rooms: 10. Double room from £99, single from £75, family from £125.
Prices: Restaurant main course from £10. Bar main course from £7.95. House wine £12.50.
Last orders: Bar: lunch 15.00; dinner 23.00. Food: lunch 14.30; dinner 22.00 (Sunday 21.00).
Closed: Rarely.
Food: Modern British.
Real ale: Phillips Heritage Bitter, Phillips Heritage Mild, Bateman XB Bitter, Everards Tiger Best Bitter, Highgate & Walsall Saddlers Strong Ale. 1 guest beer.
Other points: No-smoking area. Children welcome. Garden. Car park. Wheelchair access to the restaurant/pub.
Directions: Exit4/M54. Beside the A442, midway between Bridgnorth and Telford. (Map 3, C1)

Tourist information Bridgnorth +44(0)1746 763257
Where to shop Bridgnorth, Ludlow, Much Wenlock
Shrewsbury, Church Stretton.
Farmers' market
Bridgnorth (3rd Friday of month)
Nearest racecourse Wolverhampton, Ludlow

Local activities
Fishing on the River Severn, canoeing, horse riding and pony trekking
Events & festivals
Folk Music Festival, Bridgnorth (August)
Haydn Music Festival (June)

Exford

Exmoor White Horse Inn

Exford, Exmoor National Park,
Somerset TA24 7PY
Telephone: +44(0)1643 831229
linda@exmoorwhitehorse.demon.co.uk
www.devon-hotels.co.uk

A lovely, creeper-clad, 16th-century building, this coaching inn stands opposite the
River Exe in the heart of a small village
in the Exmoor National Park. Close to
Tarr Steps, the picture-postcard villages of
Dunster, Selworthy and Porlock, and the dramatic north Somerset/Devon coast, the White
Horse has long been a favoured pit-stop on
the tourist trail. It is also popular among
walkers and as a base for exploring Exmoor.
Downstairs in the comfortable, beamed and
carpeted bar, there are country-themed prints
adorning the walls, log fires, Exmoor ale on
tap, and an extensive menu listing traditional
pub meals. Look out for the inn's specialities,
namely venison, pheasant and partridge from
the surrounding moors, locally caught lobster
and fresh fish, and the platter of Somerset
cheeses. There is also a Sunday lunch carvery.
The inn offers en suite accommodation in
cottagey bedrooms.

Rooms: 28. Double/twin room from £80,
single from £40.
Prices: Set dinner £30 (3 courses). Main course from
£12. Bar snack menu from £6. House wine £9.50.
Last orders: Bar: 23.00. Food: lunch 14.30; dinner 21.30.
Closed: Never.
Food: Traditional British.
Real ale: Exmoor Ale, Old Speckled Hen, Marston's
Pedigree, Exmoor Gold. 2 guest beers.
Other points: No-smoking in the restaurant and food
bar. Children welcome. Dogs welcome overnight.
Garden. Car park. Wheelchair access to the
ground floor.
Directions: On B3224, midway between Simonsbath
and Wheddon Cross south of Minehead. (Map 2, D5)

Shepton Mallet

Thatched Cottage

63-67 Charlton Road, Shepton Mallet,
Somerset BA4 5QF
Telephone: +44(0)1749 342058
enquiries@thatchedcottage.info
www.thatchedcottageinn.co.uk

Sporting a new thatched roof, fresh paint-
work and a smart stone façade, this listed,
300-year-old cottage stands on the edge of
town on the old Fosse Way. Money has also
been lavished on the interior, resulting in a
cool, comfortable and contemporary open-
plan bar that blends the traditional - oak
beams, wood tiled floors and log fires - with
a stylish, modern decor, squashy sofas, and
chunky candles on pale-wood tables. Comfort
and style extend upstairs to the eight, tastefully designed bedrooms. Expect oodles of
space, movie channels, internet access and
impressive slate-floored bathrooms. Back in
the bar, tuck into liver and bacon with red
onion gravy, or the 'Thatch Burger', made
with prime beef from Brown Cow Organics.
Asian specialities feature in the restaurant,
alongside warm orange and scallop salad,
chump of Sedgemoor lamb with rosemary
sauce, and British cheeses from Longman's
Cheese. Accompany with a pint of Greene
King or with one of 20 wines by the glass.

Rooms: 8. Double/twin from £94.50, single from £77.25.
Prices: Set lunch £12. Restaurant main course from
£9.95. Bar snack from £5. House wine £11.95.
Last orders: Bar: 23.00. Food: lunch 14.30; dinner 21.30.
Closed: Rarely.
Food: Modern European and Asian.
Real ale: Greene King IPA, Bateman.
Other points: No-smoking area. Dogs welcome in bar.
Garden. Car park. Wheelchair access to public areas.
Directions: On the A361 west of the town centre at
the junction of Fosse Lane and Charlton Road.
(Map 3, F1)

South Cadbury

The Camelot

Chapel Road, South Cadbury, Yeovil,
Somerset BA22 7EX
Telephone: +44(0)1963 440448
enquiries@thecamelot.co.uk
www.thecamelot.co.uk

Formerly known as the Red Lion, the only pub in South Cadbury has undergone a major refurbishment to emerge as the distinctly jazzier and magnificent Camelot. Zizi Montgomery has created a fantastic setting in which to showcase its amazing, well-sourced and wide-ranging menu. The friendly bar, with flagstones, wooden tables and brightly coloured cushioned chairs or the relaxing lounge with comfortable leather sofas are ideal places for wining and dining. Enjoy a pint of local Butcombe Bitter with a ploughman's or something more international, culinary and wine wise. A house speciality is zakuski-Russian-style tapas starters, such as spiced lentils and chorizo, mushrooms and crème fraîche, or seafood, while the bar and carte menus offer an extensive line-up of favourites from bangers and mash to duck breast or lamb shank. A lovely beer garden extends the dining-area options.

Prices: Set lunch £13. Set dinner £19. Restaurant main course from £7.50. Bar main course from £4.50. House wine £11.
Last orders: Bar: lunch 14.30; dinner 22.00 (open all day Saturday and Sunday). Food: lunch 14.30; dinner 21.30.
Closed: Rarely.
Food: Modern British.
Real ale: Butcombe Bitter. 2 guest beers.
Other points: No-smoking area. Dogs welcome in the bar. Garden. Children welcome. Wheelchair access. Skittle alley.
Directions: Off the A303 between Wincanton and Yeovil. (Map 2, E5)

Wells

The Crown at Wells and Anton's Bistrot

Market Place, Wells, Somerset BA5 2RP
Telephone: +44(0)1749 673457
eat@crownatwells.co.uk
www.crownatwells.co.uk

Built in 1450 within sight of the Gothic cathedral and Bishop's Palace, the Crown retains many of its original features. For a traditional pub atmosphere, head for the Penn Bar, where popular bar meals are served and for a more contemporary dining experience, head to Anton's, a wine-bar-cum-bistro. The dining is casual and informal and stripped-pine tables and candles by night set a relaxed scene. Anton's menu offers modern dishes that don't stint on quality. Start with wok-steamed mussels with a creamy saffron sauce before moving on to beef fillet with a roasted garlic mash and roasted vegetables. At lunchtime and early evening Sunday to Thursday, you can choose from a specially compiled 'Les Routiers' menu, which includes good-value mains of rib-eye steaks or an asparagus and Swiss cheese tart. Bedrooms are decorated in keeping with the traditional inn.

Rooms: 15. Double room from £85, single from £55. Family room from £100.
Prices: Set lunch from £11.95. House wine £11.50.
Last orders: Bar: lunch 15.00; dinner 23.00. Food: lunch 14.30; dinner 21.30 (Sunday 21.00).
Closed: Never.
Food: Mediterranean.
Real ale: Butcombe, Oakhill Best, Smiles Best.
Other points: No-smoking in the restaurant and bedrooms. Children welcome. Dogs welcome overnight. Courtyard. Car park. Wheelchair access to the restaurant.
Directions: The pub is in the centre of Wells, in the Market Place. Follow signs for hotels and deliveries to take you into the Market Place. (Map 3, F1)

The Camelot

The Camelot opened in July 2004 after an extensive six-month refurbishment programme by the owners, the Montgomery family, who also farm the surrounding countryside as well as making award-winning handmade cheese. The result has been the creation of a great local pub, in a fantastic location, with fabulous food. Head Chef, Sasha Matkevich, first became interested in cooking when inspired by his grandmother in his home in southern Russia. He emigrated to England in 1996, having met his future wife, Ailsa, who was working in Russia (but actually hails from Compton Pauncefoot, a neighbouring village to South Cadbury). There is a lot of Spanish/Italian/Mediterranean influence in Sasha's cooking. He is a great believer in cooking with local fresh produce, organic where possible.

Taunton

A378

Burrow Hill Cider
Burrow Hill

Cantelo Nurseries Ltd,
Isle Abbotts

South Petherton

Visit the Farmers' Market

Head for Wincanton and the Memorial Hall for the monthly farmers' market on the first Friday of the month from 9am to 1pm.

A30

Burrow Hill Cider
Pass Vale Farm, Burrow Hill, Kingsbury Episcopi,
Tel: 01460 240782

Burrow Hill Cider is pressed from traditional cider apples (some of which are supplied by the Montgomerys at Manor Farm, North Cadbury). At Burrow Hill, they grow 40 different varieties of cider apples and have 150 acres of orchards from which to choose their fruit. The result is a vintage-quality cider that is the only cider to have won the Cider Championship Awards in Devon, Somerset and Herefordshire all in the same year.

**Gilcombe Farm Shop
& Somerset Organics, Bruton**

A must for its wonderful organic smoked dry-cured bacon. The shop
also stocks a wonderful range of organic products.

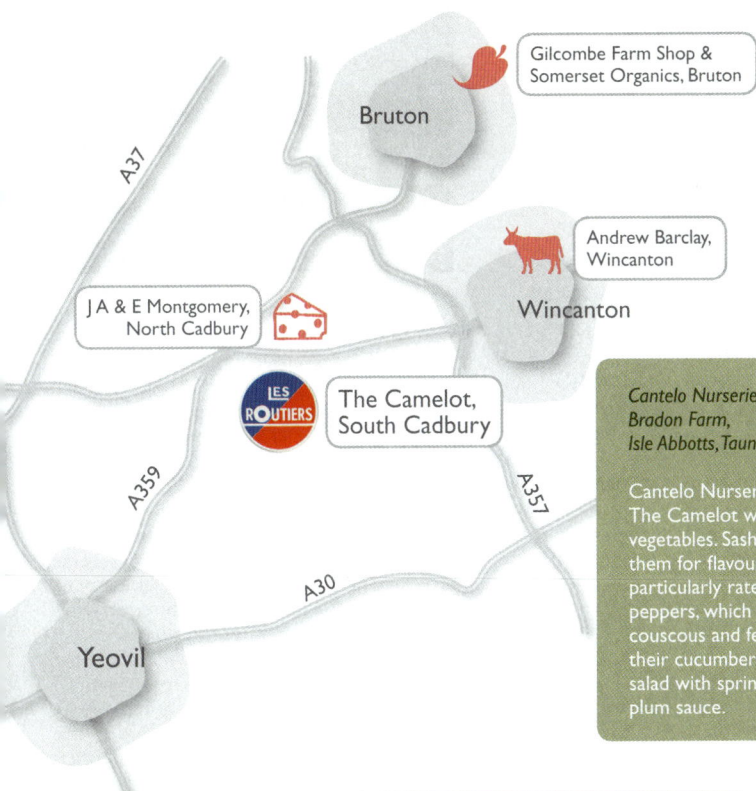

Gilcombe Farm Shop &
Somerset Organics, Bruton

Bruton

A37

Andrew Barclay,
Wincanton

Wincanton

J A & E Montgomery,
North Cadbury

LES
ROUTIERS

The Camelot,
South Cadbury

A359

A357

A30

Yeovil

**Cantelo Nurseries Ltd
Bradon Farm,
Isle Abbotts, Taunton**

Cantelo Nurseries supplies
The Camelot with organic
vegetables. Sasha chooses
them for flavour and
particularly rates their red
peppers, which he fills with
couscous and feta. He serves
their cucumbers in his duck
salad with spring onions and
plum sauce.

**J A & E Montgomery
Manor Farm, North Cadbury, Yeovil**

The Montgomerys have been farming in North and South Cadbury since
1911, and Jamie is the third generation of the family to continue this
great cheese-making skill and tradition. Jamie and his family also own The
Camelot, which is managed by his wife, Zizi, and her team. They produce
and supply award-winning Montgomery Cheddar (Supreme Champion,
British Cheese Awards, September 2004), Ogle Shield (Best English Cheese
at the same) and Montgomery Butter. Montgomery Cheddar and Ogle
Shield is made from the milk of the Montgomerys' own herd of cows
– Freisian milk for the cheddar and milk from the beautiful Jersey cows for
the Ogle Shield, which is a creamier, softer cheese.

Wells

Fountain Inn and Boxer's Restaurant

1 St Thomas Street, Wells, Somerset BA5 2UU
Telephone: +44(0)1749 672317
eat@fountaininn.co.uk
www.fountaininn.co.uk

Adrian and Sarah Lawrence's popular 16th-century pub was built to accommodate the builders working on Wells Cathedral. Today's guests come to sample pints of the local Butcombe Bitter and freshly prepared food in Boxer's Restaurant. The bar offers the main focal point on entry, along with a welcoming fire, but what hits you is the unpretentious nature of the place. Dark-wood furniture and a floral carpet happily clashing with the terracotta walls offer a no-nonsense bistro atmosphere, within a pub setting. This place is all about food, and there's a profusion of blackboards displaying the daily specials such as grilled sea bass with cumin-roasted vegetables. The printed menu cranks out a lengthy repertoire of familiar and more contemporary dishes: beef, ale and mushroom pie and ploughman's for lunch. Evening dishes take in mussels with garlic butter and parmesan and fillet steak with green peppercorn and brandy sauce. Portions are honest, robust, and prices reasonable.

Prices: Set lunch £9.75. Restaurant main course from £7.25. Bar main course from £3.50. House wine £9.95.
Last orders: Food: lunch 14.00 (Sunday 14.30); dinner 22.00 (Sunday 21.30).
Closed: Rarely.
Food: Modern British.
Real ale: Butcombe, Courage Best. Guest beer.
Other points: No-smoking area. Children welcome. Car park. Wheelchair access.
Directions: Exit J22/M5. In the city centre, 50 yards from the cathedral. Follow signs for the Horringtons. (Map 3, F1)

Wincanton

The Old Inn

Holton, Wincanton, Somerset BA9 8AR
Telephone: +44(0)1963 32002

Weary A303 travellers should look out for the Holton exit and head for this 17th-century former coaching inn for rest and refreshment - there's a lovely flower-filled terrace for summer sipping. It enjoys a peaceful village setting and is popular locally for good straightforward pub food, with produce sourced from local suppliers. The character beamed bar, dominated by a large stone fireplace with log-burning stove, boasts ancient flagstones, upholstered wooden settles, large refectory tables and a clutter of bric-a-brac. Sup a pint of local Butcombe Bitter or Otter Ale and tuck into a traditional bar meal, perhaps a ploughman's lunch with farmhouse cheddar cheese from Ditcheat, roast beef and horseradish sandwich, lasagne, or rump steak with all the trimmings. From the separate restaurant menu, perhaps choose lamb cutlets with rosemary, or peppered steak flamed in brandy and cream. A local butcher sources the meats from nearby farms.

Prices: Main course from £7.25. Bar meal from £6.25. House wine £8.25.
Last orders: Bar: lunch 14.00; dinner 22.00. Restaurant: lunch 14.00; dinner 22.00. Restaurant closed Sunday evening, bar meals available from 19.00.
Closed: Rarely.
Food: Traditional British.
Real ale: Butcombe Bitter, Wadworth 6X, Otter Ale.
Other points: No smoking in the restaurant. Garden. Car park. Dogs welcome in the bar. Wheelchair access to the restaurant/pub.
Directions: Off A303 2 miles south-west of Wincanton. (Map 2, E7)

Stafford

The Holly Bush ★

Salt, Stafford, Staffordshire ST18 0BX
Telephone: +44(0)1889 508234
geoff@hollybushinn.co.uk
www.hollybushinn.co.uk

The origins of this pretty thatched 14th-century pub are thought to reach back to 1190 - it is reputedly Staffordshire's oldest licensed premises. It maintains its historic charm throughout the cosy interior, with carved heavy beams, a planked ceiling, exposed brick walls, old oak furnishings, open fires and intimate alcoves characterising the main bar. Landlord Geoff Holland is passionate about using fresh local produce, and sources meat from W M Perry, an Eccleshall butcher with his own abbatoir, and game from local shoots. Among the good-value dishes on offer, you will find homemade soups or grilled black pudding on spinach with poached egg for starters, followed by grouse casserole, slow-cooked lamb and barley stew and steak-and-kidney pudding. Alternatives include monkfish with fennel, shallots and morels, and prime steaks, including a 20oz T-bone. Expect good lunchtime sandwiches and daily seafood specials. Round off with a traditional pudding or a selection of Staffordshire cheeses.

Prices: Main course from £6.95. House wine £7.25.
Last orders: Bar: lunch 14.30; dinner 23.00. Food: lunch 14.00 (all day Friday, Saturday and Sunday); dinner 21.30.
Closed: Rarely.
Food: Traditional and modern British.
Real ale: Adnams, Marston's Pedigree. Guest beer.
Other points: No-smoking area. Children welcome. Garden. Car park. Wheelchair access.
Directions: Exit J14/M6. Four miles along A51 Stone to Lichfield road, or half a mile from the A518 Stafford to Uttoxeter road. (Map 6, G5)

Market Drayton

Buttercross Farm Foods,
Market Drayton

Buttercross Farm Foods,
Market Drayton
Tel: 01630 656670

Fresh pork and pork products from free-range organic pigs reared at Packington Fields Farm near Lichfield are prepared and packaged at Buttercross Farm Foods. The pigs are reared to the highest of welfare standards to maximise flavour, taste and tenderness. Sample it in the form of baked pork fillet stuffed with sage, onion and apricots and wrapped in bacon at the Holly Bush.

Jolly Jersey Ice Cream,
Admaston, Stafford
Tel: 01889 881509

Natural ingredients and full-cream milk from Jersey cows grazed by the shores of Blithfield Reservoir are used to make the superb Jolly Jersey ice creams.

The Holly Bush

Thatched, and dating from the 14th-century, the attractive, flower-adorned pub is reputedly Staffordshire's oldest licensed premises and England's second oldest. Historic charm pervades the cosy interior – note the carved beams, planked ceiling and old oak furnishings. Landlord Geoff Holland is passionate about using fresh local produce, and interesting menus list local butcher meats, handmade sausages, venison from Cannock Chase, and homegrown herbs and vegetables. Don't miss the summer hog roasts and live jazz concerts.

Visit the local Farmers' Market

Head for the Market Square in Stafford on the second Saturday of the month to sample the atmosphere and produce of Stafford's farmers' market from 9am to 4pm.

Stone

Whitebridge Wines, Stone

Jolly Jersey Ice cream, Admaston

A34

A518

William Perry Butchers & Game Dealers, Eccleshall

LES ROUTIERS

The Holly Bush, Salt

A51

Stafford

A513

Parkside Bakery, Stafford

Cannock Chase

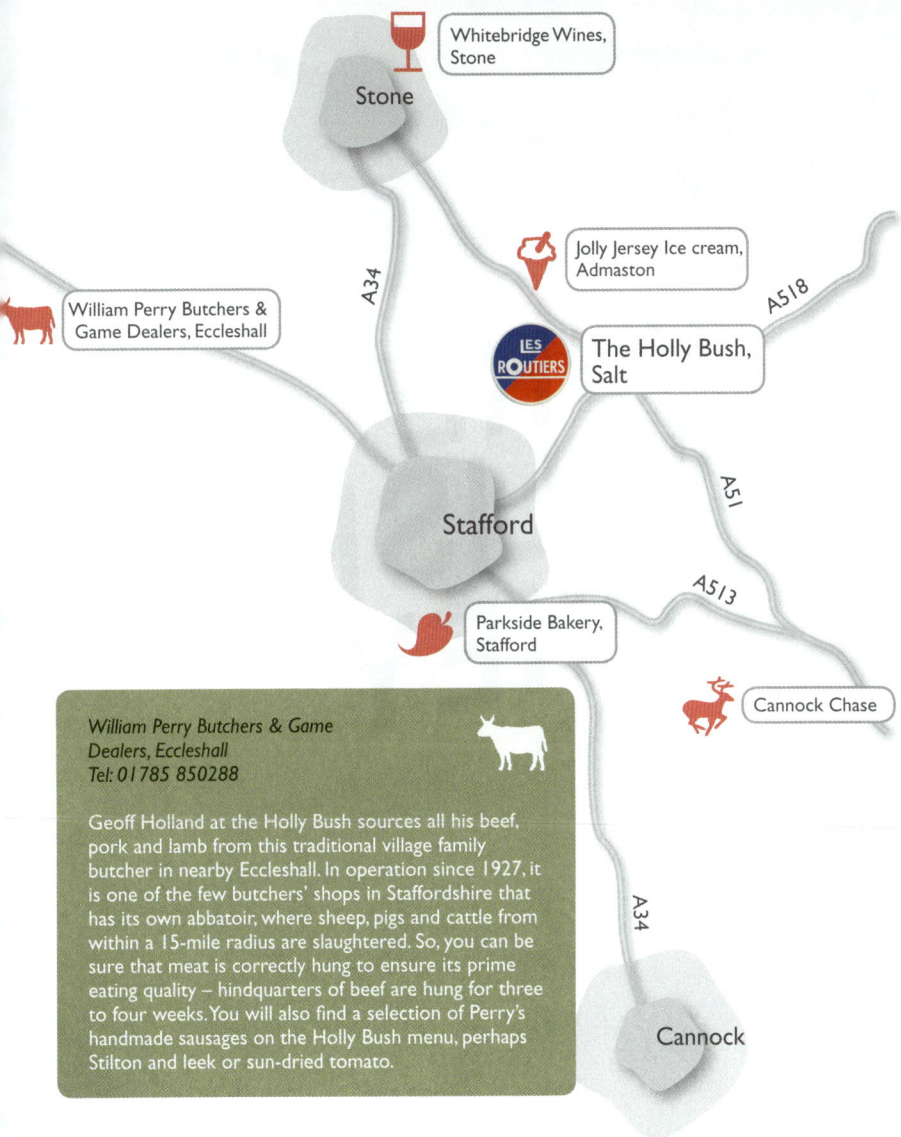

William Perry Butchers & Game Dealers, Eccleshall
Tel: 01785 850288

Geoff Holland at the Holly Bush sources all his beef, pork and lamb from this traditional village family butcher in nearby Eccleshall. In operation since 1927, it is one of the few butchers' shops in Staffordshire that has its own abbatoir, where sheep, pigs and cattle from within a 15-mile radius are slaughtered. So, you can be sure that meat is correctly hung to ensure its prime eating quality – hindquarters of beef are hung for three to four weeks. You will also find a selection of Perry's handmade sausages on the Holly Bush menu, perhaps Stilton and leek or sun-dried tomato.

A34

Cannock

Whitebridge Wines, Stone
Tel: 01785 817229

Established in 1983, Whitebridge Wines is an independent, family-owned wine merchant and is the Midlands' leading wine warehouse, with over 1,000 wines in stock. Wines on the short, reasonably priced list at the Holly Bush come from Whitebridge's warehouse a few miles up the A51.

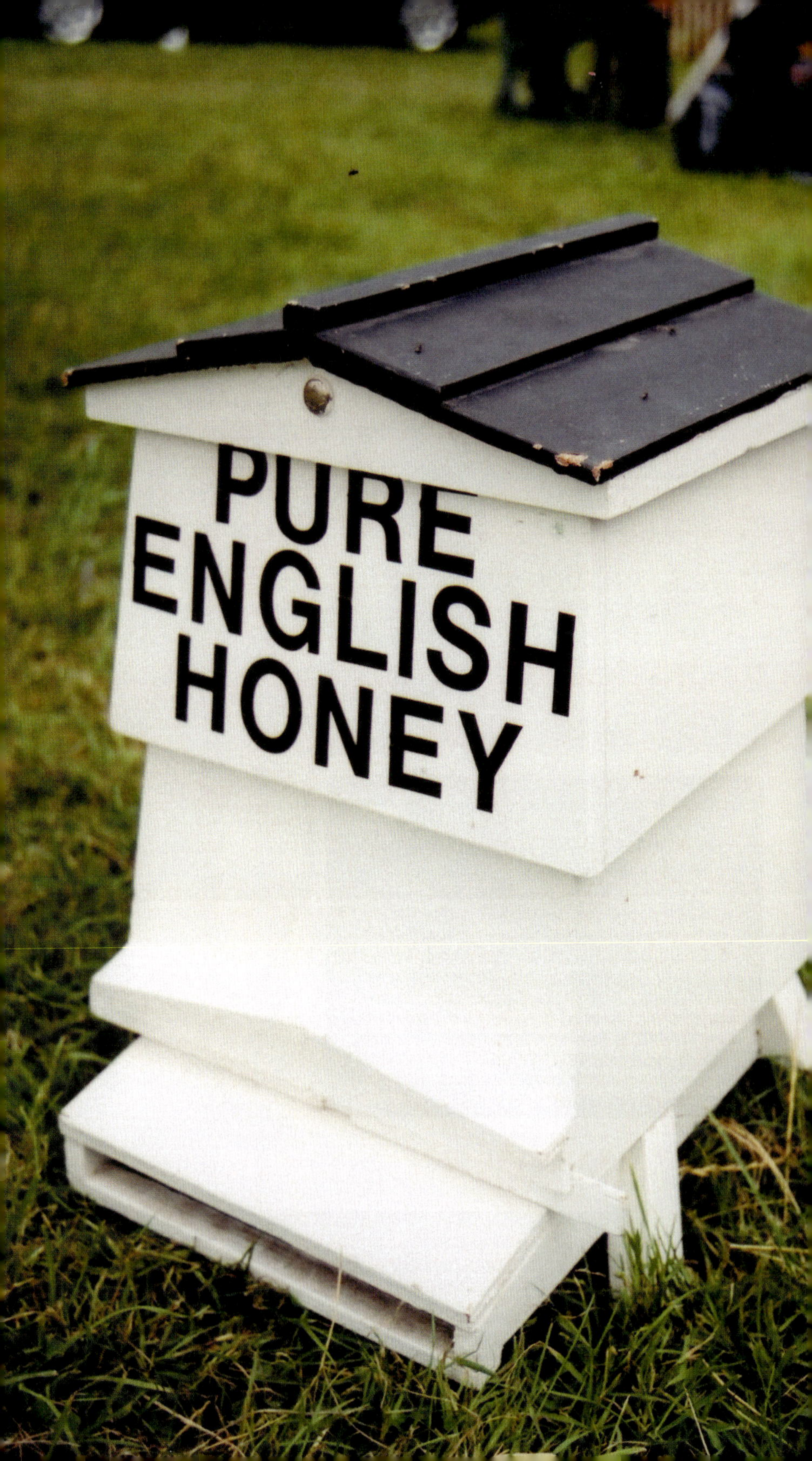
PURE
ENGLISH
HONEY

Barnby

The Swan Inn

Swan Lane, Barnby, Beccles, Suffolk NR34 7QF
Telephone: +44(0)1502 476646

This flower-adorned, pink-washed village local offers the most extensive menu of fish and seafood to be found in a Suffolk pub. The quality and freshness here is first class, thanks to pub owner and Lowestoft fish wholesaler, Don Cole, who supplies the pub with the best of the day's catch. Up to 80 different fish dishes are listed on the printed menu and ever-changing blackboards. From local sprats traditionally smoked in Don's smokehouse, and smoked haddock soup, the choice extends to lemon sole in crisp batter, and turbot fillet in prawn-and-brandy sauce. The house speciality, however, is an 18oz Dover sole, simply grilled. In addition, expect to find oysters, Cromer crabs, locally caught lobster, deep-fried fresh scampi and monkfish tails in hot garlic butter. All are accompanied with salad, new potatoes or chips and peas, and served throughout the traditional bar and restaurant. Booking is advisable. A self-contained flat is available on a nightly basis.

Rooms: 3. Rooms from £40 per person.
Prices: Set lunch £13 and dinner £18. Restaurant main course from £7.95. Bar main course £3.95.
Last orders: Bar: lunch 15.30; dinner 23.30. Food: lunch 14.00; dinner 21.30.
Closed: Rarely.
Food: Seafood.
Real ale: Adnams, Greene King Abbot Ale & IPA, Bass. Guest beer.
Other points: No-smoking area. Children welcome. Garden. Car park.
Directions: From the A146, turn into Barnby (left from the west) and follow signs to the inn. (Map 4, C7)

Brandeston

The Queen's Head Inn

The Street, Brandeston, Woodbridge, Suffolk IP13 7AD
Telephone: +44(0)1728 685307
stensethhome@aol.com
www.brandestonqueenshead.co.uk

What a difference two years make. The Stenseths have brought a smart, country look to this Adnams pub, first opened in 1811, and put good food squarely back on the menu. A complete revamp of the uninspired interiors has resulted in a warm and richly coloured decor that complements the traditional homely wood, log fire and settles setting. Suzanne Stenseth's modern menu buzzes with interest and changes weekly, depending on what's in season, with quality meat and fish all sourced locally. Start with Thai-style duck salad with chilli, lime and coriander dressing, then move onto superbly cooked fillets of sea bass or lamb cutlets, both of which come with inspired accompaniments. And Suzanne doesn't run out of steam there, as all the delicious puddings are homemade. Soups, curries and steaks are listed on the extensive daily specials board. The Queen's Head is slightly off the beaten track, but well worth the detour, especially for the lovely summer garden. See pub walk on page 248.

Prices: Restaurant main course from £7.95. House wine £9.50.
Last orders: Bar: lunch 15.00; dinner 23.00. Food: lunch 14.00; dinner 20.45 (Friday and Saturday 21.00).
Closed: Sunday evening.
Food: Modern British.
Real ale: Adnams.
Other points: No-smoking area. Children over 7 welcome. Dogs welcome in the bar. Garden. Car park.
Directions: Leave the A1120 at Earl Soham. The Queen's Head is in the centre of the village. (Map 4, C7)

Chiddingfold

The Swan Inn

Petworth Road, Chiddingfold, Guildford,
Surrey GU8 4TY
Telephone: +44(0)1428 682073
the-swan-inn@btconnect.com
www.theswaninn.biz

A hip hotel meets gastropub concept has breathed new life into this expertly reincarnated 14th-century inn, providing all the charm of the country with modern, chic Manhattan-style rooms and suites, all of which are superbly appointed. A drink in the welcoming bar is a pleasant precursor to a meal in the rustic-meets-contemporary open-plan bar area or the more formal restaurant. Chef Darren Tidd, formely of Cliveden Hotel, offers classic European dishes in the bar - calf's liver and bacon, moules, fishcakes, fresh sardines or a delectable duck confit. The carte may list poached haddock on a fricassée of broad beans, tomato, pancetta and mash, or roasted partridge with fondant potato and glazed figs. Desserts include homemade ice creams as well as classics such as crepes and crème brulée. The comprehensive wine list includes 15 house choices by the glass or bottle. There is a lovely terraced area for summer drinking.

Rooms: 10. Double room from £90, single from £70, family from £120.
Prices: Restaurant main course from £14.95. Bar main course from £9.95. House wine £9.95.
Last orders: Bar: lunch 15.00; dinner 23.00. Food: lunch 14.30; dinner 22.00 (all day at the weekend).
Closed: Accommodation closed 24 and 25 December.
Food: Traditional and Modern British and European.
Real ale: Hogs Back TEA. Guest beers.
Other points: No-smoking area. Children welcome. Dogs welcome in the bar. Garden. Car park.
Directions: The pub is in the village centre beside the A283 between Godalming and Petworth. (Map 3, F4)

Esher

The Albert Arms

82 High Street, Esher, Surrey KT10 9QS
Telephone: +44(0)1372 465290
enquiries@albertarms.com
www.albertarms.com

Nearest racecourse Sandown Park
Nearest golf course
Sandown Park Golf Centre, Esher

Must-sees
Hampton Court Palace
Brookland Museum (cars), Weybridge
Claremont Landscape Gardens, Esher
Kew Gardens
RHS Garden, Wisley
Museum of Rugby, Twickenham

Kew Gardens

Money has been lavished on this impressive, white-painted pub on the corner of Park Street and Esher's busy High Street. Swing open the doors and you are immediately hit by style, be it the sleek mahogany bar, the polished oak flooring, or the large plasma TV screen in the lively bar area. A mind-boggling range of drinks takes in 36 wines by the glass, six cask ales and a raft of spirits. If you're here to eat, you'll find the dining room decor and furnishings equally impressive. Vast menus offer an eclectic choice, from traditional favourites such as rack of lamb and Dover sole, to veal Milanese, fish stew, and fillet steak Rossini. There are good-value 'executive' lunch and set Sunday lunch menus. Style and flair extends to the five luxury bedrooms. Expect air-conditioning, tasteful furnishings, mini hi-fi system, 30-channel TV, internet access, and magnificent en suite 'wet-rooms'. Live weekend jazz and wine schools add to the appeal.

Rooms: 6. Double/twin from £100.
Prices: Set lunch £13. Restaurant main course from £10.50. Bar main course from £6. House wine £11.50.
Last orders: Bar: 23.00. Food: lunch 14.45; dinner: 21.45. (No food Sunday evening.)
Closed: 25-26 December, 1 January.
Food: Modern British with Italian influence.
Real ale: Young's Ales, Fuller's London Pride, Hogs Back TEA, Greene King IPA, Brakspear Ales, Spitfire, Bass.
Other points: Smoking throughout. Children welcome.
Directions: A3 junction A244. Follow the signs to Esher. As you come into the town the Albert Arms is in the middle of the High Street. (Map 4, F5)

Tourist information
Kingston-upon-Thames +44(0)20 8547 5592
Where to shop Kingston-upon-Thames, Richmond, Guildford, London
Farmers' market Wimbledon Park (Saturday am)
Events & festivals
Derby Festival (town & racecourse), Epsom (June)
Wisley Flower Show (June & August)
Hampton Court Palace Flower Show (July)
Open-Air Music & Theatre, Claremont Gardens, Esher (July)

Where to walk
Esher may be built-up and close to London, but there are some good walking opportunities close by. Stroll along the Thames Path between Kingston and Richmond, passing Ham House. Explore the waymarked trails around Richmond Park and enjoy good views across London. Head a few miles south to Dorking for glorious walks through the North Downs, in particular around Box Hill.

Farnham

The Pride of the Valley Hotel

Tilford Road, Churt, Farnham,
Surrey GU10 2LH
Telephone: +44(0)1428 605799
email@theprideofthevalley.co.uk
www.theprideofthevalley.com

This charming inn, dating back to 1868, is one of those places you always hope you'll come across as you wind your way down country lanes. A lovely country garden, cosy interiors and a good choice of food are just a few of its draws. Bedrooms are wonderfully spacious yet cosy, with all en suite rooms having different themes, from Moroccan to Far Eastern. The dining options are also extensive, with a wide choice of dishes, from steak-and-kidney pie, Thai green curry and paella to light bites and fish specials. You can eat in the bar, where comfy sofas, scrubbed pine tables and real fires create a warm, friendly ambience, or in the grand, baronial-style, oak-panelled restaurant. Candlelit at night, this is a very special place. There are also stunning walks from the inn - an excellent prelude to a delicious Sunday lunch and a pint of Hog's Back ale.

Rooms: 16. Double/twin from £115, single from £95, family from £125.
Prices: Restaurant main course from £12.95. Main course bar/snack from £4.95. House wine £12.95.
Last orders: Bar: 23.00. Food: lunch 14.30; dinner 21.00 (Friday to Sunday 21.30).
Closed: Never.
Food: Traditional British and Modern European.
Real ale: Hog's Back TEA, Fuller's London Pride.
Other points: No-smoking area. Garden.
Children welcome. Car park.
Directions: Exit 10/M25. Four miles from Farnham on the outskirts of Churt village; two miles from the A3. (Map 3, F4)

Godalming

The Inn on the Lake

Ockford Road, Godalming, Surrey GU7 1RH
Telephone: +44(0)1483 419997
www.theinnonthelake.co.uk

The second of Mitchell's and Butler's 'Orange' concept pubs to open in Surrey in spring 2005 stands in a cracking location beside a lake on the edge of Godalming. The successful formula that draws a well-heeled young clientele out to drink and dine in stylish surroundings has been replicated here. So, expect leather sofas, relaxing earthy colours on the walls, big chunky teak tables, and floor-to-ceiling windows overlooking a smart terrace and neat gardens. Food follows the much-loved 'Orange' style, a blend of modern British dishes with Italian pizzas, pastas and warm salads. 'Little dishes' take in sardines in garlic and tomato, shallot and goats' cheese tarte Tatin, 'leaves' offer crispy duck with watercress and plum sauce, while substantial mains range from Leffe battered haddock and spit chicken with aïoli to grilled lobster with lemon butter and chips. Much needed refurbishment of the 12 bedrooms was due to start in summer 2005.

Rooms: 16. Double/twin from £79.
Prices: Restaurant main course from £7.95.
House wine £12.
Last orders: Bar: 23.00. Food: lunch 14.30; dinner 21.30 (Sunday all day to 20.30).
Closed: Never.
Food: Modern British with Italian influences.
Other points: No-smoking area. Garden. Children over 12 welcome. Wheelchair access.
Directions: Exit 1/M25. Take the A30 towards Godalming, go through the town and the Inn on the Lake is directly ahead. (Map 3, F4)

Lingfield

The Hare & Hounds

Common Road, Lingfield, Surrey RH7 6BZ
Telephone: +44(0)1342 832351
hare.hounds@tiscali.co.uk

It might not dazzle from the outside, but this pub has reserved all its best features for inside. The old-fashioned, traditional look - old settles or Chesterfields strewn with plump cushions - is individualised by the slightly eccentric air created by a collection of old posters and art for sale. There's an ever-rolling, wide choice of exciting dishes to choose from, with specials chalked up on the giant board. Chef-proprietor Fergus Greer creates unusual and interesting dishes; Siberian ravioli filled with mince beef and pork with soured cream, caraway and tomato sauce, followed, perhaps, by rack of lamb with butternut squash and mushroom tarte Tatin and a spinach and caper salsa. Chocolate, orange and chilli panna cotta is a fitting way to finish. The wine list includes French classics at good prices. Fergus and his wife have created a convivial setting and certainly made their mark in the kitchen and brought personality to this pub.

Prices: Set lunch £18.95, set dinner £23.95. Restaurant main course from £11.50. Bar snack from £7.50. House wine £10.95.
Last orders: Bar: 23.00 (Sunday until 20.00). Food: lunch 14.30 (Sunday 15.30); dinner: 21.00 (Friday and Saturday 21.30). No food served Sunday evening.
Closed: Never.
Food: Modern European.
Real ale: Greene King, Flower's Original.
Other points: No-smoking area. Children welcome. Dogs welcome in the bar. Garden. Car park.
Directions: From the A22 follow the signs to Lingfield racecourse. (Map 4, F5)

Weybridge

The Minnow

104 Thames Street, Weybridge, Surrey KT13 8NG
Telephone: +44(0)1932 831672
www.theminnow.co.uk

The 'Orange' concept continues to roll south into the Home Counties - The Minnow in leafy Weybridge opened in March 2005. Location is paramount within the group and the Minnow is no exception. It stands smack beside the Thames and has a magnificent riverside terrace for summer drinking. Naturally, there's been no expense spared in refurbishing this old pub. Expect a tastefully reworked interior, with a series of rambling dining areas radiating out from a large central bar area filled with leather armchairs. Rustic beams and flagstones abound, walls are painted in simple muted colours, and good piped music and subtle lighting create a relaxing atmosphere. Equally impressive is the interesting, Italian-inspired menu, offering a decent range of salads, fresh baked pizzas, and more substantial main courses - try the calf's liver with onion jam, or the grilled lobster with lemon butter. There's Timothy Taylor, and a raft of wines by the glass.

Prices: Restaurant main course from £7.95. House wine £12.
Last orders: Bar: 23.00. Food: lunch 14.30; dinner 21.30 (Sunday all day to 20.30).
Closed: Never.
Food: Modern British with Italian influences.
Real ale: Timothy Taylor Best, Fuller's London Pride.
Other points: No-smoking area. Children over 12 welcome. Dogs welcome. Garden. Wheelchair access.
Directions: Exit J11/M25. Follow signs for Weybridge. At the monument in the high street, turn left for half a mile. (Map 3, F4)

Brighton

The Coach House Restaurant and Bar

59 Middle Street, Brighton,
East Sussex BN1 1AL
Telephone: +44(0)1273 719000
info@coachhousebrighton.com
www.coachhousebrighton.com

It's good to see a chain-free, original pub emerge and wow us in Brighton, as many fun cafés and bars have disappeared. The Coach House is approached through a pretty sun-trap courtyard garden, which is a lovely place to while away the time with a cool drink in the summer months, then it's into the bar area with its high glass roof and selection of plants hanging from the rafters. The wide choice of drinks extends to cocktails, bottled and draft beers, and seven wines are offered by the glass. The attractive adjoining restaurant has stone walls, plenty of character and a giant octagonal fire in the middle; to the front there are huge windows for people-watching. The cutting-edge menus are well priced and offer plenty of choice. At one end you have wraps, pastas and bangers and mash (Toulouse or vegetarian), or there are buttered tiger prawn starters, dolcelatte and herb salad or Thai mussels cooked with lemon grass, ginger and coconut cream. Steaks came in every shape and size, and other hearty meals take in lamb gigot and roasts on Sunday.

Prices: Restaurant main course from £8.95. Bar/snack from £5.75. House wine £10.95.
Last orders: Bar: 23.00. Food: lunch 17.00; dinner 22.00 (Sunday all day to 21.30).
Closed: Rarely.
Food: Modern British.
Other points: No-smoking area. Garden. Children welcome. Wheelchair access.
Directions: M23. Head towards the Brighton seafront and turn right at the pier into the Lanes. (Map 4, G5)

Lewes

The Rainbow Inn

Resting Oak Hill, Cooksbridge, Lewes,
East Sussex BN8 4SS
Telephone: +44(0)1273 400334

Built of brick and flint in the 17th century, the Rainbow makes the most of its attractive corner site, with a sun-trap enclosed rear terrace replete with barbecue and distant South Downs views. Inside, beyond the small rustic bar, where you'll find a cracking pint of local Harvey's ale, the warmly decorated dining areas sport an eclectic mix of tables and chairs and a relaxed and informal atmosphere. Fresh local produce is sourced for modern, daily changing menus and chalkboard specials, the latter listing fresh Newhaven fish, lamb from local farms and game in season. The printed menu may offer prawn and chicken ravioli with crispy leeks and saffron cream, followed by roast cod with parmesan crust with chervil butter sauce. Good puddings include bread-and-butter pudding to rhubarb crème brûlée. The short, carefully selected global list of wines complements the menu. Two upstairs private dining rooms are perfect for intimate dinner parties.

Prices: Set lunch £10.95 (two courses). Restaurant main course from £8.95. Bar main course from £3.95. House wine £11.50.
Last orders: Bar: lunch 15.00; dinner 23.00. Food: lunch 14.30; dinner 22.00.
Closed: Rarely.
Food: Modern European.
Real ale: Harvey's ales
Other points: No-smoking area. Garden. Children welcome. Car park. Private dining. Barbecue area.
Directions: Situated on the A275 between Lewes and Haywards Heath on the edge of Cooksbridge village at Barcombe Fork. (Map 4, G5)

Chichester

The Anglesey Arms at Halnaker

Stane Street, Halnaker, Chichester,
West Sussex PO18 ONQ
Telephone: +44(0)1243 773474
angleseyarms@aol.com
www.angleseyarms.co.uk

An unpretentious Georgian brick-built pub that has seen its reputation for quality food grow since Roger and Jools Jackson took over two years ago. Stripped pine, flagstones, beams and panelling, and crackling log fires draw walkers from the South Downs, Goodwood and Fontwell race-goers, and well-informed locals for pints of Adnams bitter and interesting menus that utilise topnotch local and organic produce. Come for mouth-watering Sunday roasts, lunchtime classics such as home-baked ham, free-range eggs and bubble-and-squeak, pasta meals and ploughman's, or book an evening table and tuck into one of their renowned 21-day hung steaks. Local fishermen supply the rope-grown mussels and the fish listed on the daily-changing blackboard. A hearty and robust alternative may include venison stew with polenta. Game comes from the Goodwood Estate and vegetables from the Organic Farm Shop in Chichester. The garden with petanque pitch, is the setting for the 'Moules and Boules' evenings in summer.

Prices: Restaurant main course from £9.95. Bar main course/snack from £4.95. House wine £11.
Last orders: Bar: lunch 15.00 (Saturday and Sunday 17.00); dinner 23.00. Food: lunch 14.30; dinner 21.30.
Closed: Rarely.
Food: Traditional British and Modern European.
Real ale: Deuchars IPA, Young's Bitter, Adnams Best.
Other points: No-smoking area. Dogs welcome in the bar. Garden. Car park. Wheelchair access (no WC).
Directions: On the A285 Chichester to Petworth road. (Map 3, G4)

Chichester

The Royal Oak

Pook Lane, East Lavant, Chichester, West Sussex PO18 0AX
Telephone: +44(0)1243 527434
nickroyaloak@aol.com
www.sussexlive.co.uk/royaloakinn

Where to walk
The South Downs Way runs east to west across the hills. Good walking along the coast near Selsey and Littlehampton and around Pagham and Chichester Harbours.

Must-sees
Weald and Downland Museum: fascinating collection of over 40 regional historic buildings.
Bignor Roman Villa
Parham House
Petworth House
Uppark House

Where to shop
Chichester
Midhurst
Petersfield
Arundel

Flint-built 200 years ago and accessed via a pretty raised terrace, this thriving gastropub-with-rooms comprises an open-plan bar and dining area with crackling log fires, leather sofas, fat cream candles on scrubbed tables, and Sussex ales tapped from the cask. Classy modern British food draws the discerning, the main menu and daily blackboard additions featuring quality fish and meats from London markets and vegetables from local organic farms. Typically, begin with crispy duck salad with honey, sesame, ginger and alfalfa, followed by lamb steak with rosemary mash, or whole skate with prosciutto and potato salad. Lunchtime brings sandwiches, home-cooked ham, eggs and bubble-and-squeak, and there are good homemade puddings - crisp lemon tart with raspberry sauce. Decent wines include some interesting French classics; 12 by the glass. Six stylish bedrooms feature pastel decor, smart, contemporary furnishings, high-spec CD players and flat-screen televisions, and quality tiled bathrooms with power showers.

Rooms: 6. Double/twin from £70.
Prices: Restaurant main course from £11.
House wine £9.95.
Last orders: Bar: 23.00. Food: lunch 14.30; dinner 21.30.
Closed: Rarely.
Food: Traditional English and Mediterranean.
Real ale: Badger Best, Ballards, Harvey's Sussex Bitter.
Other points: No smoking in the bedrooms. Garden and terrace. Car park. Wheelchair access to the restaurant/pub (no WC).
Directions: Village signposted off the A286 Midhurst road a mile north of Chichester. (Map 3, G4)

Tourist information Chichester +44(0)1243 775888
Nearest racecourse Goodwood
Nearest golf course Hunston

Best scenic drives
A286 north to Midhurst and Haslemere, diverting onto unclassified roads to visit Blackdown Hill. Return via B2131, B2070, B2146 and B2141. A27 to Arundel, A284 and A29 to Pulborough, then unclassified roads to Bignor and Sutton, East Dean and Charlton.

Events & festivals Chichester Festival (July)
Goodwood Revival Weekend (September)

Chichester

The Ship Inn

The Street, West Itchenor, Chichester,
West Sussex PO20 7AH
Telephone: +44(0)1243 512284

Built on the site of the original 18th-century inn, the exterior of this 1930s reincarnation belies its nicely nautical interiors and the excellent seafood to boot. Just 150 yards away from Chichester Harbour, it's decked out in ship decor; with old wood panelling with portholes, wonderfully scrubbed tables and a weather station. Apart from the appealing atmosphere - cosy fires in winter and a relaxed buzz in summer - the good local fish is the big draw. At lunch, you can simply have a filled baguette or melon with smoked salmon and prawns to start, with mains of beer-battered cod or steak-and-kidney pie. At dinner, dishes step up a gear to include large crevettes with garlic mayonnaise, followed by pot-roasted pheasant or lemon sole stuffed with salmon with a lobster sauce. Add in four locally brewed ales, decent wines, plus excellent walks and boat trips nearby, and this becomes a day-trip destination in itself. See pub walk on page 250.

Prices: Restaurant main course from £6.95. Bar snack from £4.75. House wine £11.
Last orders: Bar: 23.00. Food: lunch 14.30; dinner 21.15 (Sunday 21.00).
Closed: Afternoons of 25-26 December and 1 January.
Food: Traditional British and French.
Real ale: King Horsham Best Bitter, Itchen Valley Godfathers, Gales HSB, Ballards Best.
Other points: No-smoking area in restaurant. Dogs welcome in the bar. Patio. Car park. Wheelchair access. Separate function room.
Directions: Off the A286 six miles south of Chichester towards West Wittering. (Map 3, G4)

Midhurst

The Duke of Cumberland

Henley, Fernhurst, Midhurst,
West Sussex GU27 3HQ
Telephone: +44(0)1428 652280
gaston.duval@btopenworld.com

An unspoilt 15th-century pub, with rustic brick walls covered with roses and wisteria, hidden away in wooded hills with stunning views across the Weald. The tiny rustic bars exude atmosphere in spades, helped by painted, panelled walls, low-beamed ceilings, quarry-tiled floors, scrubbed pine tables and benches, and open fires. Relying on fresh produce, including organic beef from local farms, bar food combines both the modern and the traditional, the latter including ham, egg and chips and calf's liver and bacon with onion gravy. Alternatively, you may wish to order oak-smoked duck and orange salad and grey mullet on caper-scented mash with lemon beurre blanc. Specialities include grilled trout from the pub's own spring-fed pools and, given 24-hours' notice, traditional roasts are served as a joint at the table. In summer, order a pint of Adnams, drawn straight from the cask, and sup it on the brick terrace beside babbling streams.

Prices: Restaurant main course from £10.95. Bar main course from £6.95. House wine £12.50.
Last orders: Bar: 23.00. Food: lunch 14.30; dinner 21.30. No food Sunday and Monday evening.
Closed: Rarely.
Food: Traditional and modern pub food.
Real Ale: Adnams Broadside, Young's Best, Bombardier Premium Bitter, Wychwood Shires Bitter. 3 guest beers.
Other points: Smoking throughout. Children welcome. Dogs welcome in the bar. Gardens with ponds. Car park. Wheelchair access.
Directions: The village is signposted off the A286 north of Midhurst. (Map 3, F4)

Petworth

The Halfway Bridge Inn

Halfway Bridge, Petworth,
West Sussex GU28 9BP
Telephone: +44(0)1798 861281
hwb@thesussexpub.co.uk
www.thesussexpub.co.uk

Nick and Lisa Sutherland, owners of the hugely successful Royal Oak, Chichester (see entry), have worked their magic once again on this attractive old coaching inn. Although spruced up with style and panache, it's not a clone of the Oak, and you'll find a warren of charming little rooms decorated with a relaxed, contemporary feel. A272 travellers, local diners and the polo set are drawn here for first-class modern pub food, local ales, and decent wines. Snack in the bar on a poached-salmon open sandwich or smoked-chicken Caesar salad, or look to the chalk-board in the dining area for scallops with tomato salsa, steak-and-kidney pudding or fresh fish from Billingsgate Market. In a converted barn are six stunning en suite rooms. All have been given the Sutherland treatment - exposed beams and luxury bathrooms. A super Sussex base.

Rooms: 6. Double/twin from £90, single from £60. Family/Suite from £120.
Prices: Restaurant main course from £8.75. Bar main course from £4.95. House wine £11.50.
Last orders: Bar: 23.00. Food: Lunch 14.00; Dinner 21.30 (20.30 on Sundays).
Food: Modern British.
Real ale: Betty Stogs, Cheriton Pots, Harvey's Sussex.
Other points: No smoking in the restaurant. Children welcome. Dogs welcome in the bar. Garden. Car park. Wheelchair access (disabled bedroom suite).
Directions: On the A272 between Midhurst and Petworth. (Map 3, G4)

Poynings

Royal Oak

The Street, Poynings, West Sussex BN45 7AQ
Telephone: +44(0)1273 857389
mail@royaloakpoynings.biz
www.royaloakpoynings.biz

Set in a pretty village below the South Downs, a wonderful summer garden with barbecue facilities, serene rural views, and all-day food that utilises local produce are the major attractions at Paul Day's cream-painted pub. Add hop-adorned beams, roaring winter log fires and local Harvey's bitter on tap and you have a cracking country destination pub. Food successfully blends traditional favour-ites with more ambitious modern dishes, the extensive main menu being supported by an impressive specials board. Ingredients are carefully sourced - smoked fish arrives daily from the local smokery, beef and lamb are reared at Poynings Farm, sausages are handmade in neighbouring Henfield, and fruits and vegetables come from a farm within walking distance of the pub. So, expect oak-smoked duck with sweet mustard and honey dressing, lamb shank with mint cream and jus, and Sussex cheeses alongside steak-and-kidney pie, sausages and mash, filled jacket potatoes and a good range of sandwiches.

Prices: Restaurant main course from £8. Bar/snack from £5. House wine £12.
Last orders: Bar: 23.00. Food: 21.30.
Closed: Rarely.
Food: Traditional and Modern British.
Real Ale: Harvey Sussex Bitter.
Other points: Three no-smoking areas. Children welcome. Dogs on a lead welcome. Garden with barbecue facilities. Car park. Marquee available.
Directions: M23. From the A23, follow the A281 towards Henfield, then follow the signs to Poynings village. (Map 4, G5)

Shipley

The Countryman Inn

Countryman Lane, Shipley, Horsham,
West Sussex RH 13 8PZ
Telephone: +44(0)1403 741383
countrymaninn@btopenworld.com
www.countrymanshipley.co.uk

Just a 10-minute drive away from Horsham, the Countryman offers all you'd expect of a traditional, cosy inn tucked away down a country lane. The Vaughan family have run the pub for 16 years, and have maintained its old-fashioned charm - the impressive inglenook fireplace remains a centrepiece - while ensuring their menus have moved with the times. Alongside the good-value, hearty Countryman pies, casseroles, stews, fish and meat specials, you'll find Tuscan bean soup, moules Provençal, Malaysian chicken, and garlic monkfish. They source locally grown vegetables and meats for their menus. Add in calorie-bursting desserts, and you will never be stuck for choice or go home unsatisfied from this inn. They also serve a good range of ales and wines. You can eat informally in the comfortably seated bars or the main restaurant area, which can seat 50. This, too, has a log fire and beams, plus lovely views on to the gardens.

Prices: Set lunch £15 and dinner £22. Restaurant main course from £9.50. Bar main course from £4.50. House wine £11.95.
Last orders: Bar: Lunch 14.30; dinner 23.00. Food: lunch 14.30; dinner 21.30.
Closed: Rarely.
Food: Traditional British and Modern European.
Real ale: Horsham, Bass, Harvey's. Guest beer.
Other points: Garden.
Directions: One mile south of the A272. The pub is situated outside the village at the junction of Smithers Hill and Countryman Lane. (Map 4, G5)

Bidford-on-Avon

The Bridge

55 High Street, Bidford-on-Avon, Alcester,
Warwickshire B50 4BG
Telephone: +44(0)1789 773700

Patrick Marshall and Rosemary Willmott, a winning team of front-of-house and chef, respectively, have turned this old saddler's shop on the banks of the Avon into a stylish brasserie. Long windows look out to the ancient bridge and river. Inside, the decor is plain and simple. Upstairs there is a bar/lounge area with brick red walls, comfortable sofas and coffee tables. Firmly wedged into the brasserie tradition, the menus here draw on North European as well as Mediterranean traditions with starters including black and white pudding and char-grilled squid or chorizo and chick-pea salad. The menu is split into Char Grill and Stove & Oven sections. From the former is pork chop Dijonnaise with crackling, or there's confit of duck and crispy pork belly with cassoulet, or rack of lamb with onion sauce from the latter. Accompanying vegetables are unusual and creative. The short but effective dessert menu includes Nigella's chocolate mousse cake and a classic crème brûlée. The wine list has a majority of Old World wines.

Prices: Set lunch £20. Set dinner £25. Restaurant main course from £7.75. House wine £11.95.
Last orders: Food: lunch 14.30 (Sunday 15.30); dinner 21.30 (No food Sunday evening).
Closed: Sunday evening and 25 December.
Food: Modern British.
Other points: No-smoking area in the restaurant. Garden. Riverside. Children welcome. Car park. Wheelchair access.
Directions: Exit 15/M40. Follow signs to Stratford and Evesham. Approx six miles from Stratford. (Map 3, D2)

Stratford-upon-Avon

The One Elm

1 Guild St, Stratford-upon-Avon,
Warwickshire CB37 6QZ
Telephone: +44(0)1789 404919
theoneelm@peachpubs.com
www.peachpubs.com

In a prime town-centre location, a stroll from the river and theatre, the One Elm mirrors the chic, contemporary look and style of menus to be found at Peach Pubs flagship pub, the Rose and Crown in Warwick. Opening at 9am for coffee and breakfast sandwiches, there is an informal, almost Continental feel about the place, especially in the stylish front lounge area with its wood floor, bright painted walls and leather sofas. Beyond the central, open-to-view kitchen is the more formal dining area. From a deli chalkboard offering tapas-style starters or nibbles of charcuterie, cheese, fish and antipasti, both lunch and dinner menus list interesting modern pub food. Enjoy starter or main course size chicken Caesar salad or begin with Oriental broth with chilli, ginger and fish balls. Follow with honey-mustard pork hock with mash or 35-day dry-aged rump steak from the chargrill. Decent wines include eight by the glass.

Prices: Restaurant main course from £7.50. Bar main course from £1.35. House wine £10.50.
Last orders: Bar: 23.00.
Closed: Rarely.
Food: Modern European.
Real ale: Greene King IPA, Greene King Old Speckled Hen, Fuller's London Pride.
Other points: Children welcome. Dogs welcome. Garden. Car park. Wheelchair access (no WC).
Directions: Exit15/M40. The pub is situated in the town-centre. (Map 3, D3)

...for special offers

Warwick

The Rose and Crown

30 Market Place, Warwick,
Warwickshire CV34 4SH
Telephone: +44(0)1926 411117
roseandcrown@peachpubs.com
www.peachpubs.com

Warwick had little to offer discerning pub-going locals until the Peach Pub Company transformed this 18th-century pub in the Market Place. Now a favoured destination for food, attractions include inspired touches such as leather sofas bordering low-slung coffee tables displaying the day's newspapers, a policy of opening early to attract people throughout the day, and tables that are kept free of cutlery to encourage a mix of drinkers and diners. A deli plate chalkboard offers small tapas-style portions of cheeses, hams, salami, marinated anchovies and peppers and rustic breads. There is also a soup of the day and risotto of the week. Two printed menus offer a wide selection of options to suit the occasion and time of day, opening at 8am with breakfast sarnies, then offering shellfish linguine, confit belly pork with cider broth, and medallions of beef fillet with horseradish cream. Upstairs, five minimalist-style bedrooms are tastefully decorated.

Rooms: 5. Doubles/twins from £65.
Prices: Restaurant main course from £7.50. Bar main course from £6.50. House wine from £10.50.
Last orders: Bar: 23.00. Food: 22.00.
Closed: Rarely.
Food: Modern British.
Real ale: Fuller's London Pride, Timothy Taylor Landlord, Greene King Old Speckled Hen.
Other points: Children welcome. Dogs welcome. Garden and terrace. Parking opposite. Private dining available. Wheelchair access to the restaurant/pub.
Directions: Warwick town centre. (Map 3, C3)

Warwick

The Saxon Mill

Coventry Road, Guys Cliffe, Warwick,
Warwickshire CV34 5YN
Telephone: +44(0)1926 492255
www.saxonmill.co.uk

With unrivalled views across the River Avon and Guy's Cliffe from its decked terrace, this beautifully renovated old mill has been transformed into a stylish food venue by the hugely successful 'Orange' group of pubs. The modern, almost minimalist interior decor - wood or rushmat floors, simple muted colours, deep sofas and chunky wooden tables and chairs - works well with the original beams, open fires and bare brick walls. You will also find dressers laden with pasta jars and olive oils, and the trademark features of open-to-view kitchen, stone-fired ovens and the trendy, Italian-inspired menu. Typically, tuck into a 'little dish' of squid with coriander, chilli and salsa, or order one of the fired pizzas, or opt for something more substantial such as rib-eye steak with Café de Paris butter and fries.

Prices: Restaurant main course from £8.95. Main course bar from £5.50. House wine £11.95.
Last orders: Bar: 23.00. Food: lunch 14.30; dinner 21.30 (Sunday 20.30).
Closed: Rarely.
Food: Modern British with Italian influences.
Real ale: Bass, Brew XI.
Other points: No-smoking area in restaurant. Riverside seating. Children welcome. Dogs welcome in bar. Car park.
Directions: A46 to Leek Wootton roundabout. Do not go into Leek Wootton but continue round the roundabout to the A429 in the direction of Warwick. The pub is 400 yards on the left. (Map 3, C3)

Brinkworth

The Three Crowns

The Street, Brinkworth, Swindon,
Wiltshire SN15 5AF
Telephone: +44(0)1666 510366
www.threecrowns.co.uk

Close to the village church and green, Anthony and Allyson Windle's 200-year-old stone pub is a bustling dining destination. The traditional pubby bar features two remarkable tables created from huge 18th-century bellows and is the spot for lunchtime snacks, namely enormous ploughman's lunches and filled double-decker rolls. A comprehensive list of main courses is displayed on a huge blackboard that dominates one wall of the pine-furnished conservatory dining extension. Few people leave dissatisfied: portions are not for the faint-hearted, and food quality is well above average. The ambitious dishes make good use of local produce, including locally farmed veal and free-range poultry. Typically, tuck into homemade steak-and-kidney pie, rack of lamb, or crocodile served Thai style. Round off with a sticky toffee pudding or a plate of cheese from an impressive cheeseboard selection.

Prices: Main course from £14.95. Bar/snack £6.95. House wine from £12.95.
Last orders: Bar: lunch 15.00 (Saturday 16.00, Sunday 17.00); dinner 23.00 (Sunday 22.30). Food: lunch 14.00; dinner 21.30.
Closed: Rarely.
Food: Modern British and Traditional French.
Real ale: Archers Best, Greene King IPA, Castle Eden, Fuller's London Pride, Wadworth 6X. Guest beer.
Other points: No smoking in the restaurant. Children welcome. Dogs welcome in the bar. Garden. Car park. Wheelchair access.
Directions: Exit 16/M4. A3102 towards Wootton Bassett, then follow B4042 Malmesbury road. (Map 3, E2)

Norton

The Vine Tree

Foxley Road, Norton, Malmesbury,
Wiltshire SN16 0JP
Telephone: +44(0)1666 837654
info@thevinetree.co.uk
www.thevinetree.co.uk

This 18th-century mill is set in unspoilt Wiltshire countryside, has a tranquil suntrap terrace and a reputation for innovative modern pub food. Equally, it is popular with local drinkers in search of a decent pint or one of 20 wines by the glass. The smart, part stone-flagged interior is furnished in attractive pine, and open fires and evening candlelight enhance the relaxing ambience. Eclectic menus draw on global influences, although fish from Cornwall and local game in season are specialities, and they use organic produce. Starters and light meals may include chicken liver parfait with onion confit. For something more substantial, there may be venison-and-juniper pie, or fishy specials such as chargrilled tuna with olive and red pepper tapenade, with pink champagne and wild strawberry jelly for pudding. Popular summer barbecues.

Prices: Main course from £9.95. Snack from £5.75. Sunday lunch from £9.50. House wine £10.75.
Last orders: Bar: lunch 15.00; dinner 23.00. Food: Lunch 14.30 (Saturday and Sunday 15.00); dinner 21.30 (Saturday and Sunday 22.00).
Closed: Never.
Food: Traditional and modern British & Mediterranean.
Real ale: Tiger Beer, Fuller's London Pride, Young's Bitter, Fiddlers Elbow, Tribute, Butcombe Bitter.
Other points: No-smoking area. Children welcome. Dogs welcome. Play area. 2-acre garden and terrace. Car park. Wheelchair access (no WC).
Directions: Exit 17/M4. Take A429 towards Cirencester, then the left turn signed Grittleton to Norton, then right to Foxley; bear right over ford to pub. (Map 3, E2)

Swindon

The Sun Inn

The Street, Lydiard Millicent, Swindon,
Wiltshire SN5 3LU
Telephone: +44(0)1793 770425
thesuninnlm@yahoo.co.uk
www.cotswoldinns.co.uk

Close to the hustle and bustle of Swindon, the late 18th-century Sun Inn lies tucked away in a pretty conservation village. The refurbished interior sports tiled and wooden floors, open fires and exposed timbers, and retains much of the building's original charm and character. Food is freshly prepared from local produce, with meat supplied by Harts' specialist butchers in Cricklade, smoked fish from Severn and Wye Smokery, and first-class vegetables from Mise en Place in Cirencester. Well-presented lunch dishes may include warm ciabatta, pasta with tomato and chorizo, and liver and bacon with mash and onion gravy. Evening additions and daily dishes may feature lime-and-chilli seasoned squid, hake with wild mushroom risotto, roast pork tenderloin stuffed with apricots, wrapped in bacon and served with a cider jus, and deep-fried cod stuffed with pesto butter. There is a short global list of wines, with eight offered by the glass.

Prices: Restaurant main course from £8.95. Lunch menu from £4.50. Bar snacks from £2.50. Wine list from £9.95.
Last orders: Bar: lunch 15.00; dinner 23.00 (all day Sunday during the summer). Food: lunch 14.30 (Sunday 15.00); dinner 21.30 (Sunday 21.00).
Closed: Rarely.
Food: Traditional and modern British and European.
Real ale: Wadworth 6X, Flowers Original, guest beers.
Other points: No-smoking area. Children welcome. Garden. Car park. Wheelchair access.
Directions: Exit J16/M4. The pub is in the village centre three miles to the west of Swindon. (Map 3, E2)

The Fountain Inn

Purchased by Russell Allen and his family in 1999, a series of developments have seen an ageing alehouse transformed into an award-winning establishment. With awards for food, beer and service, the Four Diamond-rated, silver star award 11 en-suite bedroom hotel is The Fountain's newest addition. The use of fresh local produce is the key to the quality menu, which earned The Fountain the title of British Food Pub of the Year.

Visit the local Farmers' Market

The post office car park in Tenbury Wells is the location for the town's monthly farmers' market on the fourth Saturday of the month from 9am to 2pm.

Ludlow

A456

A49

Leominster

A417

Bowkett Butchers
Market Square, Tenbury Wells
Tel: 01584 810351

Roger Bowkett and his dedicated team of butchers are renowned throughout the area for their quality. Situated within the GH Bowkett supermarket in Tenbury, the butchery counter supplies The Fountain with all of its fresh meat, including the incomparable Herefordshire beef. A trip to the area can be considered incomplete without taking some of Bowketts' produce home to remind you of the visit!.

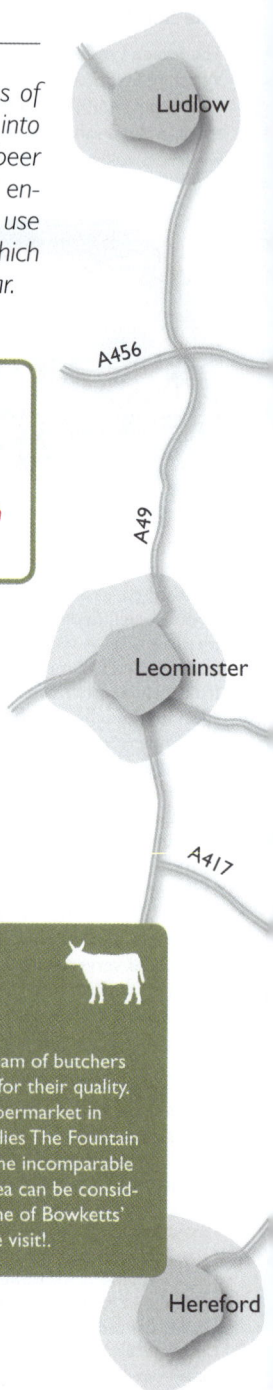

Hereford

Birmingham Market

Birmingham Market
50 Edgbaston Street
Tel: 0121 622 0200
www.bullring.co.uk

Part of the first phase of the
£400-million redevelopment of the
Bullring, this vast indoor market
houses almost 100 traders. It's
foodie heaven, and more than half
the stalls sell food fresh produce
such as fish, seafood, poultry, meat
and game, and the remainder offer
fruit and vegetables, deli fare and
Caribbean foods. You will find
plenty of bargains and choice. In
addition, there are clothes, haber-
dashery, florists, hairdressers and
cafés. There's ample parking too.

The Fountain Inn,
Tenbury Wells

Tenbury Wells

Bowkett Butchers,
Tenbury Wells

Fish from the River Tay
Scotland

Although not strictly local to The Fountain, some of the country's
finest available fish finds its way there, courtesy of owner Russell
Allen's father, Doug. A keen fisherman, he fishes the Tay and some
of Scotland's other salmon and trout rivers regularly and his
catches are some of The Fountain's best-selling dishes.

A44

Worcester

A465

Wye Valley Brewery,
Stoke Lacey

Wye Valley Brewery
Stoke Lacey
Tel: 01885 490505

Wye Valley is the leading cask ale brewery in the
county. Get together a group of 10 or more interested beer fans and you can take a guided tour of
the brewery, where you can see the ale selection being made. The latest addition to the line-up is Butty
Bach, a burnished gold full-bodied ale. Its popular
Dorothy Goodbody selection includes ales for every
season, plus a wholesome stout. You can order its
drinks memorabilia from its online shop at www.
wyevalleybrewery.co.uk

Tenbury Wells

The Fountain Inn 🛏️🍺★

Oldwood, St Michael's, Tenbury Wells,
Worcestershire WR15 8TB
Telephone: +44 (0)1584 810701
enquiries@fountain-hotel.co.uk
www.fountain-hotel.co.uk

There aren't many pubs, if any, in Britain that can boast of having a 1,000-gallon aquarium complete with a leopard shark in the bar, but then the Fountain Inn is no ordinary pub. The real draws in this striking, black-and-white 17th-century inn are the smart wood-beamed bar and the nautically styled restaurant serving fresh food using quality local ingredients. Seafood is, of course, big business, with fish bought direct from Birmingham market, but other produce is sourced more locally. Chef Paul Smith also has the pick of the pub's organic herb and vegetable garden. Diners come from miles around to see the shark and tuck into homemade soup, garlic mushrooms or terrine of the day, or mains of steak-and-ale pie, lamb Wellington and fine Herefordshire steaks, as well as the many fish options. There are smart en suite rooms, and The Oldwood Suite is ideal for wedding functions. Beer lovers will appreciate the award-winning Fountain Ale.

Rooms: 11. Double/twin room from £49.95.
Disabled suite available.
Prices: Main course from £6.95. Sunday lunch £9.95.
House wine £9.95.
Last orders: Bar: 23.00. Food: 21.00.
Closed: Never.
Food: Traditional British with Continental influences.
Real ale: Fountain Ale, Wye Valley Bitter & Butty Bach, guest beers.
Other points: No smoking in the restaurant. Children welcome. Garden. Car park. Wheelchair access.
Directions: Exit J5/M5. One mile from Tenbury Wells on the A4112 Leominster road. (Map 2, B7)

Tenbury Wells

The Peacock Inn 🛏️

Worcester Road, Tenbury Wells,
Worcestershire WR15 8LL
Telephone: +44(0)1584 810506
thepeacockinn001@aol.com
www.thepeacockinn.com

New owner Robert Cheadle has spruced up the Peacock, a rambling, ivy-clad 14th-century inn on the Shropshire border with views across the River Teme. The charming interior comprises of several low-beamed and comfortably furnished rooms, notably the oak-panelled lounge with its blazing log fire, hop-strewn black beams and relaxing dining atmosphere. Quaff local Hobson's Best in the lively locals bar, and tuck into fresh pasta dishes and good homemade pizzas from a bistro-style menu in the high-vaulted rear dining room. In the lounge bar, the modern menu highlights local produce, notably excellent fish fresh from Birmingham market and local game. Choose, perhaps, sea bass with scallops and beurre blanc, or freshly battered cod and chips. Alternatively, start with fresh oysters or goats' cheese and red onion tart with onion confit, then follow with duck breast with green-peppercorn sauce. Beams abound in the six en suite bedrooms; two have hand-crafted oak four-poster beds.

Rooms: 6. Double/twin from £75, single from £55..
Prices: Restaurant main course from £7.95. Bar/snack from £3.50. House wine £12.75.
Last orders: Bar: lunch 15.00; dinner 24.00. Food: lunch 14.15; dinner 21.00.
Closed: Rarely.
Food: Traditional British.
Real ale: Tetley, Hobson's Best, Wells Bombardier.
Other points: No-smoking area. Children welcome. Dogs welcome in the bar. Garden. Car park.
Directions: Exit 3/M5. On the A456 one mile before Tenbury Wells. (Map 2, B7)

Bedale

The Buck Inn

Thornton Watlass, Bedale, Ripon,
North Yorkshire HG4 4AH
Telephone: +44(0)1677 422461

Next to the village green cricket pitch in a beautiful Bedale village, this is a traditional, well-run, friendly institution that has been in the experienced hands of Michael and Margaret Fox for nearly 20 years. The lounge, with upholstered wall benches, several mounted fox masks and a fine mahogany bar counter is comfortably old-fashioned; adjacent to it is the dining room which overlooks the sheltered rear garden. At lunchtime, good-value dishes range from Masham rarebit (Wensleydale cheese with local ale topped with bacon) to steak-and-kidney pie. Using locally sourced produce, equally traditional evening additions may include goat's cheese-and-tomato tartlet to start, followed by baked cod with avocado pear and tiger prawns, or the generous Buck mixed grill. At the bar you'll find local ales on tap, and an impressive selection of malt whiskies. Cottagey bedrooms provide a comfortable night's sleep.

Rooms: 7, 2 with shared bathrooms. Double from £70, single from £50, family from £85.
Prices: Sunday set lunch £12.50. Restaurant main course from £9.50. House wine £9.95.
Last orders: Bar: 23.00. Food: lunch 14.00; dinner 21.15.
Closed: Rarely.
Food: Traditional British.
Real ale: Black Sheep, Theakston Best, John Smith's.
Other points: No smoking in the restaurant. Children welcome. Dogs allowed in bedrooms, not in bar. Garden. Car park.
Directions: From Bedale, follow the B6268 towards Masham. Turn right after two miles. (Map 6, D5)

Burnsall

The Red Lion Hotel

By the Bridge, Burnsall, Skipton,
North Yorkshire BD23 6BU
Telephone: +44(0)1756 720204
info@redlion.co.uk
www.redlion.co.uk

Traditional charm and hospitality abound at this stone-built 16th-century inn, which stands beside an ancient bridge in this pretty Dales village. Cosy and rambling, with lovely gardens running down to the River Wharfe, and stylish en suite bedrooms, it has long been a favoured base for exploring the Dales. In the rustic, stone-flagged bar, with its roaring fires, relaxing sofas and hand-pulled pints of Theakston ale, you can tuck into some hearty home-cooked food. Local ingredients play a big part on seasonal menus, for example, daily specials of Wharfedale lamb stew, roast grouse, and locally smoked haddock with egg, spinach and hollandaise. Light lunch options include decent sandwiches and salad Niçoise, while dinner in the restaurant could feature Whitby crab and avocado, followed by steak-and-kidney pudding, with chocolate bread-and-butter pudding to finish.

Rooms: 15 and 3 Cottages by the river. Double/twin from £60, single from £60.
Prices: Set lunch and dinner £29.95. Restaurant main course from £12.50. Bar main course from £3.95. House wine £12.50.
Last orders: Bar: 23.00. Food: Lunch 14.30, Dinner 21.30.
Closed: Rarely.
Food: Modern British.
Real ale: Theakston Ales, Timothy Taylor Ales.
Other points: No-smoking areas. Children welcome. Dogs welcome. Garden. Car park. Licence for civil weddings. Wheelchair access in the restaurant.
Directions: A65. From Leeds to Ilkley, turning towards Bolton Abbey just through the town. (Map 6, E5)

Fadmoor

The Plough Inn

Main Street, Fadmoor, Kirkbymoorside,
North Yorkshire YO62 7HY
Telephone: +44(0)1751 431515

Overlooking the green of this tranquil village high up on the edge of the North Yorkshire Moors, this stylishly refurbished old stone pub enjoys views across the Vale of Pickering. First and foremost, the Plough is a great local and walkers' pub, serving a splendid pint of Black Sheep Bitter in its snug little bar replete with black-tiled floor, simple wall benches and wood-burning old range. However, imaginative pub food is drawing discerning local diners to this moorland oasis. Neil Nicholson sources meat from local farms and butchers, fresh vegetables from Kirkbymoorside, and fish is delivered direct from Hartlepool. Dinner may begin with chicken-liver paté with fruit chutney, then follow with beef Wellington with Madeira sauce, or an excellent fishy option such as basil and parmesan crusted cod with tomato, garlic and white wine sauce. Finish with chocolate-and-orange terrine with mango-and-papaya sorbet. There are good-value two-course lunch and Early Bird menus.

Prices: Set lunch £12.95 (two courses). Set early-bird dinner £14.50. Main course from £9.50. House wine from £11.95.
Last orders: Bar: lunch 14.30; dinner 23.00. Food: lunch 13.45; dinner 20.45.
Closed: Rarely.
Food: Traditional and modern pub food.
Real ale: Black Sheep Best, Tetley's Cask. Guest beer.
Other points: No-smoking area. Children welcome. Garden. Car park.
Directions: Head north from Kirkbymoorside (off the A170), turn left and fork left to Fadmoor. (Map 6, D6)

Great Ouseburn

The Crown ★

Great Ouseburn, York,
North Yorkshire YO26 9RF
Telephone: +44(0)1423 330430

Expect high standards of service and quality food at this classic Yorkshire pub, which stands in a picturesque village close to the A1. Traditional it may be in appearance, being chock-full of character and interesting memorabilia, including that of the Tiller Girls dancing troupe who began their careers here, but the food is decidedly up-to-date with imaginative modern British dishes featuring on a variety of menus. From the extensive dining-room carte you may begin with baked queen scallops with leeks, smoked bacon and mozzarella, before moving on to a memorable 'Moby Dick' fresh haddock in crisp beer batter, or roast duck with plum and ginger sauce. In the bar, opt for chargrilled British steaks or the Crown's legendary steak, ale and mushroom pie. Leave room for caramelised fig tarte Tatin with caramel sauce. Good vegetarian options, set-price monthly menus, and decent Sunday lunches, and a well-annotated wine list.

Prices: Brasserie two-course set menu £12. Main course from £11. Bar main course from £6.50. House wine from £9.80.
Last orders: Food: 21.30 (Sunday 21.00). No food Monday-Friday lunchtime.
Closed: Rarely.
Food: Modern British.
Real ale: Black Sheep Best, Hambleton Best Bitter.
Other points: No-smoking area. Children welcome. Garden. Car park.
Directions: Exit J48/A1. Great Ouseburn is off the B6265, midway between Boroughbridge and Green Hammerton. (Map 6, D6)

Harome

The Star Inn

High Steet, Harome, Helmsley, North Yorkshire YO62 5JE
Telephone: +44(0)1439 770397
www.thestaratharome.co.uk

Must-sees

Castle Howard, Malton: a magnificent 18th-century
domed palace enjoying a dramatic setting of lakes,
fountains and extensive gardens.

Nunnington Hall

Rievaulx Abbey: Beautiful and well preserved ruins of
a Cistercian abbey founded in 1131 and set in the
peaceful Rye Valley.

Helmsley: Lively small market town with ruined
12th-century castle and Duncombe Park.

Ryedale Folk Museum, Hutton-le-Hole

North Yorkshire Moors Railway, Pickering

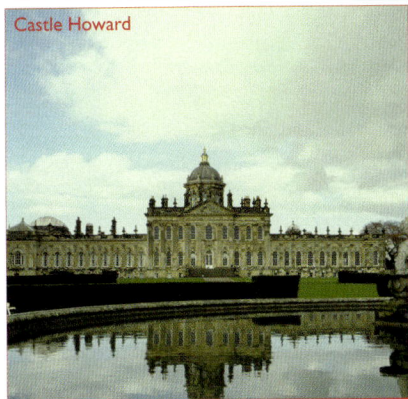

Castle Howard

The Star shines like a beacon well beyond Yorkshire since Andrew and Jacqui Pern transformed it from a neglected village local into one of the finest inns in Britain. The original 14th-century thatched building has low-beamed ceilings, wonky walls, hand-carved oak furniture, and a winter log fire in a very civilised bar. Booking is essential in the separate, beautifully decorated dining room. Andrew's culinary talent delivers outstanding pub food, and his kitchen also provides top-class goodies to their food shop-cum-deli across the lane. The cooking makes full use of homegrown herbs and seasonal produce comes from a select network of local suppliers. Weekly-changing menus, enhanced by daily specials, may list pressed oxtail terrine with Yorkshire pudding and onion gravy for starters, followed by lobster, monkfish and scallop pie, or pot-roast pigeon with bubble-and-squeak rösti and smoked-bacon gravy, with banana bread-and-butter pudding or a plate of local cheeses to finish. Accommodation is absolutely first-class.

Rooms: 11. Double/twin room from £90.

Prices: Set lunch £20 and dinner £30. Main course from £14. House wine £11.95.

Last orders: Bar: 23.00. Food: lunch 14.00; dinner 21.30; Sunday lunch 18.00.

Closed: Monday.

Food: Modern British.

Real ale: Black Sheep Best, John Smith's Cask, Theakston, Cropton Brewery. 2 guest beers.

Other points: No-smoking area. Children welcome. No dogs. Garden. Car park.

Directions: Harome is two and a half miles south-east off the A170 between Helmsley and Kirkbymoorside. (Map 6, D6)

Tourist information Pickering +44(0)1751 473791

Where to walk

For well waymarked and fairly easy circular walks head for Rievaulx Abbey, Sutton Bank, Farndale, Levisham, Rosedale Abbey and Lastingham. OS Map: Explorer OL26 & 27. For more adventurous walking undertake sections of the Cleveland Way and Lyke Wake Walk.

Events & festivals
Jorvik Viking Festival, York (Feb)
Festival of Food & Drink, York (September)

Farmers' market Cleveland Way, York
Where to shop Helmsley, Easingwold, Malton, York

The Friar's Head at Akebar

Created from old workers' cottages 15 years ago, the Friars Head stands at the heart of Akebar Park, a popular leisure facility that includes a caravan park and an 18-hole golf course. Certainly no clubhouse, the character-bar sports roaring log fires, old stone and heavy timbers, and there's a cracking conservatory dining room, festooned with vines and plants. Expect modern pub food and an emphasis on fresh local produce, not basic pub grub. Changing menus list quality meats from a local butcher and game from Constable Burton Hall across the road. Lovely views and great local walks.

Wensleydale Dairy Products
Hawes
Tel: 01969 667664

Despite a turbulent history, which saw the dairy nearly close in the 1930s, before it was rescued by passionate workers who still run the business, Wensleydale Dairy is still heralded as the official maker of real Wensleydale cheese. At Hawes they produce the mild, slightly 'fresh' white cheese and the ripe blue version, which takes six months to mature and has a smooth, creamy texture similar to Stilton but with a mellower flavour. Why not take a tour of the creamery and museum and then sample the cheese in the cheese shop. You will also find it at the Friar's Head where you can wash a wedge down with a pint of first-class Black Sheep Bitter.

JB Cockburn & Sons
Bedale
Tel: 01677 422126

For 40 years this family butcher has offered Bedale folk locally sourced meats from its shop in the town's Market Place. Beef comes from its own herd of pedigree Highlands, organic lamb is sourced from the Dales and locally shot game - including woodcock, teal and snipe - is dressed on the premises. While respectful of tradition, the shop now has a popular deli section offering ready-prepared dishes, all cooked by Jonathan Cockburn, who trained as a chef before joining the family business. Cockburn's supplies the Friar's Head with game, venison and lamb.

Wensleydale Dairy Products, Hawes

The Friar's Head at Akebar

Dents Farm Dairy, West Burton

B6160

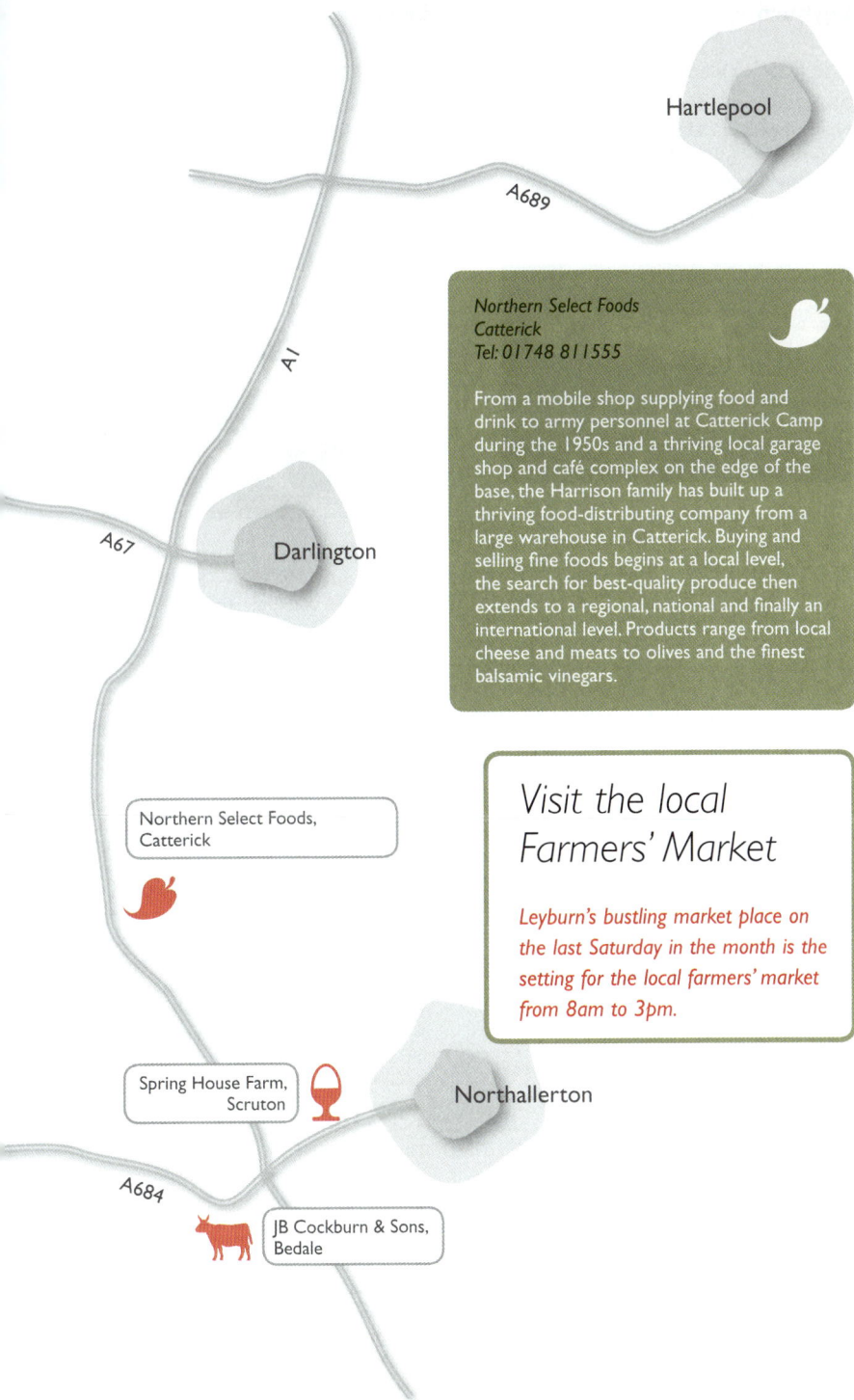

...for special offers

Hartlepool

A689

A1

A67

Darlington

Northern Select Foods
Catterick
Tel: 01748 811555

From a mobile shop supplying food and drink to army personnel at Catterick Camp during the 1950s and a thriving local garage shop and café complex on the edge of the base, the Harrison family has built up a thriving food-distributing company from a large warehouse in Catterick. Buying and selling fine foods begins at a local level, the search for best-quality produce then extends to a regional, national and finally an international level. Products range from local cheese and meats to olives and the finest balsamic vinegars.

Northern Select Foods, Catterick

Visit the local Farmers' Market

Leyburn's bustling market place on the last Saturday in the month is the setting for the local farmers' market from 8am to 3pm.

Spring House Farm, Scruton

Northallerton

A684

JB Cockburn & Sons, Bedale

Leyburn

The Friar's Head at Akebar

Akebar Park, Wensleydale, Leyburn,
North Yorkshire DL8 5LY
Telephone: +44(0)1677 450201/450591
info@akebarpark.com
www.akebarpark.com

Akebar Park is the vision of Joyce and Colin Ellwood who have transformed their historic farm into a popular leisure facility, namely an 18-hole golf course, a caravan park and the Friar's Head, a fascinating country pub created from old farm workers' cottages. Roaring log fires warm the character bar, where old stone and heavy timbers have been used to great effect in creating a traditional and very cosy pub atmosphere. The superb conservatory-style garden room is festooned with magnificent vines and plants and enjoys great country views. Here you can sit at massive, candlelit, stone tables and tuck into some good modern pub food. Meat is sourced from local family butchers and local shoots provide the seasonal game. Typically, begin with cheese-and-spinach soufflé, and move on to braised lamb with minted redcurrant and port sauce. Round off with warm chocolate caramel rice pudding. Yorkshire beer, decent wines and invigorating local walks.

Prices: Restaurant main course from £8. Bar main course from £7. House wine £9.95.
Last orders: Food: lunch 14.00; dinner 21.30 (Saturday 22.00).
Closed: Three days in February - phone to confirm.
Food: Modern British.
Real ale: John Smith's, Theakston, Black Sheep.
Other points: No smoking in the restaurant. Garden. Children welcome (must be dining with parents in the evening). Car park. Wheelchair access.
Directions: A1. Take the A684 from Leeming Bar to Bedale and continue for seven miles. The pub's entrance is on the left, signed to Akebar Park. (Map 6, D5)

Leyburn

The Sandpiper Inn

Market Place, Leyburn, Wensleydale,
North Yorkshire DL8 5AT
Telephone: +44(0)1969 622206
hsandpiper99@aol.com

In this 17th-century stone cottage, just off the market square in sleepy Leyburn, Jonathan Harrison is cooking some of the best pub food in the Dales. The comfortably spruced-up bar has an unspoilt and traditional atmosphere, with a wood-burning stove, cushioned wall benches and low dark beams, while the simple, yet stylish dining area hints at Jonathan's modern approach to pub dining. Listed on a twice daily-changing blackboard, light lunchtime options might include Caesar salad with smoked salmon and Yorkshire ham with local farm eggs and fried potatoes. However, dinner reveals a repertoire of well-balanced modern British dishes featuring the best local produce available, notably local game and farm meats. Expect, perhaps, saddle of venison with braised red cabbage and port jus or cod fillet with a herb and apple crust, followed by raspberry and almond tart with clotted cream. Two smart upstairs bedrooms and rooms in the cottage annexe are tastefully furnished. See pub walk on page 252.

Rooms: 2. Double room from £70, single from £60. Cottage annexe (double) £90.
Prices: Main course from £10.50. House wine £11.
Last orders: Food: lunch 14.30 (Sunday 14.00); dinner 21.00 (Friday and Saturday 21.30).
Closed: Monday.
Food: Modern British.
Real ale: Copper Dragon, Black Sheep Best, Daleside. Guest beer.
Other points: No smoking in the restaurant. Dogs welcome in the bar. Garden/terrace.
Directions: Off Market Square in Leyburn. (Map 6, D5)

Marton

The Appletree Country Inn 🍺🍴★

Marton, Pickering, North Yorkshire YO62 6RD
Telephone: +44(0)1751 431457
appletreeinn@supanet.com
www.appletreeinn.co.uk

A former run-down boozer that has been transformed into one of Yorkshire's top gastropubs by young, talented licensees - chef TJ and Melanie Drew. Innovative monthly menus and daily creations make the most of quality local produce, including lamb, beef and pork from surrounding farms and home-grown fruit and vegetables. Arrive for dinner and follow excellent homemade breads with crab-and-scallop risotto. Move on to confit pork belly with black pudding and diable sauce. For pudding, opt for warm chocolate pudding, but save room for TJ's delicious petit fours with excellent coffee. First-rate lunches include Marton lamb stew and black pudding with smoked bacon and scrambled egg. All are served throughout the informal and very comfortable bar/restaurant, with its deep red walls, heavy beams and open fires. In addition, expect quality wines, impeccable service from Melanie, Yorkshire ales, and a shop counter laden with homemade goodies.

Prices: Main course dinner from £9.
House wine £11.
Last orders: Bar: lunch 14.30 (Sunday 14.30); dinner 23.00. Food: lunch 14.00 (Sunday 14.30); dinner 21.30.
Closed: Monday, Tuesday and two weeks in January.
Food: Modern British.
Real ale: Three changing guest beers from Yorkshire breweries - Timothy Taylor, Black Sheep, Hambleton.
Other points: No-smoking area. Children welcome. Garden. Car park.
Directions: From Kirkbymoorside on A170 towards Scarborough, Marton is signposted right. (Map 6, D6)

Masham

The Black Sheep Brewery 🍺☕

Wellgarth, Masham, North Yorkshire HG4 4EN
Telephone: +44(0)1765 689227
sue.dempsey@blacksheep.co.uk
www.blacksheep.co.uk

Black Sheep Brewery not only brews and bottles four award-winning real ales, it has an excellent visitor centre, where you will discover how Black Sheep brew 12 million pints a year. You can take a fascinating 'shepherded' tour of the brewhouse, then enjoy a perfect pint and a meal in the spacious, split-level 'baa...r'-cum-bistro, with its wooden floors, bright check-clothed tables, brewery equipment and informal atmosphere. At lunchtime, tuck into wholemeal sandwiches of Yorkshire ham with wholegrain Riggwelter mustard, say, and haddock in Black Sheep ale batter, or one of the blackboard specials, perhaps rack of local lamb with rosemary-and-redcurrant sauce. The more imaginative evening menu (Thursday-Saturday) may offer fillet steak with caramelised shallots and bordelaise sauce, with homemade puddings or local Wensleydale cheese to finish. Afterwards, visit the Black Sheep shop. Cakes and set afternoon teas are also available.

Prices: Lunch main course £6.95. Evening main course from £8.95. House wine £9.95.
Last orders: Bar: lunch 14.30 (Monday, Tuesday and Sunday 17.00); dinner 23.00.
Closed: Monday, Tuesday, Wednesday and Sunday evening. 10 days in January.
Food: Traditional and modern British.
Real Ale: Black Sheep Ales. At least 2 guest beers.
Other points: No-smoking area. Children welcome. Garden. Car park. Wheelchair access.
Directions: Masham lies midway between Ripon and Leyburn on the A6108. (Map 10, D5)

The Appletree Country Inn

Melanie and TJ Drew have taken a loss-making village boozer and transformed it into a stylish, money-making modern dining pub, and one that holds its own against several stellar performers in the neighbourhood. Tucked below the North York Moors along winding country lanes, it's worth seeking out for innovative monthly menus that make the most of locally produced and homegrown ingredients. Hundreds of candles create a cosy atmosphere throughout the rambling bar, dining room and sofa-adorned lounge area. Delightful patio garden.

Visit the local Farmers' Market

Every Tuesday in summer a farmers' market is held in the Market Place in Malton. A big farmers' market is held at Yorks Auction Centre on the first and third Saturday of the month from 9am to 1pm.

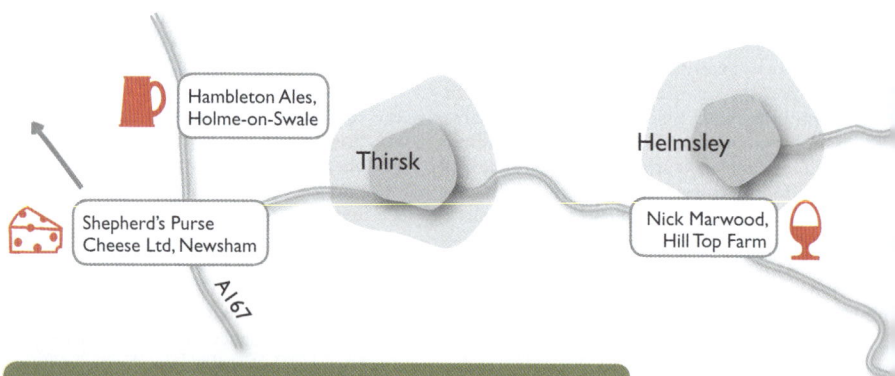

Hambleton Ales,
Holme-on-Swale

Thirsk

Helmsley

Shepherd's Purse
Cheese Ltd, Newsham

Nick Marwood,
Hill Top Farm

A167

Hambleton Ales
Holme-on-Swale, Thirsk
Tel: 01845 567460

Nick Stafford's Hambleton Ales is a small family-run business that has flourished since its inception in 1991 on the banks of the River Swale in the heart of the Vale of York. Starting in a small barn, it now produces 100 barrels a week, supplies over 100 outlets, and has a bottling plant that handles brews from over 20 micro- and larger brewers. Using malted barley and English hops, traditional ales include the award-winning Hambleton Nightmare, Stallion and Stud, a strongly bitter beer with rich hop and fruit flavours. Hambleton Ales regular feature at the Appletree, alongside Malton and Daleside beers. Arrange to tour the brewery and buy some bottles from the shop.

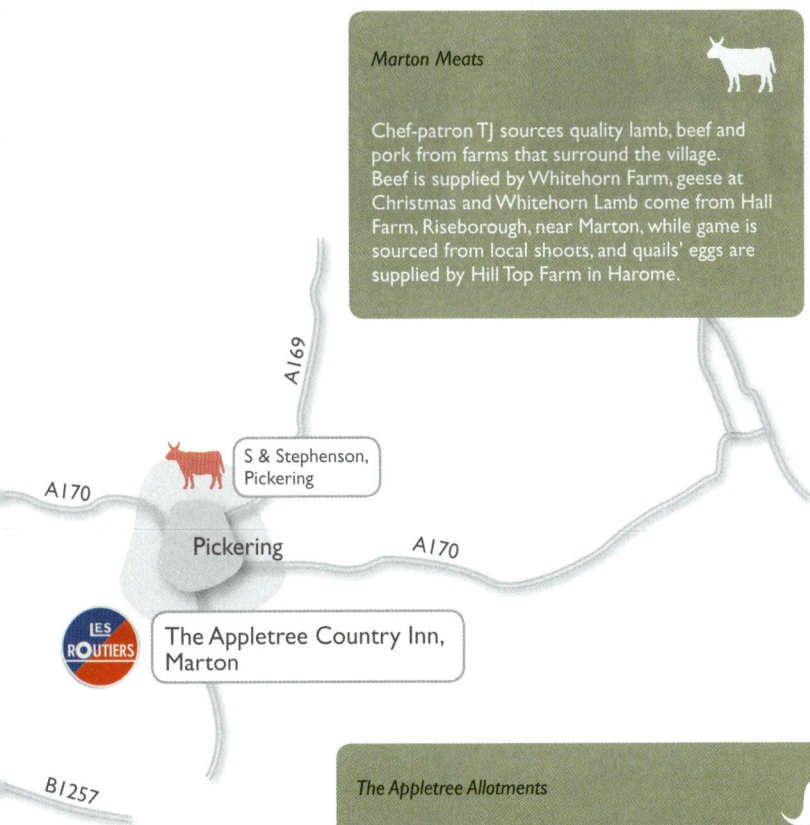

Marton Meats

Chef-patron TJ sources quality lamb, beef and pork from farms that surround the village. Beef is supplied by Whitehorn Farm, geese at Christmas and Whitehorn Lamb come from Hall Farm, Riseborough, near Marton, while game is sourced from local shoots, and quails' eggs are supplied by Hill Top Farm in Harome.

A169

S & Stephenson, Pickering

A170

Pickering

A170

LES ROUTIERS

The Appletree Country Inn, Marton

B1257

The Appletree Allotments

Venture to the end of the garden at the Appletree Inn and you will find Melanie and TJ's other passion, their rapidly developing smallholding that supplies the pub kitchen with the freshest vegetables and herbs. Developed in 2002, it has a poly tunnel and neat rows of vegetables and soft fruit, all carefully tended by Alf the gardener. The adjoining well-established orchard provides apples, pears, cherries and plums. Soft fruit and other suitable produce usually find their way into the delicious preserves, oils and pickles that are available from the shop counter in the pub.

Osmotherley

The Golden Lion

6 West End, Osmotherley, Thirsk,
North Yorkshire BL6 3AA
Telephone: +44(0)1609 883526

A wonderful old stone inn overlooking the green in pretty Osmotherley, the Golden Lion is run by Christie Connelly and chef-partner Peter McCoy. This is not only a thriving food pub that appeals to well-heeled foodies in search of imaginative, good-value cooking, but one that also welcomes walkers hiking the Lyke Wake Walk. Expect a lively and bustling atmosphere in the cosy, wood-panelled bar, with its cushioned pew seating, log fire, and inviting evening candlelight. Simple, clean and full-flavoured dishes range from fresh mussels in wine, cream and shallots, or a deep bowl of tomato-and-basil soup for a light snack or starter, to warm salads, calf's liver with mash and peas, or sirloin steak with peppered sauce and hand-cut chips. There are good homemade burgers and vegetarian options - goat's cheese and red-pepper terrine - and puddings may include fresh strawberry tart and sherry trifle plus decent coffee to finish. Booking is essential.

Prices: Restaurant main course from £6.50-£13.95. House wine from £12.
Last orders: Bar: lunch 15.30; dinner 23.00. Food: lunch 16.00; dinner 22.00.
Closed: Rarely.
Food: Modern pub food.
Real ale: Hambleton Biter, Timothy Taylor Landlord, John Smiths Cask. Guest beer on Bank Holidays.
Other points: No-smoking area. Children welcome.
Directions: Off the A19 north of Thirsk. (Map 6, D6)

Richmond

The Hack & Spade Inn

Whashton, Richmond, North Yorkshire DL11 7JL
Telephone: +44(0)1748 823721
hackandspade@ukonline.co.uk
www.thehackandspadeinn.co.uk

Peacefully tucked away off the A66, Jeremy Jagger and Joanna Millar's revitalised 17th-century country local thrives as a dining pub and is worth seeking out. Step beyond the old-fashioned stone exterior for a pleasant surprise. Here, original beams, stone-flagged floors and crackling open fires blend beautifully with the warm terracotta decor, subtle lighting and modern pictures that give this old pub a contemporary feel. Everything is immaculately maintained. Menus are chalked up on boards and dishes are dictated by the seasons and by whatever local farmers can supply. Thus, to start, there could be warm salad of smoked bacon, Stilton and pork and apple sausages, with steak, kidney and Guinness pie or roasted sea bass with baked cherry tomatoes to follow. Round off with sticky toffee pudding or local cheeses from the Swaledale Cheese Company. Light lunchtime snacks take in soup, sandwiches and salads. Excellent wines from Pagendam Pratt - eight by the glass.

Prices: Set dinner £18. Lunch from £5. Main course from £7.25. Bar snack from £4.50. House wine £9.95.
Last orders: Food: lunch 13.30; dinner 20.45.
Closed: All day Monday, Sunday evening and the first two weeks of January.
Food: Traditional and Modern British.
Real ale: John Smith's, Theakston Ales.
Other points: No-smoking area. Children welcome. Car park. Wheelchair access.
Directions: Take the turning off the A66 signed for Kirby Hill and Ravensworth, five miles west of Scotch Corner and the A1. (Map 6, D5)

Sawley

The Sawley Arms and Cottages

Sawley, Fountains Abbey, Ripon,
North Yorkshire HG64 3EQ
Telephone: +44(0)1765 620642

A fine old-fashioned village pub whose immaculate upkeep and enduring popularity are a tribute to the devotion of June Hawes, who has been in control here for some 36 years. She has built up an excellent reputation for good food, friendly hospitality and quality overnight accommodation in a newly built stone cottage. In a succession of alcoves and tiny rooms, each with winged armchairs, cushioned settles and attractive plates and prints, regulars find their preferred tables and order from June's tempting menus that are built around prime local materials, including smoked Nidderdale trout. Expect a good range of fresh-cut sandwiches, delicious soups and snacks or starters such as salmon, celeriac and herb pancake. The evening choice extends to steak pie with buttercrust pastry, braised lamb shank in Madeira gravy, and fresh Whitby cod. Available, on a self-catering basis, the two comfortable cottage suites feature spacious lounges, fully equipped kitchens and spotless en suite bathrooms.

Rooms: 2 cottage apartments each sleeping two.
Prices from £250. There are seasonal price variations, please call ahead.
Prices: Restaurant main course from £10.50. Bar main course from £7.70. House wine £10.50.
Last orders: Food: lunch 14.30; dinner 21.00.
Closed: Sunday and Monday evening.
Food: Traditional and Modern British.
Other points: Totally no smoking. Garden. Car park.
Directions: Take the B62665 from Ripon and turn at Risplith into Sawley village. (Map 6, D5)

Skipton

The Bull at Broughton

Broughton, Skipton, North Yorkshire BD23 3AE
Telephone: +44(0)1756 792065
janeneil@thebullatbroughton.co.uk
www.thebullatbroughton.co.uk

Sleepy Broughton and the rambling, stone-built Bull are part of the Broughton Hall Estate, and the pub's rear terrace overlooks the unspoilt parkland. Sister pub to the highly acclaimed Shibden Mill Inn in West Yorkshire (see entry), it shares the same reputation for honest, freshly prepared food. Using top-notch local ingredients Neil Butterworth produces robust, full-flavoured dishes on a sound, brasserie-style menu, which has proved very popular with local diners. Bread is baked daily and the sausages, sauces and ice creams are all made on the premises. Dishes range from light meals such as a classic cassoulet and a fillet steak filled ciabatta, to corn-fed chicken breast with cep sauce, and an old-fashioned shepherd's pie. Puddings include tarte Tatin and a decent cheeseboard. All food is served throughout cosy little rooms, each sporting heavy beams, log fires and a mix of quarry-tiled and wooden floors.

Prices: Restaurant main course from £7.50. Main course bar from £4.20. House wine £9.90.
Last orders: Bar: 23.00 (Tuesday-Saturday). (Monday lunch 14.30; dinner 22.00, Sunday all day until 20.30).
Food: lunch 14.00; dinner 21.00 (Friday and Saturday 21.30, Sunday 12.00-18.00). Open all day Sunday and Bank Holiday Mondays.
Closed: Rarely.
Food: Modern British.
Real ale: Bull Bitter. 2 guest beers.
Other points: No-smoking area. Dogs welcome. Children welcome. Garden. Car park. Wheelchair access (no WC).
Directions: The pub is on the A59, 3 miles from Skipton. (Map 6, E5)

PUDDINGS @ 4.25

- CHOCOLATE FUDGE 9ATEAU
- SPOTTED DICK
- APPLE CRUMBLE
- WHITE CHOCOLATE ?
- AMARETTO FORTE
- BANOFFEE PIE
- TREACLE TART
- APPLE TART
- FRENCH BRIE CHEESE   4 @ 4.95

ICE-CREAM @ 3.75

- CHOCOLATE

Shibden

Shibden Mill Inn

Shibden Mill Fold, Shibden, Halifax, West Yorkshire HX3 7UL
Telephone: +44(0)1422 365840
shibdenmillinn@zoom.co.uk
www.shibdenmillinn.com

Must-sees

Shibden Hall: house dating from the 15th century, with rooms laid out to illustrate different periods of history; craft weekends.

Piece Hall, Halifax: unique 18th-century hall now housing an industrial museum, art galleries and shops; open market and workshops.

Brontë Parsonage Museum, Haworth: family history of the Brontë sisters.

Keighley & Worth Valley Railway & Museum, Haworth

Bradford Museums & Art Gallery.

Where to shop Halifax, Bradford, Leeds

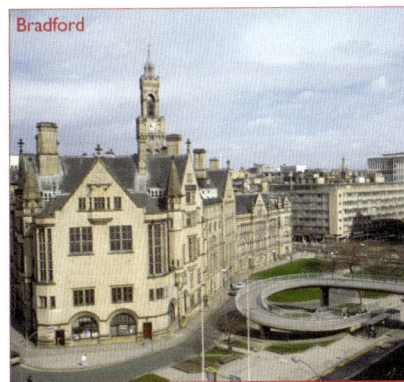

Bradford

Hidden in the folds of the Shibden Valley, overlooking the babbling Red Beck, this rambling 17th-century inn is a surprisingly peaceful spot, just minutes from the hustle and bustle of Halifax. While retaining an appealing rustic tone, sympathetic refurbishment has succeeded admirably at the difficult task of creating, simultaneously, a simple pubby brasserie, a restaurant with serious aspirations, and a rather fine place to stay the night. Simplicity and good local ingredients appears to be the key to the food operation; clear, well-defined flavours are to be seen in a starter of tea-smoked duck with warm sweet-and-sour fennel salad, and in stuffed leg of rabbit with smoked bacon, tarragon, prunes and pine-nuts. Own-baked bread deserves a special mention as does the in-house shop of homemade goodies and the excellent bar food. Wines are well chosen, with a Connoisseur Collection adding weight. There are 12 bedrooms, all comfortably decorated with warmth and style.

Rooms: 12. Double room from £72, single from £68.
Prices: Restaurant main course from £10. Bar main course from £8. House wine £9.95.
Last orders: Bar: lunch 15.00; dinner 23.00 (all day during the week-end). Food: lunch 14.00 (all day Sunday); dinner 21.30 (Sunday 19.30).
Closed: Rarely.
Food: Modern British.
Real ale: John Smith's Cask, Theakston Ales, Shibden Mill Inn Bitter. 2 guest beers.
Other points: Smoking throughout. Children welcome. Garden. Car park. Licence for civil weddings.
Directions: Exit26/M62 on A58. Turn right into Kell Lane at Stump Cross Inn (near the A6036 junction), after which the pub is signposted. (Map 6, E5)

Tourist information Halifax +44(0)1422 368725
Farmers' market Halifax (3rd Sat of month), Bingley (last Sat of month)

Where to walk

For the best walking, head for the Pennine moors. North, in Brontë country, there are good walks around Haworth, through Penistone Country Park, and through a remote valley to Top Withins, the original Wuthering Heights. From Hebden Bridge there are tracks along Heptonstall Craggs to the Calderdale Way; Hardcastle Crags and the Pennine Way are just a little further west.

SCOTLAND

Isle of Bute

Russian Tavern at
The Port Royal Hotel

37 Marine Road, Kames Bay, Port Bannatynne,
Argyll & Bute PA20 0LW
Telephone: +44(0)1700 505073
stay@butehotel.com
www.russiantavern.co.uk

Norwegian-born Dag Crawford and his
Russian wife Olga have won much deserved
praise for their recreation of a 'Russian
Tsarist tavern' on the beautiful Isle of Bute.
The stone-built Georgian building overlooks
the stunning Kames Bay from which fishermen catch fish and langoustines. Dag cooks
brasserie-style dishes that have a strong
Russian accent but he uses local fish, beef
from Orkney and vegetables from his own
garden. His beef stroganoff is outstanding,
but gets strong competition from blinis with
marinated herring, and spicy Russian sausage
with latkes, red cabbage and sauerkraut. A
typical dinner of langoustine soup, halibut
steak in cream and white wine, and fresh
fruit Russian Pavlova, is remarkable value.
Excellent real ales from Scottish micro-breweries. Five good-value bedrooms.

Rooms: 5, 3 not en suite. Room from £22 per person,
Prices: Set lunch and dinner £20. Restaurant main
course £18. Bar main course from £5.50.
House wine £5 per pint.
Last orders: Bar: 01.00 (Saturday 02.00).
Closed: 1-28 November.
Food: Traditional Russian.
Real ale: Arran Blonde & Dark, Loch Fyne's Highlander,
Houston's Peters Well, Heather Ale from Strathaven,
Loch Fyne's Pipers' Gold, Kelburn's Red Smiddy,
Other points: Totally no smoking. Children welcome.
Dogs welcome in the bar. Car park. 5 free yacht moor-
ings. Beach. Golf course at the rear. Wheelchair access.
Directions: Three miles north from Rothesay (ferry)
and six miles south from the ferry at Colintraive,
Argyll. (Map 7, E3)

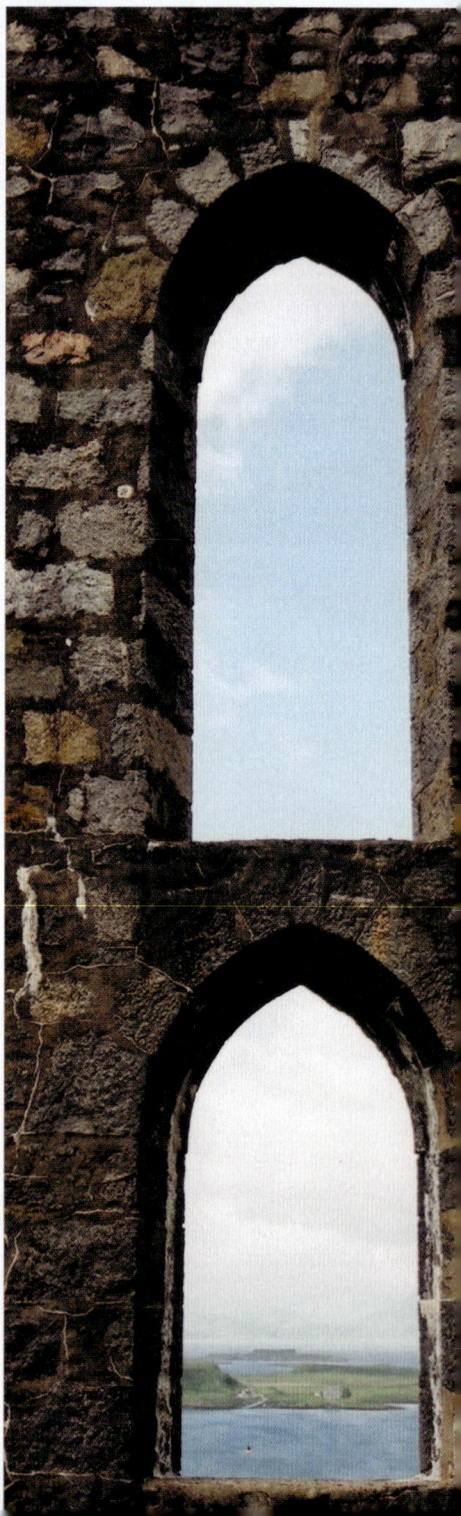

Isle of Whithorn

Steam Packet Hotel

Harbour Row, Newton Stewart, Isle of
Whithorn, Dumfries and Galloway DG8 8LL
Telephone: +44(0)1988 500334
steampacketinn@btconnect.com
www.steampacketinn.com

Large picture windows at this friendly, family-run inn take in yachts and fishing boats,
as well as the comings and goings of folk
and fishermen in what is considered one of
the prettiest natural harbours in this part of
Scotland. The Scoular family have been here
for 23 years, constantly modernising and
improving this harbourside inn. The split bar,
one side with wood-burning stove, serves a
good global list of wines, and has a relaxed,
laid-back atmosphere. Fish, landed on the
doorstep, dictates the menu, served in the
beamed, comfortable dining room and conservatory. Blackboards are scrawled with the
daily catch, dishes such as langoustines with
ginger, spring onion, lime and lemongrass,
complemented by seasonal game and prime
Aberdeen Angus steaks. Bar snacks take in
haddock and chips, and filled rolls. En suite
bedrooms are well equipped and the two
deluxe rooms overlook the harbour.

Rooms: 7. Double room from £50, single from £30.
Prices: Main course from £7. Bar snack from £5.
House wine £11.50.
Last orders: Bar: 23.00 (Friday and Saturday 24.00).
Food: lunch 14.00; dinner 21.00.
Closed: Bar 14.30-18.00 from October to March.
Food: British, with seafood as a speciality.
Real ale: Theakston XB. Guest beer.
Other points: No smoking in the restaurant. Children
welcome. Dogs welcome. Garden. Wheelchair access
to the restaurant/pub.
Directions: South of Newton Stewart on the A714 and
A746 to Whithorn, then take the B7004 to the Isle of
Whithorn. (Map 7, H4)

Edinburgh

The Café Royal Circle Bar and Oyster Bar Restaurant

19 West Register Street, Edinburgh EH2 2AA
Telephone: +44(0)131 556 1884
caferoyale@snr.co.uk

This great Edinburgh institution was founded
as a bar and restaurant in 1817 and has occu-
pied its present location since 1862. It's a glorious example of the Victorian and Baroque,
especially the elaborate plasterwork, gilding,
mahogany panelling and hand-painted windows depicting sporting life in the 19th century. Divided into two, the bar, with its dark-
brown leather banquette-style seating serves a
short, informal menu that delivers very good
sandwiches, seafood chowder, and braised
shank of lamb with rosemary-and-honey
sauce. In the richly decorated restaurant, the
emphasis is on fresh fish, shellfish and game.
Typically, start with grilled langoustines with
a tomato vinaigrette, and follow with pan-
seared scallops with crab risotto and a light
ginger and vermouth sabayon, or collops of
wild Highland venison with a bitter chocolate
and red-wine jus. France is the anchor for the
wine list, with Italy, Spain and New World
wines adding variety.

Prices: Restaurant main course from £15.50. Bar main
course from £4.95. House wine £9.
Last orders: Bar: 23.00 (Thursday 24.00, Friday and
Saturday 01.00). Food: lunch 14.00; dinner 22.00.
Bar food last orders 22.00.
Closed: Rarely.
Food: Seafood and Game.
Real ale: McEwans, Courage Directors. Guest Beer.
Other points: Children welcome in the restaurant only.
Directions: Just off the south-east corner of St
Andrew's Square, close to Princes Street. (Map 8, E6)

The Unicorn Inn

Standing beside the famous Kincardine Bridge, Liz and Tony Budde's 17th-century inn combines classic rural charm with the contemporary style of a modern dining pub. Inside, you will find a sofa-filled lounge, the casual Grill Room dining area and the intimate Red Room restaurant, where nightly menus list the best-available meat, game and seafood.

Visit the local Farmers' Market

Maxwell Place in Stirling is the nearest farmers' market. It is held on the second Saturday of the month from 9am to 2pm.

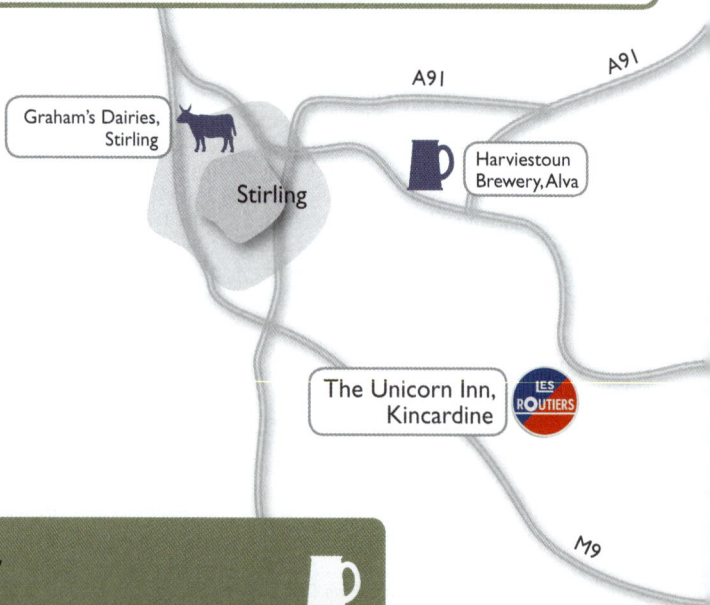

Graham's Dairies, Stirling

A91

A91

Harviestoun Brewery, Alva

Stirling

The Unicorn Inn, Kincardine

LES ROUTIERS

M9

A8

Harviestoun Brewery
Alva
Tel: 01259 769100

One of the smallest breweries in Britain, yet Harviestoun is continually nominated for and winning awards in national competitions, with the fantastically named (and flavoured) Bitter & Twisted winning Champion Beer of Britain at the Great British Beer Festival in 2003. Ptarmigan, Schiehallion and Old Engine Oil (named after its opaque nature rather than its viscosity) have also won awards. The name of the last of these is down to the man who started it all in 1985, Ken Brooker, an ex-Ford employee. He and Harviestoun have spearheaded the revival of micro-breweries in Scotland.

...for the latest news

173

Fife

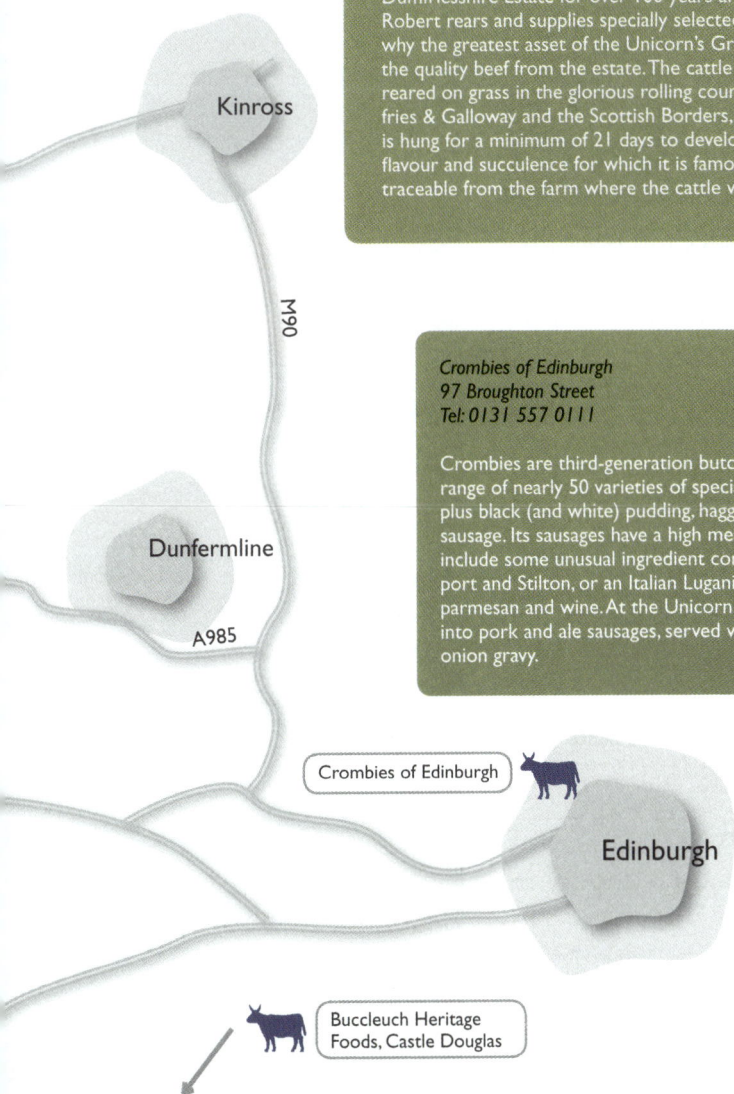

Buccleuch Heritage Foods
Castle Douglas
Tel: 01556 503399

Although not exactly local to the Unicorn, the Buccleuch Estate has close links to Liz and Tony Budde, the owners of the Unicorn. Liz's family have been farmers on the Dumfriesshire Estate for over 100 years and her brother Robert rears and supplies specially selected cattle, hence why the greatest asset of the Unicorn's Grill Room menu is the quality beef from the estate. The cattle are traditionally reared on grass in the glorious rolling countryside of Dumfries & Galloway and the Scottish Borders, and the beef is hung for a minimum of 21 days to develop the unique flavour and succulence for which it is famous. All meat is traceable from the farm where the cattle were born.

Crombies of Edinburgh
97 Broughton Street
Tel: 0131 557 0111

Crombies are third-generation butchers offering a range of nearly 50 varieties of specialist sausages, plus black (and white) pudding, haggis and Lorne sausage. Its sausages have a high meat content and include some unusual ingredient combinations, say port and Stilton, or an Italian Luganiga made with parmesan and wine. At the Unicorn you can tuck into pork and ale sausages, served with champ and onion gravy.

Kinross

M90

Dunfermline

A985

Crombies of Edinburgh

Edinburgh

Buccleuch Heritage Foods, Castle Douglas

Kincardine

Unicorn Inn ⭐

15 Excise Street, Kincardine, Fife FK10 4LN
Telephone: +44(0)1259 739129
info@theunicorn.co.uk
www.theunicorn.co.uk

Tony and Liz Budde's careful refurbishment of their lovely 17th-century inn, situated next to Kincardine Bridge, successfully combines classic rural charm with the contemporary style of a modern dining pub. At ground level is a lounge that features leather sofas around an open fire, and the more casual of two dining areas, The Grill. Its greatest asset lies in the beef from the Duke of Buccleuch estate, reared by Liz's brother Robert, which scores highly for quality and flavour. Additional selections take in fresh haddock and hand-cut chips and pork-and-ale sausages with champ. You'll find the Red Room restaurant upstairs, romantically fitted out with deep red curtains and tables clothed in white linen. Nightly menus depend on the best available fresh seafood, meat and game. Start perhaps with Loch Linnhe langoustines, before local venison medallions with sweetened haggis and red wine sauce. A classic pudding or a plate of Scottish and Irish cheeses should round things off nicely.

Prices: Restaurant main course from £7.95.
House wine £11.95.
Last orders: Bar: 24.00. Food: lunch 14.00; dinner 21.00
Closed: Monday.
Food: Scottish and Irish.
Real ale: Schiehallion, Smithwick's Bitter and Twisted.
Other points: No smoking in the restaurant. Children welcome. Garden. Car park. Wheelchair access.
Directions: From the south, cross Kincardine Bridge, then take the first then the second left. (Map 8, E5)

Fort William

Four Seasons Country Pub & Restaurant

Inchree Centre, Inchree, Onich,
Fort William, Highland PH33 6SE
Telephone: +44(0)1855 821287
enquiry@inchreecentre.co.uk
www.inchreecentre.co.uk

Outdoor types looking for high-quality budget accommodation in the Glencoe area should look no further than the Inchree Centre, a chalet-and-hostel complex hidden away in a stunning woodland setting with views down Loch Linnhe. What's more, there's a cracking pub-restaurant on site serving ale from Highland micro-breweries and imaginative evening meals. The simple wood-clad building houses an oak-panelled bar, kitted out with pine pews, traditional darkwood furniture, a curious pink-and-blue decor, and a rack of maps and walking guidebooks. As dusk settles and the fire blazes, it's a cosy place for a pint and a meal. Robust Scottish cooking comes in the form of game-liver paté with homemade chutney to start, with venison suet pudding with port and redcurrant sauce to follow. Try the excellent white chocolate and lime cheesecake for pudding.

Rooms: 8 Chalets. Chalet from £45, family hostel room from £39.
Prices: Set dinner from £11.95 (for larger parties only). Restaurant main course from £6.95.
Last orders: Food: Dinner 21.30.
Closed: Dining room open weekends only from November-Easter.
Food: Scottish
Real ale: Isle of Skye Red Cuillin, Ben Nevis. Up to 2 guest beers.
Other points: No-smoking area. Children welcome. Dogs welcome. Garden. Car park. Internet access. Wheelchair access.
Directions: 8 miles South of Fort William in Onich. 1/4 mile south of Corran Ferry. (Map 7, C3)

Fort William

The Grog and Gruel

66 High Street, Fort William,
Highland PH33 6AE
Telephone: +44(0)1397 705078
greatbeer@grogandgruel.co.uk
www.grogandgruel.co.uk

Active types fed up with bagging peaks should head for the Grog and Gruel, for great Scottish micro-brewery ales, hearty pub food and a lively atmosphere. Its tongue-in-cheek name reflects the relaxed and informal atmosphere of a traditional alehouse. Wooden floors, traditional bench seating and background rock music set the scene in which to enjoy pints of Atlas Latitude and Cairngorm Tomintoul Stag, 60 different malt whiskies, and all-day food from the 'alehouse' menu, served in the first-floor restaurant overlooking the High Street. From starters of 'Mucho Macho' nachos with 'hog's breath' chilli beef and smoked salmon with oatcakes and dill mayonnaise, the menu extends to Tex-Mex chicken fajitas with sour cream and guacamole, house-speciality pizzas, traditional steak-and-ale pie, and freshly battered cod with chips. If you're not partial to a decent pint, order a litre pitcher of Tequila Sunrise to accompany your beef-filled burritos. Don't miss the annual beer festivals.

Prices: Main course from £7.45.
Last orders: Bar: 23.00 (Thursday to Saturday 01.00). Food: 22.00 Restaurant and 21.00 Bar.
Closed: Rarely.
Food: Mexican, American and Italian.
Real ale: Isle of Skye Brewing Ales, Heather Ales, Atlas Brewery Ales, Caledonian Brewery Ales, Cairngorm Brewery Ales. Up to 10 guest beers.
Other points: No-smoking area. Children welcome in restaurant only. Dogs welcome. Garden.
Directions: Halfway along Fort William's pedestrianised high street. (Map 7, C3)

Glencoe

The Clachaig Inn ⬛▯★

Glencoe, Highland PH49 4HX
Telephone: +44(0)1855 811252
inn@clachaig.com
www.clachaig.com

Set in the heart of Glencoe, this 300-year-old inn is a favourite haunt of mountaineers and walkers. The inn has a lively atmosphere and is an activity centre in itself, offering mountain-bike hire, winter mountaineering courses and live folk music. Huge log fires provide a roaring welcome in the cosy, wood-floored lounge bar, and in the rustic, stone-flagged Boots Bar. In the latter, booted walkers can take refuge and enjoy refreshments at a bar dispensing 120 malt whiskies and up to eight Highland micro-brewery ales. The traditional pub food served in generous portions is perfect following a bracing walk, and can be enjoyed in the three bars or restaurant. The choice ranges from filled baguettes and pasta dishes to venison casserole and chargrilled steaks. If you want to sample something local, make room for the homemade ecclefechan tart. Bedrooms are split between the main house and chalet-style rooms. See pub walk on page 254.

Rooms: 23. Double room from £30, prices per person.
Prices: Restaurant main course from £5.85.
House wine from £8.25.
Last orders: Bar: 23.00 (Friday 24.00, Saturday 23.30).
Food: 21.00.
Closed: Rarely.
Food: Scottish, American, Mexican.
Real ale: Up to eight guest beers.
Other points: No-smoking area. Children welcome.
Dogs welcome overnight. Garden. Car park. Bike shed.
Wheelchair access to the restaurant/pub.
Directions: Located in the heart of Glencoe, just off the A82 Glasgow to Fort William Road. (Map 7, C3)

Plockton

The Plockton Hotel

Harbour Street, Plockton, Highland IV52 8TN
Telephone: +44(0)1599 544274
info@plocktonhotel.co.uk
www.plocktonhotel.co.uk

Must-sees
Eilean Donan Castle: a historic 13th-century
  stronghold built to deter Viking raiders.
Isle of Skye
Duirinish Lodge: woodland garden with heathers,
  azaleas and rhododendrons.

Local activities
Fishing, wildlife watching, pony trekking

Nearest golf course Kyle of Lochalsh, Isle of Skye

Where to walk
Plenty of signposted walks, including a choice at Glen
Affric, immortalised by Landseer's paintings of woods,
crags and tumbling waters. The glen forms part of
a long-distance trail to Kintail. Elsewhere paths and
tracks reach to the heart of this awesome landscape.

Eilean Donan Castle

Tourist information
Kyle of Lochalsh +44(0)1599 534276
Where to shop Isle of Skye, Dornie, Plockton, Balma-
cara

Commanding a beautiful waterfront location and superb views in an idyllic National
Trust village, the Pearson family's unique inn
stands on the shores of Loch Carron. Tom
and Dorothy are fully committed to caring
for its guests, from hot-water bottles in the
beds to cosseting sofas to flop into. Day-
rooms include a leather furnished reception
lounge, a non-smoking snug, two bars with
crackling fires, and the delightful restaurant.
Wonderfully comfortable bedrooms enjoy
stunning views. Food reflects the surrounding area. Locally caught shellfish landed
at the pier daily, fish from Gairloch and
Kinlochbervie, hill-fed lamb and Highland
beef and locally-made West Highland cheeses
feature on comprehensive, daily-changing
menus. House specialities embrace traditional
fish and chips, alongside cream of smoked-
fish soup, the celebrated Plockton Smokies,
casserole of Highland venison, and perhaps
iced cranachan parfait, among the puddings.
Real food and wine, real value and real
Highland hospitality make this a place that's
hard to leave.

Rooms: 11 rooms in hotel and 4 in the cottage annex.
£30 per person in the cottage annex, £45 per person
in the hotel.
Prices: Restaurant main course from £12. Bar snack
from £6.75. House wine £7.95.
Last orders: Bar: 23.00
Closed: Never.
Food: Modern Scottish.
Real ale: Caledonian Deuchar's IPA, Sky Brewery
Hebridean Gold. Guest beer.
Other points: No-smoking area. Children welcome.
Dogs welcome in the public bar. Garden. Licence for
civil weddings. Wheelchair access to the restaurant/pub
and one bedroom.
Directions: Seven miles north around the coast from
Kyle of Lochalsh. (Map 7, B3)

Events & festivals
Skye and Lochalse Arts and Crafts (May)
Plockton Regatta (July/August)
Highland Games, Skye (August)
Agricultural Show, Skye (August)

The Plockton Hotel

Unique in every way, where do we start in describing this Highland jewel? Think, perhaps, of sitting outdoors under palm trees, no less, on the shores of Loch Carron, with stunning views of the surrounding hills. Staff at the Pearson family's unique converted inn are really committed to caring for guests. There are beautifully furnished lounges, two bars with open fires and a raft of fine malts, cosy bedrooms with loch views, and mouth-watering menus that list fish and shellfish landed along the quay, hill-fed lamb, Highland beef, and the celebrated Plockton smokies.

West Highland Dairy
Achmore
Tel: 01599 577203

Sheep milk from the dairy's own flock of milking sheep and locally produced cows' milk are manufactured into a wide range of dairy products, including yogurt, ice cream, crème fraîche and award-winning cheeses – blue, hard, soft and bloomy-rind cheese. At the Plockton Hotel you can round off a memorable meal with a plate of these local cheeses.

Home-grown herbs
Colbost

Sleepy Hollow Smokehouse
Aultbea
Tel: 01445 731304

Sleepy Hollow Smokehouse at Mellon Charles is run by Jenny and Andrew Wiseman and is one of the few truly traditional smokehouses left, using old-fashioned techniques and skills rather than modern electronic kilns. Their smoked salmon is first class and the hot smoked salmon has won several awards for its unique flavours. As well as smoking and curing fish, the Wiseman's can supply fresh fish – lemon sole, monkfish, turbot and salmon, among others.

Portree

A850

Sleepy Hollow Smokehouse,
Aultbea

A832

Skye Food Link Van
Glendale, Isle of Skye
Tel: 01470 511349

Skye and Lochalsh has huge potential for
fresh local produce, but the problem has
been how to actually obtain it, especially
when the population of 12,000 live in an
area that is over 2700 sq km. The solution
was found in 2001 when a group of food
producers started the Skye Food Link
Van. It has been a great success and any
producer is eligible to join the group, the
simple aim being to make the fantastic
local produce of the area available to the
public, largely by selling it to restaurants
and hotels. The van runs once or twice
a week and delivers a mouth-watering
range of goodies, from herbs and fruits to
fresh oysters and chocolates.

A896

The Plockton Hotel,
Plockton

LES
ROUTIERS

West Highland Dairy,
Achmore

A850

Mussels,
Loch Eishort

Ullapool

The Seaforth Inn

Quay Street, Ullapool, Highland IV26 2UE
Telephone: +44(0)1854 612122
drink@theseaforth.com
www.theseaforth.com

Smack on the quayside, with stunning views of Loch Broom, the Seaforth has developed from a basic bar and chippy to an award-winning pub and seafood restaurant since Harry and Brigitte MacRae took over in 1995. The extended and modernised 18th-century building takes in a huge ground-floor bar with oak floors and large picture windows, an upstairs bistro for more intimate dining, and 'The Chippy', a traditional fish-and-chips takeaway. In fact, menus throughout the pub are overwhelmingly (and unashamedly) biased towards locally caught seafood. In the bar, snack on fresh oysters, steamed mussels or sweet pickled herrings, or feast on the amazing seafood platters. Linger longer in the bistro over seafood soup, fresh lobster or sea bream with tarragon and Pernod. Carnivores can tuck into Highland steaks. The Chippy menu is equally impressive - where else can you 'takeaway' scallops and chips, mussels by the kilo, and the best haddock and chips for miles.

Prices: Restaurant main course from £8. Bar/snack from £3.50. House wine from £9.50.
Last orders: Bar: 01.00. Food: 22.00. Times vary according to season.
Closed: New Year's Day.
Food: Seafood and traditional Scottish.
Real ale: Isle of Skye Ales.
Other points: No-smoking area. Garden and patio. Children welcome. Car park. Air-conditioning. Wheelchair access.
Directions: Take the A835 from Inverness. (Map 9, F4)

...for special offers

Blair Atholl

Atholl Arms Hotel

Old North Road, Blair Atholl,
Perth & Kinross PH18 5SG
Telephone: +44(0)1796 481205
enquiries@athollarmshotel.co.uk
www.athollarmshotel.co.uk

If you want a taste of the high life in the Highlands, head for this stunning grand Victorian house that is now a smart hotel. In a commanding position and commanding attention, this fine, gabled, granite-stone building was until recently owned by the Atholl Estate. The interiors reflect the house's Victorian and Scottish heritage and are sumptuously decorated in deep burgundies and greens with walls covered in baronial-style accessories, with tartan making tasteful appearances throughout. The bedrooms are smartly attired as are the Bothy Bar and Baronial Dining Room, where you can sample the best of local produce from Blair Atholl estate game to Tombuie Smokehouse meats and cheeses, fish from Kerrachers, and shellfish from Skye. The hospitality and atmosphere are amazing.

Rooms: 31. Double/twin from £50, single from £35.
Family from £50.
Prices: Set lunch from £12. Set dinner from £20.
Restaurant main course from £10. Bar/snack from £6.45. House wine £10.50.
Last orders: Bar: 23.00 (Friday and Saturday 23.45).
Food: 21.30.
Closed: Rarely.
Food: Modern Scottish.
Real ale: Moulin Ales.
Other points: No-smoking area. Children welcome.
Dogs welcome in the bar. Garden. Car park.
Directions: Six miles north of Pitlochry on A9, turn right at the T-junction and follow signs for Blair Castle. The Atholl Arms is 200 yards past the main gate on the left. (Map 8, C5)

Comrie

The Royal Hotel

Melville Square, Comrie,
Perth & Kinross PH6 2DN
Telephone: +44(0)1764 679200
reception@royalhotel.co.uk
www.royalhotel.co.uk

Finely restored in 1995, this 18th-century coaching inn exudes a country-house atmosphere, with period antiques, paintings and stylish soft furnishings complemented by the Milsom family and their staff's cheerful, helpful hospitality. The cosy lounge bar, along with the wood-and-stone public bar, are the focus of the local community, offering an informal atmosphere and a warm welcome. Here, and in the conservatory-style brasserie, venison and leek burgers or haggis with hash browns and whisky sauce may be washed down with a glass of Deuchar's IPA or one of 170 Highland malts. Dinner in the intimate restaurant can be a fixed-price three-course affair or taken from a seasonal carte, that makes full use of the markets' seasonal produce, from fresh fish, meats and game to local farm fruits and vegetables. Beautifully appointed bedrooms feature furnishings by local craftsmen and rich fabrics.

Rooms: 11. Double/twin £60 per person, single £75.
Four-poster suite from £80 per person.
Prices: Set dinner £27.50. Restaurant main course from £9.95. Bar main course from £6.95. House wine £9.50.
Last orders: Bar: 23.00 (Friday and Saturday 23.45).
Food: lunch 14.00; dinner 21.00.
Closed: Rarely.
Food: Traditional and Modern English.
Real ale: Deuchar's IPA, Bass.
Other points: No smoking in the restaurant. Garden.
Children welcome. Dogs welcome overnight. Car park.
Wheelchair access to the restaurant.
Directions: From the A9 at Greenloaning take the A822 for Crieff, then the B827 to Comrie. (Map 8, D5)

Perth

The Famous Bein Inn

Glen Farg, Perth, Perth & Kinross PH2 9PY
Telephone: +44 (0)1577 830216
stay@beininn.com
www.beininn.com

An institution and local landmark, this old drovers' inn stands alone in a deep-wooded glen, five minutes drive from the M90. Since David Mundell has been at the helm, the Bein has become famous for live-music sessions, attracting some top recording artists. Rock music fans travel miles to experience David's Rock Bar, a basement museum filled with rock memorabilia. Decor is a tad more traditional in the MacGregor Bar, with its tartan carpet and comfortable sofas, and in the more formal Balvaird Restaurant. Food is honest and home-cooked, the simple menus appealing to a loyal local clientele and passing travellers. Expect lunchtime sandwiches and light meals such as the inn's classic beefburger and pan-fried lamb's liver, to house specialities such as Shetland salmon with herb-and-prawn butter. In keeping, en suite bedrooms are clean, tidy and unpretentious.

Rooms: 12. Double from £70, single from £45, family from £65. Prices include breakfast.
Prices: Set lunch £14, set dinner £18. Restaurant main course from £10.95. Bar main course from £5.95. House wine £10.50.
Last orders: Bar: lunch 14.00; dinner 23.00 (open all day at the weekend). Food: lunch 14.00; dinner 21.00 (Sunday food served all day).
Closed: Rarely.
Food: Traditional Scottish.
Real ale: Inveralmond Independence.
Other points: No-smoking area. Children welcome. Car park.
Directions: Exit9/M90. Drive through Glenfarg. The inn is one and a half miles into the glen. (Map 8, D6)

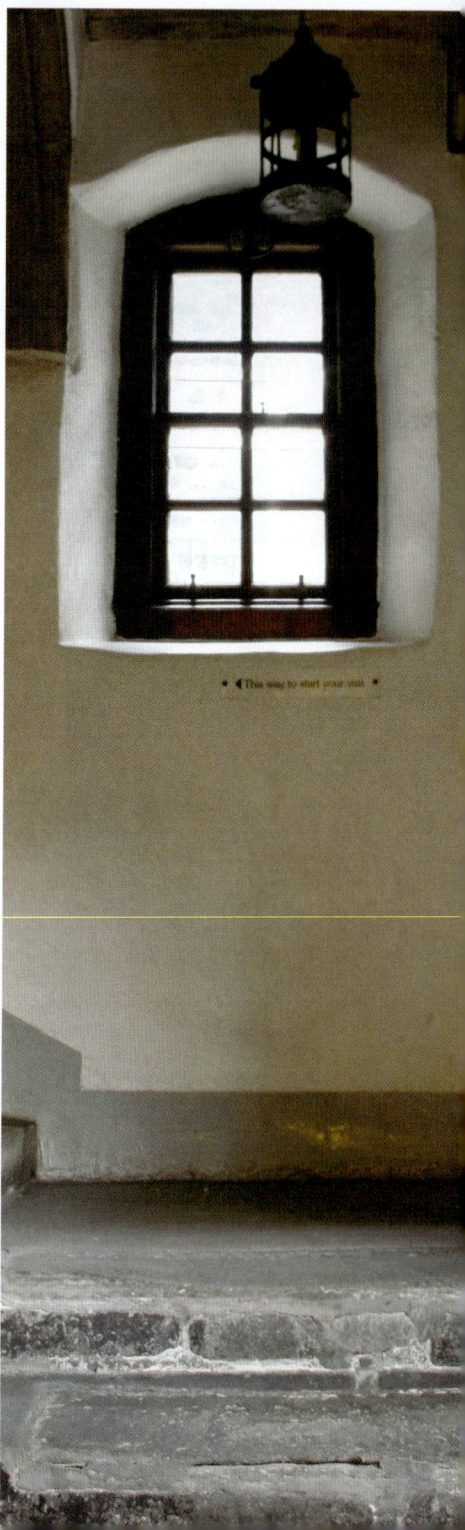

This way to start your visit

Pitlochry

Loch Tummel Inn

Strathtummel, by Pitlochry, Perth & Kinross PH16 5RP
Telephone: +44 (0)1882 634272

Local activities Cycling, fishing, horse riding, shooting, quad and mountain biking, white-water rafting

Blair Castle

Built as a coaching inn by the Dukes of Atholl, the Loch Tummel Inn enjoys breathtaking views across the loch and mountains, and landlord Michael Marsden explains that his hostelry is a place for stopping, taking in the view, and rediscovering your forgotten childhood senses of taste, touch and smell. Even on a wet summer evening, the green-and-burgundy colour scheme with cream walls decorated with deer antlers and maps makes the bar feel cosy. Here, against a backdrop of magnificent views, a dinner menu built around local lines of supply is served. This is good country cooking, with a typical meal producing own-smoked salmon, followed by venison with red wine and redcurrant sauce, and a rhubarb and fudge crumble to die for. From the guests' sitting room, warmed by a log fire, a small staircase leads to six bedrooms furnished in exquisite good taste.

Rooms: 6, 2 with private bathrooms. Single from £50, double from £75. Family room £100.
Prices: Main course from £10.
House wine £4.80
Last orders: Food: lunch 13.30; dinner 20.30.
Closed: End October to the week before Easter.
Food: Traditional Scottish.
Real ale: Moulin Braveheart.
Other points: No smoking in the restaurant. Children welcome. Dogs welcome overnight. Garden. Car park. Wheelchair access to the pub.
Directions: From Pitlochry take the Blair Atholl road (A9) At Garry Bridge turn left onto the B8019 for eight miles. (Map 8, C5)

Tourist information Pitlochry +44(0)1796 472215
Where to Shop Pitlochry, Aberfeldy, Perth

Farmers' market Occasionally at Aberfeldy
Nearest racecourse Perth
Nearest golf course Pitlochry
(with handicap certificate)

Where to walk
Good walks in Tay Forest Park and close to Loch Tummel.

Best scenic drives
B8019 to A9 and Pitlochry, on to Aberfeldy, B846 to Tummel Bridge and return to inn.

Events & festivals
Pitlochry Festival Theatre - a different production daily For other events and festivals, contact Pitlochry Tourist Information Centre.

Must-sees
Blair Castle

Pitlochry

The Old Mill Inn

Mill Lane, Pitlochry, Perth & Kinross PH16 5BH
Telephone: +44(0)1796 474020
enquiries@highlandperthshire.com
www.old-mill-inn.co.uk

In the heart of Pitlochry and accessed from the High Street along a paved path, the Old Mill, as its name suggests, is a refurbished 17th-century corn mill, replete with working water wheel and gushing burn. Like the town, the pub draws the crowds and the Smaile family work hard to meet their needs, as well as endeavouring to create a more individual inn. Space is not a problem, there's a coffee shop, a new upstairs bistro, a bustling bar area offering Scottish ales and 150 malt whiskies, a function room, and a big terrace and garden for summer barbecues. Menus are broad and cosmopolitan, with basic pub meals listed alongside more imaginative homemade dishes that utilise fresh, local produce. Typically, these include fresh haddock, local black pudding rösti stack, Dunkeld lamb chops, Perthshire venison sausages, and local butcher meats. Don't miss the Highland buffet night on Thursdays. En suite bedrooms are comfortable and well equipped.

Rooms: 6. Double/twin from £90, single from £80 and family from £120.
Prices: Restaurant main course from £5.95. Main course bar/snack from £3.95. House wine £10.95.
Last orders: Bar: 23.00. Food: 22.00.
Closed: Rarely.
Food: Modern Scottish.
Real ale: Tetley's Bitter, Jennings Bitter, Hook Norton.
Other points: No-smoking area in restaurant. Garden. Children welcome. Car park. Wheelchair access.
Directions: A9 Pitlochry. Situated in the centre of Pitlochry behind the post office. Parking available behind the inn. (Map 8, C5)

Kelso

The Border Hotel

The Green, Kirk Yetholm, Kelso,
Scottish Borders TD5 8PQ
Telephone: +44(0)1573 420237
BorderHotel@aol.com
www.theborderhotel.com

Marking the end of the 268-mile-long Pennine Way walk, this old coaching inn is a welcoming and most hospitable place to revive after any journey, be it on foot or by car. Current owners, the Blackburns, have refurbished the place and it is a comfortable place to wine, dine and stay. The hospitality starts in the stone-flagged bar with a blazing fire, where walkers who have completed the Pennine Way can claim a free ale. Quality local ingredients such as langoustines, crab, fresh fish, beef and game are used in traditional Scottish recipes, as well as international favourites; so alongside starters of cullen skink and haggis are Thai fishcakes. Mains range from smoked Eyemouth haddock to Border curry of the day. Specials take in choice cuts of meat and game, all deftly cooked. Eat in the two dining areas in the bar, the conservatory or the dining room that looks out over the patio and beer garden.

Rooms: 5. Double/twin room from £40 per person. Single from £45 per person. Family room from £100.
Prices: Restaurant main course from £8. Bar snack from £3.50. House wine £10.
Last orders: Bar: 23.00. Food: lunch 14.00; dinner 21.00.
Closed: Rarely.
Food: Traditional Scottish.
Real ale: Deuchars IPA.
Other points: No-smoking area. Children welcome. Dogs welcome in the bar. Garden. Car park. Games room. Wheelchair access to the restaurant (no WC).
Directions: From Kelso take the BB352. The Border Hotel is situated at the end of the Pennine Way. (Map 8, F7)

Tweedsmuir

The Crook Inn

Tweedsmuir, Scottish Borders ML12 6QN
Telephone: +44(0)1899 880272
thecrookinn@btinternet.com
www.crookinn.co.uk

The poet Robbie Burns wrote Willie Wastle while staying at this famous old drovers' inn, and locally born John Buchan knew the inn well and set many of his novels in the area - the glorious Tweed Valley countryside. Licensed since 1604, the Crook Inn is a strange but winning amalgam of old stone-flagged farmers' bar with open fire and bags of character, and pue 1930s Art Deco in ocean liner-style lounges. As well as providing comfortable accommodation in five en suite bedrooms with lovely valley views, the inn offers local Broughton ales on tap, a good selection of single malts, and home-cooked food with supplies of beef and lamb provided by a local farmer. Dishes range from steak pie, Crook Pillows (cheese, mushroom and leek parcels), Arbroath haddock and chips, haggis with whisky cream sauce, and shepherd's pie in the bar, to sirloin steak with Drambuie cream sauce in the dining room.

Rooms: 5. Double room from £60, single from £38.50.
Prices: Set dinner £15. Bar main course from £7. House wine £10.
Last orders: Bar: 23.30.
Closed: Third week of January.
Food: Traditional Scottish.
Real ale: Broughton Ales.
Other points: No smoking in the restaurant. Children welcome. Dogs welcome overnight. Garden. Car park. Licence for civil weddings. Wheelchair access.
Directions: On the A701 Moffat to Edinburgh road, 16 miles north of Moffat. (Map 8, F6)

WALES

St George

The Kinmel Arms

St George, Abergele, Conwy LL22 9BP
Telephone: +44(0)1745 832207
info@thekinmelarms.co.uk
www.thekinmelarms.co.uk

Farmers' market
Welsh College of Horticulture, Northop, Mold
(3rd Sunday of month)

Must-sees
Bodelwyddan Castle
Conwy Castle
Aberconwy House, Conwy
Llyn Brenig Visitor Centre, Cerrigydrudion
Bodnant Garden (NT), Tal-y-Cafn
Welsh Mountain Zoo, Colwyn Bay

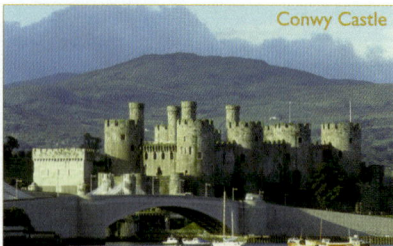

Conwy Castle

Tucked away in the beautiful Elwy Valley, this refurbished 17th-century coaching inn marches on under the touch of Lynn Cunnah-Watson and Tim Watson. Amid country furniture and polished wood floors, everything operates on clean, uncluttered lines around a slate-topped bar offering quality real ales and exceptional wines. Meals may be taken in the cosy lounge, a quieter segregated dining area or the sunny conservatory. A range of sandwiches and snacks, or 'boat-sinking battered cod' with tartare sauce make for a more than adequate lunch, with perhaps braised ham hock with white wine and herb sauce, or the award-winning dish of Welsh beef fillet with roast garlic and shallot jus, as a mainstay of a full-blown evening feast. Look out for market-fresh fish and local meats on the boards. New for 2005 are four stunning, individually designed suites, each offering handmade beds, luxurious bathrooms, a balcony or patio, and views over the Kinmel Estate.

Rooms: 4 suites from £135.
Prices: Set lunch on Sunday £13.95. Restaurant main course from £9. Bar main course from £9. House wine £11.
Last orders: Bar: lunch 15.00 (Sunday 17.30); dinner 23.00. Food: lunch 14.00; dinner 21.30.
Closed: Monday.
Food: Traditional British, Welsh and French.
Real ale: Moorhouses Black Cat, Conwy Castle Bitter, Tetley's Bitter. 3 guest ales.
Other points: Totally no smoking. Children welcome. Dogs welcome in the bar on request. Garden. Car park. Wheelchair access.
Directions: Exit16/M56. A5517 and A550 to A55; St George is 2 miles south-east of Abergele. (Map 5, G3)

Tourist information Conwy +44(0)1492 592248
Where to shop Chester, Conwy

Where to walk
Explore the Clwydian Range of hills south-east of Asaph and walk a section of the Offa's Dyke Long Distance Path, perhaps south towards Llangollen. A short drive west brings you to the beautiful Conwy Valley and those keen of mountain walking can continue into the Snowdonia National Park for invigorating hikes.

Events & festivals
Conwy Seed Fair (March)
Llangollen International Musical Eisteddfod (July)
North Wales Blues Grass Festival, Llandudno (July)
Llangollen Hot Air Balloon Festival (September)

Aberdyfi

Penhelig Arms Hotel

Aberdyfi, Gwynedd LL35 0LT
Telephone: +44(0)1654 767215
info@penheligarms.com
www.penheligarms.com

Where to walk
Hilly walks abound, particularly up the friendly slopes of Cader Idris and the hills and valleys near Llanfihangel. South of the estuary is an easy beach and nature-reserve walk from Ynyslas, and excellent rambles through the Vale of Rheidol close to Devil's Bridge. Long distance trail - Dyfi Valley Way - 108 miles circular trail to Bala Lake from Aberdyfi.

Where to shop Machynlleth, Aberystwyth

Cader Idris

Tourist information Machynlleth +44(0)1654 702401

Must-sees
Ynyshir Bird Reserve: birdwatching on the
  Dovey Estuary
Celtica, Machynlleth: history and legend of the Celts
Centre for Alternative Technology, Machynlleth
Tal-y-Llyn Railway

You can sit on the sea wall, drink in hand, or on the balcony of one of the rear bedrooms, and enjoy superb views across the Dyfi estuary at Robert and Sally Hughes's wonderful 18th-century waterside inn. In the Fisherman's Bar, locals and visitors alike congregate to enjoy traditional ales, first-class wines, and imaginative bar food. This is a true 'local' also, in that fresh fish, meats, fruit, vegetables and bakery goods all arrive at the door from local suppliers, featuring within minutes, it seems, on the daily menus that provide such excellent value for money. Diners are charged simply by the amount they eat from a host of choices: fish stew, sea bass with African spices and roasted lemon potatoes, Welsh Black sirloin steak with peppercorn sauce, and summer pudding being typical temptations to indulgence. In addition to 14 spacious and beautifully appointed bedrooms, there's a stylish loft-style apartment with its own private terrace.

Rooms: 14. Double/twin room from £118 including dinner.
Prices: Set lunch (two courses) from £10.95 and dinner £26. Restaurant main course from £8.95. Bar snack from £4.95. House wine £10.
Last orders: Bar: lunch 15.30; dinner 23.00.
Food: lunch 14.30; dinner 21.30.
Closed: Rarely.
Food: Welsh and seafood.
Real ale: Adnams Broadside, Hancock's HB, Greene King Abbot Ale, Felinfoel Double Dragon Ale. 2 guest beers.
Other points: No smoking in restaurant or bedrooms. Children welcome. Dogs allowed. Garden. Car park. Wheelchair access to the restaurant/pub (no WC).
Directions: Take the A493 to Aberdyfi from the A487 in Machynlleth. (Map 5, H2)

Farmers' market Machynlleth (every 2nd Wednesday)
Local activities Birdwatching, boat trips, sea & river fishing, swimming (good beaches)

Events & festivals
Aberystwyth International Music Festival (July), Welsh International Film Festival, Aberystwyth (November)

Abergavenny

Hunters Moon Inn

Llangattock Lingoed, Abergavenny,
Monmouthshire NP7 8RR
Telephone: +44(01873)821499
huntersmooninn@btinternet.com
www.hunters-moon-inn.co.uk

Built in 1217, this traditional rural local has been tastefully renovated to make the most of its historic setting and the building itself. A solid oak door leads through to a traditional bar with a tiled floor and a warming log fire. The comfortable dining area with carpets, limestone walls and soft lighting makes a congenial setting for dining. The menu revolves around what's available locally, notably Hereford steak, a house favourite that is hung for 28 days for a fuller flavour. Most ingredients are quality Welsh home-grown and reared and the menu majors on robust dishes best suited to pub dining. Garlic mushrooms or baked tomato stuffed with brie are satisfyingly good, as are pheasant with rich game gravy or beef-and-mushroom pie. Whiskey bread-and-butter pudding and crumbles continue the hearty theme. The well-kept ales are Welsh, too, while Gwatkins cider and perry make for a rustic treat.

Rooms: 4. Double/twin from £50, single from £25.
Prices: Restaurant main course from £8.
House wine £10.
Last orders: Bar: lunch 14.00; dinner 23.00. Food: lunch 14.30; dinner 21.00.
Closed: Sunday night, Monday, Christmas Day evening.
Food: Traditional and Modern British and Welsh.
Real ale: Brain's Rev James.
Other points: No-smoking area. Children welcome. Dogs welcome in the bar. Garden. Car park. Skittle alley. Wheelchair access to the restaurant (no WC).
Directions: A40 to Abergavenny. Take the B4347 to Llanvetherine and follow the signs to Llangattock Lingoed. (Map 2, C6)

Bettws Newydd

The Black Bear Inn

Bettws Newydd, Usk,
Monmouthshire NP15 1JN
Telephone: +44(0)1873 880701

You will be one of the family and made to feel totally at home - dogs, muddy boots and all - for there is simply no standing on ceremony at Stephen Molyneux's 14th-century timbered inn. Hidden down lanes amid rolling countryside and replete with stone walls, oak beams and log fire, it is the food and the landlord that draws regular diners here to enjoy Stephen's touches of eccentricity, produce sourced locally and unexpected food combinations and flavours that are the mark of a man who lives for his passion: somewhat quirky, always inventive and often genuinely surprising food. The best illustration is his inclusive 'whatever comes out of the kitchen' tasting menu that might include a pheasant terrine, Usk salmon, and beef medallions in Madeira sauce. After a hearty feed and pints of London Pride, sleep fitfully in one of three simply furnished en suite bedrooms.

Rooms: 3. Double/twin from £50, single from £30.
Prices: Sunday lunch £12.95. Set dinner £23. Restaurant main course from £12. Bar snack from £5.
House wine £12.
Last orders: Food: lunch 14.00; dinner 21.30.
Closed: Closed Monday lunch.
Food: Modern British.
Real ale: Bass, Fuller's London Pride, Tomos Watkin Ales.
Other points: No smoking in the restaurant. Children welcome. Dogs welcome in the bar and overnight. Garden. Car park. Wheelchair access to the restaurant/pub. No credit cards.
Directions: Exit24/M4. Take the A449 to Usk, then the B4595 towards Abergavenny; the village is signposted in two miles. (Map 2, C6)

Raglan

The Beaufort Arms Coaching Inn and Restaurant

High Street, Raglan, Monmouthshire NP15 2DY
Telephone: +44(0)1291 690412
thebeauforthotel@hotmail.com
www.beaufortraglan.co.uk

A proper 16th-century coaching inn with outstanding period features, including a huge fireplace taken from nearby Raglan Castle, Welsh slate floors and an impressive heavily carved oak bar. Renovation by the Lewis family has introduced a modern feel. Add blazing log fires and a warm welcome and you have a vibrant community inn. Chefs are committed to using first-class local ingredients. Bar menus comprise simple food, such as rustic sandwiches of Welsh ham alongside inventive modern dishes listed on the daily specials board, and overall quality and presentation is well above average. In the restaurant, imaginative cooking produces highlights such as lamb with fine green beans, warm basil and mint oil on a red wine deglaze. All en suite bedrooms have been stylishly refurbished.

Rooms: 15. Double/twin room from £55, single from £50.
Prices: Restaurant main course from £10.95. Bar main course from £5.75. House wine £8.95.
Last orders: Bar: 23.00. Food: lunch in the lounge bar served daily. Dinner: 21.00 (20.30 Sunday).
Closed: Never.
Food: Modern British.
Real ale: Brain's Rev James, Fuller's London Pride.
Other points: No smoking in the restaurant. Garden. Car park. Wheelchair access.
Directions: One minute from junction of A40 from Abergavenny and A449 to Monmouth. South to Newport M4 north to M50 M5-M6. (Map 2, C6)

Skenfrith

The Bell at Skenfrith ★ ★

Skenfrith, Abergavenny,
Monmouthshire NP7 8UH
Telephone: +44(0)1600 750235
enquiries@skenfrith.co.uk
www.skenfrith.co.uk

Janet and William Hutchings' beautifully restored 17th-century inn occupies a picturesque spot by the River Monnow. It oozes all the charming allure of an old Welsh inn, with slate floors, old settles and fireside easy chairs in the stylish open-plan bar and dining area, but it's the food and wine that really steal the show. A commitment to local produce in the results in some seriously good cooking. Bar lunches bring Old Spot pork sandwiches or venison steak with cranberry jus, followed by apple tart. The dining-room menu showcases local ingredients in ballotine of duck foie gras, followed by local venison or sea bass with crab risotto. Caramelised rhubarb and vanilla custard provides a fitting finish. William's wine list is superb. There are eight luxuriously appointed, en suite bedrooms. See Pub Walk on page 256.

Rooms: 8. Double/twin from £95. Single from £75, family room from £145.
Prices: Sunday lunch £19.50. Restaurant main course from £10.20. Bar main course bar/snack from £5.50. House wine from £10.
Last orders: Bar: 23.00. Food: lunch 14.30; dinner 21.30.
Closed: Two weeks end of January and early February. Mondays from October to April.
Food: Modern British.
Real ale: Hook Norton Best Bitter, Freeminer Best Bitter, Timothy Taylor Landlord.
Other points: No-smoking in the restaurant and bedrooms. Garden. Children welcome. Car park. Wheelchair access to the restaurant.
Directions: From Monmouth take A466 for Hereford. In 5 miles turn left onto B452 for 2 miles. (Map 2, C6)

Usk

Greyhound Inn Hotel

Llantrissant, Usk, Monmouthshire NP15 1LE
Telephone: +44(0)1291 672505
enquiry@greyhound-inn.com
www.greyhound-inn.com

Surrounded by woodland and pasture in the beautiful Usk Valley, the Greyhound is a traditional 17th-century Welsh longhouse noted for open fires and a comfortable atmosphere. Visitors will find a printed bar menu detailing traditional pub favourites alongside interesting home cooked specials listed on chalkboards. The kitchen uses fresh produce from first-class suppliers, including locally grown fruit and vegetables, and venison from the Welsh Venison Centre. Look out for the good selection of fresh fish dishes and the hearty grills. Puds are a gooey and retro selection of profiteroles, banana split and gateaux. Conversion of the former stables has produced spacious en suite bedrooms, all decorated in a cottage style that suit the rural location. Summer alfresco drinking is a real treat among the colourful flower borders and hanging baskets of the garden, a regular Wales in Bloom Gold Award winner.

Rooms: 10. Double room from £74, single from £52.
Prices: Bar main course from £7.
House wine from £12.
Last orders: Food: lunch 14.15 (Monday to Sunday); dinner 22.30. No food Sunday evening.
Food: Traditional Welsh.
Real ale: Bass, Flower's Original, Greene King Abbot Ale, Brains Bitter. Guest beer.
Other points: No smoking in the restaurant. Children welcome. Dogs welcome in the bar. Garden. Car park. Wheelchair access.
Directions: Exit 24/M4. At Usk town square, take the second left and follow signs to Llantrissant for 21/2 miles. (Map 2, C6)

Welsh Venison Centre
Middlewood Farm, Bwlch, Brecon
Tel: 01874 730929
www.welshvenisoncentre.com

Established and run by the Morgan family since 1985,
the Welsh Venison Centre is located in the heart of
the Brecon Beacons National Park and was the first to
become accredited as both a farm and processing unit
under the Quality Mark for Farmed Venison. The deer are
raised in beautiful surroundings and importance is given
to superb animal husbandry and the highest standards of
animal welfare. The result is very tender meat that has a
mild yet distinctive and succulent flavour, not at all like the
tough gamey reputation venison often has, attributed to
wild deer. Nick Davies at the Greyhound in Usk uses lean
and healthy meat in his venison and ale pie.

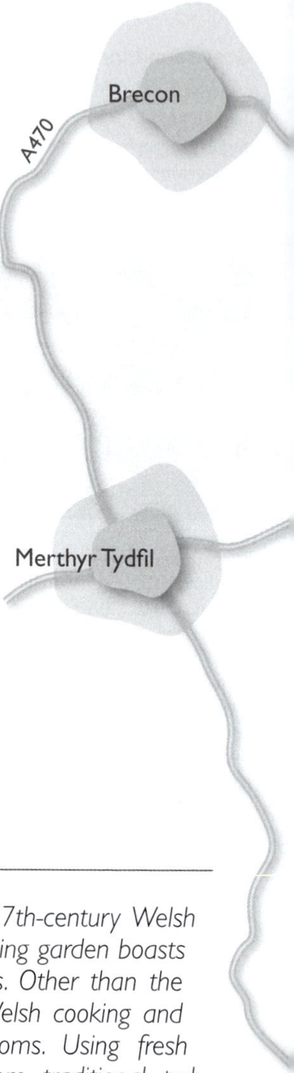

Brecon

A470

Merthyr Tydfil

The Greyhound

Summer eating and drinking is a real treat at this 17th-century Welsh longhouse overlooking the Usk Valley, as the award-winning garden boasts colourful flower borders and attractive hanging baskets. Other than the stunning hillside position, the draw is the traditional Welsh cooking and comfortable accommodation in cottagey, en-suite rooms. Using fresh produce from well-sourced suppliers, food ranges from traditional pub favourites to imaginative blackboard specials listing local venison, Usk salmon and Welsh lamb.

Visit the local Farmers' Market

The Memorial Hall in Usk is the venue for the local farmers' market on the first and third Saturday of the month from 10am to 1pm.

Vin Sullivan Foods
Abergavenny and Blaenavon
Tel: 01495 792792

From humble beginnings at its shop in Abergavenny's High Street, which opened in 1960 and continues to thrive, Vin Sullivan Foods now produces, packages and distributes over 5,000 products from an industrial-estate unit in Blaenavon. High-class gourmet products are supplied alongside more recognisable items over five main product areas – fresh fish, cheese, charcuterie, vegetables and dry provisions.

Welsh Venison Centre, Bwlch

A40

A465

Abergavenny

Vin Sullivan Foods, Abergavenny and Blaenavon

Bowers of Usk

Pontypool

The Greyhound Inn, Llantrissant

Perfect Patisserie, Cwmbran

Newport

A48

Cardiff

Snowden & Co, Cardiff

Snowden & Co
Cardiff
Tel: 029 2048 9948

Occupying city-centre premises, Snowden & Co supplies fresh fish, seafood, shellfish and frozen products to fishmongers, restaurants, hotels and fish-and-chip shops. Top-quality fish is sourced from all the major British fishing ports, from Shetland to Cornwall, Billingsgate and France. The diverse range includes exotic fish such as barracuda, red snapper and parrot fish. A fleet of vans delivers across Wales, with the Greyhound's daily fresh-fish specials being supplied by one of them.

Brecon

The Felin Fach Griffin

Felin Fach, Brecon, Powys LD3 0UB
Telephone: +44(0)1874 620111
enquiries@eatdrinksleep.ltd.uk
www.eatdrinksleep.ltd.uk

Charles Inkin's smart, ochre-coloured inn is one of the new breed of contemporary Welsh inns. Its innovative food brings together quality ingredients and mouth-watering combinations, while upstairs you can stay in chic, individually designed bedrooms. Flagstone floors, open fireplaces and stripped pine beams create an inn with character and personality. The ethos in the kitchen is to use fresh local ingredients and keep it simple to maintain freshness and flavours. Daily updated blackboard menus may list honey-roast parsnip soup followed by Welsh minute steak with béarnaise for lunch. Suppers may consist of quail skewer, braised Puy lentils and cep cappuccino with local venison with autumn fruits, with dark-chocolate mousse or exemplary Welsh cheeses to finish.

Rooms: 7. Double room from £92.50, single from £67.50. Four-poster room £115.
Prices: Main course lunch from £7.95. Main course supper from £12.95. Starters from £4.50. House wine £11.95.
Last orders: Bar: lunch 15.00; dinner 23.00. Food: lunch 14.30; dinner 21.30 (Sunday 21.00).
Closed: Monday lunch (except Bank Holidays).
Food: Modern British.
Real ale: CWRW Haf, OSB (Old Style Bitter), Tomos Watkins Ales.
Other points: No smoking in the restaurant. Children welcome. Dogs welcome overnight. Garden. Car park. Wheelchair access to the restaurant/pub.
Directions: Four miles north of Brecon on the A470. Large terracotta building on the left. (Map 2, B5)

Crickhowell

The Beaufort

Beaufort Street, Crickhowell,
Powys NP8 1AD
Telephone: +44 (0)1873 810402

Welcome refurbishment and restyling saw the Beaufort reopen as a dining venue in late 2003, the loud music and faded decor replaced by tasteful beechwood furnishings on polished boards in the bar and a relaxing, civilised atmosphere in the carpeted dining room. Local diners have also been impressed with the improvements to the food. Lunch and dinner menus are sensibly short, modern British in style, reflect the changing seasons and draw heavily on the top-notch produce that mid Wales has to offer. Welsh Black beef is sourced from the village butcher and game from local shoots, while breads are baked on the premises. A typical winter meal may kick off with pan-fried pigeon with Puy lentils and a balsamic reduction, followed by coq au vin with creamy mash or lamb shank with Toulouse cassoulet. Finish with a plate of Welsh cheese or, if you've room, try the enormous lemon posset.

Prices: Set lunch £10. Set dinner £25. Restaurant main course from £14. Bar snack from £6. House wine £12.
Last orders: Bar: 23.00. Food: 14.30 (Sunday 15.00); dinner 21.30 (Sunday 21.00).
Closed: Rarely.
Food: Modern British with Asian influences.
Other points: No-smoking area. Garden. Children welcome.
Directions: Exit 26/M4. Travel towards Abergavenny and then take the A40 to Crickhowell. (Map 2, C7)

Penpont Organic

The Felin Fach Griffin,
Felin Fach

A470

A479

P F Sweeney Family
Butchers, Brecon

Brecon

Welsh Venison Centre
Middlewood Farm, Bwlch, Brecon Powys
Tel: 01874 730929
www.welshvenisoncentre.com

Sells quality-assured farmed venison either diced, in
shoulder steaks, chops, mince, sausages and burgers,
plus other cuts. Contrary to popular opinion, this is
a low-fat, low-cholesterol meat, rich in iron. It also
sells Middlewood lamb. The shop is open Monday to
Saturday. Check the website for times.

A40

Welsh Venison Centre,
Bwlch

The Felin Fach Griffin

Head chef Ricardo Van Ede is an accomplished cook who was awarded his
Michelin star in the Netherlands. He and the Griffin's owner, Charles Inkin,
appreciate the superb ingredients available in this culinary hotspot around the
Brecon Beacons. They are big fans of the Slow Food movement and incorporate
local fresh produce into the seasonally changing menu.

Visit the local Farmers' Market

Abergavenny's farmers' market is held on the fourth Thursday of every month in Market
Hall, Cross Street, Abergavenny. There is plenty of organic produce among the fish, game,
meat, fruit, vegetables, cheese, eggs, preserves, wines and crafts. For more information, visit
www.abergavennymarket.co.uk.

Bower Farm Dairy
Grosmont

Victor and Val Collinson have developed a local market for their dairy produce, with milk from a herd of pedigree Jersey cows from which they make cream, clotted cream, yogurt and crème fraîche. They also produce rare-breed Gloucester Old Spot pork, which features on the Griffin's menu.

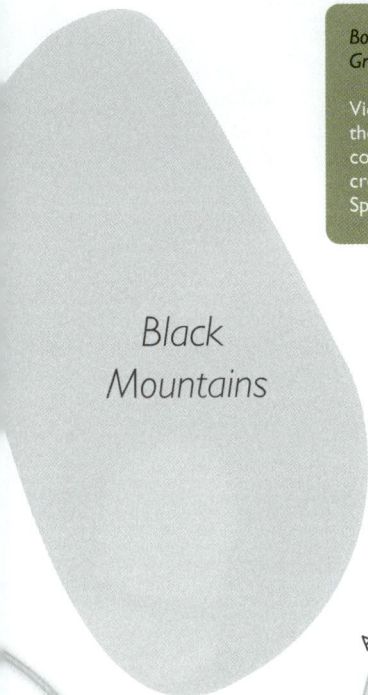

Black Mountains

Bower Farm Dairy, Grosmont

A465

P F Sweeney Family Butchers
9-11 Market Arcade, Brecon
Tel: 01874 623428

Sweeny's is a long-established family butcher that cuts and prepares meat and joints to order. Excellent local lamb and beef and that Welsh delicacy, faggots.

Black Mountains Smokery, Crickhowell

A485

Abergavenny

A40

A4042

Black Mountains Smokery
Crickhowell
Tel: 01873 811566
www.smoked-foods.co.uk

Traditional smoking methods and hand filleting and slicing from quality ingredients make for a fine product collection. The smokery sells wonderful smoked salmon and duck, plus a range of gift packs from fish or meat party platters to the incredible 'Feast'. It is possible to order a monthly supply of salmon for a year.

Wall Path

WALKS

Following his epic coast-to-coast walking adventure in 2004, Nicholas Stanley, of Les Routiers, headed north to tackle Scotland's famous West Highland Way. Here he recounts his experiences during his 95-mile, week-long ramble from the Lowlands around Glasgow to Fort William in the Highlands.

Stanley's Highland fling

I must confess that, until very recently I had regarded people in nylon anoraks plodding along, slightly stooped under the weight of their rucksacks (like a snail with its house on its back) with the gravest suspicion. I simply couldn't understand why anybody not in the army, would want to spend their holidays so engaged. As a keen photographer and a lover of beautiful scenery, I had driven widely around the Lake District, and the other better-known National Parks of the British Isles – in comfort!

But 18 months ago, resulting from a rash challenge in a pub, I found myself setting off, on foot, to walk the 196 miles of Wainwright's famous coast-to-coast walk from St Bees Head in Cumbria to Robin Hood's Bay in North Yorkshire. Once I had shed kilos of totally useless baggage from my rucksack, and blessed with 11 days of the most glorious September weather, I loved every minute of it. And resolved then and there to do another long-distance walk.

The choice between the South West Coast Path and Scotland's West Highland Way, resolved itself in favour of the romance of moorland, heather, Robbie Burns, fine whisky and mountains – and so it was that I found myself arriving at Glasgow airport at 10 o'clock on a Friday night.

Through the Lowlands

Unabashed by the late hour, my B&B host gave me exactly the sort of warm welcome that Les Routiers and other guides search out and promote to a wider public – I commend High Farm, Craigtown, near Glasgow to you in complete confidence. And breakfast the following day, the first of my 95-mile walk, was, in Michael Winner's words, 'heroic'. Intrigued by the 'Organic Farm' sign in the lane, I asked the landlady about organic farming in Scotland. 'Oh, we don't do that any more. We loved being organic farmers, but the nearest approved abattoir is in Aberdeenshire.' What a tragedy for Britain that we should put such hurdles in the way of farmers who want to plough an already difficult and exacting furrow.

My landlady insisted on delivering me to the start point of the walk, marked by a stone obelisk, and I met up with a dozen or two fellow walkers all setting off on that same sunny Saturday morning from Milngavie. My fellow walkers were mainly Scots, and comprised every age, shape and size; some walking for the joy or it, many others to raise money for cancer and other charities.

Following an impeccably waymarked trail, we wound our way through the golf courses of the northern suburbs of Glasgow and out towards the first hills. The sun shone, and spirits were high as I headed gently towards the glorious scenery of Loch Lomond. The approach to Balmaha brings you to the shores of Loch Lomond. This magnificent loch stretches for nearly 20 miles and is some four miles across at its widest point. Even in the mist and driving rain, its contours remain visible as the path wends relentlessly up and down the shoreline, requiring the most painstaking walking (and feeling your way) over the rocky outcrops and knobbly tree roots that characterise most of the path between Balmaha and Inveranan near the loch's northern extremity.

Glorious deep orange-brown bracken lines either side of the path, a succession
of small islands dot the upper section of the loch and, for more intrepid walkers
(or the historically minded), there are the (albeit underwhelming) attractions of
Rob Roy's Cave and Prison. As you reach the northern end of the loch, the Way
veers north east, and you find the splendid Falls of Falloch down below on your
left. And across the water you get a clear view of that famous old coaching stop,
the Drover's Hotel. Briefly following the course of the A82 (and attendant traffic
noise), the Way follows another section of Military Road, which, together with the
old drovers' roads, criss-crosses this part of Scotland.

Nothing daunted us during two days of rain and mist – Scotland's intrepid walkers sustain and restore their sodden spirits and blistered feet with liberal quantities of liquid spirits. Alcohol and convivial, noisy company there was aplenty, but, for three days, could I find or buy an apple or a banana? Not if my life depended on it! Chips by the hundredweight, everywhere, but fresh fruit, never.

Rain aside, and there were intervals, the lambing season was in full swing and enchanting to see. The lanes and byways were decorated and scented with the luxuriant, deep-yellow flowers of broom, and with splendid rhododendron.

Into the Highlands

I arrive in Crianlarich ("Gateway to the Highlands") in better weather, and much better spirits, to be collected by the delightful and obliging owner of the Suie Lodge Hotel. Glorious loch-side views, a comfortable bed and Highland Co for dinner marked my arrival at the Highlands. Then it was on to Tyndrum, home of Scotland's most famous restaurant/shop, The Green Welly Stop (one of Britain's best, inexpensive, large-scale catering restaurants), before setting off across the magnificent landscape of Rannoch Moor.

Whatever weather and travails had gone before, my day walking across Rannoch Moor, in glorious uninterrupted sunshine, redeemed everything. The stunning scenery constantly reminds you of the region's rich history as you join and re-join Scotland's aforementioned network of old military roads. Although I was too early to see heather in full flower, Rannoch Moor helped me make sense for the first time of the yellow, purple and green palette that characterises the canvases of Thorburn and other artists of Scottish scenery.

I arrived at around teatime at the Kingshouse Hotel with its Mountain Rescue Post, at the end of Glencoe Valley. But, having chosen the busy first week of May to do the West Highland Way, I was unable to stay at the hotel, so I decided to take a taxi off the trail and go and stay at a Les Routiers member hotel, the Clachaig Inn in Glencoe village.

The taxi drive from Kingshouse through the bleak and dramatic valley floor to Glencoe was splendid – definitely meriting le detour! The Clachaig Inn is clearly a favoured hostelry among the hiking-and-climbing fraternity – at the end of a long and weary day, this small inn provides the warmest and most obliging welcome. Surrounded by stunning scenery and fellow walkers, I enjoyed a well-earned, restorative drink. The bedrooms are warm and extremely comfortable, the hospitality friendly and attentive, and there's good local beef and venison, and some outstanding local beers. I warmly recommend the Clachaig for visitors exploring Glencoe and surrounding areas.

Walking Q&A

Q. What should I take on a country walk?
A. Enough to be dry and comfortable if the weather changes. Britain's climate is notoriously fickle and the elements will ruin the enjoyment of the walk if you don't take the proper precautions. A good pair of sturdy boots or stout walking shoes is essential. Keep your feet warm and dry at all times and take warm and waterproof clothing with you – an inexpensive, breathable jacket and waterproof trousers will easily do the job. A small rucksack is also good for carrying food and water, a camera and other essentials.

Q. How do I plan the route?
A. A good map is essential – preferably the Ordnance Survey Explorer series, which is excellent. These maps are large-scale – 1:25000 (2 1/2 inches to 1 mile or 4cm to 1 km) and clearly show rights of way as well as useful landmarks that will reassure you as you navigate your way round the walk. Many rights of way are signposted but expect to find some without any form of waymarking at all. This is where the map is especially useful.

Q. What else is there, besides a good map, to help me?
A. A reputable High Street bookstore will stock a good range of walking guide publications that will help to make the task a lot easier. Route-finding instructions and plenty of other useful information (i.e. pubs, points of interest, public transport details etc) are included. There are also guidebooks devoted to Britain's National Trails and a great many lesser-known long-distance routes besides.

GPS Systems
If you are the kind of walker who likes to know your precise whereabouts at any given time, then invest in the latest satellite-navigation equipment. The GPS (global-positioning satellite) unit, or hi-tech compass, tracks the satellites and pinpoints where you are in the countryside to a matter of feet.

Q. Where can I find refreshment?
A. To the many a walker, a good pub and beautiful countryside go hand-in-hand, providing the essential ingredient for a great day's ramble. Few things in life are as pleasurable as running a finger along the red dotted line of a map until it arrives at those magical initials, PH, in search of your lunchtime refueling stop or a cosy refuge at the end of your walk. Having stimulated a healthy appetite and a parched throat, the sight of a welcoming country pub will quicken the steps of even the weariest of walking legs. Don't forget to leave your muddy boots outside.

Q. Is there much to see and do while out walking?
A. There are lots of things to see and do. In fact, a really good country walk should be much more than just fresh air and exercise. It should be an experience – a memory to relish and treasure. Yes, the physical advantages of a long hike or a rural ramble are well documented – no one can deny walking is a healthy pastime. But exercise in the countryside is often the basis for a whole day's entertainment. You could link your walk in with a visit to a museum or a National Trust property, a country park or an animal farm for children. Devise a linear route and return to the start by train or bus, or if you are completing a long-distance trail, perhaps make a short detour in order to visit a nearby attraction just off the route.

To Fort William and the Finish

We leave Glencoe via the Devil's Staircase (the first of two long, steep climbs in the pouring rain that day), the trail heading north through pleasant valleys and forest to the undistinguished town of Kinlochleven. You are reminded of encroaching civilisation and industry as you approach the town – the woodland path brings you across the heavy plant and machinery attached to an aluminium-smelting plant. Nicely situated, Kinlochleven is notable for the impressive waterfalls that you pass as you leave the town, en route for the forests and valleys which mark the route to Ben Nevis.

The long walk from Kinlochleven to Ben Nevis and Fort William was the coldest, bleakest walk I can ever remember. Even the densely wooded forest trail seemed to offer only modest shelter or relief from the weather. But the knowledge that I would be in the warmth and comfort of Fort William before the end of the day helped to keep up the spirits! With the minimum of effort and imagination you could appreciate how stunningly beautiful the steep valleys on the last leg to Ben Nevis must be on a clear or sunny day. By teatime the sky had become grey and the lump of Ben Nevis sat mainly hidden in cloud, so it was no surprise the following morning to see a fresh dusting of snow over its upper levels.

As you descend from Ben Nevis towards Fort William, you experience that apparently inescapable feature of the last leg of any long walk – the sense that Fort William and the end of the trail – always 'around the next bend' – will ever actually be reached. Winding your way through car parks, you do finally come down over the town, the path bringing you in via a housing estate.

A busy crossroads of road, rail, and water traffic, Fort William sits in grey, northern light, but offers the warmest welcome that any traveller could ask for, especially at my blissfully friendly B&B, The Distillery House. Clothes were dried, blisters were plastered, homemade fudge was served and, most importantly, an outstanding local seafood restaurant was recommended and booked for me.

Not only was the return journey back to Glasgow by train, but the journey followed closely the route which I had just spent six days walking on foot. So, I was able to re-visit and enjoy sections of the trail that had been shrouded in cloud and rain, but this time in glorious sunshine. Stunning views, from the comfort of a half-empty carriage! Sheer bliss...

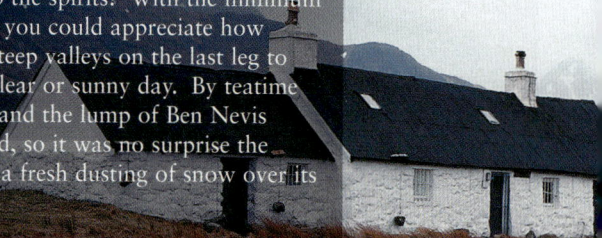

Fact File

Walking the West Highland Way

The West Highland Way runs for 95 miles/153km between Milngavie near Glasgow to Fort William. Opened in 1980, it was Scotland's first official long-distance footpath and is best tackled from south to north, striding from the industrial Lowlands to the heart of the Highlands and the foot of Britain's highest mountain. The scenery grows more magical with every step. From gentle walking through woods, low hills and alongside the eastern shore of Loch Lomond, the trail becomes more challenging as you ascend the lower slopes of Ben Lomond and then follow the old drove roads and military roads across exposed Rannoch Moor into magnificent Glencoe. The route then remains on high ground to Loch Leven and the final few miles to Fort William, with Ben Nevis firmly in sight.

Distance: 95 miles/153km
Duration: 7 days
Start/Finish: Milngavie near Glasgow to Fort William
Terrain: Moderate hills to start, followed by rough lochside paths, mountain slopes and exposed open moor
Waymarking: Excellent throughout
Information: Visit www.west-highland-way.co.uk. The website offers general information, details on where to stay, and a location map. The West Highland Way, by Anthony Burton is published by Aurum Press. For bag-carrying services, contact: AMS (01236 722795) or Travel-lite (0141 956 7890)

To Greyfield Wood from The Hunters Rest

From the word go, the views on this spectacular walk are breathtaking. Weave your way down to the village of Clutton, then follow a lengthy stretch of the popular Limestone Link path through a long valley to reach peaceful Greyfield Wood, with its fascinating industrial heritage and array of plants and flowers.

1 From the pub, cross over to the footpath opposite and follow it alongside a fence beside a white cottage. Cross two more stiles as you descend to reach double gates and the road. Don't go through them. Instead, swing left by the waymarker and follow the path down the field, keeping a line of trees on the right. Continue to a kissing gate on the right.

Cross the track here to another gate and drop down the field to the next gate by a barn. Continue down the slope, crossing a paddock to reach woodland. Cross a footbridge and follow the path through the trees. Soon swing left at some steps and emerge from the trees. Cross over a woodland path to a stile and keep ahead between houses to the road.

3 Turn right, pass the entrance to The Ramblers and turn left immediately beyond a line of cottages. Go down the field, across a stream to a gate and up the slope, keeping to the left. Pass through a gate and continue uphill to Pennyquick Cottage. Cross two stiles and turn left to the stile in the field corner and a lane. Follow it ahead through the village of Clutton. Cross the road junction into Church Lane and make for St Augustine's.

4 Go round the left bend, cross a stream and just beyond it, the road swings right. Veer off to the left here to follow the Limestone Link. Take the obvious track towards farm outbuildings, pass to the left of them and continue on the well-used trail, crossing a number of stiles and negotiating a variety of gates. Eventually you come to a kissing gate and a few paces beyond is a gate with a footbridge spanning the stream.

5

Cross the bridge and the field beyond it towards woodland and pass through a gate, following the broad path through Greyfield Wood. Cross a wide track and continue to an information board on the edge of the wood. Follow the track ahead and when you reach the road turn left and walk through Greyfield.

6

CUCKOO LANE

When you reach a footpath sign, veer off to the right up the lane. At a junction, keep left and follow Cuckoo Lane. When you reach Clutton Hill, turn left at the junction and drop down to a path on the right, immediately beyond houses. Go diagonally up the field slope, or round the right edge if it is ploughed, to a gap in the hedge, turn left along the lane and return to the pub. For pub entry see page 38

fact file

Distance 5 miles
Time 2 1/4 hours
Paths Field paths, woodland tracks, quiet roads. Undulating. Can be muddy in places
OS Map Explorer 142 (Shepton Mallet & Mendip Hills East)

look out for

Greyfield Wood is not just a wood renowned for its bluebells and wildlife. This part of the walk is closely associated with the North Somerset Coalfields, and signs of the former pits are still visible. Greyfield Colliery opened in 1833 and became one of the largest in the county, producing up to 60,000 tons of coal a year. The pit closed in 1911.

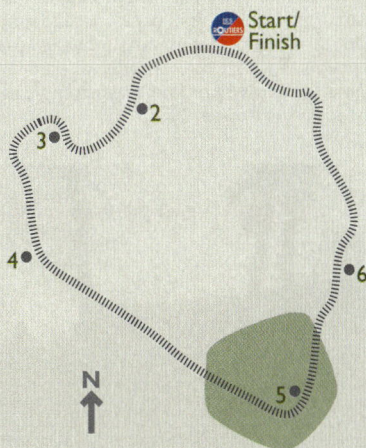

Start/Finish

2

3

4

6

5

N

Woodland

* Les Routiers logo denotes member pub / inn

To Crazies Hill from the St George & Dragon

Escape the bustle of Wargrave, renowned for its Edwardian appearance and picturesque Thames-side setting, by following peaceful paths to the heart of wooded Bowsey Hill.

1 From the St George & Dragon turn right, then left into Wargrave Hill. Go up the hill and along the road, crossing the junction with Dark Lane. Pass Wargrave Manor, ignore the left turn to Crazies Hill and continue to a path on the left just beyond Purfield Drive. Go through the kissing gate and follow the clear field path ahead. Cross a footbridge and avoid a path on the left.

As you approach the corner of the field, veer right through the hedge gap, turn immediately left and skirt the pasture. Make for two stiles and a waymarker in the field corner and keep ahead on the path. In 80 yards look for another waymarker, turn left and head north through woodland. Cross a footbridge after a few paces, ascend steps and turn right at the next obvious path junction. Follow the woodland path for some time to where four waymarked paths meet. This is Bowsey Hill.

Take the first left path and look for occasional white arrows on trees to guide you through the woodland. Reach a gate and road and turn left. Pass the entrance to Maple Croft on the right, then, in 60 yards, look for a stile heralding two waymarked footpaths also on the right. Take the right-hand path, veer right on to a track and follow it to a gateway. When you see a 'private' sign keep ahead to the next gate where there is a reassuring waymarker.

4

Continue ahead through trees to a stile and gate, go straight over into the field and follow the right-hand boundary. Make for a bungalow in the corner, skirt the garden and turn right at the road. Swing sharp left after several paces to join a bridleway, following it downhill through the trees. Keep to the tree-lined path until you reach a footpath crossing the bridleway. Turn left here, head up the steep slope between fairways and cross two more stiles to reach the road.

5

Turn right, passing the entrance to Hennerton Golf Club. When you reach a field path on the left, follow it across open pasture to a fence. Turn right to the next road and here you have a choice. The most direct route is right, then left at the T-junction, back to Wargrave. To avoid the road, turn left, take the first path right and follow it across the fields to a footbridge. Turn right and retrace your steps to Wargrave and the pub. For pub entry see page 42

fact file

Distance **6 miles**
Time **2 1/2 hours**
Paths **Field and woodland paths. Some climbing and road walking. Wet and muddy in places.**
OS Map **Explorer 171 (Chiltern Hills West)**

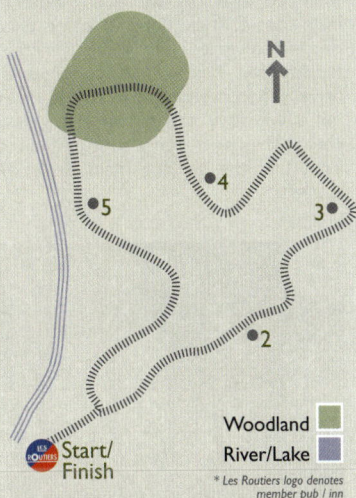

Woodland ▪
River/Lake ▪

Start/Finish

* Les Routiers logo denotes member pub / inn

look out for

The origins of Wargrave date back many centuries. Edith, the wife of Edward the Confessor, lived in the manor in the 11th-century. Much of the local church was destroyed by fire during the First World War – possibly the work of angry suffragettes who took exception when the vicar refused to withdraw the word 'obey' from the marriage service.

The pretty hamlet of Crazies Hill is located on the upper slopes of the Thames Valley. Apparently, 'Crazies' is a rustic name for buttercups, which once thrived in this area.

The Five Arrows Hotel and Waddesdon Manor

Make a day of it visiting the palatial home of a famous banking family and then enjoy this attractive walk through its extensive parkland.

1 With your back to the inn, turn left, then left again by the war memorial into High Street. Walk along to some beautifully decorated gates, the public entrance to Waddesdon Manor, and continue on the drive. When it emerges from the trees, look for a waymark and follow the grassy path ahead, keeping a hedge and pavilion on the right and the snaking main drive over to the left.

2

Cross the drive further on and follow the bridleway signposted to Windmill Hill Farm. Cut between fields and bursts of woodland and follow the drive as it bends right over a cattlegrid.

3 On the horizon now is the awesome facade of Waddesdon Manor, a jumble of exuberant architectural styles. The drive swings left at the next cattlegrid and cuts through a copse. Keep on the bridleway to Windmill Hill Farm and follow the track between the outbuildings.

fact file

Distance **3 miles**
Time **1 1/2 hours** (allow much longer to visit Waddesdon Manor)
Paths **Parkland drives, farm tracks, field paths**
OS Map **Explorer 181 (Chiltern Hills North)**

look out for

The Five Arrows Mayer Amschel Rothschild founded the famous banking dynasty in the 18th-century. The family coat of arms focuses on a red shield and includes a fist holding five arrows. The arrows represent his five sons, four of whom left Frankfurt to establish banking houses in Europe's other financial centres.

Waddesdon Manor One of England's grandest country houses. It is a magnificent French Renaissance-style chateau built by Ferdinand de Rothschild in the late 19th-century.

4 Continue between fields to a gate and along the field edge to the next gate. Turn right and keep the hedge on the right. Keep ahead in the next field and, on reaching the boundary, cross it and then turn immediately right over a stile and footbridge.

Keep along the right-hand boundary, cross the stile in the field corner and continue to two stiles and a footbridge in the right fence. Go diagonally left across the field and head up the slope towards trees. Head for a gap and follow the path up the bank to the main drive to Waddesdon Manor.

6 Turn right and, when you reach a waymark for the Tramway Trail, branch off half-left across the grassy slopes. Make for a wrought-iron kissing gate and follow the path ahead towards trees. Go through a gate on the far side of the field, cut through woodland and cross a drive to reach some lock-up garages. Ahead now are the war memorial and the Five Arrows Hotel.

For pub entry see page 48

Five Arrows Hotel

Through Teesdale from The Rose and Crown

An invigorating ramble through the heart of Teesdale, exploring rough hillside pastures dotted with isolated farmsteads, and the sheltered wooded valley beside the swiftly flowing River Tees.

1 Turn left on leaving the inn and follow the dead-end lane ahead to the left of the green. Take the arrowed path left opposite Klein Cottage and follow the walled path down to a footbridge and stile. Continue ahead across pasture behind the cemetery and bear right alongside the wall, heading uphill to a stile. Head across the field to a stile and follow the wall on your right, high above the River Tees with views of Eggleston Hall, to reach a gate beyond a stone building.

2 Turn right along the road, cross the bridge and climb the stile right to follow the Teesdale Way along a metalled drive. Just before a gate, cross the stile on the left and ascend steps through trees, the path eventually reaching a stile and field. Continue ahead beside the wall to a stile and follow the path uphill towards farm buildings. Beyond a stile, keep right along the wall and pass to the rear of the farmhouse.

3 Follow the arrow (on telegraph pole) to a gate and bear slightly right, following the path through rough pasture to cross a beck, then a wall stile. Head gently downhill to a stile and bear slightly left following the waymarker across the field to a visible stone stile. Bear left then right with the arrow, cross a stile and proceed ahead beside the wall above Shipley Wood.

4 Beyond the next stile, at the edge of the trees, bear right to reach the Perry Myre Rock viewpoint. Alternatively, keep to the path ahead and bear left down a track. Cross a beck and the stile immediately on your right. Cross a further stile and follow the defined path downhill towards Cotherstone and walk across a caravan park to a gate.

fact file

Distance 6 miles

Time 3 hours

Paths Old moorland roads,
field paths, lanes

OS Map Explorer OL31 (North Pennines)

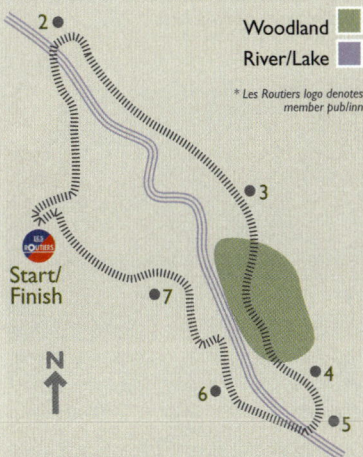

Woodland

River/Lake

* Les Routiers logo denotes
member pub/inn

2

3

Start/
Finish

7

N

4

6

5

look out for

Romaldkirk One of the prettiest villages to
be found in upper Teesdale.

Eggleston Hall Dominates the riverside
scene and the gardens can be visited.

Woden Croft One of the infamous
'Yorkshire Schools' featured in Charles
Dickens' novel *Nicholas Nickleby*.

5

Head downhill along the track, bearing
right at the bottom to cross the footbridge
over the River Tees. Follow the Teesdale
Way right along the bank, then uphill to
a stile. Keep parallel with the river, cross
a stile and bear left down stone steps to
cross a beck via stepping stones. Climb
the next stile and follow the path uphill to
a gate to the right of a stone building. Go
through the gate ahead and pass in front
of Woden Croft.

6

Cross the drive, pass in front of
cottages and keep right of a corrugated barn
to a stile. Beyond the next stile ahead, bear
immediately right downhill into woodland
beside the River Tees. Follow the undulating
woodland path - narrow and slippery in
places - close to the river. Eventually, leave
the river, cross a stile and keep to the right-
hand field edge to pass a derelict cottage.

7

Go through a gate and follow the grassy track left uphill. Bear off right to a tiny gate
and head across the field to a further gate. Maintain this direction and soon bear
slightly right through trees to a gate. Join a narrow path and follow this back into
Romaldkirk. For pub entry see page 52

A moorland and valley ramble from The Old Inn

A varied exploration of the western fringes of Bodmin Moor, through pasture fields and delightful wooded valleys, with expansive views over the moor's highest land and towards the north Cornwall coast.

Walk uphill from the pub. Turn right just before the church; then first left over a stile into a field. Bear right to a stile; keep ahead over two more stiles. Continue ahead to the next stile among hawthorns, into a big field. Keep ahead, bearing slightly left to pass a granite gatepost in a bank, and cross a stile (left of the gate) onto a lane.

Turn right and follow the lane through Treswallock Farm. Descend to cross the stream and turn left over a stile into marshy ground. Cross the stile ahead and bear right, following the wall of Mellon farmhouse. Pass through a gate and bear diagonally left across the field. Cross a stile, a narrow meadow, and another stile onto a lane.

Keep ahead over a stile, looking right for Rough Tor and Alex Tor. Continue up the field, aiming for a gate just left of conifers. The track leads to Corgelly Farm; turn right. After 50 yards, turn left over a stile. Keep ahead, downhill (a big metal barn on your left), parallel to the hedge-bank. Cross the stream on a wooden bridge. Keep ahead for 20 yards, then turn left along the field bottom, aiming for a stile onto a track.

Turn left uphill through Newton and reach a lane. Turn left again. Where the lane bears away left, bear right up a rough track. Pass between farm buildings; keep ahead through a gate on a grassy track across open ground. Pass over the hilltop and keep left of the gorse-filled track as it descends towards a wall.

...for topical features

5 Turn left. Where the wall bears away right, keep ahead over a stile. Bear left uphill to a post/steps over a wall. Keep ahead and cross the next wall corner on steps, with St Breward Church tower directly ahead. Straight across the next big field, descending through a gate left of an open barn. Follow the track downhill, passing through the right of three gates. Keep ahead, descending to meet a tarmac way through a gate.

6 Turn right. Descend over a cattle grid, ascend to a road. Turn left uphill. 100 yards beyond a sharp right bend, bear right onto a track. At the house entrance, turn left onto a narrow footpath. Eventually meet a path junction and turn right downhill to Fellover. Bear left and keep straight on above the Camel valley. Reach a lane by the tropical-bird farm; bear right to pass through the Chapel and continue uphill.

7 Turn left uphill past the holy well. Pass through a gate with a house on your left. After 100 yards, turn left through a gate and bear right over a stile. Continue uphill, over a stile, through playing fields. Cross a stile onto a track and follow the path ahead to the pub. For pub entry see page 53

fact file

Distance 5 1/2 miles
Time 2 1/2 hours
Paths Field paths, tracks, farm lanes, grassland, woodland paths
OS Map Explorer 109 (Bodmin Moor)
Note: waymarking is inconsistent, so use an OS map.

look out for

St Breward Church Dates from Norman times and is dedicated to the 6th-century saint, said to have been martyred in the neighbourhood.

Holy Well of St James Thought to have been visited by pilgrims en route to Santiago de Compostela in Spain.

N

Start/Finish

Woodland
River/Lake

** Les Routiers logo denotes
member pub / inn*

Stepping into Eden from The Dukes Head

Unspoilt. Undiscovered. The Eden Valley really does live up to these billings. Peaceful paths, spectacular scenery, dramatic views - all these are part of this superb, easy walk in the foothills of the Pennines.

1 From the inn, walk down to and cross the bridge over the river Eden. At the far end, take the steps left, and loop back beneath the bridge to join a widening path through fine oak, beech and pine woods. Through the trees are glimpses to the imposing Pele tower or castle.

The Dukes Head Inn

2 At a waymark post above an old weir, turn back-left, walk 50 paces to another waymarked post and turn right along a woodland path beside a fence. Shortly, climb a stile and keep ahead up the wide track rising gently into Coombs Wood. At one point, a narrow path diverges right to a spectacular viewpoint up the Eden Valley (Beware! This is unfenced and slippery). At any major forks ,keep left, eventually leaving the woods at a parking area and Forest Enterprise board.

fact file

Distance **5 1/2 miles**
Time **2 1/2 to 3 hours**
Paths **Woodland, field paths, quiet byroads**
OS Map **Explorer OL5 (The English Lakes North-Eastern Area)**

3 Turn left and walk to the phone box and sign for Longdales. Turn right along this lane, rising past cottages. As the tarred lane fades, turn left along a track signposted to bridleway. Passing beside a cottage, this rough lane rises gradually to a summit. At this point, turn right through a gate along the signposted bridleway to Bascodyke. Cross to the left of the hedgerow and follow it to a gate into a farm lane. Follow this to Bascodyke Head Farm.

Bear left to the farmyard; take the track to the right, just past the first barn and walk to the very top of the complex, above the front farmyard. Turn left and follow the farm lane. This soon develops as a tarred lane; follow this past farms up to a minor road. Turn left to drop to Ainstable. The way is straight over the crossroads, soon passing a mill. About 300 yards past this, turn left up the lane signed for Ainstable Church. Take the gate beside the churchyard wall and bend right to another kissing gate. Go through and turn left, dropping through a series of stiles to reach a lane.

5 Go up the entrance virtually opposite, enter the pasture and shadow the wall on the right, to reach a waymarked stile. Continue along the right-hand edge of the next few pastures to reach a stile into a green lane. Turn left, signed for Oatlands Cottage. At the road, turn left to reach a bridge over a brook. Take the footpath signed right here, joining a riverside path that returns you to the bridge at Armathwaite. Re-cross this to return to The Dukes Head. For pub entry see page 55

N

Start/Finish

Woodland
River/Lake

* Les Routiers logo denotes member pub / inn

look out for

Armathwaite A sleepy little village beside an ancient crossing of the River Eden. The church has two colourful windows, including one by Sir Edward Byrne-Jones.

Longdales A row cottages beside a no-through-road. Marvellous views up and down the Pennines unfold with every step along the lane.

From The Boot Inn to Burnmoor Tarn

Here's a walk with a steep climb. Your reward is to stand beside a remote tarn in the shadows of England's highest peaks, with views to die for and a return leg through a sublime valley and lake-speckled moors.

From the inn, walk up to the old packhorse bridge beside the watermill. Go through the gate beyond this and turn right. In about 100 yards go through the bridlegate on your right. The track rises gradually through a series of gates beside oakwoods high above the lively Whillan Beck, finally passing through a last wall to continue across gently sloping moorland.

At the first fork, keep ahead-right along the lesser path, walking in line towards the towering Scafell. Keep right at the next fork, passing well above the footbridge at Lambford. Occasional cairns mark the route. Eventually, the remote Burnmoor Tarn is revealed. To your right, Scafell scrapes the sky; ahead are the stunning peaks clustering at Wasdale Head. (An additional 2 miles return walk to the low horizon beyond Burnmoor Tarn reveals this wonderful panorama).

fact file

Railway
Woodland
River/Lake
* Les Routiers logo denotes member pub / inn

Distance 6 1/2 miles
Time 3 1/2
Paths Rough paths, moorland tracks, one short road section
OS Map Explorer OL6 (The English Lakes, South-Western Area)

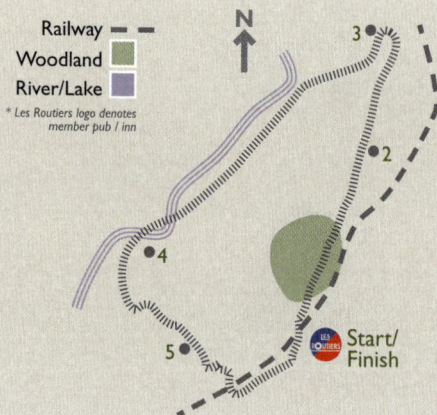

Start/Finish

3 Above the near shoreline, turn left to walk to Burnmoor Lodge. Pass just left of this and take a narrow path to the right. This soon crests a gentle rise to reveal hidden Miterdale. Pick a way down to the bank of the infant River Mite and trace a path along either side of the water. You'll ultimately need to be on the left bank to take a ladder stile near to fir woods. Walk ahead to find a stile beside a tree. Don't take this; rather turn uphill to follow the wall around to a gate at the edge of woods. Stay on this old stony lane as the woods peel away.

4

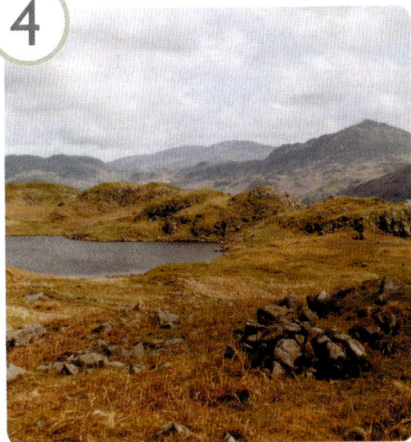

Continue along this to a gate; keep ahead to a second gate. Don't go through this; instead turn left up alongside the wall, commencing a lengthy and potentially boggy climb up to a forestry road at a woodland gate. Remain outside the woods to the point where the trees and wall turn away right. Here, bear left along an indistinct path which circles to the left of a knoll. Fork right in 200 yards through a dip in the low ridge and walk ahead to a lone rowan tree. A more obvious path now passes left of reedy Siney Tarn and crests a rise to reveal lovely Blea Tarn.

Pass right of the tarn and pick up a path which passes to the right of the snout of the knoll beyond the tarn. This bends left to start a series of lazy zigzags down into Eskdale. At the bottom, go through a gate and cross the railway to Beckfoot Station. Turn left along the road, pass Dalegarth Station to find the turn for Boot beside Brook House Inn.
For pub entry see page 57

5

look out for

Built in the 16th-century Boot Watermill is said to be the oldest working mill in England.

Burnmoor Tarn One of the largest and most remote of the tarns of Lakeland.

Miterdale Has views up its valley to Scafell and glimpses of statuesque Great Gable.

From The Inn Fox to Hardy's Evershot

An undulating and very scenic walk taking in the beautiful church at West Chelborough and the unspoilt village of Evershot, Evershead in Hardy's Tess of the D'Urbervilles.

1 From The Fox Inn, turn right along the lane, then right by the post box. Take the footpath right beside Norwood Cottage to a gate. Proceed through the wood to a gate and continue across pasture to enter a copse. Cross the footbridge, go through a gate, cross a further field and pass through another wood to a gate.

2 Follow the yellow arrow right uphill across pasture, with a farm on your left. Bear left along the fence to a gate in the field corner. Go through the gate immediately right, bear left and ignore the path left down to a gate. Keep ahead and proceed towards the houses. Bear left along the fence following the blue arrow, pass behind barns to a gate, then right in front of a farmhouse. Turn left along the drive to West Chelborough Church.

3 Take the track to the left of the churchyard, then the footpath, following the yellow arrow through a gate and right around the field edge down into the valley. Go through the second gate on the right, cross the footbridge to a gate, then head uphill across the field. Pass beneath telegraph wires, enter the next field and continue parallel with the poles, uphill to a track. Bear left through Manor Farm to a lane.

fact file

Distance 7 miles
Time 4 hours
Paths Field paths, tracks, metalled lanes
OS Map Explorer 117 (Cerne Abbas & Bere Regis)

look out for

West Chelborough Church Commands beautiful rural views and is noted for its 17th-century stone-effigy tomb of a mother and child, and a 12th-century font.

Evershot A sleepy village of mellow-stone houses set among the hills south of the beautiful Melbury Park Estate.

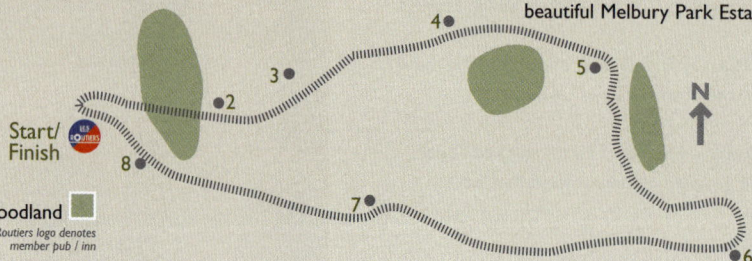

Start/Finish

Woodland
* Les Routiers logo denotes member pub / inn

4

Follow the metalled track right and climb steeply. As it levels, look for a stile in the left hedge. Follow the field edge ahead, go through the left-hand gate in the corner and cross the field to a stile. Cross the stile opposite and bear half right to a stile hidden behind the barn. Pass between the houses to a lane, turn left, then right and enter the car park behind The Acorn Inn.

Cross over and pass beside a workshop (not signed). Head downhill along the field edge, then across the field to a stile in the left corner. Cross the stream, ascend to a gate and head across a large field, uphill towards a farm. Pass between the barns, bear right to a gate and join the track at Girt Farm.

5

Turn right along the village street, pass the church and leave the village for a mile. Take the second lane right, signed Chelborough. Cross over staggered crossroads, signed West Chelborough, then, at a sharp right bend, take the track left.

6

7 Immediately bear off right steeply uphill to a gate. Keep to the right-hand field edge onto Chelborough Hill. Enter the next field and bear slightly left to a gate. Beyond the next gate, walk along the field edge towards a barn. Join the track, go through a gate and keep to the high-level track, eventually reaching a crossing of paths.

8 Go through the gate ahead and take the right-hand path to a stile in the corner. Pass through the trees to a gate and keep ahead to a futher gate. Head towards the house and bear left to enter the next field. Follow the path to a stile, pass through the trees to a stile and pass through the narrow field to a gate and The Fox Inn. For pub entry see page 70

Paglesham Creek and The Plough & Sail

An easy, level walk that takes in Paglesham Churchend, and a breezy return loop beside Paglesham Creek and the River Roach.

1 Take the arrowed footpath along the track to the left of the pub. Go through a gate beside a house called Cobblers Row, the waymarked path taking you through another gate, then along the left-hand field edge. Pass beside a brick wall, then walk around the edge of the lawn of Well House to a wicket gate.

2 Join the metalled track, ignoring the footpath on the right, and follow the lane left towards barns. Take the footpath beside the corrugated barn (East Hall), following it left behind the barn to pick up a track that skirts the left-hand edge of the field. Follow it right, then go through the gate on your left and follow the Roach Valley Way along the grassy field edge. Pass beside a paddock and a pond to reach St Peter's Church at Paglesham Churchend.

fact file

Distance **6 1/2 miles**
Time **2 3/4 hours**
Paths Field paths, grassy sea wall, unmade tracks
OS Map Explorer (176 Blackwater Estuary and Maldon)

River/Lake ▮
* Les Routiers logo denotes
member pub / inn

look out for

The remote location of Paglesham on Essex's east coast and its proximity to waterways, it attracted many smugglers to the area. One notorious 18th-century smuggler, William Blyth, is buried at Paglesham Church.

Paglesham Creek The habitat for a host of waders and wildfowl. Look out for brent geese in winter and oystercatchers, curlews and, if you're lucky, a short-eared owl.

Continue ahead along the village street, passing The Punch Bowl Inn. In a few paces, take the concrete path on your right and turn left along the field edge parallel to a waterway. Go up a grassy embankment and turn right along the sea wall beside Paglesham Creek. With views across Wallasea Island to Burnham-on-Crouch, keep to the path as it meanders beside open marsh and Paglesham Creek, with good opportunities to see wading birds.

The path eventually reaches the River Roach. Follow it right beside the river, passing oyster beds and boats to reach a boatyard. Drop down steps by the quay and walk through the boats and machinery to exit the yard via the main gate. Follow the unmade track to cottages at Paglesham Eastend. On reaching Cobblers Row, turn left and retrace your steps back to The Plough & Sail. For pub entry see page 73

From The Plough Inn at Kelmscott to Lechlade

This easy ramble beside the River Thames takes in St Mary's Church at Buscot, historic Lechlade and Kelmscott Manor, once the home of William Morris, founder of the Arts and Crafts Movement.

From The Plough, turn right along the lane beside the inn and walk through the village to a T junction. Turn right towards Kelmscott Manor, pass the entrance and continue along the track to the River Thames. Go through the gate on your right to join the Thames Path. Walk beside the river for 1 1/2 miles and cross the second footbridge over the river. Follow the path around the field edge and cross a stile to reach Buscot Lock.

To view Buscot Weir, church and Old Parsonage (National Trust), cross the lock gates on your left and follow the path over the weir. Pass Lock Cottage and take the footpath right to visit the church and adjacent Old Parsonage. Return across the weir and lock and keep ahead across the second lock to a stile. Turn left along the field edge and rejoin the Thames Path.

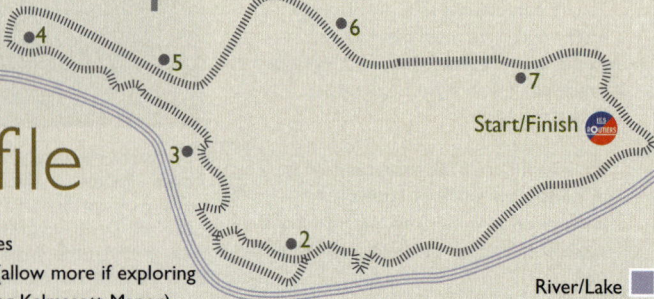

fact file

Distance 6 1/2 miles
Time 3 1/2 hours (allow more if exploring Lechlade and visiting Kelmscott Manor)
Paths Riverside and field paths, some road
OS Map Explorer 170 (Abingdon, Wantage & Vale of White Horse)

River/Lake

* Les Routiers logo denotes member pub / inn

3 Continue along the meandering path to a further footbridge. Ignore the alternative Thames Path signed right across the footbridge. Shortly, pass beneath the A417 to reach St John's Lock. With excellent views of Lechlade Church, continue for a further 1/2 mile to Ha'penny Bridge and the A361. Leave the Thames Path and cross the bridge to enter Lechlade.

4 Turn right at the T-junction in the town centre, then bear off right to the church. Take the paved path through the churchyard (Shelley's Walk) to a lane. Cross and pass through two gates, then cross a meadow to a kissing gate. Follow the raised, tree-lined path ahead to a lane opposite a caravan park.

5 Take the lane ahead beside the Trout Inn. Follow the waymarked path left just before a house and stream. Skirt the house, then follow the path across fields close to the River Leech and pass behind a house to reach Mill Lane. Turn right, cross the river and pass Lechlade Mill. Continue along the narrow lane to a T-junction.

6 Turn right, then left following the footpath sign (Willow Walk) and bear diagonally left across pasture to a stile. Keep left along the field edge to a stile in the field corner and maintain direction. Cross a footbridge and proceed across the field ahead on worn path to a lane.

7

look out for

Kelmscott Manor The country home of William Morris - poet, craftsman and socialist - from 1871 until his death in 1896.

Buscot Lock On the banks of the Thames, close to the picturesque weir and lock at Buscot, stands the 18th-century Old Parsonage (National Trust; limited opening times) and St Mary's Church, noted for its stained glass by Morris & co.

Turn right and follow the road into Kelmscott. Pass the church and turn right, signed to The Plough Inn. For pub entry see page 75

To Belas Knap from The White Hart

Follow Windrush Way past magnificent Sudeley Castle and climb the Cotswold scarp for spectacular views across Gloucestershire to one of the great burial mounds of ancient Britain.

1 Turn left downhill from the pub car park. At Sudeley Country Cottages, take the arrowed path right (Windrush Way) through a kissing gate into parkland. Follow the path across pasture, crossing a track, soon to pass through a further gate in the field corner by woods. Turn left, cross the entrance drive to Sudeley Castle and go through a gate to the left of double gates, following the green-and-white marker of the Windrush Way.

2 Continue across parkland, with Sudeley Castle visible left, keeping left through a further gateway. Here, at the fork, bear half-right and keep to the marker posts on a defined grassy path, gently descending to cross a brook. Go through a swing gate, bear right across the river and turn left to a stile beside a gate.

3 Bear half right uphill through pasture (right of telegraph pole) to a stile. Keep ahead to another stile, walk beside woodland to yet another stile and descend to a stile by a brook. Continue across a meadow final to a track. Leave the Windrush Way and turn right along the 'road used as public path'. Soon reach a gate and New Meadow Farm.

4 Beyond the gate, take the waymarked path left through a green gate. Head uphill on a track between fields to a further gate. Continue uphill and turn right through double gates at woodland. Follow the path to a T-junction of tracks by Humblebee Cottages.

5

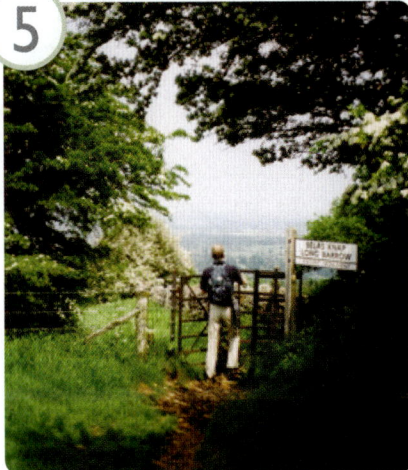

Turn left uphill along the Cotswold Way to a metalled lane. Turn right for 1/4 mile to reach a sign for Belas Knap. Climb the stile on your left, head uphill through trees to a kissing gate and follow the field edge left, soon to follow it right steeply uphill to a gate in the field corner affording superb views. Keep left to reach Belas Knap.

6

Retrace your steps back to the road and turn left. Where the road bends sharp right, take the arrowed path ahead up to a stone stile, signed Winchcombe. Head downhill across pasture following marker posts to reach a stile. Turn right along a metalled track, passing the cricket pitch. to a gate and road.

7

fact file

Distance **5 miles**
Time **3 hours**
Paths **Field paths, defined tracks, the Cotswold Way, quiet lanes**
OS Map **Explorer OL 45 (The Cotswolds)**

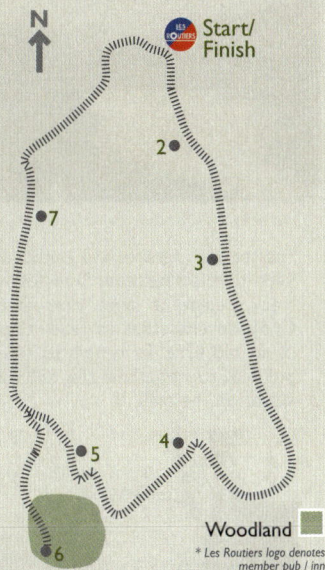

Woodland
Les Routiers logo denotes member pub / inn

look out for

Winchcombe has a considerable history. Visit the huge 'wool church' and its two interesting museums - Folk Museum and the Railway Museum.

Sudeley Castle Worth visiting for its ruined banqueting hall and immaculate, ornate gardens.

Belas Knap Dates to around 2500BC - an impressive burial mound.

Turn left, then, just beyond houses on your left, take arrowed path right, through the first kissing gate. Follow the field-edge path to a gate and continue along the narrow path to another gate. Cross the pasture to a metal gate and turn left, crossing the river, then, at the village road, turn right back to the inn. For pub entry see page 80

Titley, The Stagg Inn and the Mortimer Trail

This glorious figure-of-eight walk takes the walker right to the heart of the Welsh Marches, a wonderfully quiet and unspoilt rural district, following the Mortimer Trail, one of its loveliest upland routes.

1 From the inn, turn left and follow the road to Titley Church. Turn left immediately beyond it and follow the Mortimer Trail beside farm outbuildings. Avoid a path on the left and head up through the fields, following the frequent trail waymarks. When the path curves left in line with the field boundary, look for a gap in the hedgerow and take the Mortimer Trail across pastures to Green Lane Farm.

2 Pass to the right of the outbuildings and keep to the Mortimer Trail, following the track beside a large corrugated barn. Cross several stiles to reach the remains of an old byre. To return to Titley, go to point 6; to complete the full walk, keep ahead on the trail.

3 Skirt the pasture, keeping woodland on the left, and make for the field corner. Enter bluebell woodlands and follow the trail through the trees to a stile on the right. Cross a field and look for a stile in the top boundary. Join an enclosed path and follow it for some time to a stile. Cut through a pine forest and drop down some steps to reach a waymarker.

4 Turn sharp right here, leaving the trail, and descend steeply, bending to the left. Keep dropping, avoiding any turnings to the left and right, and eventually you reach a T-junction with a track. Turn right and walk along to a ford and some cottages. Turn right before the water, avoid a turning on the right and follow the cycle trail between trees and hedges to reach Little Brampton.

5

Look for the path signposted to Titley (1 1/2 miles) and follow the clear waymarks. The path eventually makes for the foot of the wooded escarpment and a line of coniferous trees. Cross the fields and continue on a track. Go through a gate and pass some outbuildings and a house. Turn right at the lane and return to The Stagg. For pub entry see page 85

Turn right at the footpath sign, following the track to a field. Keep ahead towards the wooded escarpment and head for a stile. Swing left and climb through the trees. This is a lengthy pull. Cross the edge of a tree-ringed field to two stiles with a path in between and turn left along the field.

6

fact file

look out for

The Mortimer Trail, 30-miles in length, running from Ludlow to Kington, takes walkers through a land of lush pastures, wooded valleys and rolling hills.

Distance 7 1/2 miles (or 4 miles for the first loop and 3 1/2 the second)
Time 4 hours for the full walk
Paths Field, woodland paths, tracks, sections of the Mortimer Trail. The full route is quite an adventurous walk, particularly the second loop.
OS Map Explorer 201 (Knighton and Presteigne)

Titley Church Mainly a Victorian restoration. In the churchyard is the grave of Lazar Meszarios, a Hungarian general who became ill and died while visiting the area.

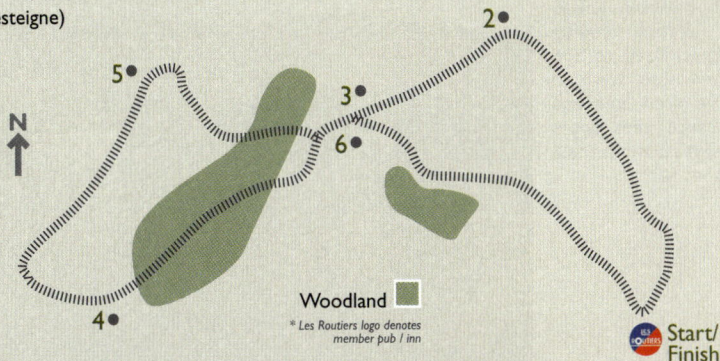

Woodland

* Les Routiers logo denotes member pub / inn

Start/Finish

N

The Alford Arms and the Ashridge Estate

A charming blend of peaceful commonland and glorious beech woodland forms the scenic backdrop of this very varied walk through the beautiful Ashridge Estate.

1 From the front of the pub, cross the road and take the path opposite, following it uphill through trees and bluebell woods. Keep to the wide path, cross a drive and continue alongside hedging. Enter woodland and bend right, keeping right after a few paces to pass by trees and private gardens.

2

Soon you reach the fairways of a golf club. Skirt the fairways, following the path through the trees to the road. Cross over, following the Hertfordshire Way across more fairways. Cut between trees and, further on, you reach a waymarked crossroads.

3

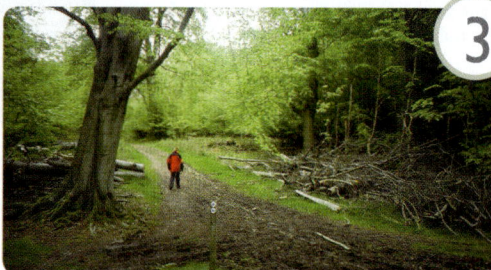

Turn right, following the bridleway down into a dip at Frithsden Beeches and ascend the other side. Join a tarmac drive and when it bends right, keep ahead along the field edge and then down through the undergrowth to reach the road.

4

Cross over and take the path signposted to Little Gaddesden. Pass the entrance to a house called Rodinghead and then follow the path ahead between fences and across rolling parkland. Keep to the left and head down to a large dead tree and two beech trees. Cross the next stile to a track and veer left.

...for special offers

5

Swing left after 120 yards and take the path up the slope to Ashridge House. Turn right at the corner of the building and follow the drive to a left bend. Turn right here by a NT bridleway sign and follow the track through the trees and across parkland. Enter woodland and as the track loops dramatically to the left, look for a path running up the bank to an adventure playground. Cross it diagonally to the right corner and turn left at a path T-junction to reach the road.

6

Cross over to a field path and follow it down through a grassy valley. Cross a track and continue through the fields, passing a solitary tree before reaching Nettleden. Join the road, pass a waymarked path to St Margaret's and turn right a few steps beyond it by Pightle Cottage. Follow the lane and further up the slope take the woodland path parallel to it on the left. Rejoin the lane and return to The Alford Arms. For pub entry see page 86

fact file

Distance **6 3/4 miles**
Time **3 1/2 hours**
Paths **Common paths and bridleways, parkland paths and drives, field paths**
OS Map **Explorer 181 (Chiltern Hills North)**

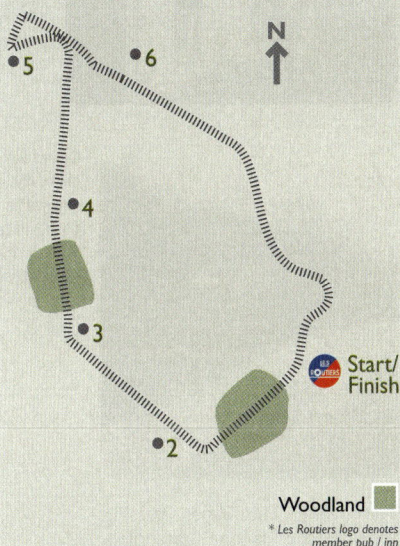

Woodland

Les Routiers logo denotes member pub / inn

look out for

5,000 acres of Ashridge Estate is characterised by sprawling woodland, farmland and open downland, now in the care of the National Trust.

Ashridge House Its vastness takes the breath away. It was built in 1276 and restored by James Wyatt in 1808.

The Freemasons Arms under Pendle's Spell

Forbidding Pendle Hill was the setting for the most notorious alleged acts of witchcraft in the early years of the 17th-century. From the skirt of the hill, this easy walk meanders to the banks of the River Calder and the village of Whalley, with its ruined Abbey.

1 Turn left from the pub, cross the lane and ascend Moor Lane. At the top, bear right into a stony field road. In 100 yards, take the stile on the right and head left to a ladder stile into woods. Keep straight ahead through stone gateposts to a stile into a field. Go ahead to decrepit sheepfolds; here drop right to a walled corner. Take the right-hand stile, then shortly, another. Turn right, aiming for the left of the woods below. Use the footbridge onto the golf course and turn right to reach a stile and nearby traffic lights.

2 Carefully cross into Accrington Road. In 300 yards, take the stile left just past the Whalley sign. Join the riverside path. Pass the weir and trace the rough lane to a village street. Turn right. In 50 yards, go left onto Abbey Mews and then wind through Cornmill Mews on a tarred path emerging beside the churchyard. Turn left to reach one of the Abbey's gatehouses. Explore!

Walk along The Sands, passing beneath the second gatehouse and the viaduct. Take the private road, passing under the bypass. Remain on this lane past the treatment works and ahead to the riverbank, then turn right. About 150 yards before the river bends, fork half-right up a scarred track and then half-left, a metal rail-fence soon on your right. Trace this track straight through a complex of gates and fences, then bend right with the rail-fence still on your right and an old orchard left. Remain on this track over a metal step stile. Continue to a road.

fact file

Distance 5 miles
Time 2 1/2 to 3 hours
Paths Mostly field paths and lanes
– expect mud and cattle
OS Map Explorer 287
(West Pennine Moors)
NB - the route at Brook House Farm complex (in Point 4) may change very slightly due to building work.

Woodland
River/Lake

* Les Routiers logo denotes member pub / inn

look out for

Pendle Hill Looms mysteriously above this walk. It was on the slopes of this hill that Alice Nutter, Demdike and other unfortunates were accused of witchcraft by the local squire, Roger Nowell, and ultimately convicted and hanged in Lancaster Castle in 1612.

Whalley Abbey Founded by the Cistercian order in 1296. Closed and looted in 1537 during the reign of Henry VIII, substantial remains survive in a tranquil setting by the River Calder.

St Mary's Church Contains some exquisite woodworking.

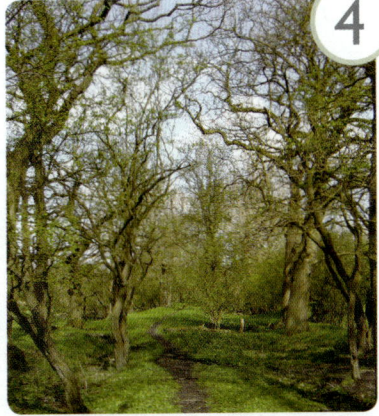

Cross and take the right-hand stile, walking to the distant farm. Use the wooden gate onto a concreted lane and go ahead to the driveway. Turn left to Brook House Farm (Whalley Cornmill). Bend left, then right (a large green barn and horse yard on your left), take the handgate and go ahead over a bridge to a gate. Drift half-right to the field edge, ignore the gate on your right and keep ahead to a bridge and stile. Cross the railway to another stile, then bend left up a wooded strip. At the end, take the stile right and walk the dirt field track through to a road.

Cross straight over into Whiteacre Lane. Remain on this over the bypass. At the junction fork right to return to Wiswell centre and the pub.
For pub entry see page 86

Into Bowland from The Inn at Whitewell

Over the stepping stones from a famous inn for a circuit amongst the Forest of Bowland's little-known limestone scenery.

From the front of the inn, pass the church on the right and walk down into the car park. Go through the gateway and turn right towards the river. The riverbank path drops down to the left below the garden wall and leads to the stepping stones. Cross the River Hodder and follow the waymarkers on the opposite side to a gate at New Launds Farm.

Go through the gate and turn left through another gate on a steep track up the bank. The track peters out but the line is clear, with woods dropping down to the river on the left and open pastureland ahead and right. Continue up through the field to a gateway. Continue over the shoulder and bear slightly right before dropping down to a stile. Follow the fence on the right, then bear right, up to a gate and stile. Through these, turn left and join the track to Fair Oak. Descend through a gateway, cross a brook and walk up the ramp into a hamlet.

3 Bear left, then turn right opposite the barn, into a yard. Pass the cowshed on the left and locate a handgate by the barn wall in the far corner. Follow the path to a stile into a field. Walk across the field, aiming to intercept the fence on the left-hand side at the far end. Cross a stile then cut off the field corner to a stile leading to the road. Turn right and follow the road for 200 yards to a crossroads.

4 Go straight ahead, over the cattle grid. Follow the track over another cattle grid and then around a bend. It becomes surfaced and crosses yet another cattle grid, heading for sheds on the left. Go through a gateway by the buildings and continue, as the track swings left to descend to Dinkling Green Farm. Crossover another cattle grid, then cross the bridge over the brook and bear left into the farmyard.

From a courtyard, turn right to a gate between a wooden shed and garden wall. Follow the snicket to a stile then cross the field ahead, maintaining direction to a stile in the fence to the left of the gate. Cross the stile and bear half-right to another stile. Cross into the paddock and turn left towards the chicken sheds. Beyond these, cross the wooden bridge over the brook. Go through the gate and up a track into the farmyard.

fact file

Distance 5 1/2 miles
Time 2 1/2 hours
Paths Field paths, farm tracks, quiet country lanes, stepping stones
OS Map Explorer OL41 (Forest of Bowland & Ribblesdale)

N

River/Lake ■
* Les Routiers logo denotes member pub / inn

look out for

Forest of Bowland Not a forest in the sense that it was wooded, but open moorland that was a hunting domain owned by the Duchy of Lancaster.

Go through the gate on the the other side, continue up the access track, bearing right at the fork. Follow the track over the saddle, then right, over the cattle grid and past Tunstall Ing. After a left turn, emerge at a minor road by a cattle grid. Turn left for 200 yards to a gate on the right. Go through and aim for the base of a round hillock. The contouring path leads round the foot of the hill to two gates. Take the left-hand gate and walk down the field with the fence on the right. At the bottom, take the right-hand gate to join the track that skirts the base of the escarpment. Through the next gate, turn right into New Launds Farm. Walk up through the yard, descend to a gate, then retrace your steps back to the stepping stones and return to The Inn.

For pub entry see page 95

Holkham Estate from The Victoria

Choose from three very different and very beautiful walks in and around Holkham Hall, taking in magnificent parkland, a wildlife-rich nature reserve and a huge sandy beach and, on the longer walk, tidal creeks and Nelson's home village of Burnham Thorpe.

1 From the Victoria, turn right up the estate drive and pass beneath the gatehouse into Holkham Park. Continue ahead on or beside the metalled drive to pass in front of Holkham Hall. Bear left with the drive by the lake and turn right, signed to the Nursery.

2 With the ice house on your left, bear off right and go through a gateway at the end of the lake. Follow the defined path across the park towards and pass St Withburga's Church. At the crossing of paths by Church Lodge, turn right (for longer walks, see point 3). Drop down through trees, pass round the top of the lake and keep to the main track. With the monument on your right, bear left and follow the track back to the gatehouse. Turn left back to the inn.

3 Keep ahead at Church Lodge, go through the gate and cross the A149. Cross a stile and walk down the track into the Nature Reserve. At a junction, keep straight on towards woodland. Follow the track left, then right through the trees (noting the hide on your left), and keep ahead at a crossing of paths.

4 Keep to the undulating path (which becomes sandy) through pine trees and soon reach Holkham Dunes & Beach. At the top of the beach, turn right (for a longer walk, see point 5) and keep to the top of the beach until reaching Holkham Gap, a significant V-shaped break in the corner of the woods. Climb the steps and head inland on the duckboard path, then follow Lady Ann's Drive back to the inn.

5

Turn left along the top of beach (for 400 yards a naturist beach), round the dune headland and look out for the coastal path marker (acorn symbol). Head inland here across the dunes and duckboards, then follow the raised dyke inland beside Overy Creek to Burnham Overy Staithe.

6

Go through a gate and soon turn left to reach the A149 opposite The Hero pub. Cross straight over into Gong Lane. Where the lane ends, proceed ahead along the track and follow this to cottages and the B1155. Turn right, cross over and take the waymarked footpath by the parish noticeboard.

7

Walk along the edge of two fields to reach a raised embankment path (an old railway) and turn left. In 50 yards, turn right through a gate and follow the defined path across a watermeadow (possibly boggy in winter). Cross a footbridge and keep left to a gate and lane. Turn right to visit Burnham Thorpe Church.

8

Turn left up a gravel track and cross a metalled lane onto a signed bridleway. Pass a flint barn, keeping ahead at the crossing of paths. At a T-junction of paths, turn left alongside the wall. On reaching a gate house (West Gate), turn right and follow the metalled drive through Holkham Estate, passing the Nursery back to Holkham Hall. Retrace steps back to The Victoria. For pub entry see page 107

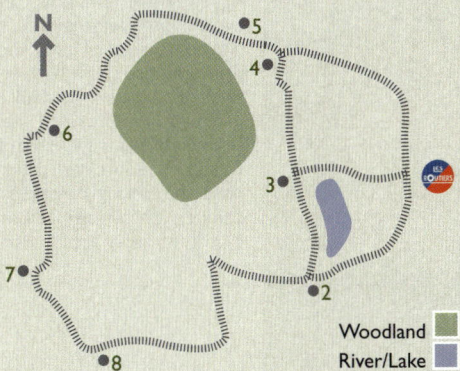

N

5
4
6
3
Start/Finish
7
2
8

Woodland
River/Lake

* Les Routiers logo denotes member pub / inn

fact file

Distance 3, 4 1/2 or 11 miles
Time 1 1/2; 2 1/2; 6 hours
Paths parkland tracks, dunes and beach, coastal path, farm tracks
OS Map Explorer 251 (Norfolk Coast Central)

look out for

Holkham Hall A classic 18th-century Palladian-style mansion set in 3,000 acres of parkland. Attractions include a Bygones Museum, History of Farming, a pottery and fine-food centre.

Holkham Beach is one of the most unspoilt and beautiful stretches of sand in the country. The Nature Reserve is home to many rare species of flora and fauna.

To Kielder Water from The Pheasant Inn

Forest roads and bridle paths take this walk to clearings high in the forest to reveal airy views across the wild Northumbrian countryside. The return route follows peaceful lakeside paths beside Kielder Water.

1 From the inn, turn left along the main road and then right, signposted Falstone. Cross the River North Tyne, pass the Blackcock Inn then turn left, having passed under the railway bridge. In 100 yards, fork left onto the former railway line and remain on this, signed Reivers Cycle Route. At a junction, keep ahead to reach a cross-tracks above a farm. Turn right and ascend the track left of a house to pass through a wall.

2

In 50 yards, fork left off the track along a grassy forestry road. Gently climb towards the woods, the track eventually emerging from the trees to reveal some excellent views across the southern end of Kielder Water. The trees gather once again before parting to allow distant views north across Kielder Forest to the Cheviot Hills. Walk down to the wide forestry road.

3

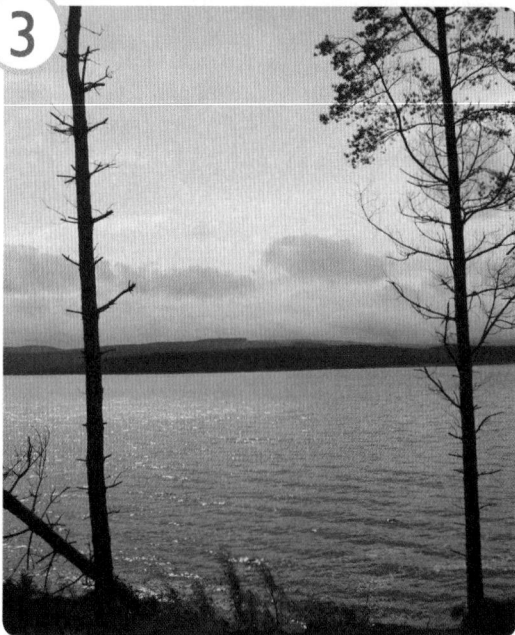

Turn left and walk downhill (800 yards) to the second white post signed Wave Chamber, and a cycle-route waymarker. Fork right onto a sandy track though the trees, then turn right in 100 yards along a waymarked path, dropping to cross a marshy isthmus. Keep right at a fork, tracing the circular path out onto the Belling Peninsula, and savour superb views across the lake from rocky promontories.

Kielder Water, Northumberland

4 Remain on the path, marked by occasional orange waymarkers, to reach a white post signed Belvedere. Turn right along a gravelly path through trees, in 100 yards gaining a wider track, along which turn right. This narrows to a delightful path around rocky inlets and bays before reaching the remains of Gordon's Walls Castle. Just beyond this, the path leaves the shoreline at some rail fencing, soon reaching a wide forestry road. Turn right along this.

Remain on this roadway, passing behind the Hawkhope car park, sited at the north end of the reservoir dam close to the immense valve tower. Don't take the road to the dam; instead take the road signed 'Forestry Vehicles only'. At Hawkhope Farm, passed earlier in the walk, turn right at the cross-tracks, pass beside the farm and take the gate on the left, joining a gated road to Falstone. At the junction by the Blackcock Inn, turn right and retrace your outward steps back to The Pheasant Inn.

For pub entry see page 112

5

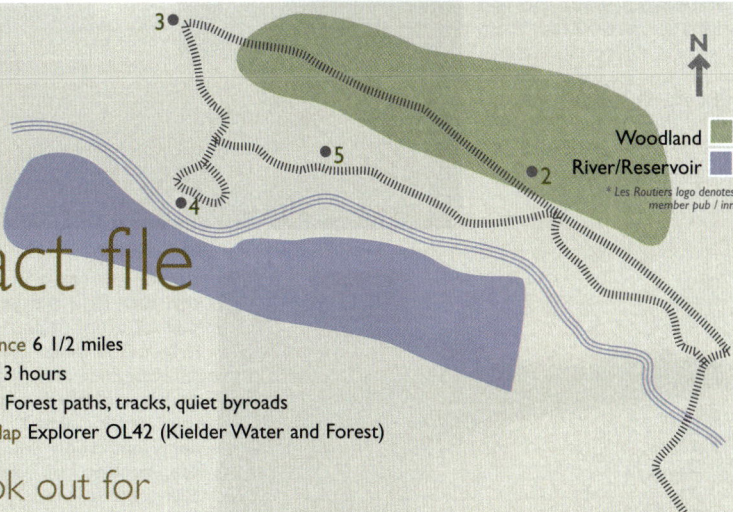

N

Woodland
River/Reservoir

* Les Routiers logo denotes member pub / inn

fact file

Distance **6 1/2 miles**
Time **3 hours**
Paths **Forest paths, tracks, quiet byroads**
OS Map **Explorer OL42 (Kielder Water and Forest)**

look out for

Kielder Forest is Europe's largest man-made forest, covering around 200 square miles. It was first established in 1926 to help reduce Britain's dependence on imported timber.

Kielder Water covers 2,684 acres and is the largest reservoir in northern Europe.

Start/
Finish

Doddington Hall from the Bottle & Glass

The flatlands of Lincolnshire dominate this attractive walk, which follows part of a popular cycle trail before making for one of the county's loveliest ancestral homes, Doddington Hall, with its colourful gardens and historic treasures.

1

Turn right out of the pub and follow the road for about 75 yards, veering right just before the T-junction to join a track running away from the houses of Harby. Swing sharp right on the edge of the village and then left. Keep to the clear path, following it as it weaves its way through open countryside. Look for some pylons ahead and make for a junction with a cycle trail just before them.

Turn right here and follow Route 64, linking Lincoln with Newark-on-Trent. Pass under the pylon cables and keep going. Farther on, pass under a road bridge, then cut between woodland and vegetation. Break cover from the trees and continue ahead on the trail until you come to a Route 64 sign. A path runs off to the left here. Ignore it and take the gated path on the right, skirting a field.

2

3

When you reach a bridleway sign, turn right and pass to the side of a lake. Keep silos and farm outbuildings over to the left. Continue on the bridleway, skirting a bluebell wood. Follow the track ahead between fields and soon you can see the rooftop of Doddington Hall against the skyline. The bridleway joins a tarmac lane and makes for the road.

4

Turn left, pass the church and keep ahead for a few paces to a post box. Turn right here for Home Farm. Follow the concrete track between outbuildings and houses. Look for a waymarker just beyond stables and swing right to join a footpath. Cross a field and over a grassy avenue lined with broad-leaved limes. To the right is a striking view of Doddington Hall.

5

Keep ahead towards trees, following the waymarked grassy path to a stile at the corner of the wood. Keep right, skirting the field, go through a gateway into the next pasture and cross it diagonally. Make for a pylon and a waymark and turn left. The spire of Harby Church is visible now. Pass through a gate and go straight ahead across the field to the next gate. Continue ahead beside the ditch, keep to the left of a paddock and turn right on reaching the recreation ground. Keep right at the road, walk straight ahead at the junction and back to the pub.

For pub entry see page 115

fact file

Distance **6 1/2 miles**
Time **2 hours**
Paths **Tracks, cycleway, bridleways, field paths**
OS Map **Explorer 271 (Newark) and 272 (Lincoln)**

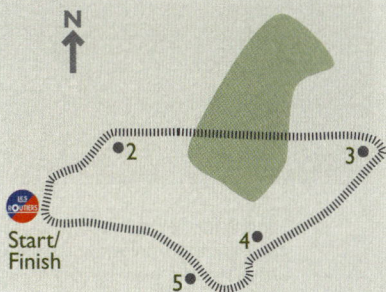

Woodland

Les Routiers logo denotes member pub / inn

look out for

St Peter's Church The precise date of this Church at Doddington is not known, but the circular font dates back to the middle of the 13th century. The older parts of the church are constructed of small, rough Lincolnshire stone.

Doddington Hall is a striking Elizabethan manor house built of mellowed brick. Inside is an impressive collection of china, tapestries and Stuart and Georgian furniture. It is open during the spring and summer months.

South Chiltern Hills from The Cherry Tree

A gently undulating ramble through the Chiltern Hills to Nuffield and the Ridgeway Path.

1 From the pub car park, turn right along the village street. Turn right just past the village hall, along a narrow path, with the exotic Maharajah's Well just a few steps further on the right. Descend to a metalled lane and turn left. This soon dwindles into a track. Continue beside a bluebell wood for 1/4 mile, then take the footpath right across a stile.

2 Climb a further stile and follow the left-hand field edge to a stile in the corner. Turn left along the bridleway, passing Oakingham House. Follow the drive out to a road. Cross straight over to join a 'right of way'. Pass the drive to Ridgeway Farmhouse and follow the lane to the entrance to Upper House Farm. Turn right along the field edge, keeping to the path towards a house, then right along the fence to a stile.

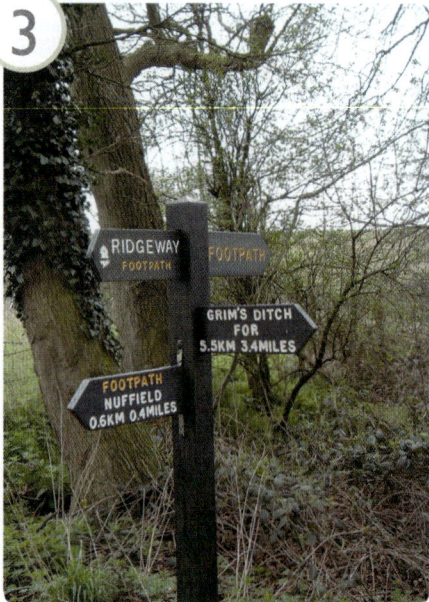

3 Cross the drive and follow the path around Ridgeway Farm. Enter a field and keep to the right-hand edge, soon to walk through a spinney, with super views west across South Oxfordshire. At a junction with the Ridgeway Path at Grims Ditch, keep ahead and then along the edge of a field to reach a lane.

4 Turn right through Nuffield, passing the church, to reach a T-junction with Timbers Lane. Turn left, then immediately right along a footpath to the left of a house called Martyn's Close. At a gravel drive, bear right past Elderberry Cottage to join a bridleway.

5

Continue on the enclosed path and soon join a wider track. Keep right, ignore the stile on your right and follow the track left for Howberrywood Farm. Pass the farm, then, where the drive becomes metalled, keep right into woodland.

At a waymarker post, follow the yellow arrow right through the trees and along the woodland fringe to a stile. Keep right along the field edge and cross a stile by a gate and barn. Turn left along the track and bear left then right downhill past cottages to a metalled lane by a house called Squirrels.

6

Take the path ahead, downhill through trees to a road, cross straight over and climb through woodland, keeping ahead at a crossing of paths. Shortly, bear right uphill to reach a road. Turn left and follow it back into Stoke Row. Turn right by the green for the pub. **For pub entry see page 120**

7

fact file

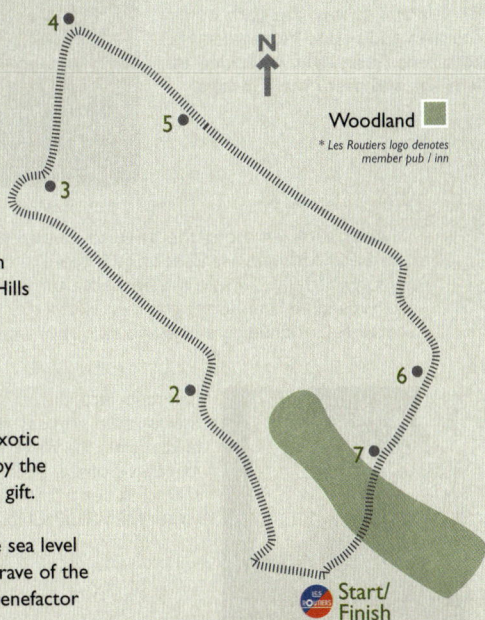

N

Woodland
* Les Routiers logo denotes member pub / inn

Distance 6 miles
Time 3 hours
Paths Bridleways, footpaths, metalled tracks, the Ridgeway Path
OS Map Explorer 171 (Chiltern Hills West)

look out for

Maharajah's Well Enclosed by an exotic cupola, it was given to the village by the Maharajah of Benares in 1863 as a gift.

Nuffield The church is 700ft above sea level and the churchyard contains the grave of the renowned car manufacturer and benefactor William Morris (1877-1963).

Start/Finish

Deben Valley from The Queen's Head

A gentle amble through rolling, unspoilt Suffolk countryside around the peaceful Deben Valley.

Leave the pub car park and turn left along the village street. In 200 yards, turn right at a grassy triangle and road, signed to Brandeston Hall. Take the waymarked bridleway ahead, soon to follow the track right and downhill to a footbridge and ford over the River Deben. Enter a field and keep left around the field edge.

At a junction of paths in the field corner, keep ahead and pass in front of a house. Join the drive and soon follow it right (note the waymarker), uphill towards a large house. Where it swings right by a bungalow, bear off left and follow the path across the lawn and beside Monewden Hall to a lane. Turn right, following the lane left, and pass Moat Cottage.

Shortly, turn left along the drive to Chestnut Tree Farm. Ignore the path left by a barn and continue ahead, soon to follow the right-hand field edge through two fields. In the third field, where the field edge turns sharp right, keep ahead across the field to a metalled lane. Turn right, then left in 100 yards along a grassy path just before a cottage. Continue to a lane and turn right into Cretingham.

Descend into the village, pass The Bell and keep ahead at the junction to pass the post office and church. Cross the bridge over the River Deben, then, at a T-junction, turn right for Earl Soham. Pass Manor Farm then, just beyond the sharp left bend, follow the unmade drive right, signposted to Cretingham Golf Club.

5 On nearing the clubhouse, bear half-left across the car park and walk in front of the clubhouse, following the footpath markers. At a crossing of paths, turn right and keep right of the tee along a defined track that cuts through the golf course and copses to reach a footbridge over a stream. Continue ahead through trees to a stile.

Proceed up the grassy track ahead to a stile and maintain this direction beside woodland to reach a stile and road. Turn right, then left up the T-road and pass Grove Farm. Take the bridleway right alongside a house and soon reach a metalled track. **6**

Turn left, then take the arrowed footpath right before the bungalow. Walk down the field edge to a metalled road and turn right. Keep to the lane back into Brandeston and turn right at the village road for the pub. For pub entry see page 137

fact file

Distance **4 1/2 miles**
Time **2 hours**
Paths Bridleways, field paths, quiet lanes, village streets
OS Map Explorer 212 (Woodbridge & Saxmundham)

look out for

Just a short drive from Brandeston is the peaceful market town of Framlingham. In addition to its many attractive buildings, there is a striking 12th-century castle that remains intact, with 13 impressive towers. You can enjoy marvellous views across the surrounding countryside from the battlements.

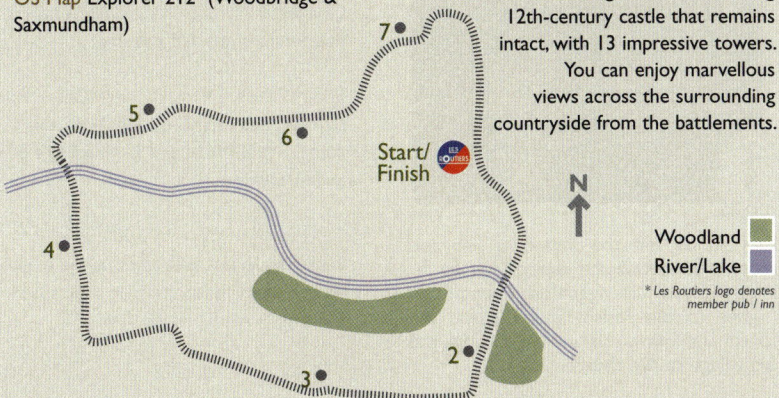

Start/Finish

N

Woodland
River/Lake

*Les Routiers logo denotes member pub / inn

The Ship Inn and Chichester Harbour

Follow peaceful field paths to West Wittering and a short, optional extension to a sandy beach and East Head, with views across the Solent to the Isle of Wight.

1 From the Ship, turn right along the lane back through the village (can be busy). In 1/4 mile, turn right into the drive to Itchenor Park House and take the footpath immediately left to the side of the memorial hall. Follow the path along the field edge, across the footbridge in the corner and keep to the field edge.

2 Cross a track and continue through the centre of a field on a defined path. Soon reach the field edge and follow the path to a track. Turn right and remain on the track to Rookwood Road on a sharp bend. Cross straight over and walk along the pavement into West Wittering.

3 Pass shops and the memorial hall and cross over, noting the wall plaque to Sir Henry Royce. Turn right along Pound Road (signed to the Parish Church), pass the toilets and follow the lane left through the old village to the church.

fact file

Distance **6 3/4 miles**
Time **4 hours**
Paths **Field paths, tracks, village streets, beach, creekside paths**
OS Map **Explorer 120 (Chichester)**

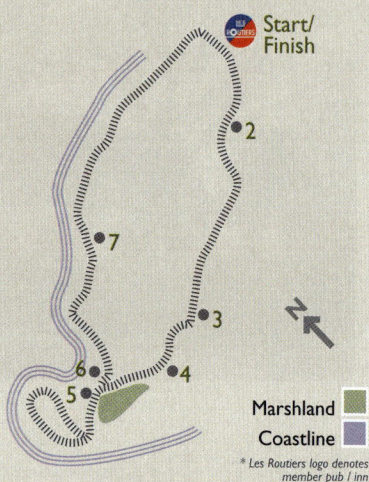

Start/Finish

Marshland
Coastline

* Les Routiers logo denotes member pub / inn

look out for

West Itchenor A sleepy village with an attractive street leading down to Chichester Harbour. King Charles kept a yacht here in the 17th century.

West Wittering Parish Church Dates from Norman and early-English periods and contains fine tombs and a remarkable old belfry staircase.

Chichester Harbour At 3,000 acres, it forms the largest area of estuarine mudflats on the south coast, and is an ideal spot for watching waders and wildfowl.

Walk through the churchyard, pass the entrance and cross the stile ahead into a field. Cross the field to a gate and join a track. At a T-junction with a metalled track, turn right and follow this past big houses, with Snow Hill Marsh to your left, to a grassy area beside Chichester Harbour.

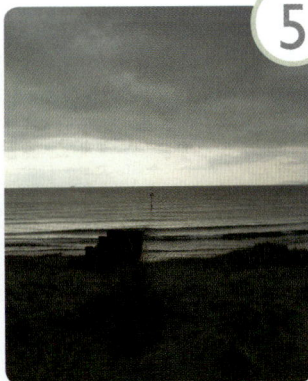

For the optional extension to the beach and East Head (sandy spit), bear left to join the footpath above the water (walk along the stony beach if the tide is out), and follow it to West Wittering beach. If the tide is out you can walk around East Head (NT) – super sea and harbour views. Return to the grassy area.

6 Follow the waymarked footpath that runs parallel with the water's edge. With good views and the opportunity to watch the wealth of birdlife, keep to this path, veering right before Ella Nore spit, and then head slightly inland by an impressive redbrick house, passing a further house called Tide's Reach.

The path continues to the right of the drive to Rednum Court soon to join the water's edge once again. Continue for 1 1/2 miles and cross a boatyard to join a fenced path leading to the quay at West Itchenor. Turn right up the lane back to the pub. For pub entry see page 145

Uphill and down dale
from The Sandpiper Inn

Walk in the footsteps of Victorian high society along the Leyburn Shawl promenade, an airy stroll rising gently above glorious Wensleydale, en route to pretty Preston, stately Bolton Hall and sublime Wensley herself, huddled around the Dales' best church.

Take Shawl Terrace, beside the Dalesman's Club in the top marketplace, Commercial Square. At the end, slip left into The Shawl, created as a promenade by townsfolk about 170 years ago to attract well-to-do visitors to take the air. Impressive views open out across Wensleydale; look back-left for Middleham Castle. Stay outside the playground and keep ahead at the gap, with the woods on your left. Remain beside these through several stiles to a final stile and gate 75 yards left of a barn and pylons. Enter the woods here.

The wide path snakes through beech and Scots pine woods clothing the steep limestone scar (edge). Keep to the upper path at old stone gateposts, remaining beside a wall. Take the stile near the end of the woods, walk 30 paces and take a stile left into the sloping field. Head half-right to a stile and then walk to the bottom-right corner to a stile and gateway. Keep the fence, then wall, on your left, ignore a field gate and continue to a rough lane beside the distant woods.

Cross slightly left into a woodland path, Keep left within a few yards, but at the next T-junction in 150 yards, turn sharp right following the blue waymarker, dropping to a culvert. On your right here, the ruined tunnel is a flue from Keld Head Lead Mine, once the largest in Wensleydale. Turn sharp left following the blue waymarker, along the well-walked path across several side streams to a gap stile into pasture. Go ahead to the far bottom corner where a gateway leads to a lane. Turn right to Preston-under-Scar.

4

At the foot of the green, go sharp left at the fingerposted footpath, down the driveway beside The Setts to a narrow path and gate into pasture. Head slightly left to a stile right of the small barn, then go ahead to a stile. Cross the railway and take the track opposite. Use the stile, but keep ahead to reach a road to the right of the house. Cross into the rough lane and follow this. At a T-junction, turn left to wind to and through the Home Farm at Bolton Hall. Bend left with the concrete driveway to pass 150 yards below Bolton Hall. Walk through to Wensley village green.

5

Join the B6108 road beside the churchyard (signed for Middleham and Masham) and remain on this. Beyond the village, wide verges soon develop, making walking easier. In a mile, pass a small derelict barn on your right. In another 50 yards look left for a narrow entrance to a hedged stony path. This is muddy underfoot for the first 300 yards before becoming a wider and firmer track. Follow it gently uphill past a barn, passing beneath the railway to gain a main road. Turn right to Leyburn and The Sandpiper Inn. For pub entry see page 160

fact file

Distance **6 miles**
Time **3 hours**
Paths **Mostly field paths and byroads**
OS Map **Explorer OL30 (Yorkshire Dales, Northern & Central Areas)**

look out for

Bolton Castle Started in 1379, for six months in 1568 this magnificent castle was prison to Mary, Queen of Scots.

Bolton Hall A stately pile in hundreds of acres of landscaped parkland beside the river Ure.

Holy Trinity Church in Wensley is oft-cited as the best in the Dales.

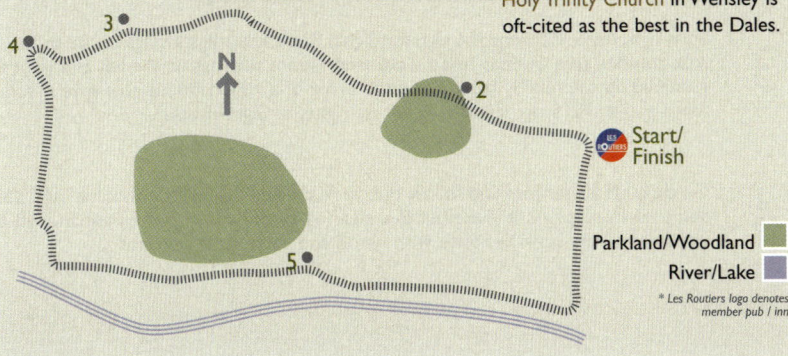

Parkland/Woodland
River/Lake

* Les Routiers logo denotes member pub / inn

Glencoe and The Clachaig Inn

A short forest walk reveals some surprising views of this great mountain valley

1 From the front of the inn, turn left up the road towards Glencoe village. After 50 yards, turn left into a car-parking area. On the far side you will see a National Trust for Scotland (NTS) sign for An Torr. Walk through the parking area and continue up the forestry track to a gate in the deer fence. Go through the gate and continue along the forest track. After 110 yards, take the path ascending on the right, signposted An Torr.

2 Follow the narrow footpath as it climbs up through woods to the high point of An Torr. There are views behind you into Clachaig Gully. From the rocky outcrop, admire the vista across Achnacon towards Meall Mor. From the summit, retrace your steps back to the larger forestry track and turn right. Continue as it winds past an area of clear felled woodland and swings left down to a junction.

3 Turn right here, following the sign for Signal Rock. The track swings round to the left past another area of clear felled woodland. Ignore turnings to the left and right and continue up the muddy bank. Over the brow of a rise, continue to a gate in a deer fence and an NTS sign explaining access rights to Signal Rock.

4 Go through a deer gate and follow the track. It leads over a little shoulder and down some rocky steps. As it levels out in a clearing, ignore paths to the right and left and continue up the bank opposite with wood and earth steps cut into it.

At the top of the hill, Signal Rock comes into view. A short scramble leads up to the summit, or you can slip round on a path to the right of the rock and ascend by the series of steps on far side. Now retrace your steps to the junction passed on your outward journey with signs to Signal Rock and The Clachaig Inn.

Bear right and carry on the good track down to the kissing gate in deer fence. Descend to the river. The bridge here over the River Coe used to give access to the old visitor centre, before its site was levelled. Don't cross the bridge but turn left along the riverside path to some stepping stones. Cross over and turn left again, now following the tributary upstream with the fence on the right. Follow the little path as it crosses another tributary and eventually emerges on a back road to Glencoe village. Turn left to return to the inn.

For pub entry see page 176

fact file

Distance 1 1/2 miles
Time 1 hours
Paths Forest tracks and paths
OS Map Explorer 384 (Glencoe and Glen Etive)

look out for

Glencoe provides walkers and climbers with a formidable range of mountains to clamber all over. The glen achieved its principal notoriety in 1692, when 38 members of the MacDonald clan were murdered here by government troops.

Signal Rock Believed to be the point from which government troopers gave the signal to move on the MacDonald clansmen.

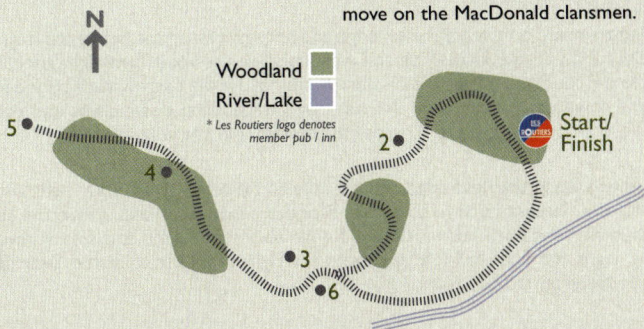

Woodland
River/Lake
* Les Routiers logo denotes member pub / inn

Start/Finish

The Monnow Valley from The Bell

A delightful riverside walk with a longer option through the peaceful Monnow Valley and a final sharp ascent to the top of Coedanghred Hill for glorious views across Skenfrith and the upper Monnow Valley to the Black Mountains.

1

Cross the river bridge on leaving the pub and take the path right, signed 'Tregate Bridge 6.5km'. Follow the path beside the River Monnow and pass in front of Sand House. Walk through a copse to a stile and bear right around the field beside the river. Bear left in the corner and follow the arrowed path right into the adjacent field. Bear slightly left towards farm buildings and silos, cross a stile and continue up the slope to a gate.

2

Walk through the Llanrothal farm and follow the access lane to cottages. Cross the stream, take the footpath right and soon follow the path left to reach St John the Baptist Church. Exit the churchyard via a stile and turn left around the field edge. Follow the river for nearly a mile to a stile and turn right across Tregate Bridge.

3 Cross the stile on your right and bear diagonally left across the field towards a farm. Pass through a gate and continue behind the farm to a gate and poplar plantation.
Short Walk:
Follow the path ahead and walk through the plantation, crossing a stream and eventually exiting the woodland on reaching the riverbank. Bear left across the field, soon to rejoin the riverbank, and keep beside the river through more woodland, soon to join the road by a house. Turn left steeply uphill, bearing right at the top (join long walk at point 8).

4 Long walk:
Turn left to a stile on the plantation edge and left again along the field edge to another stile. Bear right to the farm drive and walk uphill to the road. Turn right, then, as you begin to descend, cross the stile on the left and follow the narrow path beside fencing downhill towards a house. Pass in front of a garage, drop down steps and continue downhill (can be overgrown) to cross the stream and the stile ahead.

5 Keep ahead along the field edge, cross a stile and footbridge on your right and walk in front of a derelict cottage to a stile. Proceed across the field, ignore the stile on the boundary and turn left up the field edge to a stile. Climb the stile immediately to your right and bear half-left to pass to the right of a barn to a stile. Bear left and enter St Maughan's churchyard.

fact file

Distance 5 or 7 miles
Time 3 or 4 hours
Paths Riverside and field paths, tracks, some road
OS Map Explorer 189 (Hereford & Ross-on-Wye) & OL14 (Wye Valley & Forest of Dean)

N

Woodland
River/Lake
Les Routiers logo denotes member pub / inn

Start/
Finish

2
8
7
4
6 5 3

look out for

Skenfrith Church Noted for its massive square tower.

Skenfrith Castle Built in the 13th-century, it has a round keep, set within an imposing towered curtain wall.

St John the Baptist Church This church, in Llanrothal, dates from the late 13th-century.

6 At the road turn right, pass a farm, then at a fork of drives bear right towards Little Coxstone. Descend steeply, follow the hedged track to the left of the property uphill, then descend to a stream. Climb up the sunken path (can be very wet), the path soon becoming a track leading to a metalled drive opposite a bungalow.

7 Turn right, pass to the left of the farmhouse, then, at a track, turn left downhill to a junction of paths. Bear right, then left and ascend beside woodland towards a house on the hill. Follow the field edge left, pass below White House to reach the drive. Turn right, then turn left at the T-junction at the top of a steep hill.

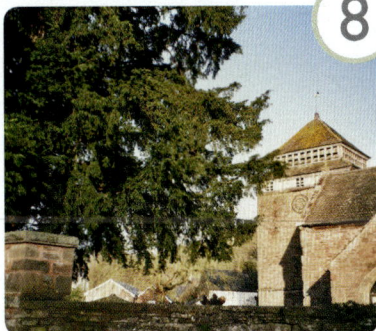

8

At a fork, keep left up the drive, pass to the left of the property and continue across the side of Coedanghred Hill. Soon steeply ascend and pass beside a house to reach a stile on the summit. Descend steeply through fields to reach a lane. Turn left back to the inn.
For pub entry see page 192

JUST OFF THE MOTORWAY

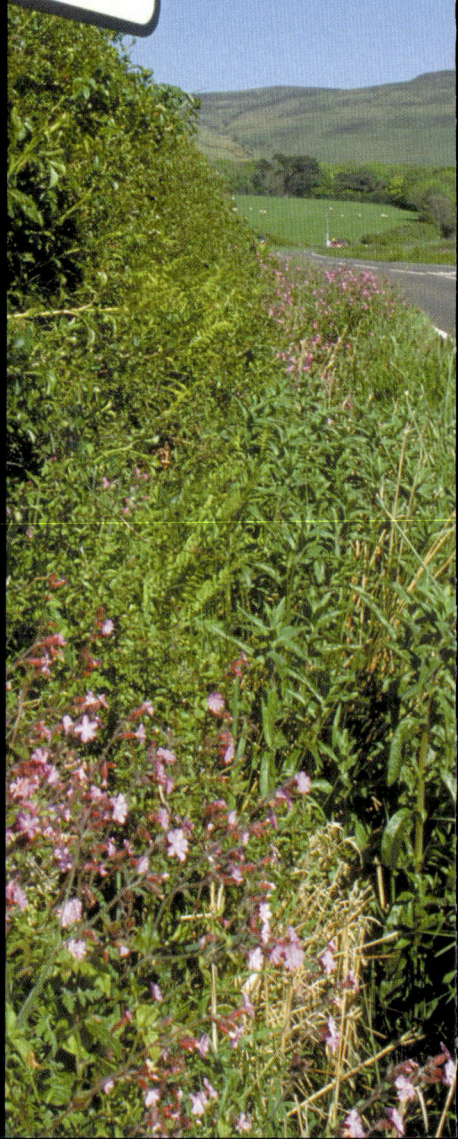

Birmingham to Bristol on the M5

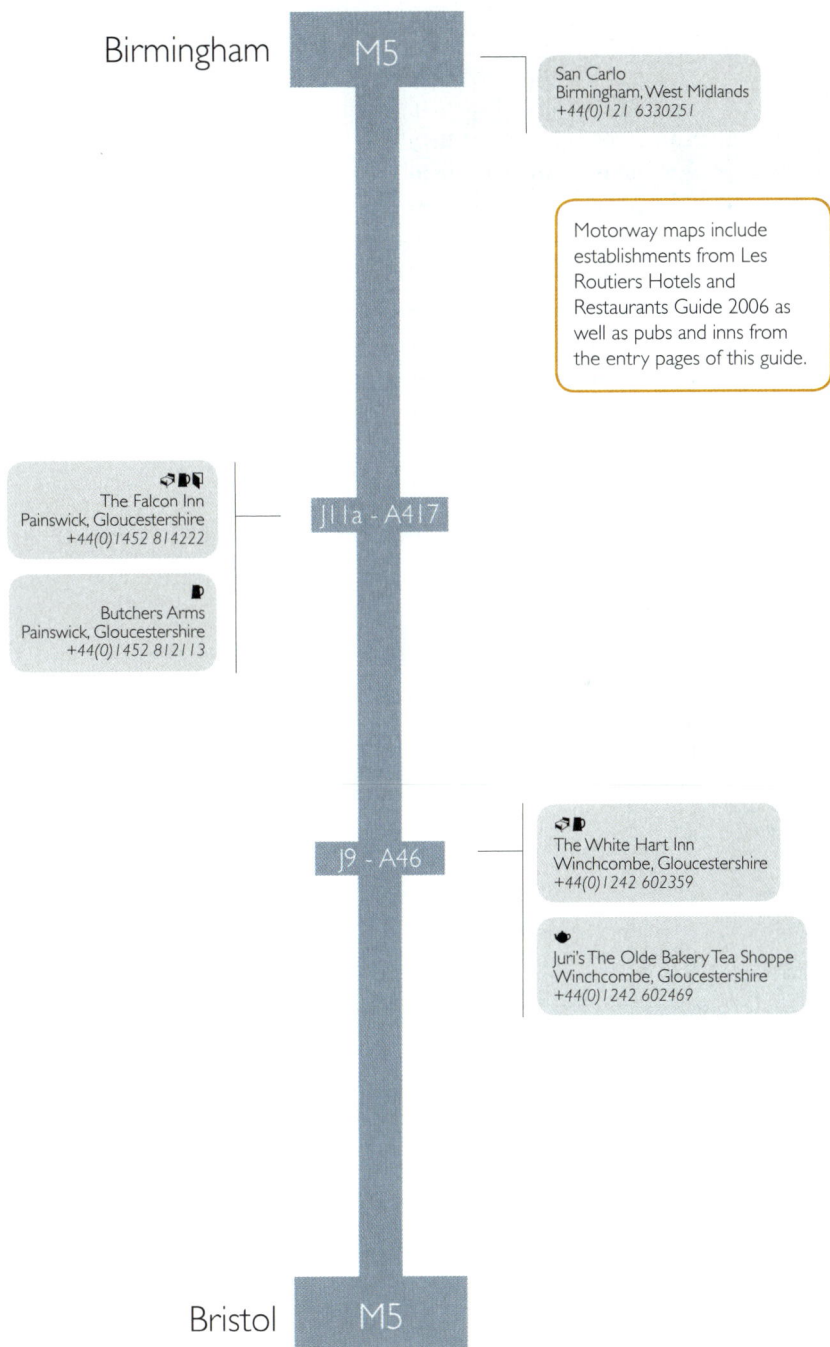

Birmingham — M5

San Carlo
Birmingham, West Midlands
+44(0)121 6330251

> Motorway maps include establishments from Les Routiers Hotels and Restaurants Guide 2006 as well as pubs and inns from the entry pages of this guide.

J11a - A417

The Falcon Inn
Painswick, Gloucestershire
+44(0)1452 814222

Butchers Arms
Painswick, Gloucestershire
+44(0)1452 812113

J9 - A46

The White Hart Inn
Winchcombe, Gloucestershire
+44(0)1242 602359

Juri's The Olde Bakery Tea Shoppe
Winchcombe, Gloucestershire
+44(0)1242 602469

Bristol — M5

Leeds to Edinburgh on the A1

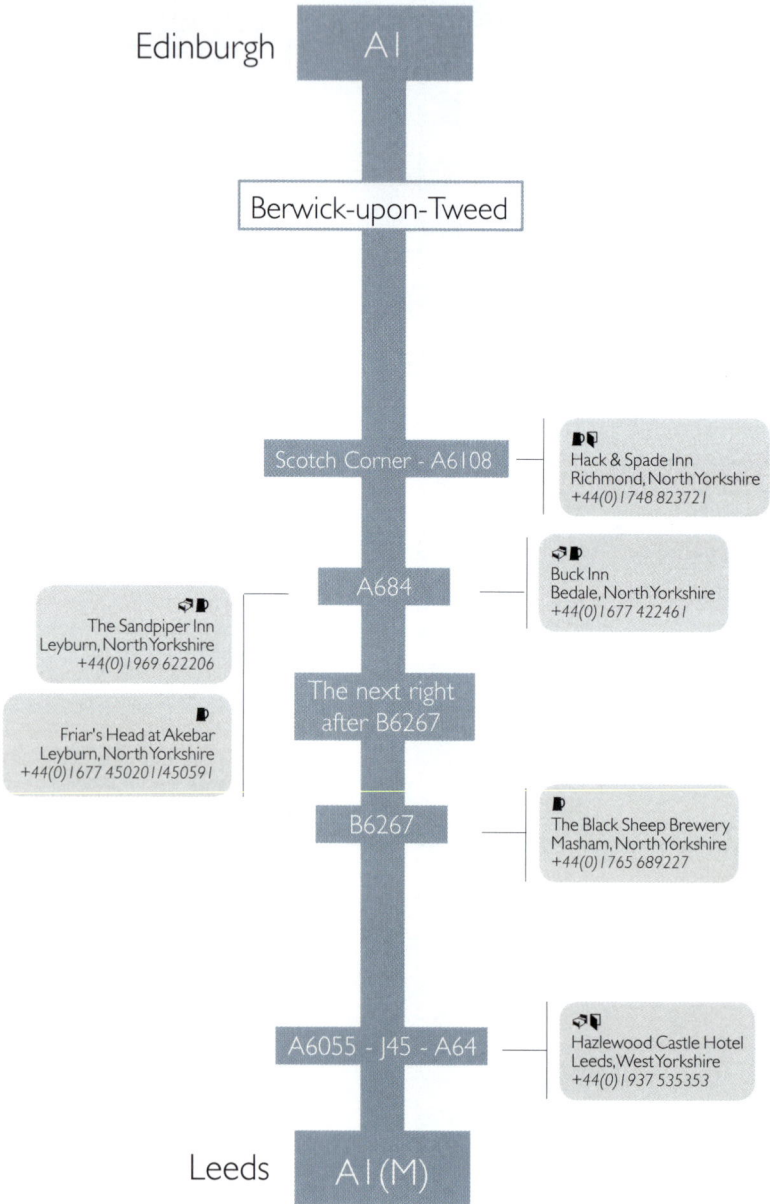

Edinburgh | A1

Berwick-upon-Tweed

Scotch Corner - A6108

Hack & Spade Inn
Richmond, North Yorkshire
+44(0)1748 823721

A684

Buck Inn
Bedale, North Yorkshire
+44(0)1677 422461

The Sandpiper Inn
Leyburn, North Yorkshire
+44(0)1969 622206

The next right
after B6267

Friar's Head at Akebar
Leyburn, North Yorkshire
+44(0)1677 450201/450591

B6267

The Black Sheep Brewery
Masham, North Yorkshire
+44(0)1765 689227

A6055 - J45 - A64

Hazlewood Castle Hotel
Leeds, West Yorkshire
+44(0)1937 535353

Leeds | A1(M)

Leicester to Norwich on the A47

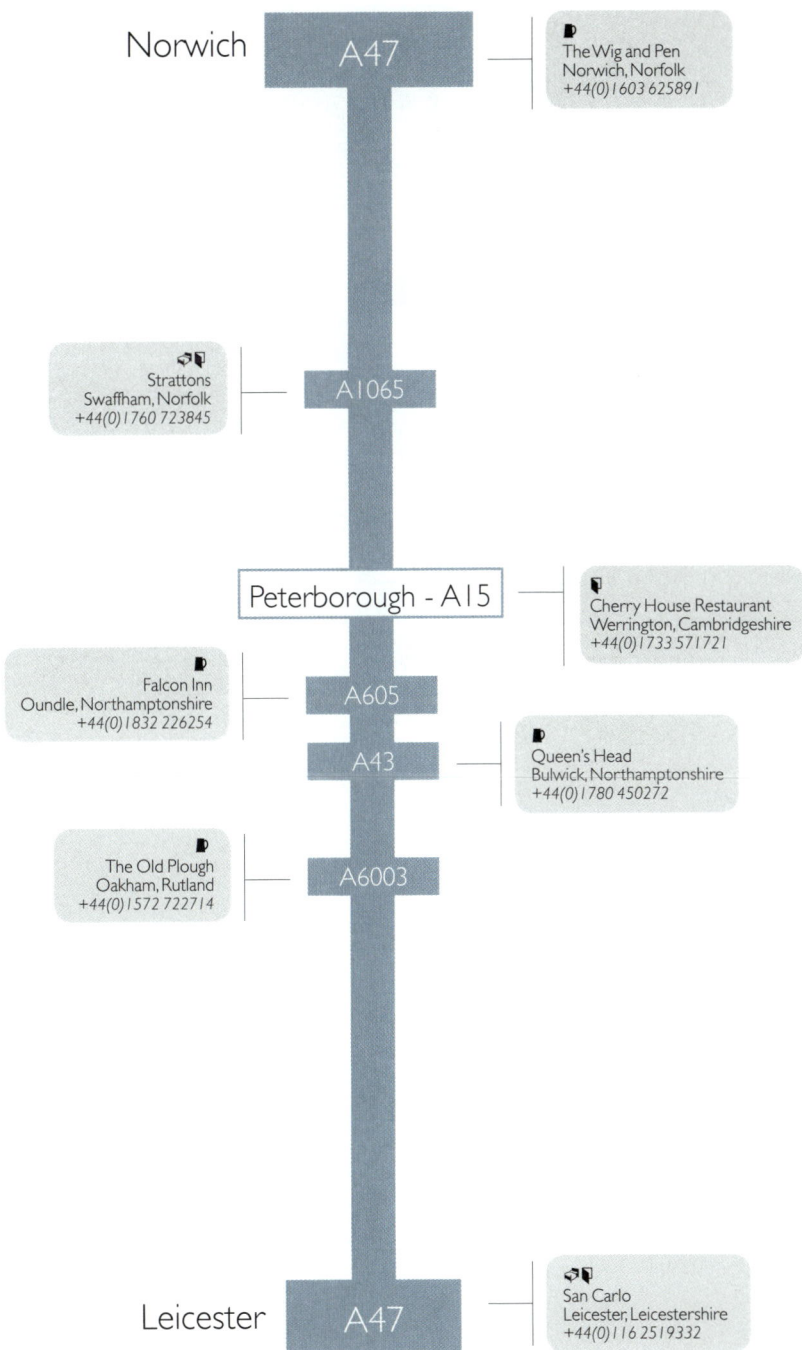

Norwich — A47

The Wig and Pen
Norwich, Norfolk
+44(0)1603 625891

Strattons
Swaffham, Norfolk
+44(0)1760 723845

A1065

Peterborough - A15

Cherry House Restaurant
Werrington, Cambridgeshire
+44(0)1733 571721

Falcon Inn
Oundle, Northamptonshire
+44(0)1832 226254

A605

A43

Queen's Head
Bulwick, Northamptonshire
+44(0)1780 450272

The Old Plough
Oakham, Rutland
+44(0)1572 722714

A6003

Leicester — A47

San Carlo
Leicester, Leicestershire
+44(0)116 2519332

London to Birmingham on the M40/M42

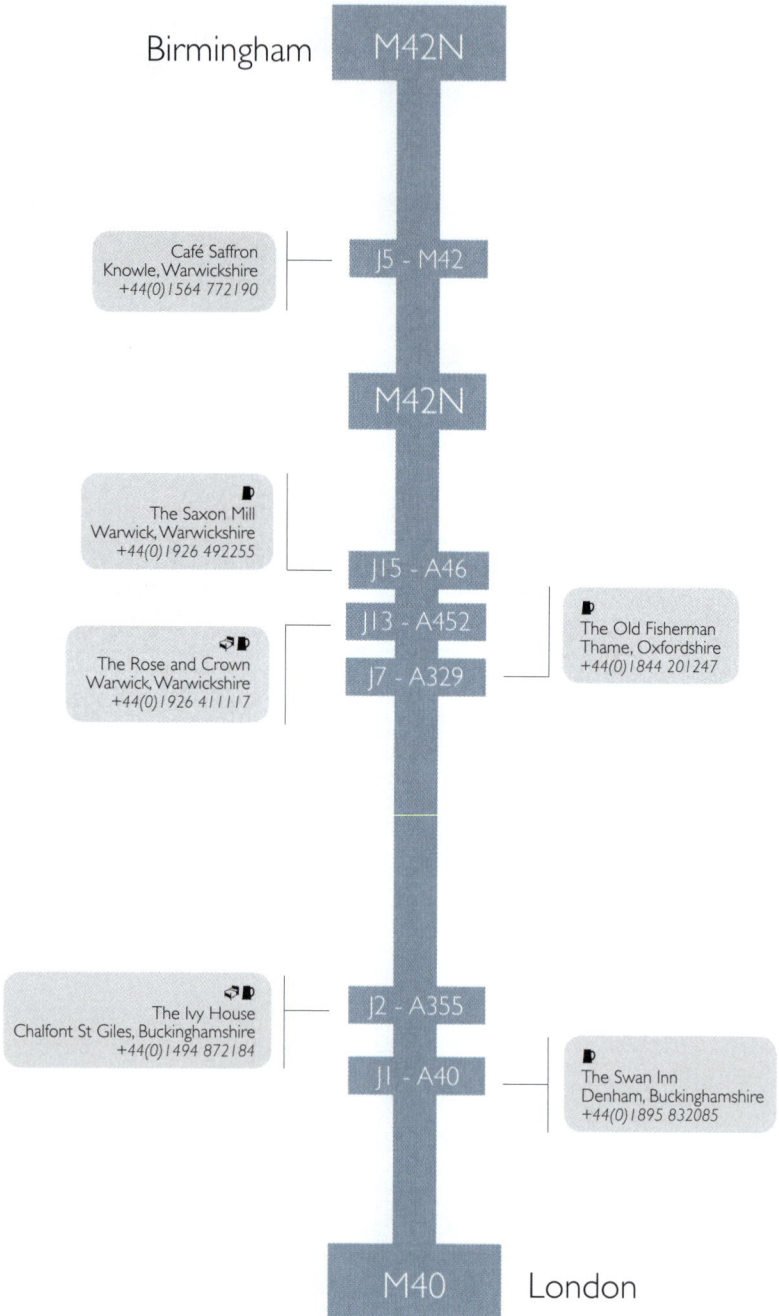

Birmingham | M42N

Café Saffron
Knowle, Warwickshire
+44(0)1564 772190
| J5 - M42

| M42N

The Saxon Mill
Warwick, Warwickshire
+44(0)1926 492255
| J15 - A46

| J13 - A452

The Old Fisherman
Thame, Oxfordshire
+44(0)1844 201247

The Rose and Crown
Warwick, Warwickshire
+44(0)1926 411117
| J7 - A329

The Ivy House
Chalfont St Giles, Buckinghamshire
+44(0)1494 872184
| J2 - A355

| J1 - A40

The Swan Inn
Denham, Buckinghamshire
+44(0)1895 832085

M40 | London

London to Cambridge on the M11

Cambridge

M11
J13 - A1303

Three Horseshoes
Madingley, Cambridgeshire
+44(0)1954 210221

The Green Man
Thriplow, Cambridgeshire
+44(0)1763 208855

J10 - A505

Motorway maps include
establishments from Les
Routiers Hotels and
Restaurants Guide 2006 as
well as pubs and inns from
the entry pages of this guide.

J8 - A120
Stansted Airport

The Swan at Felsted
Great Dunmow, Essex
+44(0)1371 820245

Oak Lodge
Stansted, Essex
+44(0)1279 871667

London

M11

From London to Leeds on the A1(M)

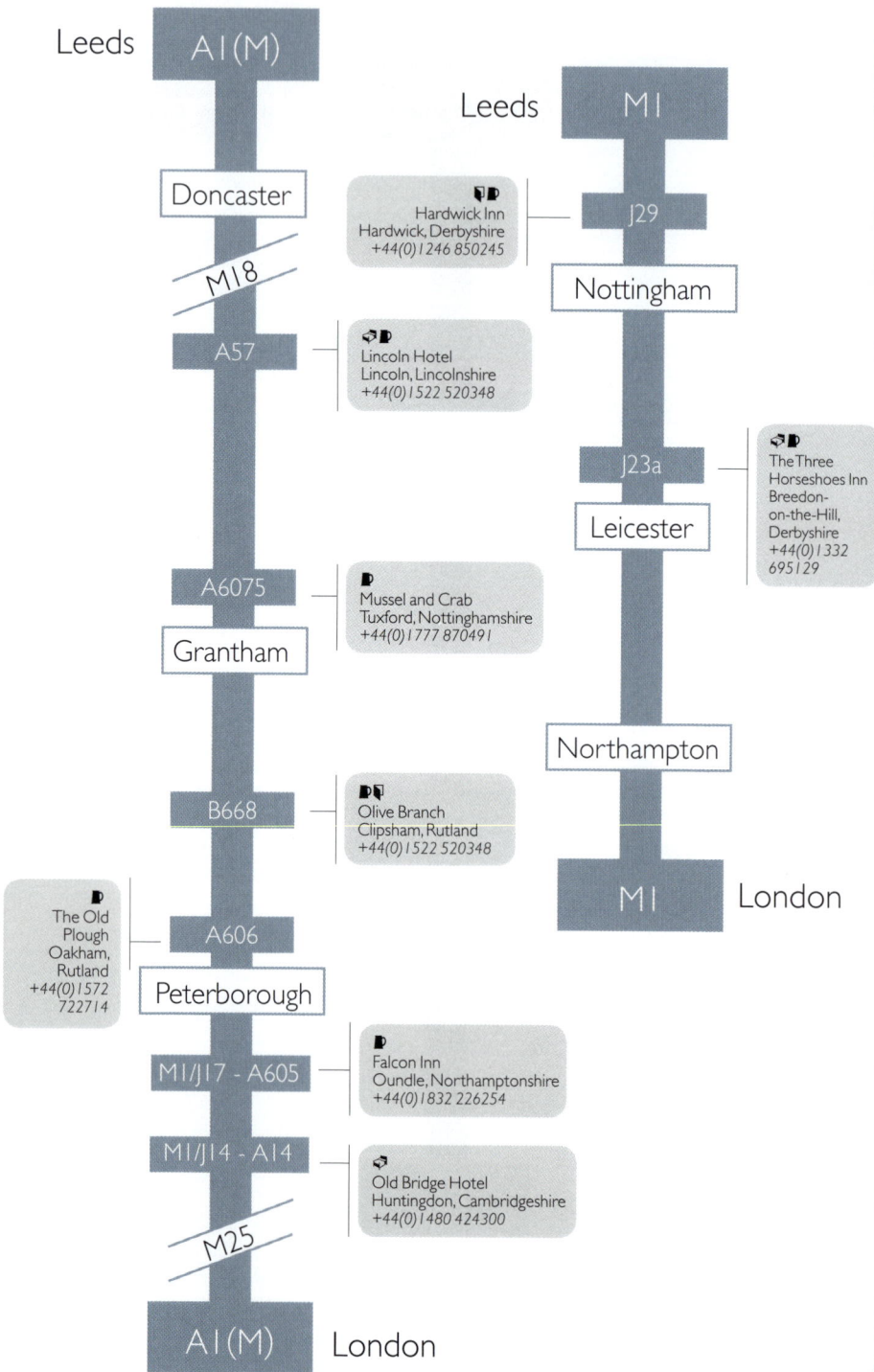

Leeds A1(M)

Leeds M1

Doncaster

Hardwick Inn
Hardwick, Derbyshire
+44(0)1246 850245

J29

M18

Nottingham

A57

Lincoln Hotel
Lincoln, Lincolnshire
+44(0)1522 520348

J23a

The Three
Horseshoes Inn
Breedon-
on-the-Hill,
Derbyshire
+44(0)1332
695129

Leicester

A6075

Mussel and Crab
Tuxford, Nottinghamshire
+44(0)1777 870491

Grantham

Northampton

B668

Olive Branch
Clipsham, Rutland
+44(0)1522 520348

The Old
Plough
Oakham,
Rutland
+44(0)1572
722714

A606

M1

London

Peterborough

M1/J17 - A605

Falcon Inn
Oundle, Northamptonshire
+44(0)1832 226254

M1/J14 - A14

Old Bridge Hotel
Huntingdon, Cambridgeshire
+44(0)1480 424300

M25

A1(M) **London**

London to Southampton on the M3

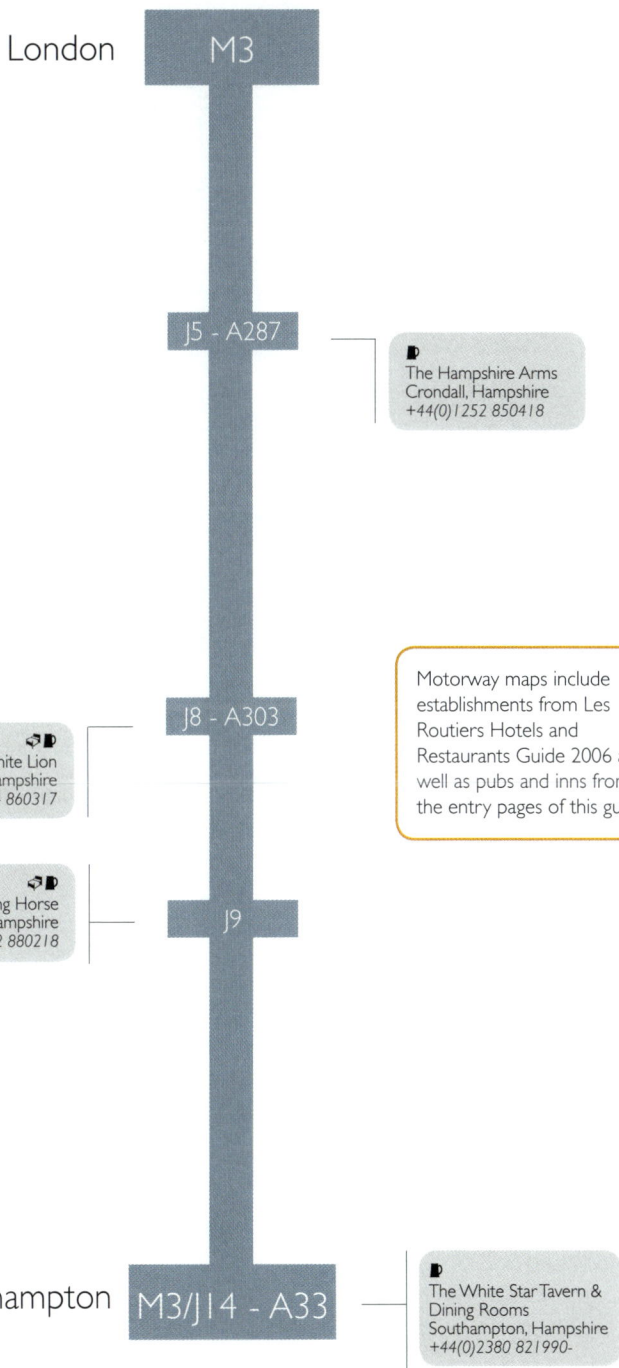

London | **M3**

J5 - A287

The Hampshire Arms
Crondall, Hampshire
+44(0)1252 850418

J8 - A303

White Lion
Wherwell, Hampshire
+44(0)1264 860317

Motorway maps include establishments from Les Routiers Hotels and Restaurants Guide 2006 as well as pubs and inns from the entry pages of this guide.

The Running Horse
Littleton, Hampshire
+44(0)1962 880218

J9

Southampton | **M3/J14 - A33**

The White Star Tavern &
Dining Rooms
Southampton, Hampshire
+44(0)2380 821990-

London to Wales on the M4

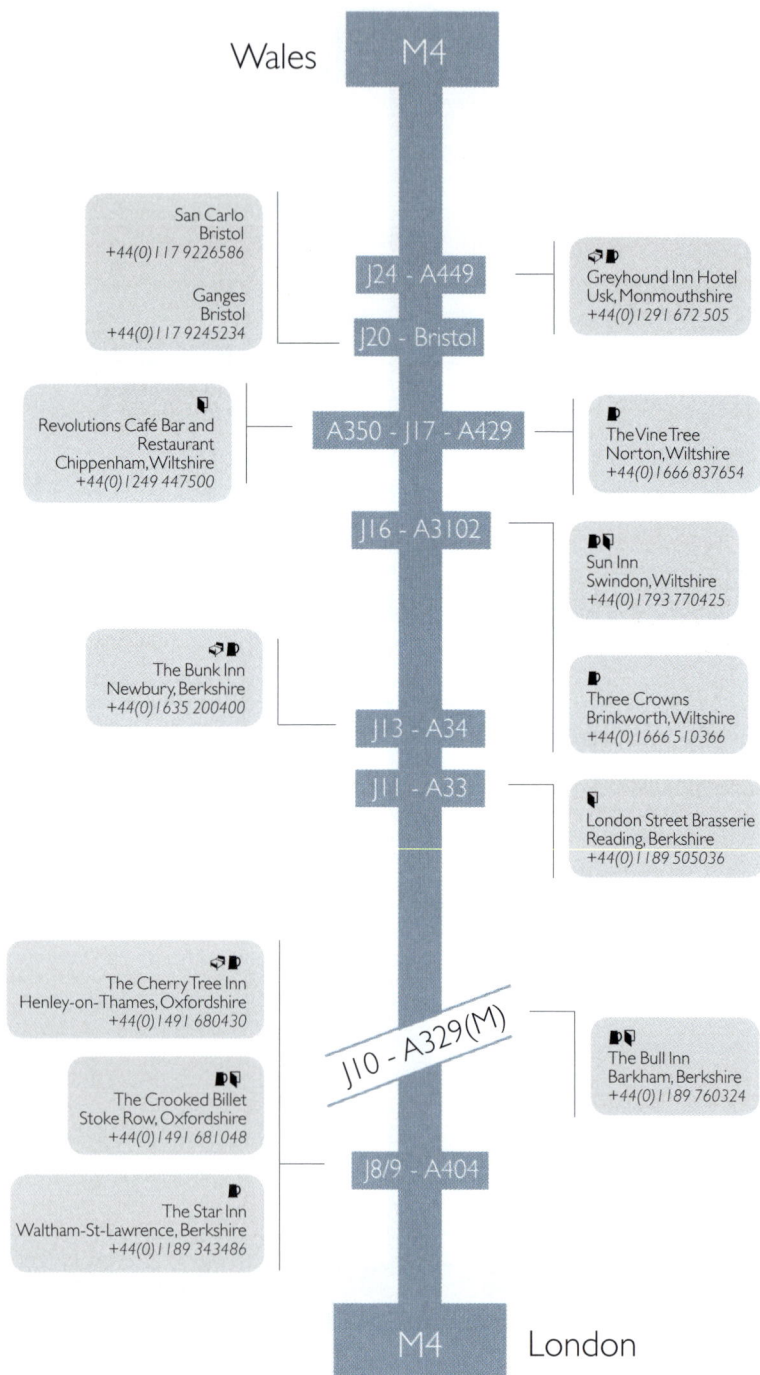

Wales

M4

San Carlo
Bristol
+44(0)117 9226586

Ganges
Bristol
+44(0)117 9245234

J24 - A449

Greyhound Inn Hotel
Usk, Monmouthshire
+44(0)1291 672 505

J20 - Bristol

Revolutions Café Bar and
Restaurant
Chippenham, Wiltshire
+44(0)1249 447500

A350 - J17 - A429

The Vine Tree
Norton, Wiltshire
+44(0)1666 837654

J16 - A3102

Sun Inn
Swindon, Wiltshire
+44(0)1793 770425

The Bunk Inn
Newbury, Berkshire
+44(0)1635 200400

Three Crowns
Brinkworth, Wiltshire
+44(0)1666 510366

J13 - A34

J11 - A33

London Street Brasserie
Reading, Berkshire
+44(0)1189 505036

The Cherry Tree Inn
Henley-on-Thames, Oxfordshire
+44(0)1491 680430

J10 - A329(M)

The Bull Inn
Barkham, Berkshire
+44(0)1189 760324

The Crooked Billet
Stoke Row, Oxfordshire
+44(0)1491 681048

J8/9 - A404

The Star Inn
Waltham-St-Lawrence, Berkshire
+44(0)1189 343486

M4 London

Salisbury to Penzance on the A303

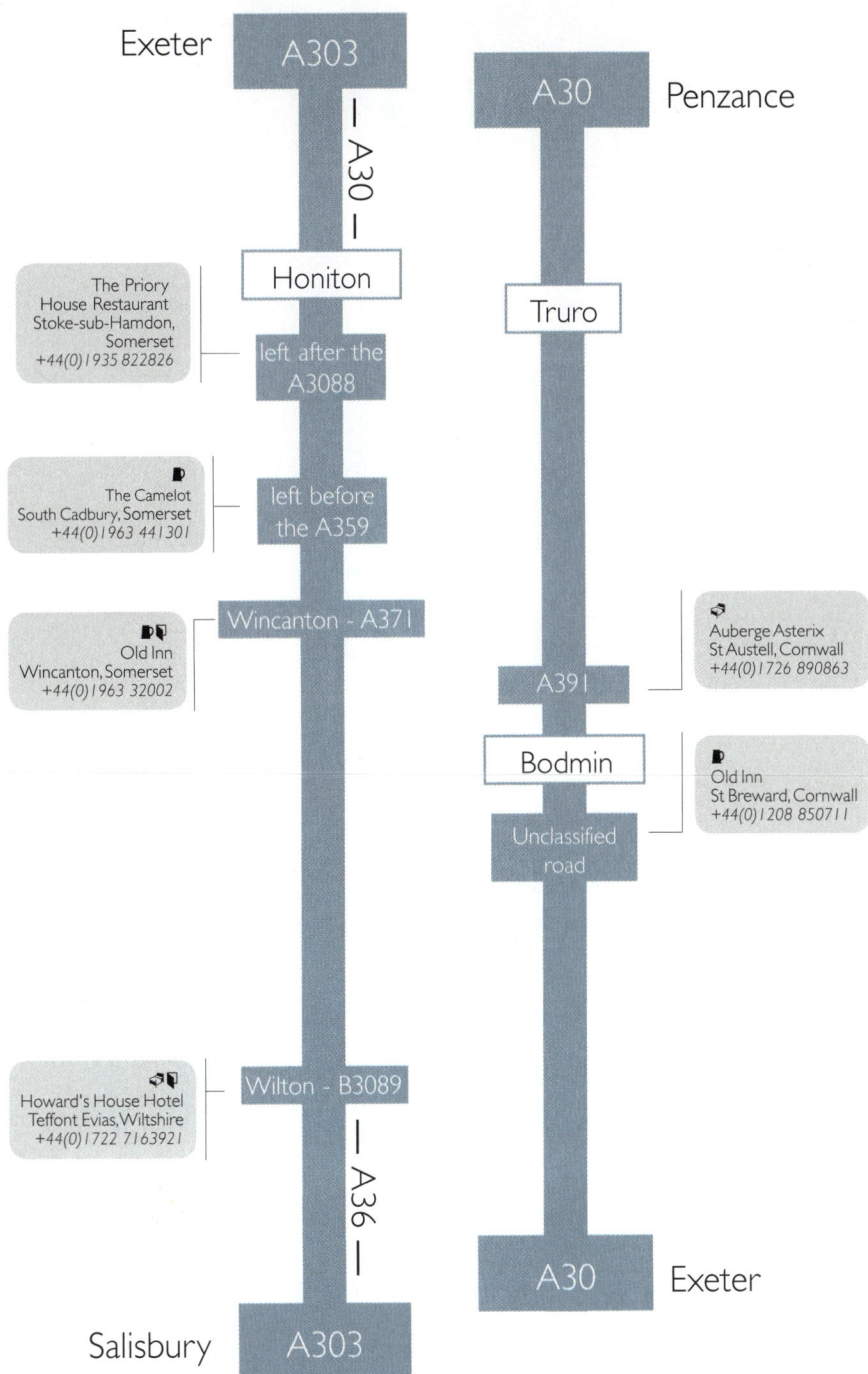

Exeter

A303

A30

Penzance

A30

Honiton

Truro

The Priory
House Restaurant
Stoke-sub-Hamdon,
Somerset
+44(0)1935 822826

left after the
A3088

The Camelot
South Cadbury, Somerset
+44(0)1963 441301

left before
the A359

Old Inn
Wincanton, Somerset
+44(0)1963 32002

Wincanton - A371

Auberge Asterix
St Austell, Cornwall
+44(0)1726 890863

A391

Bodmin

Old Inn
St Breward, Cornwall
+44(0)1208 850711

Unclassified
road

Howard's House Hotel
Teffont Evias, Wiltshire
+44(0)1722 7163921

Wilton - B3089

A36

Salisbury

A303

A30

Exeter

MAPS

9 **10**

Shetland

○ Wick

○ Ullapool

7 **8**

○ Inverness

○ Fort William

Edinburgh ○
Glasgow ○

5 Newcastle
upon Tyne **6**

○ Carlisle ○ Durham
Belfast ○

○ York
Leeds ○

Dublin ○ Liverpool ○ Manchester **4**
Llandudno ○ **3**
Nottingham ○ Norwich ○
Aberystwyth ○ Birmingham ○
1 Cambridge ○
Rosslare ○ **2**
Swansea ○ Oxford ○
Cardiff ○ Bristol ○ London ○
Dover ○
Exeter ○ Southampton ○ Brighton ○
Plymouth ○
Penzance ○

MI Motorway	National park
A1 Primary A roads	Forest
A4 Other A roads	Beach
☎ 0870I 296002 Ferry routes (with contact number)	Inn/accommodation
✈ Heathrow Airport	Pub

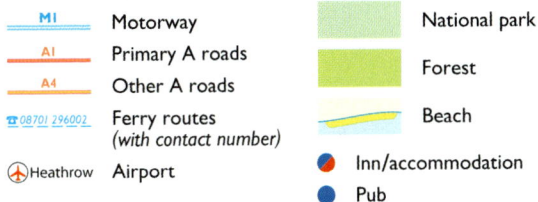

Scale 1 : 1 500 000

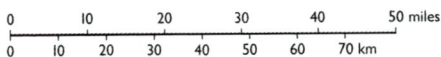

0   10   20   30   40   50 miles

0 10 20 30 40 50 60 70 km

I 1 2 3 4

5

A

Bardsey Island

Barmouth

Aberdyfi

Cardigan Bay

Aberystwyth

CE

B

Rosslare

to Rosslare ☎ 08705 707070

Aberaeron

New Quay

Cardigan

Newcastle Emlyn

Llandyssul

Cru

Strumble Head

Fishguard

PEMBROKESHIRE

CARMARTHEN

St David's Head

St David's

Newgale

Carmarthen

Ramsey Island

Haverfordwest

St Clears

Pembrokeshire Coast

Broad Haven

Amman

Milford Haven

Saundersfoot

Kidwelly

Llanelli

C

Pembroke Dock

Tenby

Linney Head

Carmarthen Bay

Swa

Caldey Island

SWA

Worms Head

Port Eyno

to Cork ☎ 01792 456116

☎ 01792 456116

Ilfracombe

Woolacombe

Br i

C e l t i c   S e a

D

Lundy ☎ 01271 863636

Sea

Braunton

B

Clovelly

Bideford

Great Torrington

E

Bude

Holsworthy

Okehampto

Port Gaverne

Launceston

Padstow

St Breward

Wadebridge

Colliford Reservoir

Tavist

F

Bodmin

Liskeard

Newquay

CORNWALL

Lostwithiel

Plym

Kelsey Head

Saltash

St Austell

Plymout

Looe

Holbe

Polperro

St Ives

Redruth

Truro

Mevagissey

Camborne

St Mawes

G

St Just

Falmouth

ISLES OF SCILLY

Penzance

Helston

Falmouth Bay

Tresco

Land's End

Sennen

St Keverne

St Martin's

☎ 08457 105555

St Mary's

Lizard

Isles of Scilly

Lizard Point

H

to New York ☎ 023 8071 6500

I 1 2 3 4

Shrewsbury Telford Shifnal Lichfield Tamworth
Welshpool Albrighton Brownhills Walsall Sutton Coldfield
Montgomery Bridgnorth Heathton Wolverhampton Nuneaton
Caersws Dudley Birmingham Coventry
Newtown SHROPSHIRE Kidderminster Birmingham Kenilworth Rugby
Llanidloes Bewdley Bromsgrove Royal Leamington Spa
Clun Ludlow Redditch Warwick
Knighton Brimfield Tenbury Wells Worcester WARWICKSHIRE
New Radnor Titley Kington Leominster WORCESTERSHIRE Evesham Stratford-upon-Avon Shipston on Stour Banbury
Llandrindod Wells Weobley Malvern Pershore Chipping Campden Broadway Moreton-in-Marsh Stow-on-the-Wold
Builth Wells Eardisley Ledbury Tewkesbury Winchcombe Cheltenham Bledington Chipping Norton
Hay-on-Wye Hereford Cotswold Hills Northleach Witney Burford
Brecon Felin Fach Ross-on-Wye Newent Gloucester GLOUCESTERSHIRE Ox
Black Mountains Llangattock Lingoed Forest of Dean Painswick Stroud OXFORDSHIRE
Brecon Beacons Crickhowell Abergavenny Skenfrith Monmouth Clearwell Frampton Mansell Cirencester Kelmscott
Merthyr Tydfil Bettws Newydd Raglan Usk Tetbury Ewen Faringdon
Aberdare Tredegar Pontypool Llantrisant Cwmbran Malmesbury Lydiard Millicent Swindon
Neath Treorchy Caerphilly Chipping Sodbury Norton Brinkworth Wantage BERKS
Maesteg Pontypridd Newport NEWPORT Chepstow BRISTOL Chippenham Marlborough Hungerford Ne
Porthcawl Bridgend Cardiff Portishead Clevedon Bristol Melksham Devizes Pewsey
VALE OF GLAMORGAN Cardiff International Barry Weston-super-Mare Bath Bradford-on-Avon WILTSHIRE Andover
Channel NORTH SOMERSET BATH & NE SOM Midsomer Norton Warminster Amesbury Wherwell
Lynton Minehead Glastonbury Wells Shepton Mallet Stockbridge Littleton Winchester
Exmoor Exford Bridgwater SOMERSET Wincanton Holton Shaftesbury Salisbury Romsey
South Molton Knowstone Taunton Langport South Cadbury Sturminster Newton Rockbourne The New Forest Southampton
Tiverton Cullompton Yeovil Fontmell Magna Fordingbridge Ringwood Lyndhurst Brockenhurst Beauli
Crediton Exeter Honiton Corscombe DORSET Blandford Forum Bournemouth -Hurn Lymington Cow
Modbury Topsham Chard Cerne Abbas Beaminster Wimbourne Bournemouth ISLE
Exeter Exmouth Sidmouth Seaton Bridport Dorchester Poole Bournemouth Freshwater
Dawlish Teignmouth Lyme Regis Lyme Bay Weymouth Swanage Isle of Wigh
Newton Abbot Torquay Easton St Alban's Head
Totnes Paignton Berry Head Brixham Portland Bill
Slapton Dartmouth Stokenham Start Point alcombe
Alderney Cherbourg
Guernsey Dielette

Liverpool St Helens
Birkenhead Warrington Glossop Rotherham Bawtry Gainsborough
Liverpool John Lennon Knutsford Manchester Stockport Marple Sheffield 6 Worksop Retford
Ellesmere Port Northwich Prestbury Macclesfield Peak Chesterfield Sherwood Forest Tuxford Harby Lincoln
Chester Cotebrook Tarporley Congleton Eaton Bakewell District Mansfield Hardwick Ollerton Thorpe on the Hill
Wrexham Nantwich Crewe Leek Matlock Newark-on-Trent
Whitchurch CHESHIRE Stoke-on-Trent Ashbourne Nottingham
Wem STAFFORDSHIRE Uttoxeter Derby Grantham
Oswestry Market Drayton Salt Belvoir Stathern
Shrewsbury Telford Stafford Burton upon Trent Breedon-on-the-Hill East Midlands Loughborough Nether Broughton Clipsham
Rugeley Ashby-de-la-Zouch Melton Mowbray
Shifnal Lichfield LEICESTERSHIRE Oakham RUTLAND
Albrighton Brownhills Tamworth Leicester Uppingham Bulwick
Wolverhampton Walsall Sutton Coldfield Corby Fotheringhay Oundle
Bridgnorth Heathton Dudley MIDLANDS Nuneaton Market Harborough Kettering NORTHAMPTON SHIRE Keyston
Kidderminster Birmingham Birmingham Coventry Rugby Northampton Wellingborough
Bewdley Bromsgrove Kenilworth Davy
Ludlow Redditch Royal Leamington Spa Daventry Towcester Newport Pagnell Salford
Brimfield Tenbury Wells Droitwich Warwick WARWICKSHIRE Buckingham Milton Keynes Wobu
Titley Kington Leominster Worcester WORCESTER SHIRE Stratford-upon-Avon Chipping Campden Shipston on Stour Banbury Brackley BUCKINGHAM SHIRE Leighton Buzzard Dunstable Mentmore
Hereford Malvern Bidford-on-Avon Evesham Broadway Waddesdon Aylesbury
Ledbury Pershore Moreton-in-Marsh Stow-on-the-Wold Bicester Stoke Mandeville Chiltern Hills
Ross-on-Wye Tewkesbury Winchcombe Cheltenham Bledington Chipping Norton Oxford Thame Berkhamsted Flaunden
Llangattock Lingoed Newent Gloucester Northleach Burford Witney Stoke St Giles Beaconsfield
Skenfrith Monmouth Forest of Dean Painswick Stroud COTSWOLDS Cirencester Kelmscott Abingdon Stoke Row Henley-on-Thames Marlow Cookham
Bettws Newydd Raglan Clearwell Frampton Mansell Ewen Faringdon Didcot Goring Rotherfield Peppard Wargrave Maidenhead
Usk Llantrisant Chepstow Malmesbury Lydiard Millicent Swindon Wantage Reading Waltham St Lawrence Windsor Slough
Cwmbran NEWPORT Chipping Sodbury Norton Brinkworth Chippenham Marlborough Hungerford Thatcham Newbury Barkham Bracknell Wokingham Weybridge
Portishead Clevedon Bristol Melksham Devizes Pewsey Basingstoke SURR
North SOMERSET Bath BATH & NE SOM Bradford-on-Avon Midsomer Norton WILTSHIRE Andover Crondall Farnham Goda
Wells Shepton Mallet Warminster Amesbury Wherwell HAMPSHIRE Churt Chiddingfold Petworth
Glastonbury Stockbridge Littleton Winchester Fernhurst Petersfield Midhurst
SOMERSET Wincanton Shaftesbury Salisbury Romsey East Lavant Halnaker Chichester
Langport Holton South Cadbury Sturminster Newton Fontmell Magna Rockbourne Southampton Bursledon Fareham Portsmouth
Yeovil Blandford Forum Fordingbridge Ringwood The New Forest Southampton Beaulieu
Corscombe Cerne Abbas Wimborne Hern Lyndhurst Brockenhurst Cowes
Beaminster DORSET Bournemouth Lymington Newport Bembridge
Bridport Dorchester Poole Bournemouth Freshwater ISLE OF WIGHT Shanklin
Lyme Regis Weymouth Swanage Isle of Wight Ventnor
Seaton Lyme Bay Easton Portland Bill St Alban's Head English

Louth   6   Mablethorpe

Horncastle   Chapel St Leonards

Partney

Coningsby   Skegness

LINCOLNSHIRE

Boston

Spalding   Holbeach   The Wash

Wisbech   Kings Lynn   Hunstanton   Brancaster Staithe   Holkham   Cromer

Snettisham   North Walsham

Peterborough   March   Downham Market   Fakenham   Itteringham   Aylsham

Swaffham   Hevingham   Norwich   Winterton-on-Sea

NORFOLK   East Dereham   Great Yarmouth

Chatteris   Ely   Wymondham   Norwich   Reedham

Huntingdon   Mildenhall   Thetford Forest Park   Thetford   Old Buckenham   Lowestoft

St Neots   Bungay   Barnby

CAMBRIDGESHIRE   Newmarket   Diss   Halesworth   Southwold

Cambridge   Cambridge   Bury St Edmunds   Eye

Madingley   Stowmarket   Brandeston

Thriplow   Hundon   Needham Market   Aldeburgh

Royston   Haverhill   Lavenham   Woodbridge   Orford   Orford Ness

Saffron Walden   Sudbury   Ipswich

Reed   Halstead   Felixstowe   to Esbjerg   to Cuxhaven

HERTFORD-   Stansted   Braintree   Colchester   Manningtree   Harwich   to Hook of Holland

Stevenage   Coggeshall   Fingringhoe   The Naze

Bishops Stortford   Great Dunmow   Youngs End   Witham   Peldon   Clacton-on-Sea

Watton-at-Stone   Hertford   Harlow   ESSEX   Maldon   Mersea Island

SHIRE   Epping   Chelmsford   Burnham-on-Crouch

St Albans   Woodford Green   Brentwood   Paglesham East End

GREATER   Hampstead   Barking   Romford   Basildon   Southend-on-Sea

London   Brompton   Woolwich   Canvey Island   Mouth of the Thames

Barnes   Wandsworth   Tilbury   Sheerness   Isle of Sheppey   Margate   North Foreland

LONDON   Swanley   Gravesend   Rochester   Whitstable   Herne Bay   Ramsgate   to Ostend

Sutton   Croydon   Gillingham   Sittingbourne   Faversham   Stodmarsh

Epsom   M26   Maidstone   Canterbury   Wingham   Deal

Featherstead   Sevenoaks   Grafty Green   KENT   South Foreland

Reigate   Bodsham   Dover

Dorking   Lingfield   Royal Tunbridge Wells   Ashford   Stowting   to Dunkerque

Gatwick   East Grinstead   Bewl Water   Folkestone   Channel Tunnel   Calais

Horsham   Crowborough   Tenterden

Haywards Heath   Heathfield   Boulogne

Uckfield   Rye   Dungeness

South   Downs   EAST SUSSEX   Battle

Poynings   Cooksbridge   Lewes   Hailsham   Hastings

Hove   Brighton   Newhaven   Eastbourne   Bexhill

Worthing   Beachy Head

Strait of Dover

C h a n n e l

Ardrossan Kilmarnock Lanark LANARKSHIRE Peebles Galashiels Melrose Kelso
Irvine EAST 8 SCOTTISH BORDERS
Troon Prestwick AYRSHIRE Selkirk
Ayr Cumnock Tweedsmuir Hawick Jedburgh
Maybole New Cumnock Sanquhar Moffat The Cheviot No
Girvan SOUTH Loch Doon Dalmellington Patna Beattock Kielder Water Stannersb
AYRSHIRE Galloway Forest Park Langholm Kielder Forest Park
Cairnryan DUMFRIES AND GALLOWAY Clatteringshaws Loch New Galloway Dumfries Longtown Brampton South Tyne
Newton Stewart Castle Douglas Gretna Longtown
Glenluce Loch Ken Carlisle Brampton
Kirkcudbright Wigton Alston
Whithorn Abbey Head Maryport CUMBRIA Armathwaite Melmerby
Drummore Isle of Whithorn Cockermouth Great Salkeld
Burrow Head Workington Bassenthwaite Lake Penrith Appleby-Westmo
Mull of Galloway Whitehaven Keswick Borrowdale Ullswater
St Bees Head Buttermere Lake District Grasmere
Egremont Wasdale Head Ambleside Windermere Kendal Sedbergh
Seascale Eskdale Boot Coniston Hawkshead Yorks
Isle of Man Ramsey Maughold Head Broughton-in-Furness Cartmel Kirkby Lonsdale
Peel Laxey Grange-over-Sands Carnforth Set
Contrary Head Douglas Barrow-in-Furness Morecambe Bay Morecambe Lancaster
Isle of Man Castletown Isle of Walney Heysham LANCASHIRE
Spanish Head Fleetwood Whitewell Clitheroe
Poulton-le-Fylde Wiswell
Blackpool Preston Blackbu
Irish Sea Blackpool Lytham St Anne's Leyland Ramsbottom
Southport Ormskirk Bolt
Wigan
ISLE OF ANGLESEY Amlwch Wallasey Liverpool St Helens
Holyhead Anglesey Great Ormes Head Llandudno Prestatyn Birkenhead Warrington
Holy Island Llangefni Conwy Colwyn Bay Rhyl Mostyn Liverpool John Lennon Knutsford
Rhosneigr Bangor St Asaph Holywell Ellesmere Port Northwich CHES
Caernarfon Llanrwst Denbigh Mold Chester Cotebrook Tarporley
Caernarfon Bay Capel Curig Betws-y-coed Ruthin Wrexham Nantwich Crewe
Beddgelert Blaenau Ffestiniog Cerrigydrudion Whitchurch
Nefyn Criccieth Porthmadog Bala Llangollen Wem Market
Pwllheli Llanbedr Snowdonia Llyn Tegid Oswestry
Absersoch Barmouth Dolgellau Dinas Mawddwy Llanfyllin Shrewsbury Telford
sey Island Cemmaes Llanerfyl Welshpool Shifnal Alb
Machynlleth POWYS Montgomery Wolv
Cardigan Bay Aberdyfi Talybont Caersws Newtown SHROPSHIRE Bridgnorth

North Sea

Bamburgh
Seahouses
Alnwick
Warkworth
Amble
gframlington
UMBERLAND
urn
Morpeth
Ashington
Blyth
Newcastle
Newcastle upon Tyne
Tynemouth
Corbridge
South Shields
TYNE AND WEAR
Stocksfield
Gateshead
Sunderland
Consett
Durham
Peterlee
Stanhope
Hartlepool
HAM
Bishop Auckland
West Auckland
Saltburn
irk
Barnard
Castle
Middlesbrough
Whitby
Whashton
Darlington
Teesside
Richmond
North York Moors
Osmotherley
Northallerton
Scarborough
Leyburn
Bedale
Fadmoor
Thornton
Watlass
Helmsley
Pickering
Filey
Masham
Thirsk
Harome
Marton
Hunmanby
les
Ripon
Malton
Flamborough Head
Sawley
Great
Ouseburn
York
Driffield
Bridlington
urnsall
EAST RIDING
OF YORKSHIRE
Bridlington Bay
lon
Skipton
Harrogate
Wetherby
Market
Weighton
Beverley
Keighley
Leeds/
Bradford
Sherburn
in Elmet
Howden
WEST YORKSHIRE
Leeds
Selby
Withernsea
ey
Bradford
Castleford
Goole
Kingston
upon Hull
Sowerby
Bridge
Shibden
Halifax
Dewsbury
Wakefield
Pontefract
Barton-upon-
Humber
NORTH
LINCOLNSHIRE
Huddersfield
Slaithwaite
Shelley
Barnsley
Scunthorpe
Grimsby
Cleethorpes
Mouth of the H
ale
Oldham
SOUTH YORKSHIRE
Doncaster
Humberside
NORTH
LINCOLNSHIRE
nchester
Glossop
Rotherham
Bawtry
Spurn Head
ster
Marple
Gainsborough
Market Rasen
Louth
Mablethorpe
rt
Prestbury
Sheffield
Worksop
Retford
Welton
Hill
Horncastle
Partney
Chapel
Macclesfield
Chesterfield
Tuxford
Harby
Lincoln
Skegne
ton
Buxton
Sherwood
Forest
Ollerton
Thorpe
on the Hill
Coningsby
A155
Bakewell
Hardwick
Mansfield
eton
Matlock
DERBYSHIRE
NOTTINGHAM-
SHIRE
Newark-on-Trent
LINCOLNSHIRE
Leek
District
Ashbourne
Stoke-on-
Trent
Nottingham
Sleaford
Boston
Hunstant
The Wash
Uttoxeter
Derby
Grantham
Snetti
RDSHIRE
Salt
Breedon
on the
Hill
Belvoir
Surfleet
Seas End
Holbeach
K
Stafford
Burton upon
Trent
East
Midlands
Loughborough
Stathern
Nether Broughton
Melton
Mowbray
Bourne
Spalding
Rugeley
Ashby-de-la-Zouch
Clipsham
Wisbech
Lichfield
LEICESTERSHIRE
RUTLAND
P
Brownhills
Sutton
Coldfield
Tamworth
Oakham
Rutland
Water
Stamford
March
Walsall
Uppingham
Peterborough
A1
Leicester
Bulwick
Dudley
Nuneaton
Market
Ha rough
Corby
Fotheringhay
Oundle
Chatteris
MIDLANDS
3
6 7 8

☎ 0191 296 1313 to Stavanger, Haugesund, Bergen
☎ 08705 333222 to Gothenburg
☎ 08705 333222
to Imuiden
Rosedale
Howden
Reservoir
Ladybower
Reservoir
Peak
Hardwick Hall
M62
M1
M18
M180
M62
M180
A1(M)
M1
M42
M6 Toll
M6
M69
A1

Leverburgh

Lochmaddy

Benbecula

Rudha Hunish

Little Minch

9 loch

Fionn Loch

Loch Maree

Kinlochewe

A832

Loch Fannich

Achnasheen

Loch Luichart

Dingwall

HIGHLAND

Muir of Ord

Beauly

Uig

Shieldaig

Loch Monar

Strathcarron

Loch Mullardoch

Cannich

Portree

Raasay

Scalpay

Plockton

Stromeferry

Kyle of Lochalsh

Invermorist

Loch Affric

Loch Ness

Sconser

Skye

Scalpay

South Uist

Rudha Hunish

Eriskay

Loch Quoich

Glenmoriston

Loch Cluanie

Loch Loyne

Fort Augustus

Invergarry

Loch Garry

Armadale

Mallaig

Loch Arkaig

Loch Lochy

Moy

Sea of the Hebrides

Canna

Kinloch

Rum

Eigg

Muck

Galmisdale

Loch Morar

Glenfinnan

Lochailort

Spean Bridge

A86

Loch Shiel

Fort William

Inner

Kilchoan

Strontian

Inchree

Glencoe

Ballachulish

Blackwater Reservoir

Loch Treig

Loch Ericht

Coll

Arinagour

Tobermory

Lochaline

Achnacroish

Loch Etive

Tiree

Scarinish

Mull

Craignure

Lismore

Connel

Oban

Loch Awe

H e b r i d e s

Iona

Fidden

Firth of Lorne

Crianlarich

Lochea

Loch Lomond and the Tro

Queen Elizabeth Forest Park

ARGYLL

Inveraray

Loch Lomond

Colonsay

AND

Strachur

Argyll Forest Park

Luss

Ardlussa

BUTE

Lochgilphead

Helensburgh

Jura

Sound of Jura

Port Askaig

Tarbert

Portavadie

Kennacraig

Kilcreggan

Dunoon

Wemyss Bay

Rothesay

Port Bannatyne

Largs

Greenock

INVERCLYDE

Johnstone

Paisley

Alexandria

Dumbar

Islay

Ardtalla

Claonaig

Bute

NORTH AYRSHIRE

Portnahaven

Port Ellen

Gigha

Tayinloan

Lochranza

Farland Head

Ardrossan

Kilmarnock

Irvine

Troon

Prestwick

Mull of Oa

Arran

Brodick

Lamlash

Ayr

Firth of Clyde

SOUTH AYRSHIRE

Campbeltown

Bennan Head

Maybole

Patna

North Channel

Mull of Kintyre

Girvan

Galloway Forest Park

Ballantrae

Kirkcolm

Cairnryan

New Stew

Stranraer

Glenluce

A75

Larne

Portpatrick

Drummore

Whith

Burro Hea

A

B

North Ronaldsay

Westray

Rousay

Sanday

Brough Head

Eday

Stronsay

Mainland

Shapinsay

Finstown

Orkney Islands

Stromness

Kirkwall

ORKNEY

St Mary's

Hoy

St Margaret's Hope

South Ronaldsay

C

Burwick

Pentland Firth

Stroma

John o'Groats

Scrabster

Thurso

Gills

Duncansby Head

Halkirk

Noss Head

Melvich

Whiten Head

Durness

Loch Hope

Tongue

Loch Loyal

Wick

D

Loch Naver

Loch nan Clar

Thurso

Altnaharra

Kinbrace

Latheron

nchnadamph

Berriedale

Loch Shin

Helmsdale

E

Lairg

Brora

Bonar Bridge

Dornoch

Tain

Loch Glass

Alness

Invergordon

Moray Firth

Lossiemouth

Buckie

Banff

F

Cromarty

Elgin

Aberchirder

Dingwall

Nairn

Forres

MORAY

Keith

Turriff

Muir of Ord

Tore

Craigellachie

Dufftown

Beauly

Inverness

Huntly

Rhynie

Oldmeldru

Cannich

Grantown-on-Spey

Glenlivet

Inverurie

Alford

Carrbridge

Aberdeen

Dyce

Boat of Garten

Invermoriston

Monadhliath Mountains

Cairngorms Park

ABERDEENSHIRE

G

Fort Augustus

Glenmore Park

Ballater

Banchory

Crathes

Invergarry

Kingussie

Braemar

Stonehave

H

Moy

Dalwhinnie

Grampian Mountains

Inverbervie

Loch Ericht

PERTH 8

ANGUS

Blair Atholl

Is it any wonder Abergavenny hosts one of the Greatest Events in Wales?

Abergavenny, the largest market town in Monmouthshire, has a history of producing food. Good food. Fresh food. Wholesome food.

The streets are lined with independent butchers, the market bustles with customers buying local fresh produce and the surrounding countryside is as stunning as the restaurants that you'll find here. It's a veritable land of milk and honey…

So no, it's no wonder, that the Abergavenny Food Festival won the Greatest Event in Wales 2003 in the National Tourism Awards. There is wonder here, however, and the wonder lies in the food.

If you're planning a visit, for the festival or at any time, why not spoil yourself in Green Dragon accredited accommodation* **www.greenbeds.adventa.org.uk**

While you're here, you can also gorge yourself on the stunning scenery by taking a day trip around Monmouthshire **www.discovery.adventa.org.uk**

If we've whetted your appetite, there is a selection of free brochures, with information on a wide range of subjects and places of interest in Monmouthshire, including local churches, gardens, and of course food. For more information email: **chepstow.tic@monmouthshire.gov.uk or call 01291 623772**

For more information about Abergavenny Food Festival: **www.abergavennyfoodfestival.com**

www.adventa.org.uk

monmouthshire
COUNTY COUNCIL
sir fynwy

WDA

LEADER+

YR UNDEB
EWROPEAIDD
LEADER +
EUROPEAN
UNION
LEADER +

Llywodraeth Cynulliad Cymru
Welsh Assembly Government

* The Green Dragon Environmental Standard is a stepped environmental management system. Wherever you see the logo you can be sure that the business is environmentally responsible and committed to supporting the local economy and culture.

A-Z by establishment name

Albert Arms, Esher, Surrey   139
Alford Arms, Berkhamsted, Hertfordshire   86
Anglers Arms, Longframlington, Northumberland   113
Anglesey Arms at Halnaker, Chichester, West Sussex   143
Appletree Country Inn, Marton, North Yorkshire   161
Atholl Arms Hotel, Blair Atholl, Perth & Kinross   181
Beaufort, Crickhowell, Powys   197
Beaufort Arms Coaching Inn and Restaurant, Raglan, Monmouthshire   192
Bell at Skenfrith, Skenfrith, Monmouthshire   192
Birdcage, Thame, Oxfordshire   124
Black Bear Inn, Bettws Newydd, Monmouthshire   191
Black Horse, Woburn, Bedfordshire   39
Black Sheep Brewery, Masham, North Yorkshire   161
Boot Inn, Eskdale, Cumbria   57
Border Hotel, Kelso, Scottish Borders   185
Bottle & Glass, Harby, Nottinghamshire   115
Brackenrigg Inn, Ullswater, Cumbria   59
Bricklayers Arms, Flaunden, Hertfordshire   86
Bridge, Bidford-on-Avon, Warwickshire   148
Bridge Pub and Dining Rooms, London SW13   103
Buck Inn, Bedale, North Yorkshire   155
Bull at Broughton, Skipton, North Yorkshire   165
Bull Inn, Barkham, Berkshire   40
Bull's Head and Stables Bistro, London SW13   103
Bunk Inn, Newbury, Berkshire   41
Butchers Arms, Painswick, Gloucestershire   79
Cabinet, Reed, Hertfordshire   87
Cadgwith Cove Inn, The Lizard, Cornwall   54
Café Royal Circle Bar and Oyster Bar Restaurant, Edinburgh   171
Camelot, South Cadbury, Somerset   129
Chequers, Chipping Norton, Oxfordshire   117
Chequers Inn, Belvoir, Lincolnshire   100
Cherry Tree Inn, Henley-on-Thames, Oxfordshire   120
Clachaig Inn, Glencoe, Highland   176
Coach House Restaurant and Bar, Brighton, East Sussex   142
Countryman Inn, Shipley, West Sussex   147
Crab & Lobster Inn, Bembridge, Isle of Wight   90
Crook Inn, Tweedsmuir, Scottish Borders   185
Crooked Billet, Stoke Row, Oxfordshire   121
Crown, Great Ouseburn, North Yorkshire   156
Crown at Wells and Anton's Bistrot, Wells, Somerset   129
Crown Inn, Fontmell Magna, Dorset   71
Dalesman Country Inn, Sedbergh, Cumbria   59
Dartmoor Union Inn, Holbeton, Devon   65
Dog Inn, Wingham, Kent   93
Duke of Cumberland, Midhurst, West Sussex   145
Dukes Head, Armathwaite, Cumbria   55
Exmoor White Horse Inn, Exford, Somerset   128
Falcon Inn, Oundle, Northamptonshire   111
Falcon Inn, Painswick, Gloucestershire   79
Famous Bein Inn, Perth, Perth & Kinross   182
Farmers Arms, Lincoln, Lincolnshire   101
Felin Fach Griffin, Brecon, Powys   197
Ferry, Cookham, Berkshire   40
Fisherman's Return, Winterton-on-Sea, Norfolk   109

Fishes, Oxford, Oxfordshire   121
Five Arrows Hotel, Waddesdon, Buckinghamshire   48
Fleece, Witney, Oxfordshire   125
Fountain Inn, Tenbury Wells, Worcestershire   154
Fountain Inn and Boxer's Restaurant, Wells, Somerset   132
Four Seasons Country Pub & Restaurant, Fort William, Highland   175
Fox and Barrel, Tarporley, Cheshire   51
Fox Inn, Corscombe, Dorset   70
Freemasons Arms, London NW3   104
Freemasons Arms, Clitheroe, Lancashire   94
Friar's Head at Akebar, Leyburn, North Yorkshire   160
Froggies at the Timber Batts, Bodsham, Kent   91
Gamekeeper Freehouse, Old Buckenham, Norfolk   108
George and the Dragon, Watton-at-Stone, Hertfordshire   87
Golden Lion, Osmotherley, North Yorkshire   164
Green Dragon, Braintree, Essex   72
Green Man, Cambridge, Cambridgeshire   49
Greyhound Inn Hotel, Usk, Monmouthshire   193
Grog & Gruel, Fort William, Highland   175
Hack & Spade Inn, Richmond, North Yorkshire   164
Halfway Bridge Inn, Petworth, West Sussex   146
Hampshire Arms, Crondall, Hampshire   81
Hardwick Inn, Hardwick, Derbyshire   64
Hare & Hounds, Lingfield, Surrey   141
Highland Drove Inn, Penrith, Cumbria   58
Holly Bush, Stafford, Staffordshire   133
Hundred House Hotel, Telford, Shropshire   127
Hunters Moon Inn, Abergavenny, Monmouthshire   191
Hunters Rest Inn, Bath & NE Somerset   38
Inn at Whitewell, Whitewell, Lancashire   95
Inn on the Lake, Godalming, Surrey   140
Ivy House, Chalfont St Giles, Buckinghamshire   43
Kings Head, Ivinghoe, Bedfordshire   38
Kings Head Inn, Bledington, Oxfordshire   116
Kinmel Arms, St George, Conwy   188
Loch Tummel Inn, Pitlochry, Perth & Kinross   183
Marsham Arms Inn, Hevingham, Norfolk   105
Minnow, Weybridge, Surrey   141
Mussel and Crab, Tuxford, Nottinghamshire   115
Old Fisherman, Thame, Buckinghamshire   124
Old Inn, St Breward, Cornwall   53
Old Inn, Wincanton, Somerset   132
Old Mill Inn, Pitlochry, Perth & Kinross   184
Old Plough, Oakham, Rutland   126
Olde Ship Hotel, Seahouses, Northumberland   113
Olive Branch, Clipsham, Rutland   125
One Elm, Stratford-upon-Avon, Warwickshire   148
Peacock Inn, Tenbury Wells, Worcestershire   154
Peldon Rose Inn, Colchester, Essex   72
Penhelig Arms Hotel, Aberdyfi, Gwynedd   189
Pheasant Inn, Keyston, Cambridgeshire   50
Pheasant Inn, Kielder Water, Northumberland   112
Plockton Hotel, Plockton, Highland   177
Plough at Kelmscott, Kelmscott, Gloucestershire   75
Plough Inn, Fadmoor, North Yorkshire   156
Plough & Sail, Paglesham East End, Essex   73
Port Gaverne Hotel, Port Gaverne, Cornwall   53
Pride of the Valley Hotel, Farnham, Surrey   140
Puesdown Inn, Northleach, Gloucestershire   78
Queen's Head, Bulwick, Northamptonshire   111

Queen's Head, Brandeston, Suffolk	137
Queen's Head Hotel, Hawkshead, Cumbria	58
Rainbow Inn, Lewes, East Sussex	142
Red House, Nether Broughton, Leicestershire	96
Red Lion, Stodmarsh, Kent	92
Red Lion Hotel, Burnsall, North Yorkshire	155
Red Lion Inn, Stathern, Leicestershire	97
Rose and Crown, Snettisham, Norfolk	109
Rose and Crown, Warwick, Warwickshire	149
Rose and Crown at Romaldkirk, Romaldkirk, Co Durham	52
Rose and Thistle, Fordingbridge, Hampshire	81
Royal Hotel, Comrie, Perth & Kinross	181
Royal Oak, Cerne Abbas, Dorset	69
Royal Oak, Marlow, Buckinghamshire	46
Royal Oak, Chichester, West Sussex	144
Royal Oak, Poynings, West Sussex	146
Running Horse, Littleton, Hampshire	82
Russian Tavern at The Port Royal Hotel, Isle of Bute, Argyll & Bute	170
Sandpiper Inn, Leyburn, North Yorkshire	160
Sawley Arms and Cottages, Sawley, North Yorkshire	165
Saxon Mill, Warwick, Warwickshire	149
Scafell Hotel, Borrowdale, Cumbria	57
Seaforth Inn, Ullapool, Highland	180
Shibden Mill Inn, Shibden, West Yorkshire	167
Ship Inn, Chichester, West Sussex	145
Ship Inn, Spalding, Lincolnshire	101
Snooty Fox Inn, Faringdon, Oxfordshire	117
St George & Dragon, Wargrave, Berkshire	42
Stag, Mentmore, Buckinghamshire	46
Stagg Inn & Restaurant, Kington, Herefordshire	85
Star Inn, Harome, North Yorkshire	157
Star Inn, Waltham St Lawrence, Berkshire	41
Steam Packet Hotel, Isle of Whithorn, Dumfries and Galloway	171
Sun Inn, Swindon, Wiltshire	151
Swag and Tails, London SW7	104
Swan, Milton Keynes, Bedfordshire	39
Swan at Felsted, Great Dunmow, Essex	73
Swan Inn, Barnby, Suffolk	137
Swan Inn, Denham, Buckinghamshire	43
Swan Inn, Chiddingfold, Surrey	138
Thatched Cottage, Shepton Mallet, Somerset	128
Three Crowns, Brinkworth, Wiltshire	150
Three Horseshoes, Madingley, Cambridgeshire	50
Three Horseshoes Inn, Derby, Derbyshire	64
Tiger Inn, Ashford, Kent	91
Tower Inn, Slapton, Devon	68
Tradesmans Arms, Stokenham, Devon	68
Tufton Arms Hotel, Appleby-in-Westmorland, Cumbria	55
Unicorn Inn, Kincardine, Fife	174
Victoria at Holkham, Holkham, Norfolk	107
Victoria Inn, Salcombe, Devon	65
Vine Tree, Norton, Wiltshire	150
Walpole Arms, Itteringham, Norfolk	107
Wasdale Head Inn, Wasdale, Cumbria	60
Wheatsheaf Inn, Northleach, Gloucestershire	78
White Hart Inn, Winchcombe, Gloucestershire	80
White Horse, Brancaster Staithe, Norfolk	105
White Horse, Frampton Mansell, Gloucestershire	75
White Lion, Wherwell, Hampshire	83
White Star Tavern & Dining Rooms,	
Southampton, Hampshire	82
Who'd A Thought It, Maidstone, Kent	92
Wig & Pen, Norwich, Norfolk	108
Wild Duck Inn, Cirencester, Gloucestershire	74
Woolpack, Stoke Mandeville, Buckinghamshire	47
Wyndham Arms, Clearwell, Gloucestershire	74

A-Z by listing town

Aberdyfi	189
Abergavenny	191
Appleby-in-Westmorland	55
Armathwaite	55
Ashford	91
Barkham	40
Barnby	137
Bath	38
Bedale	155
Belvoir	100
Bembridge	90
Berkhamsted	86
Bettws Newydd	191
Bidford-on-Avon	148
Blair Atholl	181
Bledington	116
Bodsham	91
Borrowdale	57
Braintree	72
Brancaster Staithe	105
Brandeston	137
Brecon	197
Brighton	142
Brinkworth	150
Bulwick	111
Burnsall	155
Cambridge	49
Cerne Abbas	69
Chalfont St Giles	43
Chichester	143
Chiddingfold	138
Chipping Norton	117
Cirencester	74
Clearwell	74
Clipsham	125
Clitheroe	94
Colchester	72
Comrie	181
Cookham	40
Corscombe	70
Crickhowell	197
Crondall	81
Denham	43
Derby	64
Edinburgh	171
Esher	139
Eskdale	57
Exford	128
Fadmoor	156
Faringdon	117
Farnham	140
Flaunden	86
Fontmell Magna	71
Fordingbridge	81
Fort William	175

Frampton Mansell	75	Sedbergh	59
Glencoe	176	Shepton Mallet	128
Godalming	140	Shibden	167
Great Dunmow	73	Shipley	147
Great Ouseburn	156	Skenfrith	192
Harby	115	Skipton	165
Hardwick	64	Slapton	68
Harome	157	Snettisham	109
Hawkshead	58	South Cadbury	129
Henley-on-Thames	120	Southampton	82
Hevingham	105	Spalding	101
Holbeton	65	St Breward	53
Holkham	107	St George	188
Isle of Bute	170	Stafford	133
Isle of Whithorn	171	Stathern	97
Itteringham	107	Stodmarsh	92
Ivinghoe	38	Stoke Mandeville	47
Kelmscott	75	Stoke Row	121
Kelso	185	Stokenham	68
Keyston	50	Stratford-upon-Avon	148
Kielder Water	112	Swindon	151
Kincardine	174	Tarporley	51
Kington	85	Telford	127
Lewes	142	Tenbury Wells	154
Leyburn	160	Thame	124
Lincoln	101	Tuxford	115
Lingfield	141	Tweedsmuir	185
Littleton	82	Ullapool	180
Lizard	54	Ullswater	59
London	103	Usk	193
Longframlington	113	Waddesdon	48
Madingley	50	Waltham St Lawrence	41
Maidstone	92	Wargrave	42
Marlow	46	Warwick	149
Marton	161	Wasdale	60
Masham	161	Watton-at-Stone	87
Mentmore	46	Wells	129
Midhurst	145	Weybridge	141
Milton Keynes	39	Wherwell	83
Nether Broughton	96	Whitewell	95
Newbury	41	Wincanton	132
Northleach	78	Winchcombe	80
Norton	150	Wingham	93
Norwich	108	Winterton-on-Sea	109
Oakham	126	Witney	125
Old Buckenham	108	Woburn	39
Osmotherley	164		
Oundle	111		
Oxford	121		
Paglesham East End	73		
Painswick	79		
Penrith	58		
Perth	182		
Petworth	146		
Pitlochry	183		
Plockton	177		
Port Gaverne	53		
Poynings	146		
Raglan	192		
Reed	87		
Richmond	164		
Romaldkirk	52		
Salcombe	65		
Sawley	165		
Seahouses	113		

Quick-reference guide

Best for cheese

The Pheasant, Keyston, Cambridgeshire — 50
Three Horseshoes, Derby, Derbyshire — 64
Dartmoor Union Inn, Holbeton, Devon — 65
Rose & Crown, Romaldkirk, Co. Durham — 52
Unicorn Inn, Kincardine, Fife — 174
Stagg Inn, Kington, Herefordshire — 85
Inn at Whitewell, Whitewell, Lancashire — 95
Red Lion, Stathern, Leicestershire — 97
Farmers Arm, Lincoln, Lincolnshire — 101
Bell at Skenfrith, Skenfrith, Monmouthshire — 192
Kings Head Inn, Bledington, Oxfordshire — 116
Crooked Billet, Stoke Row, Oxfordshire — 121
Felin Fach Griffin, Brecon, Powys — 197
Olive Branch, Clipsham, Rutland — 125
Thatched Cottage, Shepton Mallet, Somerset — 128
The Camelot, South Cadbury, Somerset — 129
Royal Oak, Poynings, West Sussex — 146
Three Crowns, Brinkworth, Wiltshire — 150
Star Inn, Harome, North Yorkshire — 157
Hack & Spade Inn, Richmond, North Yorkshire — 164

Best for game

Café Royal, Edinburgh, City of Edinburgh — 171
Dukes Head, Armathwaite, Cumbria — 55
Three Horseshoes, Derby, Derbyshire — 64
Unicorn Inn, Kincardine, Fife — 174
Wyndham Arms, Clearwell, Gloucestershire — 74
Stagg Inn, Kington, Herefordshire — 85
Froggies at the Timber Batts, Bodsham, Kent — 91
Inn at Whitewell, Whitewell, Lancashire — 95
Chequers Inn, Belvoir, Lincolnshire — 100
Victoria at Holkham, Holkham, Norfolk — 107
Bottle & Glass, Harby, Nottinghamshire — 115
Crooked Billet, Stoke Row, Oxfordshire — 121
Felin Fach Griffin, Brecon, Powys — 197
Exmoor White Horse, Exford, Somerset — 128
Holly Bush, Stafford, Staffordshire — 133
Star Inn, Harome, North Yorkshire — 157
Friars Head, Leyburn, North Yorkshire — 160

Best for seafood

Cadgwith Cove Inn, The Lizard, Cornwall — 54
Victoria Inn, Salcombe, Devon — 65
Tradesmans Arms, Stokenham, Devon — 68
Fox Inn, Corscombe, Dorset — 70
Steam Packet Hotel, Isle of Whithorn, Dumfries & Galloway — 171
Unicorn Inn, Kincardine, Fife — 174
White Horse, Frampton Mansell, Gloucestershire — 75
Penhelig Arms Hotel, Aberdyfi, Gwynedd — 189
Plockton Hotel, Plockton, Highland — 177
Seaforth Inn, Ullapool, Highland — 180
Crab & Lobster Inn, Bembridge, Isle of Wight — 90
Ship Inn, Spalding, Lincolnshire — 101

White Horse, Brancaster Staithe, Norfolk — 105
Mussel and Crab, Tuxford, Nottinghamshire — 115
Swan Inn, Barnby, Suffolk — 137
Anglesey Arms, Chichester, West Sussex — 143
Ship Inn, Chichester, West Sussex — 145

Best summer gardens

Royal Oak, Marlow, Buckinghamshire — 46
The Stag, Mentmore, Buckinghamshire — 46
Three Horseshoes, Madingley, Cambridgeshire — 50
Tower Inn, Slapton, Devon — 68
Wild Duck Inn, Cirencester, Gloucestershire — 74
Wheatsheaf Inn, Northleach, Gloucestershire — 78
Rose & Thistle, Fordingbridge, Hampshire — 81
Stagg Inn, Kington, Herefordshire — 85
Bricklayers Arms, Flaunden, Hertfordshire — 86
Chequers Inn, Belvoir, Lincolnshire — 100
Greyhound Inn Hotel, Usk, Monmouthshire — 193
Rose & Crown, Snettisham, Norfolk — 109
Queens Head, Bulwick, Northamptonshire — 111
Hundred House Hotel, Telford, Shropshire — 127
Swan Inn, Chiddingfold, Surrey — 138
Royal Oak, Poynings, West Sussex — 146
Vine Tree, Norton, Wiltshire — 150
Sawley Arms, Sawley, North Yorkshire — 165
Shibden Mill Inn, Shibden, West Yorkshire — 167

Best for views

Kinmel Arms, St George, Conwy — 188
Old Inn, St Breward, Cornwall — 53
Scafell Hotel, Borrowdale, Cumbria — 57
Boot Inn, Eskdale, Cumbria — 57
Brackenrigg Inn, Ullswater, Cumbria — 59
Wasdale Head Inn, Wasdale, Cumbria — 60
Victoria Inn, Salcombe, Devon — 65
Butchers Arms, Painswick, Gloucestershire — 79
Four Seasons Bistro & Bar, Fort William, Highland — 175
Clachaig Inn, Glencoe, Highland — 176
Crab & Lobster, Bembridge, Isle of Wight — 90
Inn at Whitewell, Whitewell, Lancashire — 95
White Horse, Brancaster Staithe, Norfolk — 105
Victoria at Holkham, Holkham, Norfolk — 107
Loch Tummel Inn, Pitlochry, Perth & Kinross — 183
Duke of Cumberland, Midhurst, West Sussex — 145
Royal Oak, Poynings, West Sussex — 146

Best for wine

Five Arrows Hotel, Waddesdon, Buckinghamshire — 48
Pheasant Inn, Keyston, Cambridgeshire — 50
Three Horseshoes, Madingley, Cambridgeshire — 50
Peldon Rose Inn, Colchester, Essex — 72
Penhelig Arms Hotel, Aberdyfi, Gwynedd — 189
Dog Inn, Wingham, Kent — 93
Freemasons Arms, Clitheroe, Lancashire — 94
Inn at Whitewell, Whitewell, Lancashire — 95
Farmer Arms, Lincoln, Lincolnshire — 101
Bell at Skenfrith, Skenfrith, Monmouthshire — 192
Walpole Arms, Itteringham, Norfolk — 107
Rose & Crown, Snettisham, Norfolk — 109
Bottle & Glass, Harby, Nottinghamshire — 115

Crooked Billet, Stoke Row, Oxfordshire — 121
Royal Hotel, Comrie, Perth & Kinross — 181
Olive Branch, Clipsham, Rutland — 125
Albert Arms, Esher, Surrey — 139
Royal Oak, Chichester, West Sussex — 144
Vine Tree, Norton, Wiltshire — 150
Star Inn, Harome, North Yorkshire — 157

Food and drink courses

Brackenrigg Inn, Ullswater, Cumbria (Wine) — 59
Puesdown Inn, Northleach, Gloucestershire (Wine) — 78
Olive Branch, Clipsham, Rutland (Cookery) — 125
Albert Arms, Esher, Surrey (Wine) — 139

Private dining

Kings Head, Ivinghoe, Bedfordshire — 38
The Swan, Milton Keynes, Bedfordshire — 39
Old Fisherman, Thame, Buckinghamshire — 124
Swan at Felsted, Great Dunmow, Essex — 73
Unicorn Inn, Kincardine, Fife — 174
Wyndham Arms, Clearwell, Gloucestershire — 74
Hampshire Arms, Crondall, Hampshire — 81
The Fleece, Witney, Oxfordshire — 125
Albert Arms, Esher, Surrey — 139
Rainbow Inn, Lewes, East Sussex — 142
Duke of Cumberland, Midhurst, West Sussex — 145
Rose & Crown, Warwick, Warwickshire — 149

Waterside pubs
(we have listed all our pubs that have a waterside location)

Russian Tavern at the Port Royal Hotel, Isle of Bute, Argyll & Bute — 170
The Ferry, Cookham, Berkshire — 40
St George & Dragon, Wargrave, Berkshire — 42
Old Fisherman, Thame, Buckinghamshire — 124
Port Gaverne Hotel, Port Gaverne, Cornwall — 53
Victoria Inn, Salcombe, Devon — 65
Steam Packet Hotel, Isle of Whithorn, Dumfries & Galloway — 171
Penhelig Arms Hotel, Aberdyfi, Gwynedd — 189
Plockton Hotel, Plockton, Highland — 177
Seaforth Inn, Ullapool, Highland — 180
Crab & Lobster Inn, Bembridge, Isle of Wight — 90
Inn at Whitewell, Whitewell, Lancashire — 95
Ship Inn, Spalding, Lincolnshire — 101
Bull's Head and Stables Bistro, London SW13 — 103
Bell at Skenfrith, Skenfrith, Monmouthshire — 192
White Horse, Brancaster Staithe, Norfolk — 105
Anglers Arms, Longframlington, Northumberland — 113
Kings Head Inn, Bledington, Oxfordshire — 116
Loch Tummel Inn, Pitlochry, Perth & Kinross — 183
Inn on the Lake, Godalming, Surrey — 140
The Minnow, Weybridge, Surrey — 141
The Bridge, Bidford on Avon, Warwickshire — 148
Saxon Mill, Warwick, Warwickshire — 149
Red Lion Hotel, Burnsall, North Yorkshire — 155
Shibden Mill Inn, Shibden, West Yorkshire — 167

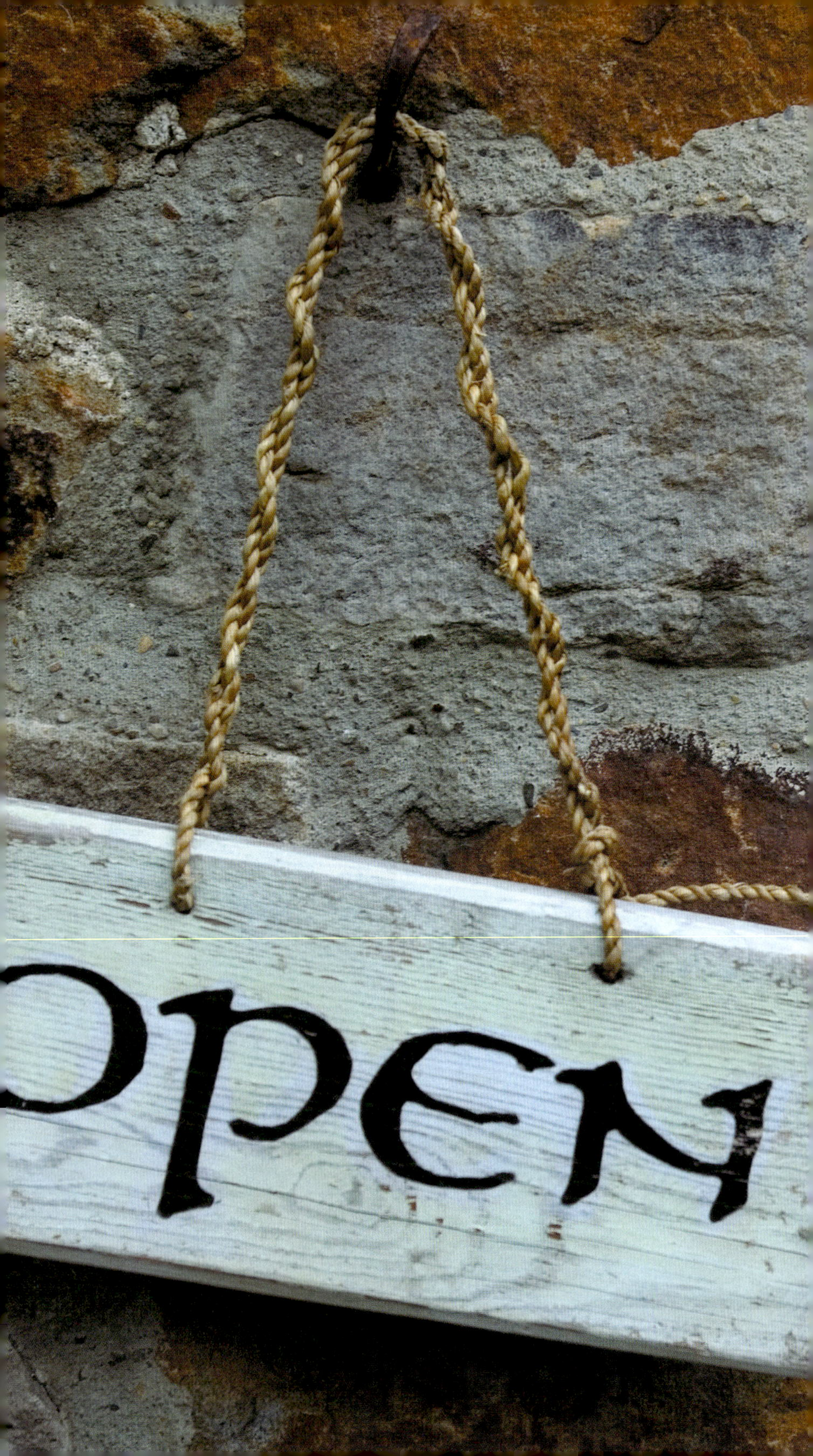
open

To the Editor, Les Routiers Guide 2007
Report Form

☐ From my personal experience the following establishment should be
a member of Les Routiers.

☐ From my personal experience the following establishment should
not be a member of Les Routiers.

Establishment   PLEASE PRINT IN BLOCK CAPITALS

Address

I had ☐ lunch ☐ dinner ☐ stayed there on (date)

Details

Reports received up to the end of May 2006 will be used in the research
of the 2007 edition.

☐ I am not connected in any way with management or proprietors.

Name

Address

As a result of your sending Les Routiers this report form, we may send you information on Les Routiers in the future.
If you would prefer not to receive such information, please tick this box ☐

To send your report...
Fax: Complete this form and fax it to 020 7370 4528
Post: Complete this form and mail it to
The Editor, FREEPOST, Les Routiers, 190 Earl's Court Road, London, SW5 9QG
Email: info@routiers.co.uk